THE
RUSSIAN EMPIRE
IN THE
EIGHTEENTH
CENTURY

The New Russian History

Series Editor: Donald J. Raleigh,
University of North Carolina, Chapel Hill

This series makes examples of the finest work of the most eminent historians in Russia today available to English-language readers. Each volume has been specially prepared with an international audience in mind, and each is introduced by an outstanding Western scholar in the same field.

THE REFORMS OF PETER THE GREAT
Progress Through Coercion in Russia
Evgenii V. Anisimov
Translated with an introduction by John T. Alexander

IN STALIN'S SHADOW
The Career of "Sergo" Ordzhonikidze
Oleg V. Khlevniuk
Translated by David Nordlander
Edited with an introduction by Donald J. Raleigh,
with the assistance of Kathy S. Transchel

THE EMPERORS AND EMPRESSES OF RUSSIA
Rediscovering the Romanovs
Edited by Donald J. Raleigh
Compiled by Akhmed A. Iskenderov

WOMEN IN RUSSIAN HISTORY
From the Tenth to the Twentieth Century
Natalia Pushkareva
Translated and edited by Eve Levin

THE RUSSIAN EMPIRE IN THE EIGHTEENTH CENTURY
Searching for a Place in the World
Aleksandr B. Kamenskii
Translated and edited by David Griffiths

THE RUSSIAN EMPIRE IN THE EIGHTEENTH CENTURY

SEARCHING FOR A PLACE IN THE WORLD

Aleksandr B. Kamenskii

Translated and edited by
David Griffiths

M.E. Sharpe
Armonk, New York
London, England

Copyright © 1997 by M. E. Sharpe, Inc.

All rights reserved. No part of this book may be reproduced in any form
without written permission from the publisher, M. E. Sharpe, Inc.,
80 Business Park Drive, Armonk, New York 10504.

Library of Congress Cataloging-in-Publication Data

Kamenskiĭ, A. (Aleksandr)
The Russian empire in the eighteenth century / searching for
a place in the world / by
Aleksandr Borisovich Kamenskii; translated by David Griffiths.
p. cm. — (New Russian history)
Includes bibliographical references and index.
ISBN 1-56324-574-4 (cloth: alk. paper). —
ISBN 1-56324-575-2 (pbk.: alk. paper)
1. Russia—History—1689–1801. I. Title. II. Series.
DK127.K36 1997
947—dc21 97-5683
CIP
Printed in the United States of America

The paper used in this publication meets the minimum requirements of
American National Standard for Information Sciences—
Permanence of Paper for Printed Library Materials,
ANSI Z 39.48-1984.

BM (c) 10 9 8 7 6 5 4 3 2 1
BM (p) 10 9 8 7 6 5 4 3 2 1

For Sasha

Contents

Author's Note	ix
Translator's Note	xi
Introduction	3
Chapter 1: The Third Rome on the Eve of the Petrine Reforms	9
Chapter 2: The Birth of the Great Reformer	39
Chapter 3: The Origins of Empire	72
Chapter 4: "The Era of Palace Revolutions"	122
Chapter 5: "You Know Whose Daughter I Am"	165
Chapter 6: The Age of Catherine the Great	194
Chapter 7: The Empire Advances	244
Chapter 8: "He Wanted to Be an Ivan IV"	265
Conclusion	281
Notes	287
Index	297

Author's Note

A book such as this, devoted as it is to an entire historical epoch, might more appropriately be written at the end of one's life, when there is no longer any chance that one's views will change fundamentally or that one will have to blush at judgments that have not withstood the test of time. After all, such a book is the essence and the sum of one's scholarly activity. Considerations notwithstanding, it proved impossible for me to resist the proposal to write this book, which was a challenge and an opportunity to try my skills. For that reason, I am extremely grateful to Professor Donald J. Raleigh of the University of North Carolina at Chapel Hill, who first suggested the idea, and by so doing, forced me to attempt to comprehend eighteenth-century Russian history as a whole and to ponder issues with which I had not previously grappled.

I began work on the manuscript in the spring of 1993, while visiting Stanford University as a Fulbright lecturer. There I started to write the first chapter, which for me was the most difficult. Conversations with Nancy Shields Kollmann, an outstanding specialist on early Russian history, proved particularly useful to me, as did the chance to attend the Workshop on Early East Slavic Culture at Stanford in June 1993. That same spring, I also gave a series of public lectures at a number of American universities, including the University of North Carolina, where I put forward some ideas that later made their way into this book. My most attentive listener and discussant was Professor David Griffiths, whom I had long known as the author of some of the most interesting work on Catherinean times. I was delighted to learn that he had agreed to translate my book into English. As I had anticipated, Professor Griffiths did not confine himself merely to translating the manuscript. He also offered numerous valuable observations on the text and drew my attention to several inaccuracies. I am extremely grateful for his efforts.

AUTHOR'S NOTE

At the start of my scholarly career I had the good fortune to make the acquaintance of the late Professor Alexander Stanislavskii, one of Russia's foremost specialists on sixteenth- and seventeenth-century Russian history, who soon became my close friend as well as my teacher. The breadth of his view of history was reflected in the fact that the dissertation topic he proposed for me to tackle was far removed from his own scholarly interests. Yet nothing exerted greater influence on my formation as a historian than my personal contact with this remarkable man and the chance to witness his scholarly inquiries, doubts, and discoveries. From the beginning, this experience inspired me to strive to analyze all problems within their broad historical context, avoiding narrower intellectual frameworks.

Professor Stanislavskii also introduced me to Evgenii Anisimov, who is without a doubt today's leading specialist on eighteenth-century Russian history. Zhenia and I became fast friends, quickly discovering that we shared a common vision of many historical issues of the time period with which we were dealing, the discussion of which has been our mutual need for the past dozen years. In the course of these discussions, many ideas for this book were spawned. Zhenia even helped me formulate its title more precisely.

Finally, this book could not have been written without the support of my family, particularly my wife, Sasha, who graciously tolerated the incursion of the stormy eighteenth century into our lives at the end of the no less stormy twentieth century. To her I dedicate this book.

* * *

The author wishes to thank the administration of the Russian State Archive for Ancient Acts (Rossiiskii gosudarstvennyi arkhiv drevnikh aktov) in Moscow for permission to publish the copy of Catherine II's draft legislative project with her doodling in the margins. The remaining illustrations are drawn from: A.G. Brikner, *Istoriia Ekateriny II* (St. Petersburg, 1885); V.V. Kallash, ed., *Tri veka: Rossiia ot smuty do nashego vremeni,* vols. 3 and 4 (Moscow, 1912); M.I. Semevskii, *Tsaritsa Katerina Alekseevna, Anna i Villem Mons, 1692–1724: Ocherk iz russkoi istorii XVIII veka* (St. Petersburg, 1884); O. Tuberovskaia, *V gostiakh u kartin* (Leningrad, 1964); and Konstantin Valishevskii, *Doch′ Petra Velikogo* (St. Petersburg, 1911).

—A.K.

Translator's Note

The Gorbachev era launched a national dialogue on the past and future of Soviet society that eventually contributed to the collapse of the system. But *perestroika* and *glasnost* initially had little impact on the writing of prerevolutionary Russian history. There were no dramatic revelations, no "blank spots" filled in, no suppressed works pulled out of the drawer for publication. Yet, important changes were in store. A new generation of historians was eager to deliver Russian history from the constraints of the official paradigm and to rediscover its personalities, its accidents, its variety, and its uniqueness.

One of the pioneers of this new literature was Aleksandr Borisovich Kamenskii, who came to prominence in 1989 when he published, in the journal *Voprosy istorii* (Problems of History), the first reconsideration of Catherine II to appear in Russia since 1917.[1] Together with Petrine specialist Evgenii Viktorovich Anisimov, Kamenskii has since written a splendid new Russian history textbook, winner of a Soros Foundation–sponsored competition.[2] He has also published two full-length studies of Catherine.[3]

It is thus a great pleasure, with this translation, to make available to the wider English-speaking world Kamenskii's interpretation of eighteenth-century Russia. Of course, many people helped along the way. First and foremost, I am grateful to the author for a much valued friendship and for his careful review of two rounds of revisions of this translation. At the University of North Carolina, thanks are due to Nadia Zilper, Slavic bibliographer at the Davis Library, to whom I know I can always turn when I encounter an unyielding problem of the Russian language in its historical context; she never fails me. In the History Department, my friend and colleague Donald J. Raleigh, the editor of the New Russian History series, read through my original draft and made many helpful suggestions. Graduate students Betsy Hemenway and Jeff Jones also helped with the text and Anthony Young prepared the index.

Finally, I thank my wife, Karin, who is not governed by the laws of translation. She occasionally wonders just why eighteenth-century Russia should be so important, but always accepts my assurances that it is.

—D.G.

Notes

1. A.B. Kamenskii, "Ekaterina II," in *Voprosy istorii*, 1989, no. 3, pp. 62–88. The essay was translated in *Soviet Studies in History*, vol. 30, no. 3, pp. 49–91 and reprinted in *The Emperors and Empresses of Russia: Rediscovering the Romanovs*, ed. Donald J. Raleigh, comp. A.A. Iskenderov (Armonk, N.Y.: M.E. Sharpe, 1996), pp. 134–76.

2. *Rossiia v XVIII–pervoi polovine XIX veka. Istoriia, Istorik, Dokument. Eksperimental'noe uchebnoe posobie dlia starshikh klassov* (Moscow, 1994).

3. A.B. Kamenskii, *"Pod seniiu Ekateriny": Vtoraia polovina XVIII veka* (St. Petersburg, 1992), and *Zhizn' i sud'ba Imperatritsy Ekateriny Velikoi* (Moscow, 1997).

THE RUSSIAN EMPIRE IN THE EIGHTEENTH CENTURY

Introduction

A serious and thoughtful student recently complained to one of my colleagues that she simply could not understand how rational philosophy could readily coexist with baroque art in eighteenth-century Russia. My colleague responded by citing several works that seemed to him to contain definitive answers to the puzzle. The student remained skeptical: she read the works, but the answers they put forward failed to satisfy her. After all, it is one thing to explain a given phenomenon in logical terms, as scholars are wont to do, and another entirely to comprehend it. Comprehension, needless to note, conflicts—or at best, coexists uneasily—with what seems unnatural in the baroque. This is but one of the many paradoxes that pervade eighteenth-century Russian history.

Such was the world into which Peter the Great intruded. The name of the Russian tsar is probably known around the world, although not everyone knows exactly when he lived or what he accomplished. For many he is nothing more than a legendary figure associated with the emergence of Russia as a great power. Those who are more familiar with Russian history are aware that during his reign, which covered the first quarter of the eighteenth century, Russia underwent a rapid and thoroughgoing transformation unparalleled in world history. As a result of the change, Russia began to play a major role in international politics, becoming a powerful empire whose political system and state institutions, at least on the surface, differed little from those of their European counterparts.

Yet with the passage of a century some Russians began to voice the opinion that the Petrine reforms had been a huge mistake, that Russia had departed from what they termed its special path, one unique unto itself and ordained by God. Russia's mediating position between Europe and Asia, its foreordained role as defender of the true Christian faith—Eastern Orthodoxy—and finally, its apparent inability to unite national cultural traditions with the values of European civilization, led some Russian thinkers to conclude that their native country constituted a world apart. Neither European nor Asian, Russia seemed to them unique, with a quality that in the twentieth century would be identified as Eurasian. From the perspective of those who espoused such views, the Petrine modernization of Russia along Western lines had proved tragic for the Russian people who were facing a resultant loss of their national identity. These thinkers found confirmation for their line of thinking in the Bolshevik Revolution of 1917, which they viewed as God's punishment for the sins of their forefathers.

But if Russia from Peter's time on was really following the path of European civilization, why were the country and its populace condemned to undergo the terrible communist experiment? Why did Russia maintain its multinational empire until near the end of the twentieth century? Was the October 1917 coup merely the result of an unfavorable conjuncture of circumstances, or the predictable outcome of the nation's historical development? And just what was that "special path" from which Russia should not have deviated, and what made it special?

A multitude of answers to these questions have been proposed both in Russia and abroad. Much has been written about Russia as a special civilization and about its proclivity for despotism; about the great historical role of the Russian people and about the actions of the Soviet Union—that "evil empire"; about the great spirituality of Russia's culture and about the expansionist tendencies of its foreign policy; about the great friendship of the peoples of Russia and about Great Russian chauvinism; about the wealthy and powerful state and about a poverty-stricken, half-starving country of peasants. The theme of Russia's fate, it seems, will never be exhausted; the disputes about it seemingly will never subside. If someday they do begin to subside, it will only be because sufficient time has passed to permit memories of the terrible shocks Russia experienced in the twentieth century to fade.

Time and again, new hypotheses and theories will be put forward. Diametrically opposed opinions and judgments will be voiced. The events of the early part of the twentieth century, which lie at the heart of the Russian tragedy—the seemingly eternal conundrum of Russian

Warrior at a Crossroads. Painting by V. M. Vasnetsov, 1882.

history—will long remain the focus of debate. More than one generation of historians will struggle over its resolution, with each new interpretation stimulating new questions and new debates. Thus, for example, if we concede that the events that took place in October 1917 were the historically determined outcome of the nation's course of development, then the question immediately arises as to just what events or features of Russian history, what moment or period, can be considered pivotal, fatal, or decisive? The possible answers are as numerous as those engaging in the debate. It would seem that history, the past, is granted to us but once and forever; for we are not free to alter or influence its course. Yet the attitude of the Russian people toward their history has always been unique. As Sidney Monas has noted, the past "has always held [for Russians] a compelling power over the future, exerting a force so constraining that it might foster the illusion, in an extreme instance, that if one changed the *accounts* in which the past is recorded and interpreted, one might well lay a magical hold upon the future."[1]

This peculiar Russian understanding of history is not coincidental. It has been spawned by an unusually large number of catastrophes, of sharp reversals the people have had to endure, especially in the present century. Unlike the American, who according to Monas does not feel the limiting effects of the past on the future, the Russian, finding himself or herself at another crossroads in history (like the subject in the painting by the Russian artist V.M. Vasnetsov above), pauses, ponders, and involuntarily glances back at the road already traveled, seeking in it the answer to the question of which road to take.

Unfortunately, one can pause and ponder the historical perspective only in the abstract. The passage of time is inexorable, and before the debates can be extinguished on one historical level, they flare up with increased intensity on another. Moreover, Russian history, as presented and interpreted in scholarly works and textbooks published in Russia and the Soviet Union, has constantly been rewritten and appropriated for the sake of political convenience. "What we remember," wrote Aleksandr Solzhenitsyn in his *GULAG Archipelago,* "is not what actually happened, not history, but those hackneyed impressions they tried to hammer into our memories by constant repetition."[2] As the contemporary Russian historian and political figure Iurii Afanasiev so wittily noted in the same vein, "We live in a country with an unpredictable past." The great paradox, however, lies in the fact that we ourselves, at each new stage of our development, may see the significance of any given event of the past either more clearly or even in an entirely new light. What seemed unimportant may suddenly acquire new significance or take on a different coloration, for the ordinary person as well as for the historian.

Like every historian, I have my own perspective on Russian history, on the causes of given events in its past, on its ups and downs. It is only natural that like all authors, I am persuaded of the validity of what I write; but I am far from convinced that I have answers to all the questions. I willingly concede that my interpretation is but one among many possible variants.

It seems to me that the Russian Revolution of the early twentieth century was actually the logical outcome of the nation's course of development over the centuries, although such an interpretation by no means signifies that this revolution was inevitable. In order to understand the causes of the event, it strikes me as necessary to delve once more into the more distant Russian past; for, as the sociologist Iurii Levada once noted, "we cannot remake history, but we have an obligation to rethink it."[3] I do not intend to argue in favor of any systematic rewriting of history. The objective behind my reconsideration of Russia's past is only to elucidate the conditions that rendered the Russian Revolution possible, the peculiar features of the nation's sociopolitical development that made its history so special and unique.

Clearly, the history of any given nation and any given people is special and unique. Thus, England in the late seventeenth century, following on the heels of Cromwell's Commonwealth, had already delineated in broad outlines the political system that exists up to the present day. In order to achieve the same ends, France first had to undergo a century of wars and revolutions. Having long remained fragmented, Germany achieved unification as a consequence of wars with its neighbors in the second half of the nineteenth century, only to lose it again in the mid-twentieth and then reclaim it after the collapse of communism. The list of such examples of the uniqueness of national history could be extended indefinitely. But we all know that, despite the distinctions and contrasts, England, France, and Germany all belong to a common European civilization. The best values of that civilization were adopted by the people of the United States who, developing and adding to them, contributed in no small measure to the fact that, in the twentieth century, European civilization has become the civilization of the entire Western world. Many of the fundamental values of this civilization have proved universal, available for adoption by various peoples, regardless of their national, racial, or religious affiliation.

As we approach the end of the twentieth century, Western civilization has shown itself more effective than any other in securing the highest quality of life. It is possible that within a few decades humanity's priorities and definitions of quality will change; but today, as I write, this is the prevalent view. That is why, in exploring the uniqueness of the Russian historical path, I have chosen the standard Western model as my point of departure. The problem lies in the fact that over the course of its history Russia has displayed another set of values, developed along a different path, although it has selectively adopted and integrated the achievements of Western culture and scientific thought. Russia's trajectory led it to a revolution that transformed it into a world unto itself.

With the aid of military force, the structures of what was termed this "new [Soviet] civilization" were even transferred to a number of East European and Asian nations. But the fact that the majority of these nations have managed to extricate themselves from their communist past rather quickly and relatively painlessly only goes to show how incompatible these structures were with their own national traditions. The situation was different with regard to Russia itself. For what reason? Why has the process of integration into world civilization proved so laborious for Russia? It would seem that Eastern Orthodoxy, as one of the major branches of Christianity, should in no way be blamed for separating Russians from Europeans. Then, too, the achievements of a wonderfully rich Russian culture have long been acknowledged and esteemed throughout the world as universal achievements. Finally, the world that surrounds Russia is no longer hostile and presents no threat to its national independence. Nonetheless, the process of Russia's integration into Europe proceeds with the utmost difficulty.

We cannot adequately explain this phenomenon without analyzing Russia's historical past anew—a complicated task that will require the combined efforts of many. I do not suggest that historians abandon their usual scholarly concerns for the sake of vague philosophizing. By no means. I am persuaded that every scholar, by focusing within his or her (at times narrow) special sphere, will make a substantial contribution to a resolution of the common task: that of elucidating the nature of that uniqueness in Russia's sociopolitical development, a uniqueness that has determined its truly special historical path. To my way of thinking, Russia followed this special historical path throughout its entire history: before and after Peter I, before and after the Revolution of 1917.

The study of eighteenth-century Russia will play a prominent role in any reconsideration of the course of Russian history. It has a long and rich tradition in Russia as well as beyond its borders. During the Soviet period, glaring distortions were introduced into Russian historiography. The Petrine period—that is, the first quarter of the century—was studied intensively, while the three-quarters of a century following the death of the great transformer, especially the political history of the period, was relatively neglected. To some degree this gap was filled by our Western colleagues of the postwar generation, primarily American and English scholars. In recent years, monographs on Russia in the middle and second half of the eighteenth century have begun to appear again in Russia as well. This serious and meticulous work on the part of several generations of historians from various nations has made possible my attempt to produce this synthesis of Russian history and to explain which events and processes were of greatest importance in transforming Russia into one of the world's most powerful empires.

Chapter 1

The Third Rome on the Eve of the Petrine Reforms

"The need to pursue a new path was recognized, the necessity to do so was defined: the people bestirred themselves and intended to take the path; but they awaited something; they awaited a leader; the leader appeared." This was how the great nineteenth-century Russian historian Sergei Soloviev described Russia's situation on the eve of the Petrine reforms.[1] In order to understand the thought behind these words, let us look still further back into the past to ascertain just what Russia was like in the seventeenth century, and why change became not only possible but necessary.

It has long been accepted wisdom in Russian historiography to divide the history of prerevolutionary Russia into two periods: the Muscovite and the Petersburg. Many historians still employ the term "Muscovite Rus" to denote the state of which Moscow was the capital and which existed up to the reforms of Peter the Great, only to disappear in the course of its transformation. It is assumed that Moscow, among a number of towns of northeastern Rus, was founded by Iurii Dolgorukii, the Prince of Rostov, in approximately 1147. The town was remote from Rostov, not to mention Kiev, which was then the center of the state. Soon, however, Kievan Rus fragmented into a number of petty principalities, which were conquered a few decades later by nomadic hordes from the East. Tatar-Mongol rule was imposed. Beginning with the mid-thirteenth century, the historical fates of northeastern and southwestern Rus began to diverge, and by the beginning of the next century Moscow had become one of the centers of the emerging nation's political life.

Historians frequently debate why the Russian nation coalesced around Moscow. They mention its remoteness from the Golden Horde, the fact that it was located at the crossroads of important trade routes, and the administrative talents of the Muscovite princes. As is usual in such circumstances, each explanation is partially correct, since a combination of favorable circumstances obviously contributed to the emergence of Moscow. In the course of the fourteenth century, the Muscovite princes steadily expanded their domains, triumphing over their rivals, and all the while becoming more independent of the Tatar khans.

The question of the impact of the Tatar-Mongol yoke on Russia likewise has attracted the attention of several generations of historians, and continues to elicit debate. Most agree that Tatar-Mongol rule dealt a crushing blow to the emerging nation's economic life and significantly retarded Russia's social and political development. Many have found the source of Russian backwardness in comparison with the West in the two centuries of Tatar occupation and accompanying death and destruction. While some historians see the yoke as an alien imposition against which the Russian people were forced to struggle for two centuries, others see the Golden Horde's influence as the source of Russian despotism and totalitarianism. The latter point out that Muscovite Rus borrowed taxation and principles of military organization from the Tatars as well as the pattern of social relations associated with them. For these reasons the Russian émigré historian George Vernadsky saw Muscovite Rus as the direct heir to the Golden Horde.[2]

Still other scholars maintain that both the extent of the devastation and the burden of the Tatar-Mongol yoke have been greatly exaggerated. Lev Gumilev, one of the most interesting twentieth-century observers of Russian history, has argued that in terms of the damage it inflicted, Khan Batu's military campaign was consonant with the internecine warfare endemic to those unruly times.[3] Historians of this school point out that the conquerors did not infringe on the national traditions and cultural values of the Russian people; they did not destroy churches and monasteries aimlessly. Their relations with those they conquered were based on the vassal–suzerain foundations prevalent in medieval times. Just as the appanage princes formerly had recognized the seniority of the Kievan prince, they now readily accepted their position as vassals of the khan of the Golden Horde, whom they addressed as "tsar." They did not scruple to take advantage of links to his court, including matrimonial ties, to settle old scores with their political enemies. The proponents of this interpretation, minimizing in every way possible the negative impact of the Tatar-Mongol conquest, emphasize that it was a lesser evil than Roman Catholic influence, for it allowed Russia to preserve its own religion, and therefore its culture.*

Because it seems obvious today that the profound influence of Mongol domination upon Russian development can no longer be denied, I have not devoted much space to this question in my book.[4] Suffice it to say that the Mongol conquest was an important landmark in Russian history: The difference between Kievan Rus and Muscovite Rus was, as Gumilev accurately noted, at least as great as that between the Rome of the caesars and the Rome of the popes, affecting not only the overall culture but morals and customs as well.[5] But where did these morals and customs come from? It is worth dwelling on this question just a bit, for the factors that contributed to the appearance of these morals continued to exist until the eighteenth century and even beyond.

Granted, both destructive internecine warfare and devastating nomadic raids were common occurrences in Rus even prior to the Mongol conquest. In instances of internecine warfare, however, one or another Russian principality had always emerged the victor. And an indisputably more powerful Rus had always succeeded in defending itself against nomadic raids. These events were, as a rule, strictly local in character. But this time, nearly all the territory of Rus was conquered by invaders. The Mongol conquest was not confined to a relatively small number of towns that were burned to the ground, as Gumilev would have us believe, but rather extended to the largest and most important of them. Even granted that towns made of wood could be rebuilt relatively quickly, that the Tatars did not even bother to station garrisons in those towns that remained intact after having surrendered without a struggle, and that the inhabitants of those that resisted frequently managed to flee to the woods and wait there until it was safe to return to the smoldering ruins, still it was one thing to rebuild several small towns that had been burned to the ground and another entirely to rebuild dozens of large towns. A town that put up any resistance to the invaders was put to the torch, and the entire male population capable of bearing arms perished with it in the flames.

---

*Elements of a nationalist ideology based on the presumed superiority of Eastern Orthodox culture obviously pervade such thinking.

Even in the best of cases, only women, children, and old men managed to save themselves. Even a town that placed itself at the mercy of the invaders would be thoroughly sacked before they departed, carrying with them all its agricultural stores. I find no evidence to support denials of Russia's devastation by the Mongols. One of the conquest's most important consequences clearly was the destruction of those still weak economic ties that bound together the individual Russian lands. It is no coincidence that Russian artisans in the thirteenth and fourteenth centuries sought work in Karakorum, the capital of Mongolia; understandably, there was no market at all for their goods in their homeland.

The Mongol invasion also had political consequences. The towns that were destroyed were rebuilt in what was in effect a different country and under different sociopolitical circumstances. At one time, Russian princes themselves had launched distant campaigns of conquest, reaching the very walls of Constantinople. Now Prince Alexander Nevskii, after defeating the Swedes in 1240 and the Swordbearers of the Teutonic Order two years later, had to kowtow before the khan in order to obtain a charter to rule his own principality. It is quite clear that Rus's international importance had declined precipitously and that the country would be excluded from international politics for years to come.

The impact of the Mongol yoke on the development of Kievan Rus's sociopolitical arrangements was even greater. According to most historians, the old Russian state had developed along the same lines as other European nations, on the whole. The question is merely one of Kievan Rus's stage of development, or, more specifically, whether it harbored feudal relations prior to the conquest. I would suggest that certain conclusions can be drawn from simple logical deduction, without resorting to a detailed analysis of the nature of one or another institution or the pattern of social relations.

As we know, the old Russian state had taken shape by the end of the ninth century. By this time, statehood in Western Europe had already enjoyed a long history, while the pattern of its social relations, too, had assumed many of its characteristic features—features that certain scholars of Kievan Rus assiduously and unsuccessfully seek in that state. By the time Christianity finally took root and a culture based on literacy began to spread in Rus, Western Europe already had a tradition not only of religious but also of secular literature and historical writing. Several centuries were to elapse between the compilation of the so-called barbarian law of Western Europe and the *Russkaia pravda,* or

Russian Law Code, the first Russian codification of the laws known to us.

Was it possible for a developed pattern of feudal relations similar to that of Western Europe to arise in Rus simultaneously with the appearance of the state?* The posing of such a question is by definition ahistorical, for in order to do so Rus would have had to pass through specific stages of development, and that required time.

The Petersburg historian I.Ia. Froianov has concluded that at the peak of Kievan Rus's development, large-scale landholding was but poorly developed and feudal relations had barely begun to take root, while the charters of judicial and financial immunity granted by the princes exhibited the character of "prefeudal arrangements."[6] This line of argument brought down upon its author a steady stream of invective from official Soviet historians. But even if one attempts to find some sort of golden mean between Froianov's position and that of his critics, we are still faced with a significant lag in the level of historical development of Rus as compared with its West European counterparts. This lag cannot of course be measured in miles or in kilometers, much less in units of time. What is important to note is that at the time of the conquest, Rus's political structure was still in its formative stages, and therefore fragile. Hence, the direction of its development could be easily altered. We might also note that after the conquest, when the grand prince was in reality appointed by the khan, conditions for the appearance of classical feudal immunities, seigniories, and the like were hardly propitious. Although the Muscovite principality increased in strength so greatly by the fourteenth century that the crown had in effect become hereditary, it was still a new state and only beginning to create its own political traditions.

---

*The use of the term "feudalism," especially with regard to Russia, has fueled huge debates. Insofar as these debates are but part of a larger problem of terminology, I cannot address them at length in this book. I will confine myself to noting that in contemporary Western literature the concept of "feudalism" is employed primarily to describe a period of fragmentation of political authority. A recent attempt has been made in Russia to describe medieval Rus as "a system of state feudalism," fundamentally different from the feudalism one sees in the nations of Western Europe: see L.V. Danilova, "Stanovlenie sistemy gosudarstvennogo feodalizma v Rossii: Prichiny, sledstviia," in *Sistema gosudarstvennogo feodalizma v Rossii: Sbornik statei* (Moscow, 1993), part 1, pp. 40–92. Because in-depth examination of this concept would require too much space, I will confine myself to noting that despite its undoubted virtues, the concept seems to me burdened with serious contradictions.

One more extremely important factor deserves mention. It has long been assumed in our historical literature that the aristocracy served to inhibit despotism. In ancient Rus, where relations between the prince and his retinue preserved to a significant degree the elements of communal democracy, such an aristocracy did not yet exist. Granted, the social stratum out of which such an aristocracy might have emerged under favorable conditions did exist. But it was precisely this stratum of the population, according to V.B. Kobrin, that was obliterated during the Mongol conquest.[7] Hence, the Muscovite state's aristocracy had to emerge anew from those strata of the population that had previously been situated at lower rungs of the social ladder. The psychology of this new aristocracy's members and their relations with princely power were different from those of the old aristocracy. On the other hand, the institution of princely power had not been destroyed by the Mongol conquest, but on the contrary had been strengthened.

If the prince previously had been "first among equals" within his military retinue,[8] just as the West European kings of early medieval times were first among their knights, now he was elevated above those around him by the will of the khan, his suzerain. The *iarlyk,* or charter, granted the prince by the khan changed the former's juridical status, transforming him into the khan's commander-in-chief within a specified territory. By the time a complement of prominent families had appeared, from which a ruling elite, the privileged stratum of the new state, might be formed, the institution of princely power was already well developed and independent enough to assert its authority. Pretenders to the status of aristocrats, on the other hand, found themselves more dependent on the prince than would have been the case had the institution of princely power and the aristocracy arisen simultaneously.*

A unified Muscovite state took shape in the midst of its princes' fierce struggle to annex neighboring principalities. Every one of those principalities had its prince with his court—the "great servitors," as the

---

*A somewhat different variant of this interpretation is found in L.V. Danilova's book: "Ruling estates emerged here [in Northeast Rus] from the military retinue and administrative-financial servitors who arrived with the princes. They had no deep local roots, and therefore their social position and the possibility of acquiring land and dependent people from whom income could be extracted depended directly on princely power" (Danilova, *Stanovlenie sistemy gosudarstvennogo feodalizma v Rossii,* p. 58).

boyars were traditionally termed. Each prince considered the principality his *votchina,* or allodial landholding: that is, hereditary property conquered by his forefathers.* But the boyars also possessed allodial estates. They enjoyed certain immunities, chiefly judicial and fiscal, on their lands. Just how highly developed boyar landholding was is unknown, for very few sources dating from before the mid-fifteenth century have been preserved.[9] Feudal immunity was also limited in character, for it had to be confirmed by a princely charter. In case of disgrace, allodial estates could be confiscated, as happened, for example, with the Muscovite boyar A.P. Khvost in the middle of the fourteenth century. At the end of the fifteenth century, Ivan III, the grand prince of Moscow, and then his son Vasilii III confiscated without hesitation the allodial estates of dozens of Novgorodian and Pskovian boyars and deported whole clans to other regions of the country.

Moreover, the concept of the allodial landholding, as Danilova has demonstrated, signified at that time not only a landed possession but inheritable property (in the form of land, a right to the princely title where appropriate, or even an administrative position). Insofar as the boyars were concerned, princely power was the sole source of allodial estates. Princely landholding, moreover, was more widespread than any other, and therefore the boyars' chief source of income was not landed possessions but provincial and district maintenance: that is, the income derived by boyars at the local level from governing territories assigned to them.[10] If we add to this the absence of special legislation dealing with the rights of possessors of allodial estates, it becomes clear that it would be stretching the point greatly to speak of the existence of the right of private property in land in fourteenth- and fifteenth-century Russia.**

At first, the boyars formally held the right to serve the prince of their choice, even if their allodial estates were located in other principalities. Early on, however, the concept of treason emerged to undermine this right. In 1375, the boyar Ivan Veliaminov departed from Moscow for Tver, to an enemy of the Muscovite prince, only to be

---

*As Richard Pipes notes, this attitude was attributable to the fact that northeastern Rus had been colonized largely on the initiative of the princes and under their auspices. In this region, political authority preceded settlement (Pipes, *Russia under the Old Regime* [New York, 1974], p. 40).

**Here we have, it seems to me, the primary problem with Alexander Yanov's thesis (see *The Origins of Autocracy: Ivan the Terrible in Russian History,* translated by Stephen Dunn [Berkeley, 1981]).

captured four years later and publicly executed. From the middle of the fifteenth century on, when the formation of the unified state entered its final stage, the boyars lost their right of departure from the prince altogether. Given the fierce conflict between proponents and opponents of centralization, the Muscovite princes accepted into their service their opponents' "free servitors," as well as the appanage princes and Tatar and Lithuanian princes. Unwilling to take any chances, the Muscovite princes extracted oaths of loyalty from them all, sworn not only in their own names but also those of their posterity. From that time on in Russia, the avoidance of state service, not to mention the expression of a desire to emigrate, was considered treason.

In addition to the former ruling princes and boyar landholders who entered the Muscovite prince's service, we find large numbers of landless people who received land from the grand prince on conditional tenure, as a form of reward for service. The latter's dependence on princely power was, naturally, even greater than that of the former. The more dependent a given stratum of the population, the more useful it would be to the prince as a pillar of support. It is therefore understandable that the state had to strive to transform the greatest possible number of free allodial landholders into dependent "servitors." On the other hand, the state itself, the princely power, depended on those who provided it with social and military support. When rewarding the service person with payment in the form of "inhabited property" (the term, meaning landed property together with the peasants who worked it, dates from a later time), the state had to guarantee a steady flow of revenue from these estates, sufficient first of all for him to subsist, and secondly to render his service obligation possible. But income depended on peasants. If they were allowed to move around freely, the state could not guarantee a stable income for conditional, or even allodial, landholders. Thus, the peasants gradually became attached to the land, or enserfed, a process completed by the end of the sixteenth century and confirmed by the Law Code of 1649.

The enserfment of the peasantry was characteristic of every medieval society. In Russia, however, this process began later than in Western Europe and coincided not with the issuance of rights of immunity to landholders but, on the contrary, with their curtailment. Hence, the nature of serfdom in Russia was different, imposed as it was at the national rather than the local level. It is also important to bear in mind that in any given society a pattern of mutual relations within the upper social stratum will, to one degree or another, be reproduced at the lower levels. The pattern of suzerain–vassal relations between royal power and the nobility in Western Europe guaranteed that serfdom would be confined there to a relatively brief existence. The denial of the boyars' right of departure, the emergence of a stratum of service people obligated to serve the ruler and tied to its service estates, and the strengthening of relations of subordination within the upper stratum all guaranteed the replication of these relations in each of Russia's social strata.

It is obvious that the processes and events described here did not all appear at once. Old Russian traditions disappeared slowly, as they were long preserved in the habits and customs of the new nation's founders. It is also obvious, however, that the model provided by the Golden Horde inevitably exerted its influence on morals as well as on the newly emerging political traditions. Here I have in mind the model of a centralized government with a strictly hierarchical, militarized social structure; a despotic regime; and an infrastructure developed specifically to assist in repressing and governing the population. Again, the influence of this model on Muscovite Rus cannot be measured in mathematical terms. Yet this influence was unavoidable because the new state took shape in such a fashion that its political structures could successfully compete with the Golden Horde's. The Horde was strong and powerful, and it would be strange indeed if the Russians of the thirteenth and fourteenth centuries—above all, the rulers—did not view it as a model worthy of emulation.

Let us turn our attention to one more potentially important consideration. As I have already mentioned, the Mongol conquerors did not encroach on the religious foundations of Russian society. Given the reality of the Tatar yoke, Eastern Orthodoxy helped to maintain the cohesion of the Russian people, playing a role analogous to that played by Judaism over the centuries for the Jews of the diaspora. Religious cohesion was extremely important, for it served as the ideological basis for the new notion of statehood. Had there been no Mongol conquest, one can assume that Eastern Orthodoxy in Russia would have been subjected to the strong influence of Catholic Europe, and its fate might have paralleled that of the lands of southwestern Rus, where a significant portion of the population was Catholicized. Thus, the Tatar yoke helped preserve Orthodoxy. But this Orthodoxy could be preserved only by conserving all of the church's fundamental tenets without subjecting them to any questioning whatever and without permitting any free thinking with regard to them. This situation hampered the development of an independent theology and philosophical thought, which in turn took a heavy toll on the development of the Russian Orthodox Church. The role of the church in the unification of the Russian lands likewise bestowed upon it characteristics of a state institution, rendering its eventual collision with state power unavoidable.

The international situation was equally important. When Constantinople fell to the Crusaders in 1204, the loss, in Lev Gumilev's words, "struck Rus like the unexpected death of a close relative.... Rus ceased to be part of a world system, finding itself instead isolated." And although the Crusaders were soon defeated, "the sense of bitter isolation remained."[11] Over the next two and a half centuries, as the decline of Constantinople became more and more apparent, culminating in its fall to the Turks in 1453, this sense of spiritual separateness increased. Along with it grew the perception that Russia had an exclusive role to play as preserver of the true Christian faith, as well as the perception that Moscow was the direct successor to Byzantium, the Third Rome. In order to conserve the Byzantine inheritance, it was necessary not only to cling to the ancient traditions of Eastern Orthodoxy but also to replicate Byzantine political traditions as closely as possible. It should be noted that Byzantium's political structure differed markedly from that of most West European nations. In Byzantium the basileus's authority was practically limitless, and his relations with the privileged strata of the population were based not on the principles of vassalage but on those of unlimited political subordination. Unlike West European society, in which it was primarily birth that dictated membership in the privileged stratum, in Byzantium the concept of "distinction" was in reality either absent or played almost no role over the course of the centuries. Much more important were service career, rank, and position. Many of these characteristics of the political structure, as we know, were reproduced in Muscovite Rus.

Such in my opinion were the most important factors contributing to the formation of the new Russian society with its unique political structure, which combined indigenous traditions with borrowings from various sources. Just what did this state look like, and how did it develop?

The year 1480 is usually considered the date when Rus finally emancipated itself from the Golden Horde. That year, Moscow's grand prince, Ivan III (1462–1505), stopped paying tribute to the Golden Horde and refused to travel to the khan at Sarai to receive his charter. When Khan Akhmat led his troops into Rus in person to punish his unruly vassals, he was forced to pull back and return home empty-handed. By this time, historians agree, Muscovite Rus had already been transformed into a unified state with a single political center and a single effective government.[12] Of course, the emancipation did not occur overnight but as the result of a long struggle, one occasionally compared with the Spanish *reconquista*.

The comparison with Spain is not entirely apt, for the lands on which the Mongol state was situated were not traditionally considered Russian. Therefore, their annexation to the Muscovite state, which occurred much later, did not represent the reestablishment of the state in its earlier borders but the conquest of new territories. A century before emancipation, in 1380, the combined Russian forces under the leadership of Muscovite Prince Dmitrii (Donskoi) had defeated the Tatar armies commanded by Mamai at Kulikovo field. This event left a deep imprint on the public consciousness, demonstrating the growing strength of the new state. But, unfortunately, it did not lead to unification. Two years later, Khan Tokhtamysh, whom the Russian princes considered their legitimate suzerain (unlike Mamai), burned Moscow to the ground. Another century would pass before Rus would win its emancipation.

The acute rivalry between Moscow and the principality of Tver persisted, and within another half-century, a twenty-year internecine "feudal war" broke out. By the time it concluded in 1453, the formerly powerful Golden Horde had disintegrated under the blows administered by Tamerlane and his successors. Meanwhile, Moscow, as so often happens in such circumstances, emerged from the civil war further strengthened and war-hardened. The victory of the Muscovite princes, the descendants of Alexander Nevskii, enhanced their authority significantly. Attempts to limit the political independence of all social strata in order to enhance autocratic rule became more noticeable at this time. The tsardom of Muscovy had replaced the principality of Moscow.

In the 1460s and 1470s, during the reign of the capable tsar Ivan III, first Pskov and then Novgorod fell under Muscovite control, the appanages of the Rostov and Iaroslavl princes were eliminated, and the war with the khanate of Kazan concluded victoriously. In 1485, Tver fell.

At the end of the fifteenth century and the beginning of the sixteenth, Moscow waged a successful war against the grand prince of Lithuania. The treaty of 1503 provided for incorporation by Rus of the extensive territories conquered during this war. In 1521, the grand principality of Riazan and the appanage of Uglich were absorbed, and in 1533, the appanage of Dmitrov. Over the course of seventy years, from the accession to the throne of Ivan III in 1462 until the death of his son Vasilii III in 1533, the nation's territory increased by six-and-a-half times, attaining a size of 2,800,000 square kilometers. In terms of ethnic composition, however, the nation remained relatively homogeneous. This situation changed in the mid-sixteenth century when Ivan IV ("the Terrible") conquered the khanates of Kazan and Astrakhan, and then Siberia. Native peoples of tribes both large and small in number found themselves under the control of the Muscovite state. Their fate for centuries thereafter would be tied to that of Russia.

The expansion of the state's boundaries required a refinement of the methods and instruments of control. At first, while the Muscovite principality still harbored the surviving appanages, their possessors exercised relatively extensive sovereign rights and were invited to render the grand prince "counsel" on the most important domestic and foreign policy questions of the day. But by the reign of Ivan III, such invitations had already begun to be viewed as mere formalities, more an obeisance to tradition than a political reality. The rights and obligations of the appanage princes were enshrined in special documents, and the princes were kept under close surveillance at their courts by the grand princes' spies.

Another significant group within the elite of the Russian state in the first half of the sixteenth century were the so-called service princes, who administered their former principalities, or parts of them, as hereditary property and were obligated to perform military service for the Muscovite prince. This obligation alone rendered them politically dependent, and by the mid-sixteenth century they had merged with the old Muscovite boyars, receiving their ranks at the grand prince's court. The holders of the highest ranks—the boyars and *okolnichie*—joined the Boyar Duma, or council.

As Richard Pipes has noted, Russian historians have spilled a lot of ink over whether the Duma enjoyed legislative and administrative power or merely ratified decisions already taken by others.[13] Not long ago, the historian G. Galperin asserted that the Boyar Council was a higher state institution that, together with the tsar, exercised the state's legislative functions.[14] As A. Zimin noted, however, the council gathered irregularly, its various members were not equal in status, and the most important government assignments frequently went to those who were not even members of the council. Moreover, there was no clear line demarcating the functions of people and institutions at this time. Rather, the secretaries were the real executors of the will of the grand prince.[15] If it were not for Zimin's observation, one might possibly agree with Pipes's suggestion to consider the council a "proto-cabinet," but a cabinet nonetheless, and the government an organ of executive authority. But it turns out that the council's functions were performed not by boyars but by secretaries, those high-level civil servants who were usually non-noble in origin. In this fashion we approach the most important of the peculiar traits of the Russian state's political structure in the sixteenth and seventeenth centuries.

As we have already seen, the highest social stratum of Russian society was made up of members of the grand princely family, service princes, the old Muscovite boyar families, and "defectors" from the Golden Horde, Lithuania, and other foreign countries. The role these people played at the Muscovite prince's court was determined not by birth but by rank—that is, by the grade to which they had been elevated by the sovereign. True, ranks were to a substantial degree bestowed on the basis of heredity, and so the scion of an old Muscovite boyar family had the right to count on a council rank for that reason alone. Tradition, however, played a major role, as a consequence of which service princes, for example, did not gain admission to the council until much later, not because they were undistinguished (the very concept of distinction in the European sense was still virtually unknown) but because it was not in keeping with tradition. When tradition was violated, as it was starting in the second quarter of the sixteenth century, when representatives of all the above-mentioned groups began gradually to infiltrate the council, the body could no longer claim to be a government. It could not do so because it numbered no more than several dozen people (by the end of the seventeenth century, somewhat more than a hundred and fifty), and because, as formerly, it functioned sporadically and without any specific guidelines. The Boyar Council never was a state institution, a situation mirrored in the fact that it had no set procedures.

Over time, the tsar's consultations with the council acquired an ever more traditional, ritualistic character,* as the Muscovite ranks of boyar, *okolnichii,* and *stolnik* qualified their holders chiefly for honorary positions in the social hierarchy. To receive a rank it was necessary to belong by birth to a specific social stratum. But when all was said and done, promotion depended on the sovereign's will. Real power accrued to a boyar when his rank was accompanied by a high administrative, judicial, or military post. Rank and function, of course, were interdependent: the state's higher officials were drawn from the same social stratum as the members of the council. As a rule, these were the same people. But function rather than rank was characteristically the main consideration in the peculiarly Russian phenomenon of *mestnichestvo,* or the allotment of high office on the basis of precedence, which was in turn a reflection of family lineage, one's position in that family line, and that line's past service in relationship to that of other family lines.

When one contested for precedence, one litigated with another servitor over an office, a position, or the right to rise above another in the service hierarchy. To bestow or not to bestow boyar rank was the prerogative of the sovereign. But if one boyar was appointed to a higher position than another, the other could contest for precedence, claiming that his ancestors traditionally had served in higher positions than the ancestors of his rival. Therefore, for him to serve at a lower level than his rival was "not in keeping with precedence," that is, it was an insult to his dignity, his honor. Thus, the very concept of honor was linked with position, with service function: position in the service hierarchy determined family honor. However, that did not make rank insignificant. Material reward depended on rank, and only those who occupied the higher ranks could contest for precedence. Only they were considered "people distinguished by the fact that they were listed in the genealogical registers."[16] The others were simply "service people." They also served the sovereign, but in the lower ranks, for the most part as *deti boiarskie,* or middle service people, and in towns other than Moscow. They were identified as "those not listed in the genealogical registers," even if they happened to bear the same names and titles as their Muscovite relatives "who were distinguished by the fact that they were listed in the genealogical registers." Thus, the sys-

---

*This was true except at isolated periods, such as during the childhood of Ivan IV, when the Boyar Council's importance increased dramatically.

tem encompassed the concepts of distinction, wealth, high rank, high position (this last was the most important), function, and state office, the receipt of which depended on the tsar and tradition and was regulated by the institution of *mestnichestvo*. As the conservative nineteenth-century Russian philosopher Konstantin Leontiev put it: "The term *mestnichestvo* bore a thoroughgoing service, statist, bureaucratic nature.... Our aristocracy adopted ... a bureaucratic nature. This bureaucracy for its part was genealogically oriented and hereditary. Service conveyed hereditary rights."[17]

In the middle of the sixteenth century important events associated with the name Ivan the Terrible took place in Russia. When his father died in 1533, Ivan was only three years old. Until he came of age, the nation was run by a clique of boyars who constantly contended among themselves for power. Their arbitrariness, which exposed the shortcomings of "collective" rule, elicited from others dissatisfaction and a desire for "a firm hand." Here were favorable conditions for the further strengthening of the autocratic regime, a prospect that corresponded to the hopes and character of the young tsar, who officially received the title in 1547. During the reign of Ivan the Terrible, tsarist power emancipated itself from many practices dating from the appanage period that tended to inhibit its exercise. The tsar's key achievement in this regard was the redistribution of land, at first by means of political and administrative reforms and then by open terror visited upon the population at large, known in the literature as the *oprichnina*.

Debates about the objectives and nature of the *oprichnina* have been going on for ages. Whatever the true nature of the phenomenon, after the *oprichnina* many former allodial land holdings either ended up in tsarist hands or were distributed as service estates, while their former holders were either destroyed or transformed into service-estate holders in other regions of the country. The *oprichnina* doubtless strengthened the autocratic aspect of tsarist power. It is indicative that it was just at this time, in the mid-sixteenth century, that a number of documents of an official nature were compiled that served to confirm and strengthen the emerging state structure. We have a compilation of a new law code (the *Sudebnik* of 1550); an official genealogical chart tracing the lineage of the royal family back to the Emperor Augustus and delineating just who would be listed in the official genealogical and service registers (*Gosudarev rodoslovets*); official guidelines for settling disputes over genealogical precedence (*Gosudarev razriad*); an official history justifying the pretensions of the Muscovite tsars to the patrimony of the princes of Kievan Rus (the *Stepennaia kniga*); and finally, a grandiose compilation of historical chronicles, in which the tsar himself participated.

By the mid-sixteenth century, those who surrounded the tsar and looked after his affairs—Muscovite service people of various ranks—composed of the *Gosudarev dvor,* or Sovereign's Court, a specifically sociopolitical grouping of an estate-bureaucratic nature in which ranks were conveyed hereditarily. The members of the Sovereign's Court represented the upper stratum of the Russian elite, whose registration was conducted on special governmental forms. The remaining service people were ascribed to the provincial towns, and for all practical purposes were attached to them, much as the serfs were to the land. There they periodically were required to appear at musters in order to demonstrate their preparedness "in terms of horses and men" to serve their sovereign. The so-called "service town," an urban gentry corporation organized around service to the state, with its own customs, traditions, and socioeconomic interests, took shape in this way. It existed until the end of the seventeenth century, when in conjunction with the reforms in the organization of the army the service town gradually fell into desuetude.

It was also at this time that the instruments of state administration emerged. At first, so-called courts, which directed the former appanage principalities, were established in the territories newly annexed to Moscow. At the same time, the large towns and their surrounding territories were assigned as "feeding," or maintenance, to boyars, who collected taxes from the population, in effect becoming the unlimited petty sovereigns of these territories. But such a situation proved uncongenial to central authority, and in the middle of the century "maintenance" was discontinued. In its place Ivan the Terrible instituted a local-government reform, creating the functions of elected district judge (chosen from the among the local middle service people) and district assistant (chosen from among the peasants). District offices, the members of which were also chosen on the basis of election, served as the organs of local administration in the towns. At first they were subordinated to the district judges, and from the seventeenth century on, to the *voevody,* or commanders, who were assigned by the tsar and administered the towns and adjoining districts through their central offices. Under Ivan the powers of the local authorities were severely restricted, as the most important matters were forwarded to the center for resolution.

Likewise, *prikazy,* or chancelleries, which were special organs of central authority combining the functions of local, estate, and territorial administration, began to emerge in Moscow during the reign of Ivan the Terrible. A number of chancelleries also exercised judicial functions. The chancelleries were headed by boyars. It was not uncommon to find several chancelleries headed by the same person, in which case the chancelleries were in reality merged. This very fact makes it clear that the directors of chancelleries served as the personal representatives of the sovereign. The tsar simply ordered one of his boyars to "direct" specific affairs on his large landed estate (which might, from another perspective, be viewed as a petty state), just as in the years to come a merchant would assign an assistant to run his kiosk or shop or keep his accounts. Given the absence of any clear functional differentiation among the chancelleries and the facts that they arose spontaneously, as the need appeared, and that their authority depended on tradition, the chancelleries were far from state institutions in the modern understanding of the term. Rather, they were offices responsible for the direction of specific aspects of the tsar's economic and political interests.

For the boyar, assignment to the chancellery was an honor, and a profitable one at that. But since he was in all likelihood illiterate and often had little claim to competence, he depended all the more on the chancellery's *diak,* or secretary, a high-level administrator who for all practical purposes ran the chancellery. Chancellery secretaries accumulated great power and were generously rewarded for their services with salary and inhabited lands. The most successful and highest in rank received the rank of *Dumnyi diak,* or Council Secretary. Yet the nature of Russian society of the sixteenth and seventeenth centuries was such that allures such as this were insufficient to attract those listed in the genealogical registers, who, if assigned as secretaries, petitioned the sovereign not to dishonor them: that is, not to consider the assignment in official *mestnichestvo* calculations. By the end of the seventeenth century, there were 55 chancelleries in all, which were directed by 31 chancellery directors, and 79 chancellery secretaries, to whom were subordinated 1,702 undersecretaries. More than eighteen hundred additional undersecretaries served in local government.[18] In its entirety this group was referred to as "chancellery people"—those of varied social origins, means, and education, who were extremely influential because they were responsible for the direct administration of the nation, and as such served as the early model for the future Russian bureaucracy.

The service people of various ranks, together with the "chancellery people," made up what might be described as the top of a huge social pyramid capped off by the tsar. At the base of the pyramid, one finds a multitude of social groups, the most numerous of which were townspeople and peasants. We have already discussed the peasants and their enserfment.[19] Here we might add only that the enserfed peasantry was composed of three primary categories: those belonging to the seigniory, the monastery, and the court (that is, belonging directly to the royal family). Then there were the state peasants* who lived on "black" lands, chiefly in the north of Russia. The land they worked was not claimed by any landlord aside from the tsar. These peasants were not formally enserfed, and the burden of their obligations was somewhat lighter than that of their enserfed counterparts. Nonetheless, they were legally bound to their hamlets and villages and lacked freedom of movement. Moreover, they were bound by a system of mutual responsibility, via the peasant commune, for the payment of their state taxes. The townspeople found themselves in essentially the same situation.

The towns in northeastern Russia were founded by a process that differed markedly from that in Western Europe. Most of the towns were founded by princes as their principalities' trade and administrative centers. Thus, from their very beginnings, the towns were considered private property, and their inhabitants, subjects of the princes. The rulers of towns were naturally also interested in the attachment of the townspeople to their towns, just as the peasants were attached to the land. There were no special municipal privileges that regulated the rights of town dwellers or delineated their special status. In the process of creat-

---

*The category of state peasants (*gosudarstvennye krest'iane*) eventually encompassed several types of peasants that will be mentioned in the chapters that follow: "black plough peasants" (*chernososhnye krest'iane*), who lived on state lands in the Russian North and in Siberia and had no seigniorial lords; "one-court peasants" (*odnodvortsy*), who were descendants of service people settled along Russia's southern and southeastern frontiers in the sixteenth and seventeenth centuries to prevent a Tatar incursion; and "economic peasants" (*ekonomicheskie krest'iane*), who formerly belonged to monasteries and other religious bodies but were placed under the supervision of the Collegium of Economy when Catherine II secularized Church lands.

ing a unified state, Ivan III and Vasilii III energetically carried out a policy of liquidating privately owned towns, transforming their inhabitants into "state *posad* people."

The trade and handicraft part of the town was termed a *posad,* distinguishing it from the fortified part. The *posad* people, or urban dwellers, shouldered a *tiaglo,* or state obligation: that is, they were required to pay taxes and fulfill certain state functions, such as collecting taxes or serving in elected posts in organs of local urban administration. The last of these obligations was far from being either honorary or profitable but rather was considered burdensome, a situation reflected in the fact that election did not signify independence. When performing his elected function, the urban dweller was not so much in a position to resolve any of his town's problems as he was responsible to the sovereign for the collection of taxes. Under the circumstances, there could be no question of any sort of "citizenship." It is true that there was a small group of privileged townspeople composed of the richest merchants: they were the *gosti,* or leading merchants, and the members of the two merchant guilds. Again, their rights were defined by charters issued by the tsar rather than by general legislation. Although some leading merchants possessed hereditary estates, an important factor in comprehending the specific features of private property in Russia in this time period, they were ineligible for entry in the genealogical registers. They were, by the way, few in number: in the first half of the seventeenth century, there were but thirteen in all of Moscow, by far the largest town in the state.

During the reign of Ivan the Terrible, yet another unique sociopolitical institution emerged, which at first glance would seem to contradict the trend toward the strengthening of autocracy. Embarking on a program of broad-based reform, the young tsar decided to balance off the boyars' advice with that of other social strata. Thus we have the appearance of the first *Zemskii sobor,* or Assembly of the Land, a gathering of representatives of various ranks, with whom he took counsel on important political questions. The composition of the assembly varied over time, but generally included the upper clergy, members of the Sovereign's Court, representatives of the urban gentry corporation, and occasionally even townspeople and state peasants.

The questions of how and why the Assembly of the Land originated, evolved, and then disappeared have captured the attention of various representatives of public opinion as well as of historians, starting with the Slavophiles of the mid-nineteenth century. The latter searched anxiously for signs of political independence on the part of the Russian people, for a form of popular sovereignty that was peculiarly Russian. Soviet historians were inclined to view the Assemblies of the Land as a representative organ based on sociojuridical estates that supported the state's policies, while appealing both to society on behalf of the state and to the state on behalf of society and its public needs. L.V. Cherepnin, the respected Soviet authority on the history of the Assemblies of the Land, expressed this view, which seems strange, coming from the pen of a Marxist-Leninist. For what public needs could be enunciated in a society that according to Marxist theory is divided into antagonistic classes? In the same work, Cherepnin goes on to claim that the Assemblies of the Land were born in acute class conflict, and "had to provide the ruling class of feudal lords with a rallying point, and secure the subordination of the people to it."[20]

Furthermore, could there really be a "society" in the contemporary understanding of the term in sixteenth-century Russia? Berlin historian Hans-Joachim Torke has suggested that there was, for the state recognized the possibility of utilizing the various social groups to help administer the nation. According to Richard Pipes, however, "the idea of society . . . entails recognition by the state of the right of social groups to legal status and a legitimate sphere of free action. This recognition came to Russia only with the reign of Catherine II."[21] With regard to the assemblies as organs of estate representation, Torke noted that such bodies emerged in Europe in the struggle between the provinces and the center, as organs limiting the sovereign's power. Such could not have been the case in Russia, for there was no notion of citizenship that could serve as an embryonic cell of the modern era.[22]

On the one hand, the Assemblies of the Land played a critical role in Russian history, for they adopted legislation and elected tsars. On the other, they never served as permanent organs: they were convened irregularly and remained in session from one or two days up to a few months. The assemblies' composition, function, and rights were never legally established. Participation in the assembly by representatives of the various ranks was viewed as a form of state service, for which they were duly compensated. Under Ivan the Terrible, assemblies convened a few times in order to confirm decisions that had already been taken by the tsar. After the tsar's death, the assemblies failed to convene at all for twelve years, a strange pattern of behavior for an organ of authority, given the fact that Russia was ruled by Ivan the Terrible's weak-willed and sickly son, Tsar Fedor Ivanovich. With his death in 1598, the Rurikid dynasty died out.

After Boris Godunov's relatively brief reign (1598–1605) came the Time of Troubles, an era of civil war and royal pretenders, during which Poland and Sweden dispatched their armies to Russian territory in an attempt at aggrandizement. Given the utterly chaotic situation, the role of the assembly as a forum for the exercise of state authority and public reconciliation naturally grew. But even then, according to Cherepnin, the assemblies were utilized by Russian feudal parties and foreign interventionists who were struggling to achieve control.[23] In 1613, an Assembly of the Land elevated the first Romanov to the throne, and over the course of the seventeenth century, up to the 1680s, assemblies convened rather frequently, no longer electing tsars but rather confirming them, while the legislative decisions they adopted were designed to strengthen the autocratic regime, as had previously been the case.

There would seem to be a paradox here: after placing a new dynasty on the throne, the Assembly of the Land should have assumed added significance, wielding its newfound authority to limit state arbitrariness. Yet the reverse happened. Soviet historians wrote of the evolution of the Russian monarchy of this time into an absolute monarchy, claiming that the Assemblies of the Land simply aided the process. But in actuality, there is no paradox here. Simply put, despite all the dislocations of the Time of Troubles, the socioeconomic system of the Russian state survived intact. Its social strata, as they had before, formed a peculiar type of pyramid of interdependent, enserfed people under the authority of one ruler and master of their lives and property. When addressing him, even the most distinguished of boyars had to refer to themselves as his servants and slaves. The Assembly of the Land was but one of a number of tools the tsar used to control his subjects. Although with time it had become a political tradition, it quietly and painlessly expired with the dawn of the new era.

Such were the basic features of the sociopolitical structure of sixteenth- and seventeenth-century Russia. I will not attempt to bestow upon this structure any particular designation: there is an abundance of terms applied in the scholarly literature. I will only repeat that I consider it absolutely unwarranted to identify sixteenth- and seventeenth-century Russia as an estate-representative monarchy.[24] It is unwarranted because one could speak of estate representation only if estates and a corresponding estate structure existed in Russia at this time. Various reference works provide differing interpretations of the term "estate." Yet all agree on one thing: estates imply inherited status for their members, as defined by law. That is, it is not simply a question of situating members of a corporation on a social ladder, but of rights, privileges, and obligations.[25] There was, however, no such law in Russia, for law was weakly developed at the time. Even such a compilative and apparently all-encompassing codex as the 1649 Law Code was not devised to formulate the rights of given groups but to place restrictions and limitations on them.* It is true that there was always custom,** but superior to it was the tsar's will, before which all social groups were completely devoid of rights, possessing only obligations. The unusual nature of the social structure—the absence of estates in the generally accepted sense of the term, and as the embodiment of this system, serfdom—was the most important determinant of the Muscovite state's pattern of development during the first few centuries of its existence.

The unusual nature of the sociopolitical structure was firmly linked with the equally unusual nature of the spiritual and popular cultures, on which an essential imprint was left by the sense of Russia's spiritual uniqueness, mentioned above. Given this situation, the whole world lying outside Eastern Orthodoxy was viewed as hostile, and salvation was thought to lie in self-imposed isolation. Inasmuch as the preservation of Orthodoxy became the fundamental objective, the everyday behavior of the individual was subordinated to a harsh canon based on tradition, every violation of which was treated as a threat to the very pillars of the Orthodox state. Struggling for survival in this fashion, Eastern Orthodoxy lost the ability to develop further, which explains the absence in Russia of a native philosophical tradition as well as of a secular culture. Thus, until the seventeenth century, Russian literature

---

*I cannot agree with L.V. Danilova, who claims that the Novgorodian and Pskovian judicial charters, like the Law Code of 1649, established "a clear juridical formulation of feudal estates" (Danilova, *Stanovlenie sistemy gosudarstvennogo feodalizma v Rossii,* p. 52). These legislative enactments were intended to regulate "law and justice," but they did not include stipulations defining the rights of estates.

**The relationship of customary law to written law is one of the most critical and least-studied problems of early Russian history.

was highly stylized and depersonalized. Traces of non-religious painting, portrait painting in particular, did not appear until the end of the seventeenth century. Sculpture and theater as aspects of art were entirely absent.

The populace, apart from functionaries staffing state institutions and clergymen, was illiterate. The nation had no system of education as we know it today. Not only was there nothing similar to European universities (not until the end of the seventeenth century was the Slavonic-Greco-Latin Academy opened in Moscow), but there was no network of primary schools. One could receive any sort of education only on an individual basis. Even basic literacy was a rarity among the upper stratum of Russian society, being considered somehow demeaning. While the study and teaching of science had become an art, one of many forms of activity that were specialized in urban life [26] in medieval Europe by the twelfth century, there were no students or teachers or scholars among the Russian population. Scholarship did not exist as an independent sphere of social activity, while mathematical and other natural scientific knowledge had a narrowly applied significance (to architecture, commerce, fiscal needs, etc.). For all practical purposes, jurisprudence as a sphere of professional activity likewise did not exist. Historians of Russian law note that knowledge of laws and the ability to deal with them were acquired almost exclusively in the process of administering the law or when drawing up official papers. Such knowledge and ability accordingly were harbored almost exclusively by those who served in the state bureaucracy.[27] I will note in passing that this lack of development of science and law distinguished Russia not only from European countries but also from Asian countries, such as China, for example.

The individual's family life was subordinated to custom and tradition, which were based on the injunctions of the *Domostroi,* or Book of Household Management, a literary product of the seventeenth century. The Russian woman of this time did not participate in social life, had no right to select her own husband, had to subordinate herself meekly to her husband, and lacked even the right to leave the "women's quar-

---

*It is true, as Nancy Shields Kollmann has noted, that women were especially revered in Muscovite Rus, a situation that was reflected in the large fine paid for dishonor (N.Sh. Kollmann, "Problema chesti zhenshchiny v Moskovskoi Rusi," in *Realizm istoricheskogo myshleniia: Problemy otechestvennoi istorii perioda feodalizma. Chteniia posviashchennye pamiati A. L. Stanislavskogo. Tezisy,*

ters" and stroll freely about town without his permission.* For several centuries, not a single aspect of people's daily life—food, clothing, housing, or occupation—changed in any perceptible way. The same was true of the economic sphere. The village and the town provided the state with as many products as were necessary to support its survival, but no more.

The level of development of the economy and of trade was tightly bound up with the peculiar nature of the sociopolitical system, society's cultural-religious outlook, and Russia's specific geographical and demographic features. This is not to assert, however, that when evaluating Russian development one ought to shy away from the concept of "backwardness" by suggesting that, given the context of Russian realities, the Russian path represented sensible choices.[28] In Russia we are indeed dealing with backwardness: backwardness, moreover, that grew more pronounced, and ever more dangerous, with time. For, as contemporary scholars point out, referring to the works of Max Weber, the consolidation of the world into a "single civilization" was taking place in the modern era, with each element acting only as a part of the whole system. Given these conditions, a nation's lag in the pace of development and rationalization posed a threat to its sovereignty.[29] This general proposition is fully applicable to Russia in the seventeenth century, when this typically patriarchal, traditional society entered a period of acute crisis.

The first indication of this crisis came with the Time of Troubles at the start of the seventeenth century. The civil war was attributable, among other reasons, to the unusual nature of the nation's social structure, in which the conflict between the Cossacks and the nobility played a key role.*[30] In 1613, the Assembly of the Land elevated Mikhail

---

dokladov i soobshchenii [Moscow, 1991], pp. 133–34). See also her "Honor and Dishonor in Early Modern Russia," in *Forschungen zur Osteuropäischen Geschichte,* vol. 46 (1992), pp. 131–46. In general, it should be noted, the *Domostroi* reflected not so much norms of behavior as desires on the part of its author to achieve these norms. For an English translation of the *Domostroi,* see Carolyn Johnston Pouncy, ed., *The "Domostroi": Rules for Russian Households in the Time of Ivan the Terrible* (Ithaca, N.Y., 1994).

*The Cossacks were a special social grouping that gradually started to take shape on the nation's borderlands at the end of the fifteenth century. This grouping was composed of runaway peasants and townspeople and was utilized by the government to protect its borders. The Cossacks had a special, somewhat democratic but also archaic and militarized, form of organization.

Fedorovich Romanov to the Russian throne. It is not hard to see that the boyars and leaders of the various military groupings assumed it would be an easy matter to run the country by manipulating the seventeen-year-old, unambitious Mikhail.

At first glance they appeared to have been right, leading several historians to conclude that the authority of the first of the Romanovs must have been severely curtailed by the Boyar Council and the Assemblies of the Land. Others conclude that given the new conditions, authoritarian power was bound to collapse, inasmuch as the self-consciousness of the various strata of the population had increased.[31] Self-consciousness grew of course; but there was something that was much more important: the striving of the people to choose a new tsar bears witness to their desire for a firm government, one that could cope with the disorder and its consequences, one that, given the outlook of the Russian people of the day, could only be authoritarian. Since Cossack detachments opposed to the government controlled the various borderland regions, parts of the country were still occupied by Swedes and Poles, and the country itself lay in ruins, only a firm hand buttressed by firm support could hope to cope with the disorders. In 1617, Mikhail's government finally managed to sign a peace treaty with Sweden, and at the end of 1618, it arranged a truce with Poland. By terms of the agreements, Russia surrendered the Baltic Sea coast and a segment of traditionally Russian land, including the town of Smolensk, which remained in Polish hands. Russian prisoners of war, among whom was Filaret, the young tsar's father, however, were sent home from Poland. In June 1619, Filaret, who in Tsar Boris Godunov's reign was forced to take the cowl, was named Patriarch of Moscow: that is, head of the Russian Orthodox church. At the same time he received the title of Great Sovereign, ostensibly sharing power with his son, although in practice he concentrated all governmental power in his own hands. For the first time in Russian history, secular and religious authority converged in one person.

The fundamental thrust of Filaret's policy—the strengthening of the state and royal power—was continued after his death in 1633. In 1649, during the reign of Mikhail's son, Tsar Aleksei Mikhailovich, the *Sobornoe ulozhenie,* a new compilation of the laws, solidified definitively a political and social structure that had gradually been taking shape: an administrative system coupled with "the sovereign's service" and a form of conditional land tenure coupled with serfdom. The number of chancelleries grew constantly as the Boyar Council played an ever diminishing role. While there were other, competing tendencies in the nation's development at the time, this tendency dominated.

After the Time of Troubles, Russia's international situation changed. While under Ivan the Terrible, Russia's foreign policy had a Western orientation, its priority was now defined by the necessity to liberate the Russian lands still occupied by Poland. The government readily recognized, moreover, that an army relying upon gentry cavalry could never hope to contend successfully with the Poles. The formation of the so-called foreign-style regiments—of infantrymen, dragoons, and light cavalry, staffed by volunteers and officered by foreigners—was inaugurated at the end of the 1620s. Several years later, the formation of such regiments was reinstituted, this time for the defense of the nation's southern frontiers. In the period from 1658 until 1660, a draft of "recruits," or men handed over to the state by local communities, was conducted: one man for every twenty to twenty-five peasant and urban households. In essence, this was the first Russian permanent, standing army, in which the infantry rather than the cavalry predominated. It presaged the end of the old service system and the urban gentry corporation associated with it. By the 1680s, the gentry cavalry was approximately half the size it had been at mid-century.

The military reforms (an attempt also was made to construct a navy) represented what might roughly be termed an effort at modernization. But they proved glaringly inadequate, as the Russian army's failures in the Smolensk war of 1632–33 and the wars with Poland and Sweden of 1654–66 clearly revealed. To complicate matters, the Ottoman Empire emerged as a new enemy to the south. Although Russia managed to prevent any seizure of its lands in the course of the war of 1677–81, the result was attributable more to Turkish weakness than to the Russian army's strength. Military expeditions against the Crimean khanate in 1687 and 1689 proved unsuccessful. It was generally understood that the creation of a viable and well-equipped regular standing army had become a vital necessity. But a radical reform of everything associated with the system of "state service," with the organization of commerce and industry, and therefore a change in society's social structure, was required. All of this was necessary in order to establish equality with the other European powers. Without it, a successful conclusion to the struggle with the Turks was impossible.

Still another circumstance dictated the need for radical reform. Over the course of the seventeenth century, the state's territory had increased significantly: to the conquests of Siberia and the Volga region under Ivan the Terrible, the Ukraine was added by mid-century. This valuable acquisition, which was followed by massive Russian migration into the Ukraine, likewise resulted not so much from Russian strength as from Polish weakness. And although most Ukrainians were Eastern Orthodox, their political past and traditions differed dramatically from those of the Russians. On the one hand, the Cossack element in the Ukraine was strong, and on the other, certain towns were regulated by the principles of the Magdeburg Law, which provided for municipal autonomy. There was no serfdom in the Ukraine, while the Ukrainian gentry was to a substantial degree Polonized. When Russia annexed the Ukraine, it agreed to recognize the nation's autonomous political and administrative structures, including the election of its Hetman, or commander. But unification soon gave way to massive anti-Russian activity, which presented entirely new problems for the Russian government, problems with which it had not had to cope previously. To govern a huge country as it had earlier been governed, relying on outmoded institutions and methods, was impossible. Without radical reform, Russia would risk losing the territories that had been acquired at such expense and compromising its national security.

Russia's ever-increasing economic backwardness also played a major role in the gathering crisis. Over the centuries no real changes had been introduced into Russian agriculture, while serfdom and what might be termed the serf-like dependence of the urban population hindered the development of trade and industry. The further behind Russia fell, the more likely it became that it would share the fate of an ever weaker Ottoman Empire, which was undergoing an analogous crisis. What sort of crisis was it that Russia faced? From all that has been said, it seems clear that it was a crisis of traditionalism: that is, a situation in which traditionally shaped forms of social and political organization, entailing a specific system of obligations of various social groups toward each other and the state, had exhausted their potential, revealing themselves incapable of abetting the nation in its further development. The traditional forms required fundamental structural reorganization.

The crisis of traditionalism was also apparent in the intellectual and spiritual realm. Scholars speak ever more frequently of the seventeenth century as a watershed for Russian culture, as a time of transformation for the entire system, when secular and religious culture stood juxtaposed.[32] Playing an essential role in these processes was the Ukrainian annexation, after which the influence of Polish culture increased substantially. This influence was reflected in the translation of Polish books, the spread of luxury items imported from Poland, Polish dress, and so forth. Also very influential were the Ukrainian Orthodox clergy, most of whom had received their education in Peter Mohyla's celebrated Kiev Academy, where the teaching had been Latinized to a significant degree. Some of the academy's graduates became tutors to children of the Muscovite elite. In this milieu, elements of European education began to take root: We find people able to read and write not only in Russian but also in other languages, and even people who had a thorough knowledge of the natural sciences.

The religious schism of the mid-seventeenth century proved decisive for the transformation of Russian culture and for the spiritual life of Russia's subjects. It was spawned by the reform of certain aspects of church ritual that was carried out by Patriarch Nikon starting in 1652. Here in essence was another facet of the crisis of traditionalism. Henceforth, Russia would harbor a whole stratum of inhabitants, the Old Believers, who refused to accept the reform, ending up in opposition to the Nikonian church as well as to the tsarist authority that supported it. The reform turned out to be a double-edged sword for the church. As M.S. Anderson has noted, the implementation of the reform signified that as Russia's contacts with the outside world developed, its religious life had to be placed on a firmer intellectual basis than that of mere blind acceptance of tradition. This step marked the victory of an attitude toward church affairs that was critical, and at least to some extent rational, over one that was traditionalist and essentially uncritical. The effects of this victory, as Anderson noted, inevitably spilled over from the purely religious sphere into other aspects of Russian life, slowly eroding old, conservative values and accelerating the pace of change.[33] On the heels of the schism came a predictable increase in tension between the secular and ecclesiastical authorities, with the latter insisting on their rights. The conflict culminated in the removal of Nikon and the subordination of the church to secular power.

The authorities accepted the new patterns of behavior evident in Russian life, especially those associated with foreign influence, in a far-from-consistent manner. Thus, toward the end of his reign, Tsar Aleksei Mikhailovich promulgated a number of decrees banning European dress, shaving, smoking, and short haircuts. In the reign of Alexei's son Fedor, who ascended the throne in 1676, many of these banned patterns of behavior began to be accepted. In 1682, Fedor carried out an extremely important reform by abolishing *mestnichestvo*. Here we have a direct response to the need to reorganize the whole system of service, to processes occurring at the Grand Court and in the "service town." The project to compile new genealogical registers for the Russian nobility proposed at this time demonstrated the desire to create and juridically define a noble estate.

Tsar Fedor's reforms were continued after his death by his sister, Tsarevna Sophia.* The phenomenon of a woman at the head of the Russian state was doubtless a manifestation of the crisis of traditionalism. Sophia and her chief minister and favorite, Prince Vasilii Vasilievich Golitsyn, as one scholar has recently noted, updated legislation, struggled to combat the arbitrariness of local authorities, encouraged the development of trade and industry, unified and enriched the nobility, and strove to create a regular standing army.[34]

Still and all, the reforms carried out over the seventeenth century by the first Romanovs, from Tsar Mikhail to his granddaughter, Tsarevna Sophia, were quite moderate in scope.** Moreover, repetitive societies, a category in which Nancy Kollmann justifiably places seventeenth-century Russia, react to change with attempts to diffuse conflict and restore the status quo. Kollmann has noted that regardless of the degree of the particular change brought about by the resolution of disputes, conflict resolution in repetitive societies emphasizes the continuation or restoration of essential social and political structures.[35] Thus, the domestic crisis experienced by the Russian state in the seventeenth century could be resolved only by more radical reforms, which had become a critical necessity, as they alone could transform a repetitive society into a changing society.

But what sort of radical reform are we talking about, and what direction was it to take? Timothy Colton has defined radical reform as an "all-encompassing change containing as an essential component the restructuring of the country's political institutions and central legiti-

---

Tsarevna was the title bestowed on daughters of tsars.
**One cannot help but note in these reforms the tendency toward Europeanization, which is also observable to one degree or another throughout the existence of the Muscovite tsardom. It bore witness to the fact that this Europeanization was necessary for the state's development.

mating beliefs and myths."[36] Although Colton applied this definition in a different context, it applies equally to this period of Russian history. The direction the reform took was determined by the crisis of traditional institutions as well as by the modernizing character of reforms that previously had been undertaken. The necessary goals of the reform were modernization, aimed at the elimination of backwardness, and the transformation of Russia into a great world power. This last point deserves special examination.

The fundamental thrust of the changes taking place in Russian intellectual and spiritual life at the end of the seventeenth century, according to A. Panchenko, a historian of Russian culture, was directed toward overcoming Russia's cultural separateness, linking it to European civilization, and permitting it to join the ranks of the great powers.[37] Given the conditions of the time, if Russia were to become a "great power," it had to wield sufficient economic and military might to play a leading role in international politics and to conduct an active, aggressive foreign policy, as aggressive and expansionist as that of the other great European powers. The process of territorial expansion that was launched in the sixteenth and seventeenth centuries in Siberia, the Volga region, the Crimea, and the Ukraine, could not simply be brought to a halt: it had to be either continued or reversed. Continued expansion was impossible without a strong, professionalized army and an up-to-date industrial base. That, as we have seen, demanded radical reform. Without it, defeat and national catastrophe were inevitable.

Thus, the circle was closed. Radical reform became for late seventeenth-century Russia an unavoidable necessity, the only escape from crisis and the only way to save the state. The concepts of "crisis" and "radical reform" were interrelated. Not only did the crisis call forth radical reform, but reform was feasible only within the context of crisis. For only under such circumstances were the powerful conservative forces capable of resisting all-encompassing transformation relegated to the background. Radical reform had to modernize the country and render it a full-fledged member of the "Respublica Christiana." It was to Peter the Great that the task of implementing this reform fell.

Chapter 2

The Birth of the Great Reformer

All of Peter I's biographers have had to confront the question of how and why the fourteenth child (born in 1672) of Tsar Aleksei Mikhailovich, who was called "The Most Serene," turned out to be a man of such boundless energy, and why he channeled that energy into reform, attempting to remake the huge nation he had inherited. What were the origins of Peter's dislike for the old Russian patterns and customs and the insouciance with which he violated time-honored norms of behavior and rejected the "world of ceremonies and conventions," the "closed system, hallowed by tradition,"[1] that had surrounded him since childhood? Yet another of Peter's traits, so uncharacteristic of seventeenth-century Russians, strikes the observer: his inquisitiveness, his desire to comprehend everything that lay beyond the confines of the traditional world of the tsarist court.

Many authors try to explain the tsar's unusual traits by his childhood experiences. Indeed, at four years of age Peter lost his father. With the subsequent coronation of his older half brother, Fedor, Peter and his mother, Tsaritsa Natalia Kirillovna,* were pushed into the background of court and political life. In keeping with Russian tradition, relatives of the tsar's wife were always found in the tsar's intimate circle. Such had been the case in 1671, when the widowed forty-year-old Aleksei Mikhailovich married for a second time, taking for his wife the twenty-year-old daughter of the Smolensk nobleman Kirill Naryshkin. She had been raised in the household of the tsar's

---

Tsaritsa was the title bestowed upon wives and mothers of tsars as well as female sovereigns who ruled in their own right.

Peter I. Engraving taken from a portrait by Carel de Moore.

favorite, Artamon Matveev, a talented diplomat and state figure and a lover of foreign innovations, who was married to an Englishwoman, Lady Hamilton. Over the course of the next five years the "Naryshkin party" established itself firmly at court, and Matveev became what would be termed today a prime minister.

With the coronation of Fedor, however, the Naryshkins had to yield to the Miloslavskiis, the relatives of the young tsar's deceased mother. Matveev was exiled and even accused of plotting against the life of the tsar. The great prerevolutionary historian Sergei Soloviev described the repercussions for the youthful Peter in this fashion:

> He is faced with a mother who is always sad and forever discussing with her confidants her troubles and the exile of her brothers and her patron Matveev. The ardent youth, sensitive as he is, absorbs and is annoyed by, the family enmity. Things that most youths only hear about in childhood tales—how evil relatives pursue innocent children and how the latter either perish or triumph—the young Peter experiences in reality. He is already the hero of his own dramas, a leading character. He detests his persecutors with a passion, and his sympathy for his heroes is stronger than that of other youths toward the heroes of their tales; for he himself, his mother, and his uncle are his heroes.[2]

Just how closely the sketch drawn by Soloviev corresponds to reality is hard to say. The tsaritsa, merry and lighthearted by nature, according to contemporary accounts, was widowed and deprived of Matveev's support at such a young age that she could not help but grieve. And the Miloslavskiis probably treated her with condescension. Tsar Fedor, however, showed his stepmother obvious respect. Nor did he neglect his younger half brother, who was also his godson. It was he who, when Peter completed his fifth year, reminded the widowed tsaritsa of the need to start the young tsarevich's education.* An undersecretary in one of Moscow's chancelleries, Nikita Zotov, a calm and pious man, was selected as Peter's tutor. It is indicative that before the assignment was announced, Zotov was examined in the presence of the tsar himself. The tsar and the patriarch attended Peter's first lesson as well, richly rewarding the newly appointed tutor. Soon thereafter, the situation at court started to change to Peter's advantage. By 1680, the Miloslavskiis' influence began to wane, while the Naryshkins'

Tsarevich was the title bestowed on sons of tsars.

waxed. Contributing to the change was Fedor, who was becoming more independent (when he ascended the throne he was not quite fourteen years old), and the circumspection of certain boyars, who foresaw that the sickly tsar's reign would not last indefinitely. Indeed, at the end of April 1682, Tsar Fedor died. Subsequent events were to reflect remarkably well both the peculiarities of the seventeenth-century Russian political structure and its crisis situation.

Since Fedor Alekseevich died childless,* all the rules of succession (which were mandated by custom rather than written law) dictated that the crown pass to his sixteen-year-old half brother, Ivan. But Ivan was a weak child and obviously incapable of ruling by himself. Taking advantage of the turmoil at court, and probably still several hours before Fedor breathed his last breath, the Naryshkins and their adherents had Peter proclaimed tsar. But their triumph proved short-lived. Barely more than two weeks later an uprising of the *streltsy,* or musketeers, constituting what was in essence a palace guard and the chief police force of the time, broke out in Moscow. It was called forth by the careless measures of the inept Naryshkins and fanned by the Miloslavskiis.

On May 15, 1682, in full view of Peter, who at the time was standing on the porch of the Kremlin's women's quarters together with his mother and his older half brother, Ivan, the musketeers hoisted Artamon Matveev, who had just returned from exile, onto the tips of their pikes. According to contemporaries, the ten-year-old Peter displayed remarkable composure. Many historians assume, however, that the convulsive twitchings of the head and other parts of the body that were to become so characteristic of the adult Peter, especially when he was extremely agitated, were connected with this childhood trauma. Such assertions can be traced back to the memoirs of Andrei Nartov, who recalled that the tsar had once told him: "The memory of the rebelling musketeers, the hydra of the fatherland, causes every bone in my body to tremble; when I think of them, I cannot sleep."[3]

It should be noted that the musketeer uprising of 1682 had a distinct Old Believer cast to it. The prerevolutionary historian A.P. Shchapov suggested that the musketeers hoped to establish "an Old Believer state or a schismatics' democracy"[4]: that is, a state more archaic in form than the existing one. After the uprising, Peter associated the muske-

---

*Fedor's only child, a son named Ilia, died in infancy.

teers, the Moscow Kremlin where the uprising took place, and the schismatics all together in his mind. They became for him the embodiment of an old Russia that was hostile to him. At the subconscious level, in Vasilii Kliuchevskii's words, he sensed that "rebellion meant schism, and schism meant the old Russian past; therefore the old Russian past meant rebellion."[5]

In keeping with the demands of the musketeers, Ivan was placed on the throne along with Peter, although as "first tsar," while their older sister, the tsarevna Sophia, was named regent until they attained their majority. It should immediately be noted that these arrangements were highly unusual and ran counter to tradition. For that reason they testified to the existence of a domestic crisis.* Up until this point two tsars had never occupied the Russian throne at the same time, while the last time a woman regent shared power was in the first half of the sixteenth century, during Ivan the Terrible's minority. Even then she was a tsaritsa, the mother of the young tsar, rather than an unmarried tsarevna, or daughter. This alone created a highly unstable situation, one in which the state was bound to experience new shocks.

The claim that Sophia herself was the chief organizer and instigator of the musketeer uprising dominates the historical literature. The surviving documents do not permit one to either confirm or reject the thesis. However, Sophia and the Miloslavskiis, who backed her, took full advantage of the uprising. The tsarevna was without doubt an unusual woman, if only because she had already decided to break with the tradition whereby daughters of Russian tsars were condemned to spend their days confined to the women's quarters of the palace, were not married off, usually lived out their lives in nunnery cells, and of course had nothing to do with politics. By the standards of the day, Sophia received a fairly good education at home; was intelligent; and most important, was ambitious and decisive. Taking advantage of the rebellion in order to seize power, she soon cleverly dispatched its ringleaders and began to rule by herself. Prince Vasilii Vasilievich Golitsyn, a man of European-style education who knew several foreign languages, became her chief minister and favorite.

---

*Yet it is also true that there had been an instance in Russian history, at the start of the sixteenth century, when Ivan III proclaimed his grandson Dmitrii his successor and co-ruler, and for a brief period of time the two ruled together. And, for all practical purposes, the Patriarch Filaret served as co-ruler with his son, Tsar Mikhail Fedorovich.

Sophia's rule has met with divergent evaluations in the historical literature. Her contemporary, Peter's colleague Prince Boris Kurakin, wrote: "The reign of Tsarevna Sophia began with great conscientiousness and justice, to the satisfaction of the people, because the Russian realm had never before known the likes of such a wise reign. The whole realm experienced great prosperity during the seven years of her reign, trade and commerce multiplied . . . and the people relished their freedom."[6] Historians who sympathize with Peter consider this praise exaggerated. Nonetheless, Sophia's government did manage to stabilize the domestic situation, attempted to combat the arbitrariness of local officials, encouraged the development of trade and industry, and adopted measures to reorganize and re-equip the army. In 1688, it achieved an important foreign-policy objective with the signing of eternal peace with Poland. From that time on, according to some sources, the regent began to ponder the possibility of having herself crowned autocratic tsaritsa.

While recognizing the political talents of Sophia and her first minister and acknowledging that the measures they undertook pacified the country, one must also admit that they did not resolve the domestic crisis.[7] The two could not accomplish the latter because they lacked a suitably broad political program. Rather, all their efforts were directed at maintaining power, regardless of the cost. For precisely this reason, military campaigns were launched against the Crimean khanate in 1687 and 1689. A victory over the khanate would have decisively strengthened the authority of Sophia, who dreamed of becoming a full-fledged tsaritsa. But the Crimean campaigns proved disastrous, at least in the view of most historians. Granted, there is another point of view, holding that the Russian army's performance in these campaigns represented one of the great achievements of the military science of the day.[8] Yet few would agree with that assessment, for the fact remains that the campaigns' objective was not attained and the Crimean khan was not transformed into a Russian vassal. Instead, succeeding decades brought the Russian government no end of complications on that front.

To return to Peter, how did he fare during his half sister's seven-year reign? Peter's family and entourage, excluded from participation in the discussion of political questions, for all practical purposes abandoned the Kremlin, preferring instead to divide their time among their various suburban residences, at Vorobievo, Kolomenskoe, and Preobrazhenskoe. Historians often refer to the disgrace and near exile of

Natalia Kirillovna and her courtiers, asserting that "bitterness and complaints" reigned at the "disgraced court," that without informing the young tsar, his mother and those close to her hatched a conspiracy, once again putting Peter's life at risk, while simultaneously frightening him and instilling in him a hatred for his half sister and her advisers.[9] In fact, the situation was not quite so straightforward.

Although effective power was vested in Sophia's government, the legal basis of this power remained quite shaky. Every time there was an official ceremony in the Kremlin—and in the schedule of the royal court such events were both frequent and long—it was first and foremost Peter and Ivan who appeared in their royal finery and with all the accompanying regalia. It was in their names that royal decrees were signed, official exchanges with foreign governments conducted, war declared, and peace concluded. Thanks to these appearances, Ivan's incapacity for rule became obvious. As for Peter, the older he grew the more self-sufficiency he manifested. As the secretary of the Swedish embassy, Engelbert Kämpfer, informs us, by the age of eleven Peter was boldly violating strict court etiquette. According to Kämpfer,

> When the [Swedish] envoy submitted his letters of credence and both tsars were to stand at the same time to inquire about the king's health, the younger, Peter, did not give his uncles time to help him and his brother up, as etiquette required. Instead, he leaped from his place, doffed the tsarist crown himself, and impetuously recited the customary greeting: "And our brother, His Imperial Majesty Karl of Sweden—is he healthy?"[10]

Let us dwell a bit on the impetuosity noted by the Swedish diplomat. Manifesting itself also as fidgetiness, restlessness, and excitability, this impetuosity was to remain embedded in Peter's character throughout his life. It bore direct testimony to the unbalanced state of the tsar-reformer's psyche, embodied in the need for constant trips and physical activity, be it military exercises, rowdy drinking bouts, or physical labor. Whether this unbalanced state was innate or a consequence of troublesome childhood impressions, it undoubtedly exerted a great influence on Peter's actions and way of life. It certainly contributed to his frequent attacks of rage, which became so characteristic, and possibly to his brutality, which shocked even his contemporaries.

In terms of his personality development, however, Peter's removal from court proved beneficial. At Preobrazhenskoe he could find an outlet for his energy far more readily than he could have in the Kremlin. Here Peter was left substantially to his own devices, and he spent the lion's share of his time at play. From early childhood on, he had displayed a fascination for handicrafts and had learned how to use various tools. Military games, however, were his real love. He devoted an especially large amount of time to them, at first playing with toy soldiers and then with real people, forming "play" regiments with his stable boys and playmates, and taking real weapons from the Kremlin's armory to equip them. An entire wooden fortress for his military games sprang up at Preobrazhenskoe, at which real cannons were fired and for which manuals of arms were drawn up.

In a shed at the Izmailovo palace Peter stumbled across an English boat, which he wanted to try out on the spot. But the boat had to be repaired before it could be sailed, and someone had to figure out how to work the sails. No one from Peter's entourage was able to help him, just as no one could explain to him how to use the astrolabe that had been brought from France. He did, however, manage to locate experts not far from Preobrazhenskoe, in the German Quarter of Moscow, a suburb where, in Evgenii Anisimov's words, he found a "peculiar model of Europe," one in which "Catholics and Protestants, Germans and Frenchmen, Englishmen and Scots" lived side by side.[11]

In the German Quarter, the young Peter was exposed to utterly new impressions: to a different pattern of life, a different system of interpersonal relations, and a multiplicity of objects he had never before seen, all alluring because of their unfamiliarity. The impatient Peter, who hated the interminable Kremlin ceremonies, found this style of life attractive in its rationality, simplicity, and naturalness. The tsar became a frequent guest in the quarter. There he found his bosom buddies and the first real love of his life, Anna Mons, the daughter of a Dutch wine merchant.

The older Peter grew, the more strained relations between his court and Sophia's became.* The tsarevna understood that once Peter reached maturity, she might lose her grip on power, for she would have no more legal claim to direct the government. Moreover, the active nature of her younger half brother began to frighten her. After all, he

---

*At this time, each of the members of the royal family maintained his or her own court retinue.

was conspicuously gathering together at Preobrazhenskoe what were in effect his own personal armed forces. In addition, the patriarch and several other high church hierarchs supported Peter. In their turn, Natalia Kirillovna and her court retinue began to grow more and more confident as time went on. At Preobrazhenskoe they started speaking ever more critically of Sophia and her ministers, realizing full well that their comments would reach the tsarevna's ear.

But Sophia, too, seemed bent on a collision course. Her name began to appear on official documents alongside those of Ivan and Peter. She even tried to inject herself into court ceremonies in which the participation of women was not traditionally permitted. The tsarevna began to hatch a conspiracy, convinced that was her only hope of preserving and continuing to wield what power she had. Once more the musketeers were called upon to carry it out. They were persuaded to raise a rebellion with the demand that Sophia be crowned ruler. The commanders of the musketeer regiments, however, wavered. In order to spur them to action, rumors were spread around Moscow on the night of August 7, 1689, that "play" soldiers from Preobrazhenskoe were marching on the town. The musketeers took up arms. In the resulting confusion, Peter's adherents concluded that on the contrary, the musketeers intended to march on Preobrazhenskoe, and they warned the tsar accordingly. A frightened Peter sought refuge that night behind the thick walls of the Holy Trinity Monastery outside Moscow. The next day, the tsar's mother, Natalia Kirillovna, arrived, as did all of his entourage, along with his "play" soldiers and a number of musketeers.

Conflict appeared inevitable. Faced with competing demands on their loyalty, the courtiers, Muscovite nobles, musketeers, and other service people were forced to take sides. One might well have expected them to choose Sophia, for she held formal power in her hands. But subsequent events revealed that Sophia lacked sufficient support among the populace. Apparently, the very prospect of a woman exercising authority by herself, especially given the presence of a living male heir to the throne, struck God-fearing Muscovites as so unacceptable that it frightened them. At the time the events took place, moreover, Sophia was serving merely as regent, with rather ill-defined status from a legal point of view, while Peter was the legitimate tsar. Then, too, the emotional factor should not be discounted: A feeling of pity for the persecuted has always animated the Russian people. As Nikolai Pavlenko has noted, "in the eyes of the capital's population, including certain elements of the musketeers, Peter seemed to be the victim, forced to save himself from persecution by fleeing his residence."[12]

During the next several days, military forces stationed in Moscow wended their way steadily to the Holy Trinity Monastery to offer their fealty. Setting off with the intention of entering into negotiations with her half brother, Sophia was stopped and ordered to return to Moscow. This was soon followed by a demand to hand over one of the tsarevna's favorites, Fedor Shaklovityi, who was accused of plotting against Peter. He was duly handed over, tortured horribly, and executed on September 11. At the end of the month Sophia was confined to the Novodevichii Convent, where she remained until her death in 1704. Together with his entourage, Peter returned to Moscow in triumph. Along the way he was met by kneeling musketeers, next to each of whom stood an executioner's block with an ax imbedded in it as a sign of submission. In such fashion began the autocratic reign of Peter I.

During the first years of Peter's exclusive rule, his way of life did not change, at least on the surface. Preobrazhenskoe remained his main residence, and he agreed to take part in palace ceremonies only at his mother's insistence, and even then with great reluctance. All his thoughts were directed at military and naval games, as before. He spent his time arranging everything for his "make-believe" battles, which entailed the capture of fortresses, cannon fire, and real casualties. As the scale of these games grew more and more extensive, they came increasingly to resemble actual military maneuvers. In the guise of bombardier Petr Alekseevich, moreover, the tsar personally participated in the battles. As for the repaired English boat, even before the coup d'état he had tried it out on the narrow Iauza River in Moscow, and then on a pond in the village of Izmailovo. Finally, in the spring of 1689, unbeknownst to his mother, he left for Lake Pereiaslavl, where at his command the construction of new vessels had begun.

In the winter of 1692, Peter again headed for Pereiaslavl, taking with him large supplies of construction material. But it did not take long for Lake Pereiaslavl to strike him as too constrictive. So in the summer of 1693, the tsar headed for Archangel, the only seaport Russia had at the time. There he caught his first glimpse of the sea and real seagoing ships, completed his first sea voyage in a yacht, and laid the keel for a new ship. He also worked with an axe, spending what spare time he had in the company of simple shipwrights. The sea and shipbuilding became and remained the passions of his life. The ship in its turn was transmuted into the symbol of the entire Petrine reign, the embodiment of Russia's transformation.

Meanwhile, the tsar's highly unusual behavior distressed Tsaritsa Natalia Kirillovna, who literally showered her son with letters during his trips to Pereiaslavl and Archangel. But neither the prayers of his mother, nor the acquisition of a young wife (Peter had married Evdokia Lopukhina early in 1689 at his mother's insistence), nor the birth of a son in 1690 could deter the tsar from whatever happened to attract him. Peter loved and esteemed Natalia Kirillovna, but by the beginning of the 1690s he had gathered around himself a circle of friends whom historians subsequently labeled his companions, and whom the great Russian poet Alexander Pushkin termed "the fledglings of Peter's nest." These people, most notably the jovial Swiss jokester Franz Lefort, Scottish mercenary Patrick Gordon, and former pie seller Alexander Menshikov, among a number of others, exercised great influence over Peter not only by refusing to discourage him from the pursuit of his amusements but also by actually egging him on.

In books about Peter I, one occasionally comes across the assertion that the tsar was something of a democrat, surrounding himself with people of "commoner" origins. Such, however, was not his intention. Those who were close at hand in critical times, who were sufficiently active and decisive and, most important, completely devoted to him, were those who became his companions. Hence it was that not only commoners but also representatives of distinguished Russian families—Prince B.A. Golitsyn, B.P. Sheremetev, F.M. Apraksin, P.A. Tolstoy, Prince F.Iu. Romodanovskii, T.N. Streshnev, and others—who early on perceived the potential benefits of proximity to the young autocrat, became his boon companions and advisers. These people varied in their level of education, their capacities, and even their ages. Their roles likewise varied. It was to Lefort, whom he loved so much, that the tsar owed much of his familiarity with European life. Peter was beholden to Lefort also for his generous and good advice and for serving as a go-between in the tsar's relationship with Anna Mons. Lefort, however, seldom meddled in governmental affairs. Menshikov, in contrast, gradually became Peter's right-hand man in the full sense of the term. He became, in Pushkin's words, "a semi-sovereign lord," the listing of whose titles, ranks, and posts alone would require an entire page. Within the tsar's intimate circle, surprisingly familiar relations prevailed, constantly reinforced by drinking bouts. This familiarity, however, never deterred Peter from severely reprimanding even the closest of his friends for the slightest offense.

These relationships, established in the pursuit of amusement, continued to preserve their game-like, jocular, populist aspect over an extended period of time. Thus, paralleling official state structures and the established system of relations between the tsar and his people was a special, imaginary realm, known only to a narrow circle of friends, which was headed by "Prince-Caesar" Fedor Romodanovskii, among whose subjects the tsar was numbered. The latter addressed the "Prince-Caesar" deferentially, as a sovereign, while the former could even upbraid the tsar for appearing before him without removing his hat. Evgenii Anisimov appropriately compares this situation with a similar one evident in the reign of Ivan the Terrible, who in 1575 ostensibly raised Khan Simeon Bekbulatovich to the Muscovite throne, and then proceeded to pretend to play the role of his humble subject for several years.[13] Despite the obvious masquerade quality of the latter episode, it had a rather prosaic political purpose to it, while the presence at Peter's court of the "Prince-Caesar," with all his purported attributes, represented a continuation of the tsar's childhood games.

It is indicative that the capital of the imaginary kingdom was named Pressburg, which was the old German name for Bratislava, the capital of present-day Slovakia, while Peter's letters to Romodanovskii opened with the Dutch address "Min Heer Konig," or "My Lord King." The transition from games to serious politics was effected effortlessly and almost imperceptibly by Peter himself and those around him. There is an important psychological point to be made here. One is struck by the fact that from childhood on Tsar Peter never assumed the role of commander in his military and naval games, preferring instead to participate in them as a regular member, or even an apprentice. He genuinely attempted to learn both military and naval affairs from the ground up, receiving the military ranks appropriate to his actual service rather than his royal birth. The existence of a "Prince-Caesar" who promoted the tsar in orderly fashion in effect helped legitimize the mechanism established for receiving these ranks. By the same token, the tsar, by pursuing a service career along with others, served as an example for his subjects, pointing out to them that ardent service alone could procure a high position in society. From another perspective, the very idea of service to the fatherland as society's supreme virtue became ever more firmly embedded in Tsar Peter's own mind.

At the beginning of 1694, Tsaritsa Natalia Kirillovna died. Her death became one more landmark in the history of Petrine Russia, for from this time Peter's independent reign could be said to have begun in earnest. Until then the tsar had displayed little interest in domestic affairs of state, not even deigning to drop in on either the Boyar Council or the chancelleries. Instead, he entrusted the direction of the government primarily to his uncle, L.K. Naryshkin. Returning to Moscow from Archangel in the early fall of 1694, Peter staged his regular large-scale maneuvers, after which he decided to undertake a real military campaign.

The direction in which he chose to move—the south—was traditional for Russian military forces of the time, which since the 1670s had joined with Polish, Habsburg Austrian, and Venetian forces in an anti-Turkish alliance. The direction chosen clearly demonstrates that Peter did not yet harbor any new foreign policy concepts or intentions. But while up to this time Russia had directed its major efforts against the Ottoman Empire's ally, the khanate of the Crimea, it was now decided to attempt to conquer the Turkish fortress of Azov, which lay on the left bank of the Don River, where it flows into the Sea of Azov. A successful campaign would provide Russia with access to open water, and the tsar with the opportunity to satisfy his passion for the sea. Peter organized his campaign in a manner similar to his "play" maneuvers: that is, the three columns of Russian troops each had their own commanders, while the tsar himself marched in one of them as commander of a company of bombardiers. The real war, however, turned out to be far more complex than his previous war games.

After reaching Azov in June 1695 and laying siege to the fortress, the Russian forces soon discovered the inability of their engineers to conduct siege warfare, the impossibility of coordinating activity in the absence of a unified military command structure, and in general, their inadequate preparation for serious military undertakings. Most glaring of all was the need for a navy, without which Azov could not be encircled. Two attempts to storm the fortress proved unsuccessful, while Turkish sallies inflicted heavy losses on the Russian forces. In October the siege of Azov was lifted, and the forces headed home. It was precisely at this point that Peter's character, including his remarkable ability to learn from his mistakes, manifested itself most starkly. Peter refused to let his spirits drop. Rather, he returned to Moscow with plans for another campaign, one organized along different lines.

On September 27, a mere two days after the tsar's return, a new campaign was announced to the state's servitors. In January 1696, volunteers began to gather at Preobrazhenskoe, including those *kholopy,* or bondsmen, who were willing to enlist in order to win their emancipation. Meanwhile, a huge effort to construct a fleet unfolded simultaneously at Preobrazhenskoe and at Voronezh on the Don River. Herded together in the latter place were about twenty thousand workers from all over Russia, most of them peasants, who were handed axes and transformed into carpenters. This was the first huge mobilization of the population carried out by Peter. It achieved the construction of about thirty ships of various sorts within a few short months. In April the ships were launched, and at the beginning of May they set sail for Azov. This time the campaign proved successful. The Russian galley fleet managed to cut off Turkish access to Azov by sea, while the armed forces began the intensive construction of siege works, accompanied by effective artillery fire directed at the fortress. Without awaiting a decisive attack, the Turkish forces capitulated on July 18.

The capture of Azov, the young tsar's first important military victory, had the consequence of significantly increasing his domestic political authority. This he badly needed because his friendship with foreigners and his lifestyle, so uncustomary for a Russian tsar, had long since aroused dissatisfaction among various elements of the population. Even more, the victory at Azov represented the first Russian military victory in a long time. Peter apparently recognized this fact, and accordingly ordered preparations for an especially festive entry into Moscow, organized not along traditional Russian lines but in the European manner. The tsar himself participated in the triumphal parade on foot, dressed in Western-style clothes. He marched, it should be noted, not at the head of his troops but on the heels of his generals.

Early success can completely turn a young man's head, leading him to conclude that he has achieved his goal and can now rest on his laurels. But success served merely to arouse Peter and to energize him still more. His activities became broader in scope, more independent, and more purposeful. Less than three weeks after his triumphal entry into Moscow, the tsar convened the Boyar Council: not in the Kremlin chambers, where the boyars felt at home, but rather at Preobrazhenskoe. Two crucial problems were posed to the boyars: how to establish and maintain Russian control over Azov and the surrounding territory, and how to construct a sailing fleet capable of continuing the prosecution of the war. The resolution of these problems would require substantial human resources and vast financial expenditures. Under other circumstances, the council members might have demurred; but now Peter was dealing with them from a position of strength.

As a result, Peter resolved to resettle three thousand Russian families from towns along the Volga River to Azov and to introduce a special shipbuilding obligation, imposing the cost of constructing a fleet on monasteries, service people, and merchants. To that end, special *kumpanstva,* or companies, were to be formed by the members of these groups, with each company made responsible for the construction of one ship. In keeping with Peter's plans, all landholders owning more than one hundred peasant households were summoned to Moscow to form such companies. They were threatened with confiscation of their property for failure to appear.[14] The Boyar Council was also forced to sanction a new mobilization of hundreds of thousands of people for the actual construction of the fleet. And there was still more to come. Although the Russian peasants mobilized at Voronezh proved adequate carpenters, the construction of sailing ships was a new and unfamiliar business to them. The nation also lacked people who knew how to sail the vessels. Highly qualified specialists were needed, and they could be found only abroad.

So it was that in November Peter promulgated a decree calling for the dispatch of several dozen scions of the most aristocratic families to study in Western Europe. The tsar's decree represented a real tragedy for the young Russians affected, who were unaccustomed not only to trips abroad but to trips in general. They knew no world other than that into which they had been born, they were unaccustomed to any form of study, and they were imbued with numerous prejudices against Europe, which was thought hostile to Russia and to Orthodoxy. No one had asked them if they wanted to go, and no one had looked into their capacity for learning. They were simply mobilized. Just as the tsar by an act of will had transformed peasants into shipwrights, so he transformed young nobles into navigators, captains, engineers—in sum, into whatever he thought the nation needed. As always in such situations, he did not spare himself from the ranks of those being mobilized; even he set off to study abroad.

On December 6, 1696, a decree was promulgated concerning the dispatch abroad of "the Grand Embassy," to be headed by three ambassadors: Franz Lefort, Fedor Golovin, and Peter Voznitsyn. Accompanying them was to be a delegation, the likes of which had never before been seen, including the tsar himself, who had assumed the name of Peter Mikhailov.* He would be the first Orthodox sovereign in Russian history to travel beyond the frontiers of his fatherland in order to visit those who had "abandoned" the true Christian faith, and the first to conduct negotiations personally with foreign royalty. Such intentions represented not only a departure from the customs of his ancestors but a direct challenge to Russian antiquity, with its ideology of isolation and xenophobia. The primary goal of Peter's journey, aside from the satisfaction of his natural curiosity, was to study the ways in which foreigners had surpassed Russians. As Sergei Soloviev so grandiloquently put it, Peter's desire to visit the West reflected "the irresistible striving of an uncivilized but historic, noble people toward civilization."[15]

Before starting out on his pilgrimage to the source of civilization, Peter managed to manifest the barbarian side of his nature when, a few days prior to his departure, he got word that the musketeers had hatched another plot against him. As a result, five conspirators were executed and their heads stuck onto sharp metal spikes and set on a wooden column that had been specially constructed for the purpose on Red Square in Moscow. Peter, moreover, ordered unearthed the coffin containing the body of Prince Ivan Miloslavskii, who had died twelve years earlier, and whom he thought to have been involved at one point in the conspiracy. Placed on a sledge harnessed to pigs, the coffin was carted off to Preobrazhenskoe, where the executions were to occur. There it was laid under the executioner's block so that the blood from the executed men would flow down into it. Five days after the executions, on March 9, 1697, the embassy, including Peter, departed from Moscow, while the frightful column, with the heads of those who had been executed held aloft and their bodies lying at the base, was left standing on Red Square until July as a reminder of the tsar's terrible wrath.

The route followed by the Grand Embassy led first through Riga, which at the time belonged to Sweden, to Mitau, the capital of Courland (now Jelgava, located on the territory of present-day Latvia, and at the time a fief of Poland), and from there to Königsberg (belonging

---

*One meets with various explanations in the scholarly literature for Peter's insistence on traveling abroad incognito. The simplest of them is that official visits to foreign countries by heads of state were not yet accepted practice in Europe at that time.

to the Electorate of Brandenburg at the time, but now known as Kaliningrad, located on Russian territory). The reception granted the tsar in Riga was cold, a fact that, according to some historians, contributed to his subsequent decision to declare war on Sweden. The receptions in Mitau and Königsberg, on the other hand, were warm. The Duke of Courland and the Elector of Brandenburg fêted the tsar with lavish banquets, fireworks, and hunts. Peter learned something about artillery from the chief engineer of the Prussian fortresses, embraced Elector Frederick II at their meeting, managed to conclude a treaty of alliance with him, and then headed off to Holland.

Along the way, Peter dined with two ladies who were anxious to make his acquaintance: Princess Sophie of Hanover and her daughter, Princess Sophie Charlotte of Brandenburg. Both left interesting accounts, from which it seems that Peter at first felt shy in their presence, even hiding his face in his hands. But once they "domesticated" him, he began to chat merrily, coerced all those present to drink three or four glasses of wine, and showed them his hands, which were calloused from physical labor, after which he enjoyed himself immensely. He even attempted to teach his hostesses "to dance in the Muscovite style." The ladies noted that the tsar did not know how to eat properly or use his napkin, while Peter, who had no idea about women's corsets, which were not worn in Russia, observed that German women had "devilishly hard bones." The older of the women, more experienced and insightful, added that "the sovereign is at one and the same time very kind and very evil; his character is completely that of his country."[16]

Upon his arrival in Holland, Peter first worked in the Saardam shipyards, and then moved on to Amsterdam, where the directors of the East India Company had the keel of a new ship laid especially for him, so that he could follow the entire construction process from beginning to end. Over the course of several months, Peter worked as a simple ship carpenter, taking breaks from his work only to participate in official ceremonies and meetings with the king of England and the stadtholder of the Netherlands, William of Orange, or with Dutch scholars, one of whom was the first to show the tsar a microscope. Meanwhile, members of the embassy conducted official negotiations with the Dutch government for an alliance against the Turks and privately purchased weapons and hired masters for Russia's metallurgical works and armories as well as experts in maritime matters. Neither the purchases nor the hiring proved a simple matter. The Russians were unable to persuade the Dutch to sign a treaty, but they did manage to purchase fifteen thousand weapons and hire several hundred sailors for service in the Russian fleet.

After spending four and a half months in Holland, Peter moved on to London in January 1698, where all sorts of introductions and excursions awaited him. The tsar visited Oxford University, the Greenwich Observatory, the Royal Society of England, and the Royal Mint. He had at least two meetings with King William III and apparently was introduced to Sir Isaac Newton.[17] He also met with the Archbishop of Salisbury, Gilbert Burnet, and convinced the Scottish mathematician Andrew Farquharson to move to Russia. It was with particular joy that Peter and those accompanying him signed a trade treaty by which Vice Admiral Peregrine Osborne, Marquis of Carmarthen, leased a monopoly on the export of tobacco to Russia. In England Peter once again worked in the shipyards, scrutinized naval vessels, observed demonstration naval maneuvers specifically organized for his benefit by the English government, learned to assemble watches, studied the casting of artillery pieces, and did other useful things. Still, the tsar and his traveling companions evidently had enough leisure time to themselves, because after their departure the owner of a house in which they stayed presented a bill to the English government for broken furniture, ruined pictures and carpets, and even damage to the gardens surrounding the house.

On April 25, 1698, Peter left England to return to Holland. From there his route took him to Vienna. Along the way he stopped for several days in Dresden, where he met Saxon Elector Augustus II ("The Strong"), who had recently ascended the Polish throne with the help of Russian troops. In Dresden the tsar was especially interested in the Royal Chamber of Curiosities, in which he spent many hours attentively examining the exhibits. In June, Peter, together with the entire Grand Embassy (except for those who were remaining in the West to study), arrived in Vienna, the capital of the Holy Roman Empire. The stay there was relatively brief and was devoted chiefly to diplomatic negotiations, which this time the tsar himself conducted with Chancellor Count Stephan Wilhelm von Kinsky and with Augustus II's minister, Major General Georg Carl von Carlowitz. In the middle of July, just as he was about ready to set out for Venice, his plans unexpectedly changed, for he was informed from Moscow that the musketeers had revolted yet again.

The Birth of the Great Reformer

It is worth noting that while the letter containing the information had taken a whole month to reach Peter, and in this interval events back in Russia could have taken any of a number of turns, the tsar never hesitated. The next day he sent word to his "Prince-Caesar" that "although we regret having to put off a potentially useful affair [the trip to Venice], because of this matter we will be home sooner than you expected."[18] While he was at it, the tsar demanded that Romodanovskii brutally suppress the rebellion. Historians usually see in Peter's words a primordial intent "to punish rebels harshly and without mercy."[19] Soloviev adds to this: "To strike fear into the hearts of opponents, to extinguish resistance with blood—this thought usually enters the heads of revolutionary figures in the heat of battle, in bitterness at the resistance, in fear of their own future and the future of that which would come afterward."[20] Undoubtedly, Peter had no intention of playing games with the hated musketeers, but on the contrary was happy to be presented with the opportunity of dealing with them once and for all. He may well also have feared for the security of his throne. It would be wrong, however, to see Peter in 1698 as "a revolutionary figure." That still lay in the future.

* * *

While Peter, looking forward with eagerness to dealing with the musketeers, is racing back to Moscow, we will take the opportunity to remain behind in order to survey the international situation that was taking shape in Europe. Johan Huizinga, the outstanding twentieth-century Dutch historian, has characterized the political life of the eighteenth century in this way:

> Statecraft had never been so avowedly a game as in that age of secret cabals, intrigues, and political filibustering.... Ministers and princes, as irresponsible as they were omnipotent, and unhampered by any troublesome international tribunals, were free to gamble any time they liked with their countries' destinies, a smile on their lips and with an exquisitely polite flourish, as though they were making a move on a chessboard. It was fortunate indeed for Europe that the effect of their short-sighted policies was limited by other factors, such as the slowness of communications and relatively inferior instruments of destruction. But the results of this playing at politics were deplorable enough, in all conscience.[21]

The game-like quality of the era's foreign policy is indeed quite striking. Diplomacy itself was transformed into something like a game, one in which ever more complicated concepts and norms of international law became the rule. This game spawned its own systems of defense and attack, of strategy and tactics, which remind one of elaborate chess matches with their long pauses to ponder every move and their crafty combinations. This is the kind of diplomacy that a relatively inexperienced Peter and his aides encountered during the Grand Embassy.

Historians disagree about the embassy's primary goals. Most assume that they corresponded to those laid out in the official instructions to Russia's ambassadors abroad, that is, to strengthen, and, where possible, expand the anti-Turkish coalition. The historian V.E. Vozgrin has recently posited another explanation, suggesting that in addition to the stated goal, the embassy had an objective that Peter considered more important—diplomatic preparation for war with Sweden over an outlet to the Baltic Sea.[22] Nikolai Pavlenko categorically rejected this assertion; Evgenii Anisimov rejected it less categorically.[23] The latter has assumed that the Grand Embassy was undertaken for the purpose of deep diplomatic reconnaissance, and that it sought to ascertain the real balance of forces in Europe in order to take it into account when setting Russia's future foreign policy.[24]

In point of fact Peter had started out on his embassy immediately following the capture of Azov and the adoption of decisive measures to reinforce the fortress. It is logical to assume that the solidification of his victory and the acquisition of an outlet on the northern littoral of the Black Sea must have been the immediate objectives of the young tsar's foreign policy. It was a question of full-scale war with the Turks, which was impossible without the support of his allies in the coalition. The apparent inaction of the latter annoyed and surprised Peter. The necessity and importance of war with the Ottoman Empire, it seems, struck him as so obvious that he had harbored no doubt about the success of the embassy's mission. That the tsar formulated his objective in these terms testifies to the fact that the Russian government was poorly informed about the actual state of affairs in Europe, and about the plans and objectives of the great powers.

All of this is not to suggest that the thought of war with Sweden had not crossed Peter's mind prior to his departure from Moscow. It had, but it had yet to become the chief goal of his foreign policy. Russia's new foreign policy direction took shape only during the course of the Grand Embassy, when first Danish diplomats and then the Elector of Brandenburg raised the possibility of a joint war against the Swedes. As the historian of Russian foreign policy G.A. Sanin has noted, the Baltic question had just entered into the formulation of Russian diplomacy. The situation that would allow for its resolution had not yet matured; but to reject the new possibilities that had surfaced would have been precipitate.[25]

Once in Europe, Peter immersed himself in international politics, and probably could not but marvel at the complex and confused nature of relations among the individual nations. In Riga the Swedish commandant viewed him as a spy; it was in conversation with the Duke of Courland that the subject of Russia's Baltic policy first came up; and the Elector of Brandenburg sought an alliance with Peter to assist him in his struggle for independence from Poland. Reluctant to spoil his relations with Poland, and fearing that the initiative in that country would be seized by the Ottoman Porte's ally, France, if he did, the tsar was forced to equivocate. In Holland, Peter's inexperience led to a complete collapse of the embassy's mission, while just prior to the departure for Vienna it was discovered that England and Holland were serving as intermediaries in the negotiations between Austria and the Ottoman Empire, then being conducted in secret. The attention of all of Europe, moreover, was fixed on a nation far removed from Russia, on Spain, where an elderly Charles II had no heirs. Both the Austrian Habsburgs and the French Bourbons had claims to the Spanish throne. Preparations for war over the rich "Spanish succession" were under way.

Given the complex situation, war with the Turks seemed of secondary importance to the European powers. To all appearances, Peter realized by the end of the Grand Embassy's mission the impossibility of creating a firm anti-Turkish league. On the other hand, the possibility of cobbling together an anti-Swedish bloc had presented itself. Denmark, long hostile to Sweden because of its struggle for control of the duchy of Schleswig, and Poland, whose new king, Augustus II, was beholden to Peter for his crown, were candidates for alliance with Russia in this new bloc. The election of the Polish king had been resolved by Peter decisively, by resorting to force: Russian troops had been sent into the country in order to obtain the election to the throne of a puppet loyal to Russia. Russian–Polish relations would be conducted in this same vein throughout the eighteenth century. On August 31, 1698, while on his way back to Moscow, Peter met with Augustus. They took an immediate liking to each other, became good friends, and in secret face-to-face negotiations laid the groundwork for an anti-Swedish Northern Accord.

The history of the Grand Embassy points to an extremely important fundamental difference in the foreign policies of Russia and the leading European powers of the day. The latter had already mastered the rules of the game, as it were, and were thinking several moves ahead. Russian diplomacy was still learning the craft, still operating on a haphazard basis, according to the old rules, being guided in many respects by spur-of-the-moment considerations. But the Russians were learning quickly. The active intrusion of the nation into European foreign policy during the Petrine period would lead to the creation of an imperial foreign-policy doctrine, one successfully carried out by Peter's successors.

Most historians assert that the quest for an outlet to the sea was the chief goal of Peter's foreign policy, and that the goal in its turn was dictated by purely economic considerations: by the desire to establish an extensive transit trade from the shores of the Baltic to Central Asia. By the same token, they emphasize that the strategic goal was an age-old one, that the exhausting wars that Peter fought were of vital importance for Russia, and that without access to the Baltic, the nation's further economic development was impossible. Therefore, they argue, territorial expansion was justified. It should be noted, however, that Russia already possessed access to the sea via Archangel. This port continued to play an essential role in the nation's foreign trade up to the end of the eighteenth century. Trade with Asia in the eighteenth century, as it had been in the seventeenth, was conducted primarily through Astrakhan.

More importantly, although Russian foreign trade increased over the course of the century (which undoubtedly would have been the case without wars, since Russia represented an almost unlimited market for overseas goods), the role of Russian merchants in that trade remained negligible. For, when all was said and done, they proved incapable of competing with their foreign counterparts. Just why this should have been the case we will examine below. When speaking of the historical necessity for a Russian outlet to the sea, however, it is important to stress that the economic results hoped for were never realized. Russia did not take over England's position in international trade. It did not become the new mistress of the seas. In fact, it did not even come close. In effect, it did nothing more than open its market to foreign goods.

One encounters other points of view in the historical literature. Russian historian Pavel Miliukov claimed that Peter was guided by neither the nation's commercial nor its economic interests when it came to foreign policy, but merely by his own ambitions.[26] Other scholars insist that the tsar acted in the interests of either the Moscow merchantry or the nobility, or else in accordance with Russia's military and strategic interests.[27] Each is correct in his own way. Peter, of course, broke through to the sea in order to satisfy his own passion for navigation. To do so he had to struggle, to go to war; but his active nature was equal to the task.

The Grand Embassy also became for Peter a peculiar form of university. In the words of V.O. Kliuchevskii, the tsar must have returned to Russia with an impression of Europe "as a noisy and smoky workshop, full of machines, ships, wharves, factories, and mills."[28] Peter probably also experienced what many succeeding generations of his countrymen experienced when returning home from abroad: a feeling of disappointment, irritation, even resentment, at one's own nation, whose backwardness smacks one in the face. Peter hoped that the Russia he ruled would become just as prosperous a commercial and industrial power as the leading nations of Central and Western Europe, with its own wharves and factories, chambers of curiosities, and anatomical theaters. Achieving this goal required radical reform of just about all aspects of Russian life, and one of its components was the quest for an outlet to the sea.

Thus, a realization of the strategic goal of his reign gradually took shape in the tsar's mind. In this program there was also an intellectual strand, likewise introduced into Russia from the West. Here is what Marc Raeff had to say on the subject:

> Geographical and scientific discoveries, as well as a quickening of the intellectual and scientific pace, gradually gave rise to the notion that God's universe was infinite and its productive potential limitless. Furthermore, man had the ability to discover the laws that regulated nature and, based on this knowledge, he could apply his will to maximize resources in both the material and the cultural realm. An increased

productive potential would first benefit the state and its rulers, but eventually also augment the prosperity and happiness of all, or most, members of society. . . . Such results could best be achieved by an educated elite of administrators under the guidance of a sovereign . . . who would "discipline" the population for productive work through the regulatory and planned action of a central authority. . . . This new political culture is usually called the "Well-Ordered Police State."[29]

To mankind, adds Evgenii Anisimov, it seemed that the key to happiness had finally been found. One need only formulate laws properly, perfect the organizational structure of society, and obtain absolute, universal, and exact fulfillment of the state's initiatives. This accounts for the optimistic, rather naive faith of people of the seventeenth and eighteenth centuries in the unlimited powers of rational man, who was thought to be able to construct his own house, ship, town, and state on the basis of experimental knowledge and according to a preconceived plan.[30]

We cannot be absolutely certain of the degree to which Peter was familiar with these ideas, although we do know that he corresponded with the German philosopher and mathematician Gottfried Wilhelm Leibniz and promoted the translation of German legal historian Samuel von Pufendorf's writings into Russian. There can be no doubt but that the tsar grasped at least the spirit of these ideas. From these ideas and principles emerged his conception of service to the fatherland as the supreme virtue for the monarch and the citizen. So throughout his reign he ardently promoted the idea of the "common good," or the "general benefit," as the goal of this service. It was service to the fatherland, to the state, that provided meaning to the life of Peter the tsar and Peter the person, whose every activity was permeated with practicality and rationality.

In significant measure the tsar's conceptions of what had to be done and how to do it were formed during his trip abroad. It is no accident that upon receiving word from Moscow of the suppression of the musketeers' uprising he did not resume his journey. Having already seen and learned enough, he was impatient to put his newly acquired knowledge into practice.

* * *

On August 25, 1698, Tsar Peter suddenly reappeared in Moscow. By the next morning, when Muscovites became aware of his presence, they understood that something terrible was about to happen. The tsar visited Anna Mons and Franz Lefort, and then, without bothering to see his wife, headed for Preobrazhenskoe. On the following day the tsar received his boyars at Preobrazhenskoe and listened to their reports on the state of affairs. He then received the leading people of the realm with scissors in hand, and proceeded to cut off the boyars' well-groomed and cherished beards, which they had been cultivating for years. To the boyars the beard was a sign of respect and honor, but to Peter it was a symbol of the Russian past and of backwardness. Debates over "the shaving of beards" had already been raging in Russia for several decades. The Orthodox Church had come out openly against the practice, doing battle against the "lascivious image" of the beardless man. In the words of Sergei Soloviev, "The beard had become a banner in the battle of the two sides," for it was "in his exterior, in his clothes and in the arrangement of his hair that a man chiefly attempts to express the condition of his soul, his feelings, his views and desires."[31] Peter decided the question in his own way, with the aid of scissors, demonstrating and predetermining, as it were, that coercion would be the chief vehicle for carrying out all his future reforms.

Soon thereafter followed the corresponding decree requiring everyone except priests and peasants to shave their beards. Those who wished to keep their beards would have to pay a special tax. Two additional aspects of this measure deserve mention. First of all, by requiring that his subjects shave their beards Peter was following through on something that henceforth he considered his prime obligation: the education of his people. Second, the minute regulation of the whole fabric of life, down to the outer appearance of his subjects, corresponded fully with his conception of the well-regulated state. But while importing from abroad his new ideas and projects concerning morals and customs, Peter remained quite Russian, as the events of the next few months were to demonstrate.

By the time the tsar had returned to Moscow, 122 participants in the uprising had been executed and about 2,000 led away to prison in chains. Peter ordered that the imprisoned musketeers be brought back and the investigation resumed. Throughout September the musketeers delivered to Preobrazhenskoe were mercilessly beaten and tortured until they confessed that they had intended to take the life of the tsar, the members of his family, boyars, and foreigners. They also implicated Sophia in the conspiracy. Peter personally participated in the torture, himself beheading five musketeers. Wasting no time, the tsar dashed off to the Novodevichii Convent in order to interrogate his older sister personally. Sophia refused to confess, and it would have been highly improper to torture her to gain a confession. Peter then forced his closest advisers to participate in the torture and execution of the musketeers. By their ardor in chopping off heads they could show their loyalty to the tsar. Like members of a gang of bandits, all of these people were now bound together, as it were, by the blood of their victims. Now they had no choice but to accompany Peter to the end of the journey. Only the foreigners refused to participate in the executions, insisting that in their countries such conduct was not accepted.

Public executions began at the end of September and continued on through October. In all, about 1,000 musketeers were executed,* of whom about 200 were hanged at the walls of the Novodevichii Convent, three of these directly under the windows of Sophia's cell. "Hangings were now taking place throughout Zemlianoi gorod," recalled a contemporary, "and even in Belyi gorod,** beyond the town, on both sides of every town gate. Logs were pushed through the merlons of the city walls, with the ends of these logs jammed in from inside Belyi gorod. From the outer ends of the logs, which protruded out from the walls, the musketeers were hanged."[32] At the beginning of 1699, about 700 more musketeers were brought to Moscow. They suffered the same fate as their predecessors, and their decomposing bodies were left hanging for several months.

Barred from Moscow, the wives and children of the musketeers were dispersed around the country. The regimen under which Sophia was kept was made much harsher, so that now even her sisters were allowed to see her only once a year, at Easter. One of them, by the way, Tsarevna Marfa Alekseevna, who was found to be a participant in the conspiracy, was also forced to enter a nunnery. Peter dealt in similar fashion with his wife Evdokia, who was guilty of nothing more than being unable to make her husband love her. To his favorite sister, Natalia, Peter assigned the education of his son and heir to the throne, Aleksei Petrovich. The tsar spared no one, took mercy on no

---

*Soloviev cites the figure of 971 executed (Solov'ev, *Sochineniia,* book 7, p. 552), while Pavlenko mentions 799 (Pavlenko, *Petr Pervyi,* p. 91).

**Zemlianoi and Belyi gorod were areas of Moscow.

The Birth of the Great Reformer

Execution of the musketeers in Moscow in 1698. From an eighteenth-century engraving.

one, as he pressed on persistently toward his predetermined objective, leaving in his wake mountains of corpses and ruined lives.

At the end of October, Peter again dashed off to Voronezh in order to try out the shipbuilding skills he had acquired in Europe. On Christmas Day he returned, feasted immoderately, engaged in revelry with his friends, participated in another round of torture and execution of musketeers, and yet again returned to the shipyards. On January 30, 1699, before his departure, he managed to sign several important decrees laying the groundwork for the reform of the civil administration. One of them concerned urban administration. In keeping with the wishes of the urban dwellers themselves, he introduced a new administrative organ, the elective Town Chamber, which was to supervise the collection of taxes and carry out judicial responsibilities. Thus the urban population was removed from the authority of the commanders (who had controlled government at the local level, and had been the subject of constant complaints) and given organs of self-administration. Peter apparently assumed that he was doing the urban dwellers a favor and that they, once liberated, would apply themselves to trade and enterprise with a passion. To enable the government to benefit from the reform as soon as possible, however, the towns whose residents chose this form of self-administration were to pay a double tax.

The reform's results demonstrated as well as anything could Peter's lack of familiarity with the nation's real conditions as well as Russian society's lack of preparedness for change along West European lines. Most of the town dwellers announced that they were quite satisfied with their commanders and could wish for no better fate. Some towns elected a Town Chamber but pretended that they had forgotten about the double tax. Only a handful of towns lived up to the government's conditions. Peter learned quickly; by October 1699, the imposition of the double tax was dropped and the election of members to the Town Chamber made mandatory.

In February 1699, likewise prior to his departure for Voronezh, Peter managed to get busy with his scissors once again. This time he shortened the sleeves and lengths of the caftans of those *gosti,* or privileged merchants, who showed up for the consecration of Lefortovo Palace in traditional Russian garments. The legal regulation of dress was accomplished only a year later, in 1700, when a series of decrees appeared, prescribing the wearing of European clothes and shoes for all but clergymen, peasants, and cab men. At the beginning of 1701, these decrees were supplemented by a ban on making and selling the traditional Russian robe.

Let us once more turn our attention to several special features of these innovations. By shaving and reclothing substantial numbers of his subjects in foreign dress, Peter had in effect divided the populace into two parts: one that was to live in the European manner and one whose style of life was to remain traditional. It is self-evident that in order to become true Europeans, the first part had to adopt a different attitude toward life, and to do so required substantial time. But the swiftness of the Petrine transformation, the unusual nature of the activities into which people were plunged, and eventually, the major changes in their lifestyle and the way they spent their leisure time had an almost immediate impact. The beard and the clothes were for Peter merely annoying symbols of antiquity. Instinctively but unerringly, he was groping for the right path. Dressed in more reasonable European clothes, relieved of the long sleeves, high collars, heavy high caps, and fur coats reaching to the ground, Russians began to move in a different way, and therefore to live and think in a different way.

Not everyone, of course, was able to adjust to all of this. The changes were especially hard on older people. But they were already fading into the background in the first years of Peter's reign, and as a result, Russia's ruling elite as a cohort grew much younger. A rapid change of generations, one typical of periods of radical reform, was taking place. This was most noticeable in the fate of the Boyar Council, which at the end of the seventeenth century and the beginning of the eighteenth all but died out, having seen its membership decline by half within a decade, a consequence of the tsar ceasing to hand out boyar ranks. It is indicative that this seemingly most powerful segment of Russian society faded into oblivion without putting up any resistance, as if sensing from the start its own predestination. As Robert Crummey put it, "When Peter made radical Europeanization official policy, [the boyars] went along—reluctantly perhaps, but without protest."[33]

After spending the spring of 1699 at the wharves in Voronezh, Peter sailed from there down to Azov in April at the head of a squadron of twenty-two galleys, and from there headed for the Turkish fortress of Kerch, where he arrived in the middle of August to a salute of cannons. From there the Russian ship *Krepost* (Fortress) sailed on farther, to Constantinople, with the tsar's ambassador, Emelian Ukraintsev, on board. The ambassador was assigned the mission of concluding peace with the Turks at any cost. The tsar himself returned to Moscow at the end of September to begin intensive preparations for war with Sweden. These preparations took place not just in the military sphere but in all spheres of society. By October, for example, Peter declared the need to set up secular education in Russia, and enlisted teachers of mathematics, engineering, and navigation from England.*

In November, the tsar turned to the reorganization of the army. First a call went out for volunteers for military service, and then for "recruits," or men to be handed over to the state by local communities, each one to be raised from a specified number of peasant and urban households. As a result, 32,000 men were drafted, from whom twenty-nine foreign-style regiments commanded by foreign officers were formed. In the same month, an important diplomatic success was achieved: the con-

---

*Having enlisted the teachers, Peter, as was so characteristic of him, forgot about them for more than a year while dealing with more pressing matters; not until January 1700 was the School for Mathematics and Navigation opened in Moscow.

clusion of a treaty of alliance with Saxony, in which a joint struggle against Sweden was expressly stipulated. Earlier Saxony had concluded a similar agreement with Denmark. Thus, the anti-Swedish coalition was in place, and Peter awaited only the conclusion of peace with the Turks in order to initiate military action. True, each of the allies was pursuing its own goals, although Russia stated its directly (the return of land seized by Sweden at the beginning of the seventeenth century and consolidation of a foothold in the Baltic), while Saxony and Denmark remained silent about theirs. As Anisimov accurately noted, Russia was assigned the unenviable task of supplying cannon fodder in the forthcoming war, while Peter was to act as some sort of "mighty bear with an iron ring through its nose that would dance to its trainer's tune."[34]

The year 1699 closed with one more notable event: at the end of December a reform of the calendar took place. Until that time Russians had used the Julian calendar but counted the years from the purported creation of the world, and celebrated the new year on the first of September. Thus, the year 1699 was the year 7207–7208 according to the Russian calendar. Peter ordered that henceforth the years be counted from the birth of Christ, as in all the rest of Europe, and that the new year 1700 be observed on January first. No decision was taken to switch to the Gregorian calendar, which was increasingly being used by Europeans. As a result, the gap between the Russian and European calendars grew by one day per century, from eleven to thirteen days, until another reform in the twentieth century brought the Russian calendar into line. The tsar's decrees also mandated the way in which the new year was to be celebrated. The courtyards of homes were to be decorated with evergreen branches and trees, and cannon salvos and fireworks, which Peter adored almost as much as his naval affairs, were to be arranged.

January 1700 was notable for still one more innovation. B.P. Sheremetev's butler, Alexei Kurbatov, wrote to the tsar suggesting the introduction of stamped paper; that is, paper with an embossed stamp in the form of the state's coat of arms, which would be required for the registration of all official documents, including financial and commercial transactions. The paper was to be purchased at a cost that would be determined by the nature of the document to be registered, a requirement that Kurbatov predicted would produce a large profit for the state. The suggestion was adopted and its originator rewarded accordingly. Kurbatov subsequently made quite a career for himself, while the tsar announced that he would reward anyone who could find additional sources of revenue for the state. The introduction of stamped paper and a number of other measures that followed enabled the government to concentrate in its own hands the function of notary public, which had formerly been lodged in private hands. The system by which government documents were to be drawn up, one elaborated in the sixteenth and seventeenth centuries, was also reformed by a series of special decrees. Until Peter's day they were composed on scrolls of paper called columns; now they were to be written on both sides of the pages of notebooks, a practice that was intended to produce a significant savings in paper, which had to be purchased abroad.

The same month brought the promulgation of a decree on the opening in Moscow of the School for Mathematics and Navigation, for which teachers had been recruited from England. From that point on it was possible to receive professional training not only abroad but in Russia itself. Then in February, Peter signed a decree announcing the opening of a Russian printing press in Amsterdam for the publication of practical books of a secular nature "for general public use and profit."[35]

The very first reforms dealing with the administration and reorganization of the army necessitated changes in the structure of the governmental apparatus. A number of old chancelleries disappeared, while new offices, better suited to the nation's new tasks, emerged to take their place. Among the new administrative offices were the Admiralty and the Mining Chancellery. The latter was ordered to intensify the search for the ore the state so badly needed. In February 1700, Peter also established the Codification Chamber, which he called upon to review and systematize existing legislation. The measure was noteworthy because it showed that the state was already aware of the inadequacy of its legislative foundations. The chamber's efforts, however, proved fruitless, and the problem of codification remained unresolved throughout the eighteenth century.

The first reforms Peter undertook were marked by traits that proved so characteristic of his later reforms: on the one hand, their extent and their penetration into all spheres of life, and, on the other hand, their unsystematic nature and the absence of any coherent plan or notion of consistency. Many vital decisions were made on the spur of the moment, in response to specific situations.

Throughout the first half of 1700, however, Peter concerned himself primarily with preparations for war and anticipation of news that peace had been concluded with the Ottoman Porte, after which he could launch his war against Sweden. The long-awaited news arrived on August 8. Although by now Russia's allies had managed to demonstrate their total ineffectiveness (Denmark had suffered a crushing defeat at the hands of Sweden and was compelled to pull out of the war, while Polish forces had besieged Riga unsuccessfully and would soon be forced to pull back without anything to show for their efforts), war with Sweden was officially declared ten days later. The Russian army promptly launched a campaign against the Swedish-held fortress of Narva, located in present-day Estonia.

To judge by the evidence, Peter was, as they say, just itching for battle, and the sooner the better. Clearly, he had grossly overestimated his own army's military capabilities, which was why he was so sure of success. It took almost a month to get the army to Narva, while an additional several weeks were spent getting the troops organized. Bombardment of the fortress did not commence until October 20, and it continued for only two weeks, until the powder and shot gave out. Thanks to the inferior quality of the Russian cannons, the effects of the bombardment proved negligible. While the Russian side was awaiting the delivery of more ammunition, news arrived of the disembarking of Swedish troops under the command of King Charles XII at Pernau and Revel (now the cities of Pärnu and Tallinn in Estonia). By November 18 the Swedish forces had reached Narva, and on the next day they attacked the Russian forces, which were at least twice as numerous. After a battle that lasted the entire day, the Russian army, having already lost about 6,000 men, capitulated.

There are a few details that need to be addressed when describing the battle of Narva. First and foremost, there is the fact that the tsar abandoned the Russian camp and headed for Novgorod without even awaiting the start of the battle. Peter's action has stirred debates among historians who, dismissing charges of cowardice out of hand, strive to find a rational explanation for his behavior. Some claim that Peter departed as soon as he got wind of Charles's approach, convinced as he was that to remain would be dangerous and useless and that his presence would prove more useful elsewhere.[36] Others are more specific, arguing that the tsar headed for Novgorod either to prepare for the defense of the troops stationed there and, while he was at it, to speed the dispatch of reinforcements and ammunition to Narva, or to hasten the dispatch of the troops left there.[37] Still others are convinced that the tsar's behavior revealed the harsh rationalism so typical of him: a sober recognition of the approaching inevitable battle, and a desire to survive in order to continue the struggle with redoubled energy another day.[38] Then there are those who see in the tsar's actions a desire not to inhibit the commander of the army by his presence.[39] Nikolai Pavlenko probably comes closest to the truth when he suggests that Peter simply underestimated the degree of danger hanging over the Russian army.[40] Indeed, enjoying a substantial superiority in manpower over the Swedish army, lacking experience in battle with the Swedes, and burning with military ardor and a craving for battle, Peter could hardly envision defeat. Presumably, he would not have abandoned his camp had he known that Charles, flying in the face of all the tenets of military doctrine known to the tsar, would attack the next day.

Regardless of what may have motivated it, the tsar's departure made manifest the lack of experience and the lightheartedness with which he had approached the war. We find confirmation of this also in the case of Charles Eugene, Duke de Croy, who presented himself to Peter a few days before the battle. Bearing a letter of recommendation from the Holy Roman Emperor, he was appointed commander-in-chief of the Russian army on the spot. It will hardly come as a surprise to learn that he was one of the first to surrender to the Swedes, taking other foreign officers with him. Nor was he unjustified in subsequently proclaiming his lack of responsibility for the debacle and demanding compensation from the tsar; for prior to the battle, he had not even had time to familiarize himself with the condition of the troops entrusted to him.

"The first pancake always turns out lumpy," runs an old Russian adage that is certainly apt for Russia's initial foray into the Great Northern War, the cost and duration of which no one could have foreseen. In commemoration of the battle of Narva, a medal was struck in Europe depicting Tsar Peter, along with his soldiers, taking flight. His sword and hat are thrown away, and he is wiping the tears from his eyes with a handkerchief. The depiction is accompanied by a quotation from Scriptures: "He went forth and wept bitterly."

Chapter 3

The Origins of Empire

After returning from abroad at the end of 1698, Tsar Peter established the first Russian knightly order. In March 1699, the first knight of this order, boyar Fedor Alekseevich Golovin, boasted of his membership to Habsburg minister Johann Georg Korb. The pedantic diplomat wrote in his diary that the order had been established by the tsar to reward those who had distinguished themselves in battle against the Turks. For understandable reasons, the symbolism underlying the creation of the order had gone unnoticed by the participants in this scene, as a result of which the Austrian assumed that it was simply one more reflection of the tsar's drive to imitate Europe. In fact, the name of the order—that of Saint Andrew the Apostle—did indeed reflect that of an old Scottish order that had been disbanded after the unification of Scotland with England and then reestablished in 1687. But the Holy Roman Emperor's envoy should have been more discerning, for the tsar's selection of this particular saint's name bore profound political significance.

According to legend, Saint Andrew was the first to preach the Gospel to the Balkan peoples and those living along the northern littoral of the Black Sea, including the Scythians, who were considered the ancestors of the Slavs. Even back in the days of the Byzantine Empire, this claim had been exploited by the Orthodox in their disputes with representatives of Latin Christianity. Now the tsar, bearing the name of Saint Andrew's brother, seemed to be reinforcing Russia's claim to precedence over the Second Rome. The apostle Saint Andrew, moreover, was considered the patron saint of travelers and sailors. His help was therefore essential in Russia's attempt to break through to the sea in pursuit of an ambitious new foreign policy. At Peter's command, the

The Origins of Empire

diagonal blue "Saint Andrew's cross" (Cruz Decussata) soon appeared on Russia's maritime flag. But there was more: for if the selection of Saint Andrew emphasized the adherence of the tsar to Eastern Orthodoxy, it also drew attention to the unity of Russia with the whole Christian world as well as its claim to one of the leading roles in that world. But then disaster struck.

The defeat at Narva must have had a sobering effect on the tsar. After all, the cherished goal proved much more remote than it had once seemed, and it could be achieved only by indefatigable effort. This was the most important lesson to be derived from the Narva debacle. "When this misfortune (or, better, great fortune) was visited upon us," wrote Peter subsequently, "necessity drove away idleness and compelled us to resort night and day to diligence and skill."[1]

We have no way of knowing whether Peter wept when he heard of the catastrophe at Narva. But we do know that his spirits never flagged. Rather, failure served only to provoke him. It aroused his fury and stubbornness, thus enabling him to tap his storehouse of indomitable energy, thanks to which he began to achieve his objectives. Narva banished whatever feelings of giddiness he might still have harbored, and became yet another divide, one more stage in the development of Peter as reformer. From this point on, his actions became, if not less chaotic, at least more conscious. For Narva had served as one more object lesson, highlighting Russia's most glaring weakness: its army. Henceforth, reform of the army, along with the prosecution of war in general, would become Peter's chief concern, bringing in its train reforms in other areas as well.

In November 1700, without knowing what the Swedes would do next, Peter hastily fortified the towns of Novgorod and Pskov, and issued orders for the formation of new regiments and the casting of more cannons. Ten additional regiments were soon raised, and by November 1701 about three hundred heavy weapons had already been cast. Clearly, mineral resources and money were indispensable to Peter's efforts. He therefore ordered that iron and copper ore be obtained from all over Russia, even if that meant taking down church bells. In December he was supplied with the first cast iron produced by a blast furnace at a metallurgical plant located in the Ural Mountains, construction of which had begun at the tsar's orders back in 1698. So successful was the enterprise that by the beginning of 1702 the iron produced there surpassed European iron in quality.

By March 1700, the minting machines at the state mint had swung into full operation, minting copper money of a lesser weight than the old, as a result of which the state turned a tidy million-ruble profit. But it came at a cost: the value of the ruble began to plummet. Starting in 1701, the *Blizhniaia kantseliariia,* or Privy Chancellery, a central administrative organ that coordinated and supervised the activities of all the chancelleries, began to function. And it was at this time that the tsar began to concern himself with the upbringing of his subjects, taking on responsibility for all aspects of their lives, including their faith.

When in October 1700 Patriarch Adrian died, Peter decided that Russia had no need of another patriarch, and so in his place he appointed a *locum tenens*, or *Mestobliustitel,* of the patriarchal throne. He followed this up with a decree on the creation of a Monastery Chancellery, to be headed by a civil servant, which was assigned the task of overseeing all the monasteries as well as the affairs of the clergy. In addition, a registration of all monks was carried out, after which they were forbidden to transfer from one monastery to another. To add insult to injury, they were deprived of paper and ink, preventing them from composing broadsides against the tsar's measures. And just how much was to be spent on the maintenance of each monk was clearly stipulated so that the remaining monastic funds could be siphoned off into state coffers. Only with the permission of the tsar could one now take the vows of a monk or nun. Thus, state regulation of the Russian way of life touched yet another social group: the clergy.

Yet the tsar still drew a clear distinction between faith and the church as an institution, intending to transform the latter into his pliant instrument, while not infringing on the former. Therefore, in February 1701, when a Polish Senator suggested that the tsar unite Orthodoxy with Catholicism, Peter responded that "God indeed has granted sovereigns power over their subjects; but Christ alone rules over people's consciences; and the unification of the churches can be achieved only by God's will."[2] That December, Peter promulgated a decree forbidding his subjects to use demeaning diminutive names when addressing the tsar in writing, as had been traditional, even for those of the very highest rank. He also prohibited them from falling on their knees before the tsar or doffing their caps before the royal palace in winter, with the justification that one ought not to render unto the tsar homage equal to that due God. According to the decree, "Less bowing and

The Origins of Empire

scraping, and more ardor for service and fidelity to me and the state—that is the homage due a tsar."[3] Nevertheless, within a few months, in March 1702, a new form of petition to the tsar was mandated that was to conclude with the formulaic "Your Majesty's Most Humble Slave" [*rab*]. This was to replace the word "bondsman" [*kholop*] for those in the tsar's service, and "orphan" [*sirota*] for those who were not in service. Step by step, the tsar was becoming master of the entire population.

In order to stretch his subjects' minds, the tsar in December 1702 established the first newspaper to be put out in Russia, *Vedomosti* (News), in which information on the achievements of the Russian state was published. The same year, a "Hall of Comedy" was constructed on Red Square in Moscow. It was Russia's first public theater, and it produced plays about Alexander the Great, Julius Caesar, and Tamerlane, among others. It even staged Molière's *The Doctor in Spite of Himself*. Medicine and the health of his people, likewise attracted the tsar-reformer's attention. The uncontrolled sale of medicinal herbs and grasses in Moscow was outlawed in 1700, while eight state-run apothecaries were opened under the supervision of the Office of Foreign Affairs. A decree was promulgated that banned, under pain of knouting and exile, the carrying of sharp knives, which Russians so often wielded in the course of drunken brawls. At the beginning of 1704 still another decree appeared, forbidding the murder of infants born with physical deformities and requiring burial no more than three days after death. Even the institution of marriage was regulated: a royal decree mandated that betrothals take place six weeks prior to marriage ceremonies, and that during this period, future brides and bridegrooms be free to change their minds. For the first time in Russian history, women were granted the legal right to have a say in the choice of their husbands. All of this was made possible only because of a fatal blunder committed by King Charles XII of Sweden.

After his victory over the Russian forces at Narva, the king faced a choice: either to pursue Tsar Peter or else to go after the tsar's ally, King Augustus of Poland. Charles opted for the latter course, thereby granting Peter and Russia a reprieve. It is of course impossible to assert with absolute certainty just what would have happened had the Swedes decided to pursue the Russian army. But in any case, it is readily apparent that the course of Russian history would have taken a different turn. Granted, the Russian forces had not been destroyed completely at Narva. When all was said and done, the tsar still had more than twenty thousand troops available to him. But the army had lost all its artillery at Narva, and was demoralized. It would hardly have been possible to defend the Russian towns of Novgorod and Pskov, which were in the vicinity of Narva, if Charles had decided to attack. Once these two towns were lost, Peter would have been forced to make peace with the Swedes as soon as possible and on their terms. But Charles opted instead to invade Poland. He did so because he considered Augustus a more formidable opponent than Peter, because he bore a personal animus against the king, and because the Polish lands were richer than the Russian. By leading the main forces of his army off into Poland, however, Charles in effect freed Peter for action in the Baltic region.

Throughout 1701, minor clashes took place between Russian troops and the detachments of the Swedish army that had been stationed by Charles on Russia's Baltic frontier. First one side would triumph, then the other. But at the very end of the year, Russian regiments commanded by Boris Petrovich Sheremetev overtook and defeated an enemy unit at Errestfer, south of Dorpat (present-day Tartu in Estonia), killing three thousand Swedes, thus proving for the first time that the Swedish forces were not invincible. Half a year later, in summer 1702, the Russian army had launched another campaign. By this time it had become clear that the main Swedish forces had been diverted into Poland and that those remaining in Livonia could not expect to be reinforced. The combined Russian forces enjoyed a substantial numerical superiority, and in July they defeated the Swedes in battle. Thanks to his victory, Sheremetev acquired what proved to be a free hand in Livonia, receiving direct orders from the tsar to lay waste the territory. As for the tsar himself, in the summer of 1702 he headed for Archangel, on the White Sea coast, where he spent three months, during the course of which two new frigates were launched and the keel for a twenty-six-gun ship laid. While at Archangel, Peter got the idea of attacking the Swedish fortress of Nöteborg, which lay at the source of the Neva River where it flowed out of Lake Ladoga. By the end of September, the Russian forces were assembled there, and on October 11, after a twelve-hour assault, the fortress surrendered. Peter renamed the fortress Shlisselburg, which in the original German means "key fortress," a reference to the fact that it opened to the Russians the road into enemy territory. Then in April 1703, the Russian army conquered another fortress on the banks of the Neva: Nyenskans (Nienshants in

Russian). Now the entire Neva, from its source to its mouth, was in Russian hands. In order to secure the Russian presence in this area a new fortress was constructed. Its foundations laid on May 16, it was named St. Petersburg. It was destined to become the new capital of a new nation.

Legend has it that Peter himself laid the city's foundation stone. In conjunction with the ceremony, it is claimed, a small trench was dug, in which "a box hewn out of stone was placed. The clergy sprinkled this box with holy water; and the sovereign placed in it a golden shrine containing the earthly remains of the apostle Saint Andrew."[4] Some historians remain unconvinced, arguing that Peter was nowhere near the site of the future St. Petersburg on May 16, and that the decision to build the town had been taken at a council of war convened immediately after the conquest of Nyenskans. Others, the St. Petersburg historian A. Sharymov included, attempt to prove that Peter was actually present at the ceremonies.[5] Whatever the case, this newly constructed city soon became Peter's pet project, the place he loved with all his heart, referring to it as his "paradise."

One of the most beautiful cities in the world, Petersburg has served as the symbol of the Petrine period for nearly three hundred years, embodying in full measure the dream of Russia's great transformer. In this symbol one finds conjoined all the contradictions inherent in Peter's activities: the elegance, luxury, and refinement of the boulevards, squares, embankments, and palaces, set against the backdrop of a sky that is all too often gloomy, a bone-chilling wind, and lapping water that forever threatens to inundate the town. From a rational point of view, it is hard to conceive of a place less conducive to human habitation. But there is symbolic meaning in even this: that of Russia overcoming nature, in accordance with its master's will. "Built on the unstable, swampy shores of the Neva, which took its present form back in the days of Jesus Christ and Pontius Pilate," noted one contemporary historian, himself a resident of the city, "Petersburg did not seem firm or solid, much less permanent. . . . This wind from the sea, strong to the point of viscidity, and this black rising water, ominously lapping at its embankments, penetrate every nook and cranny of the city, instilling in its inhabitants little cause for optimism."[6] "Nature also conspires with a climate so severe that it permanently impresses humans with the indelible awareness that this is in no way their native habitat," added one of his American colleagues.

Even the city's faded northern light seems to transmute solid matter into subdued shadows.... In such an area, the construction even of a village, let alone a world-class metropolis, demanded the kind of perseverance and obstinacy that could be assured only by unrestrained greed for gain or by the iron-willed determination of an autocrat. In either case, the resulting settlement could never emerge as a "natural" extension of its environment. Peter's city—or any other community imposed upon this bleak landscape—would have to be an artifact of human will-power.[7]

Yet it was precisely this—the artificiality of the town, the possibility of creating something from scratch, on vacant land, contrary to nature, but in accordance with his notions of the ideal town—that attracted Peter. Petersburg was designed to become for all of Russia an example of regularity, of rationality, of properly organized life: that is, of life ordered in accordance with specified principles. It was to have straight streets and boulevards, intersecting at right angles (in the old Russian town, the ring pattern of construction prevailed: that is, concentric circles extending out from the center of town). The types of houses to be built along the streets were mandated by decree for each category of the population, with the facades facing the street (in Russia at the time it was common to build houses with interior courtyards), and the color and height of houses, chimneys, ceilings, and so forth stipulated by decree. Finally, the inhabitants, all of whose lives—private as well as public—were to conform to strict order, were to dress in European-style clothing. Just as in the Russia of old, when each subject was considered a serf of the tsar, there had been no notion of "privacy," so there was no room for it in the Petrine "paradise."

Two additional aspects associated with the construction of Petersburg merit our attention. The first foreign merchant ship to drop anchor at the fortress, which was then still under construction, made its appearance in November 1703, to the delight of Alexander Menshikov, who had been appointed governor of Petersburg. He richly rewarded its sailors. From the very outset the town had been designated not only a fortress and a capital but also a gateway through which trade would pass on its way to Europe. Here again one is tempted to juxtapose the new Russia to the old, in which the major port city had been Archangel: The Archangel Michael, considered the protector of Archangel, was one of the patron saints of Russia as a whole. Thus, "the victory of the city of Saint Peter over the town of the Archangel Michael could be interpreted symbolically."[8] The secular city had replaced the religious city. Over the course of the eighteenth century, the center of Russia's foreign trade did indeed shift gradually from Archangel to Petersburg, even though Russia acquired other, more suitable, ports on the Baltic Sea at the conclusion of the Great Northern War.

Petersburg served also as a symbol for the foreign policy ambitions of the new Russia, attesting to the transformation of the old doctrine of "Moscow as the Third Rome" from an ideology into policy. The naming of the new capital "the Citie of Saint Peter," in the words of Lotman and Uspenskii,

> bore unavoidable associations not only with the glorification of the heavenly protector of Peter the First but with the concept of Petersburg as the new Rome. This orientation toward Rome is revealed not only in the name of the town but on its seal. . . . The blatant propagation of the cults of the apostles Peter and Paul in Petersburg assumes special significance. It was to them that the cathedral in the Peter and Paul Fortress was dedicated, a fortress that according to the original plan was to coincide with the center of town. In this [project] it is impossible not to espy a line of filiation with the space . . . occupied by St. Peter's basilica in Rome.

They go on to note, moreover, that

> the genuineness of Petersburg's claim to be the new Rome is to be found in the fact that its sanctity does not dominate, but rather is subordinated to, its statism. State service is transformed into service to the Fatherland and at the same time contributes to the worship of God, which contributes to the salvation of the soul.[9]

Peter's efforts to open "a window onto Europe," as Alexander Pushkin termed it, were not limited to the construction of St. Petersburg. A "Manifesto on the Invitation of Foreigners to Russia" saw the light of day as early as April 1702. According to one of Peter's biographers, it "unfolded the program of the reign and pointed the way to its realization."[10] Indeed, the manifesto confirms that from the very beginning of his reign, Peter sought to establish "the common good." He strove constantly to improve the "condition" of his subjects, the security of the state, and the extent of its commerce. To that end he introduced several changes in administration, "to enable our subjects to study more effectively and readily the knowledge that has hitherto remained unknown to them, so that they will become more skillful in all commercial matters."[11] The manifesto cited the need to spread education, strengthen the army, and so forth.

The appearance of the manifesto provides indubitable evidence that by this time Peter had a more or less clear conception of his policy goals, although that does not mean that one can speak of the manifesto as a program of reform. It is obvious that the tsar lacked any concrete understanding of the necessity for systematic and comprehensive measures or of the tactics to be employed in such a transformation. His grasp of the means necessary to attain the desired ends was primitive. It is no accident that the manifesto's message was directed not at his fellow countrymen but at the foreigners he was trying to convince to come serve. He was attempting to persuade them that Russia was a thoroughly civilized country, one in which they were promised they would be judged not by Russian law but in accordance with Roman law.

It must be noted that inviting foreign specialists to contribute to the expansion of the economy was common practice throughout Europe at the time, although in Petrine Russia it was resorted to on an extraordinary scale. The European nations usually issued invitations to specialists with very specific skills, and only when the corresponding national cadres proved inadequate. Russia had need of every sort of specialist. Peter excluded only one group from his guest list: Jews, whom he considered to be nothing but "cheats and swindlers." The Greeks, it might be noted, were treated in similar fashion because, according to one of the tsar's closest confidants, Petr Andreevich Tolstoy, "from the greatest to the least they all lie, and one should never believe them."[12]

To return to the war, Peter was determined to consolidate and expand on the military successes of 1703. In the spring of the following year, Russian forces again headed for Estonia, this time, for the fortified towns of Narva and Dorpat. Both towns were taken that summer. Polish and Turkish ambassadors soon arrived in Narva, which had become a symbol of Russia's victories in its own right. With the former Peter signed a treaty of alliance, and soon detachments of Russian troops were being dispatched to Poland to aid King Augustus II. To the latter Peter handed a response for the Sultan, decisively rejecting the Sublime Porte's demand that the Azov fleet be scuttled. At the end of the year the tsar returned to Moscow, where on December 19, he staged a victory celebration in which captured Swedish officers headed by General Henning Rudolf von Horn, the commandant of Narva, were involuntary participants.

The year 1705 began with the launching of new ships at Voronezh. Then, in the summer, a Russian detachment of eleven thousand men marched off to conquer Courland. The campaign began with a Russian defeat at Mur-myza (Gemauerthof in German); but in September, Mitau was taken, and along with it about two hundred cannons. While it would seem that fortune was smiling on the tsar everywhere, in reality the nation's domestic and foreign policy situations were extremely complicated.

While military concerns were now relegated to the background, they nonetheless spurred the process of domestic transformation. References to the Boyar Council disappear from the documents at precisely this time, to be replaced by a Council of Ministers, composed of the directors of the most important state institutions. Here we have a truly bureaucratic institution, marked by a clear division of functions and therefore of responsibilities, a well-defined work routine, and an established protocol for processing papers. A few years later, when requiring that each minister personally sign the minutes of the sessions of the Council, Peter clearly enunciated the objective he attached to the process: "for thereby the stupidity of each will be apparent."

The government continued to search for new sources of revenue, and in 1704 decreed that all inns be appropriated by the treasury so that they could then be farmed out. Peter's regimentation of the lives of his subjects also continued apace. In January, a decree was issued requiring that all buildings in the central part of Moscow be constructed of stone. Moreover, they were to be built facing the street rather than the courtyard. The owners of urban property who could not afford to rebuild in stone were forced to sell it. Then, ten years later, construction in stone in Moscow and other towns was banned altogether. The resources of the architects and construction people were to be channeled exclusively into the construction of St. Petersburg.

In 1705 a new approach to filling the ranks of the army was introduced: recruits were to be raised directly from the peasant and urban populations. A specified number of recruits was to be taken from a specified number of peasant and urban households. The recruits were to serve for life. The entire peasant or urban commune, moreover, was made responsible for the delivery of its quota of recruits. The commune was to establish the order in which they would be drafted, and was bound by mutual obligation to see that they were all handed over to the state. Relatives had to provide surety for the new recruits, to guarantee that they would not flee. If they nonetheless fled, those who had provided surety for them were to be taken in their stead. Later, in 1722, Peter ordered that recruits be branded with a cross, which was to be carved on their left arms and then gunpowder rubbed in, so that runaway recruits could be readily identified by the populace and reported to the authorities. The latter action, denunciation, was considered a civic obligation. Thanks to measures like these, "the source from which the army could supply itself with recruits had become truly inexhaustible," as Evgenii Anisimov has noted.[13] The recruitment system created by Peter survived in Russia for more than one hundred and fifty years.

The construction of Petersburg, in which tens of thousands of people were forced to participate, living and dying there under inhumane conditions; the introduction of the recruitment levy; the constant increase in the tax burden and in every conceivable labor obligation; and the forced introduction of foreign ways and other unaccustomed and alien aspects of life and culture—could not but elicit consternation and exasperation among all strata of the population. The Petrine reforms rocked the country, affected all its inhabitants in one way or another, undermined their normal way of life, and deprived them of their sense of stability. It was becoming obvious that Peter's prime means to achieve his goals were deliberate coercion and terror.* One would have thought that the nation would rise up and overthrow the tyrant. But that did not happen. "The explanation," concluded Soloviev, "lies in the fact that the best and strongest people sided with the transformer.... Hence, the powerful, all-encompassing movement that attracted some also prevented the hostile attitude of others from taking hold. The machine was going full speed ahead; one could cry out, complain, or

---

*"You yourself know," wrote Peter, "that although it is often right and proper, our people will not undertake anything new unless forced to do so" (*Polnoe sobranie zakonov Rossiiskoi imperii,* first series, vol. 6 [St. Petersburg, 1830], p. 388). "Our people are like children," he writes in another place, "who out of ignorance refuse to learn how to read and write unless forced to do so by a master" (ibid., vol. 7, p. 150). "Go ahead and apply the death penalty," the revenue finder Kurbatov advised the tsar, "for it is difficult to reform without terror" (Solov'ev, *Sochineniia,* book 7, p. 313).

curse, but one could not stop the machine."[14] It is difficult to judge whether the people surrounding Peter were indeed "the best,"* but they were unquestionably "the strongest." Given the crisis of traditionalism, with the corresponding decline of the old organization of service people, which culminated in Peter's administrative and military reforms, the country simply could not muster any organized political force capable of offering meaningful resistance to the transformer and his radical designs.

There were, by the way, attempts at resistance. In the autumn of 1705, a revolt of musketeers and Cossacks broke out in Astrakhan, while in 1707 another revolt enveloped the Don Cossack region. About three hundred people were executed in the aftermath of the first, while more than twenty thousand perished in the second, which was more large-scale and dangerous. In response to the latter the tsar ordered Cossack villages "burned to the ground, the people hacked to death, and the instigators broken on the wheel and impaled. This is the most effective way of discouraging the urge of people to engage in banditry; for this mob can only be pacified by brutality."[15] But while dealing with those who rebelled, Peter was unable to appreciate the mounting tension within society.

The goal for the sake of which the war with Sweden had been launched—the seizure of the Baltic lands, which Russians considered theirs by tradition—had been achieved. Yet, because Peter had no real confidence in his own forces, the prospect of confronting the main body of Swedish forces was still a fearful one. At the beginning of 1706, Charles XII's army blockaded the Russian army around Grodno, and the latter just barely managed to avoid total defeat by beating a hasty retreat toward Kiev. Again the Swedish king committed a fatal error by treating the Russian tsar as a less formidable enemy than his Polish counterpart. He therefore invaded Saxony and compelled Augustus II to sign a peace treaty in which he renounced his claim to the Polish crown, which passed to the Swedish puppet Stanislaw Leszczynski. What was in effect Augustus's betrayal came as a serious

---

*As the legal historian Oleg Omel'chenko accurately observed recently, "With all due respect to the activities of Menshikov and Iaguzhinskii, Shafirov and Tolstoy, and their allegiance to the 'reform program', it must be noted that literally all of those people 'called' by Peter were, irrespective of the time frame, swindlers and scoundrels" (see his review of N.I. Pavlenko's *Petr Velikii* in *Voprosy istorii*, 1991, no. 12, p. 228).

blow to Peter. He now found himself alone, one on one, with a terrible enemy who was considered unbeatable. The Russian government initiated desperate attempts to conclude peace.

When reading the diplomatic documents of the time, one cannot escape the impression that by 1707 Russian diplomacy was far more sophisticated than it had been at the time of the Grand Embassy. Russian envoys at European courts and at the Sublime Porte constantly spun their fine webs of political intrigue, bribing foreign ministers and civil servants, refusing to trust anyone completely, and cynically evaluating how much it would cost to buy which ministers. They entered into alliances with the envoys of certain powers and feverishly sought to counter the efforts of others. And when they found it necessary to locate mediators in order to conclude peace advantageously, they spared neither flattery nor promises. So, for example, the Duke of Marlborough was promised principalities composed of, variously, Kiev, Vladimir, or Siberia, with yearly revenues of fifty thousand *efimki*.* Cynicism, calculation, a lack of principle, and a desire to attain a given objective at any cost began to dominate the implementation of Russia's foreign policy.

In the period 1705–06, Peter's desire for peace became so great that he was prepared to return all the conquered lands to Sweden, categorically refusing only to raze St. Petersburg. Meanwhile, the tsar was cobbling together a faction of his own supporters in Poland, likewise sparing no promises, assuring them in particular that Livonia would be handed over to the Polish Commonwealth as soon as the war was over. Charles, however, did not want to hear of peace. He saw himself as a new Alexander the Great and dreamed of dealing with the tsar just as he had with King Augustus. He spent almost all of 1707 in Saxony, enjoying the homage that all the European powers were rendering him. In August, Swedish forces again began to move, but then set up camp in Poland for several months. These troops began mercilessly to pillage the local inhabitants, rich and poor alike, in the process fanning anti-Swedish sentiment.

In December, Charles moved his forces into Lithuania, forcing the Russian army to beat a retreat. At the end of January 1708, the Swedes occupied Grodno, and from there headed eastward. The Russian army,

---

Efimki were Austrian thalers and other European silver coins that had been restruck in Russia since the mid-seventeenth century.

in keeping with a strategy already worked out, stayed ahead of the Swedes, destroying supplies and forage along the route. By the second half of March, the Swedes had reached the little town of Radoszkowicze in Belorussia, halting there for three months. Not until the beginning of June did they again go on to the offensive, crossing the Berezina River and heading eastward. Careful to avoid a pitched battle, the Russian army retreated. On July 7, the Swedes seized Mogilev and halted there, ostensibly to await the arrival of a corps commanded by General Adam Löwenhaupt together with a supply train carrying provisions for Charles and his forces. Yet without awaiting their arrival, the king once more set off, although not to link up with Löwenhaupt. Instead he headed northeast, toward the ancient Russian town of Smolensk.

At the end of August, six battalions of Russian infantry (three regiments)* suddenly fell on five Swedish regiments near the village of Dobroe and, exploiting blunders by the Swedish command, routed them to a man, leaving up to three thousand enemy soldiers behind on the field of battle. Peter was ecstatic, remarking in one of his letters that "I have not heard of or seen such intense fire or such exemplary conduct from our soldiers since I began my service."[16] The Swedish march on Smolensk, however, continued. The Swedes did not halt until the middle of September when, according to Soviet military historians, their "offensive capabilities were exhausted."[17] They had consumed all their provisions and were faced with starvation. The victorious Swedish army was now confronting difficulties such as it had never experienced in its preceding campaigns. Charles decided to abandon the march on Moscow, turning instead toward the Ukraine.

The reasons for Charles's decision are not hard to understand. In the Ukraine he hoped to find the necessary provisions; he counted on the assistance of the Crimean khan; and he intended to lure the Turks into war with Russia, and the hetman of the Ukraine, Ivan Mazepa, into treason. But by turning toward the Ukraine, the Swedish king was abandoning Löwenhaupt's corps to its fate. The Russian command swiftly sized up the emerging situation, and within two weeks, on September 28, the army overtook the enemy corps at the village of Lesnaia. Over the course of the battle, which lasted several hours, the Russians administered the Swedes a decisive defeat. Up to eight thou-

---

*Some sources claim there were eight battalions.

sand enemy bodies were left behind on the field of battle at the end of the day. Instead of a sixteen-thousand-man corps of crack soldiers and a supply train bulging with provisions and stores, Charles received about six thousand five hundred stragglers who barely made it into his camp, demoralized by the unparalleled disaster. After this the king's hopes rested on Mazepa's forthcoming treason.

From the moment when Tsar Peter heard news of the Ukrainian hetman's betrayal, on October 27, 1708, official Russian propaganda and, subsequently, Soviet historiography, did all they could to portray Mazepa as some sort of monster, a veritable wellspring of evil. Even a very recent and reputable biographer of Peter, N.I. Pavlenko, could not refrain from claiming that Mazepa "harbored just about all the shortcomings to be found in human nature: suspiciousness and secretiveness, arrogance and cupidity, extreme egoism and a lust for revenge, perfidy and brutality, lechery and cowardice." The hetman "managed . . . to disguise the evil, to cleverly weave intrigues. He shrank from nothing, and nothing left a mark on his conscience . . . [as] he marched over bodies."[18] Alas, such a subjective approach to a historical figure is unproductive; for under the historian's pen, Mazepa is transformed into nothing but a caricature. Soloviev came much closer to the truth when he described Mazepa as "a weak person entangled in a struggle among the powerful."[19] Seconding Soloviev's verdict, Evgenii Anisimov noted that "In the saga of Mazepa we find reflected, as in a drop of water, the problems and tragedy of all the Ukraine."[20]

During the half-century since its integration into the Russian state in 1654, the Left-Bank Ukraine had preserved vestiges of autonomy. It had its own unique administrative-territorial divisions and system of government headed by an elected hetman and an elected council of elders. Among the latter were the chief minister and those who supervised finances, the chancelleries, and the troops. Administrative, military, and judicial authority was vested in the hetman, who had to be confirmed by a charter from the tsar. The regiments of the Ukrainian army, which were coterminous with administrative-territorial units, were made up of Cossacks who elected their own atamans and preserved vestiges of traditional Cossack freedom and self-government, which the tsarist government was formally bound to respect. Moscow, however, did not hesitate to violate its obligations on a consistent basis, a pattern of behavior that called forth constant dissatisfaction and anti-Russian movements in the Ukraine, and forced Ukrainian het-

The Origins of Empire 87

men to turn hopefully to Poland, Sweden, or to the Ottoman Empire and the Crimea.

With the start of the Petrine reforms, pressure on the Ukraine increased, if only because military activity was unfolding in close proximity to its borders. Peter, to draw on Evgenii Anisimov's phrase, viewed the hetman as "nothing but a privileged executor of his own will,"[21] while the Ukraine itself became in essence a pawn in his grand game. Thus, ignoring the hopes of the Ukrainians for the reunification of their country, the tsar callously promised the Poles who were supporting him to hand over Right-Bank Ukraine, where an anti-Polish uprising had recently taken place. Russian military units, constantly crisscrossing the Ukraine, treated the local populace as they habitually treated the populations of conquered lands. According to the great Ukrainian historian Nikolai Kostomarov, Cossacks "were beaten with sticks, their ears were cut off, and they were subjected to every kind of degradation. . . . Cossack wives and daughters who remained at home were raped, horses and cattle were seized or destroyed, and the Cossack elders themselves suffered beatings."[22] But what especially frightened Ukrainian Cossacks was the Muscovite state's intention of transforming their regiments into units of Russia's regular standing army. For Cossacks this signified the loss of traditional freedoms and privileges, an alteration for the worse in their customary way of life. They resisted the principle of the regimented state, which had been so ardently extended by Peter to the whole of the Russian land.

As regards Mazepa, he truly was caught between the proverbial rock and a hard place. On one side was the tsar, demanding unequivocal execution of his will, and on the other, the Cossacks, pleading with the hetman to save them from the new form of enslavement, as once Bohdan Khmelnytsky had saved them. Mazepa was a clever and experienced politician. It was no accident that he had held the hetman's office for so much longer than any of his predecessors and had managed to convince the tsar of his absolute fidelity. In order to ease his position, he even suggested that the Russians destroy the Zaporozhian Sich, the Cossack military settlement on the lower reaches of the Dnieper River and the center of Cossack freedom. But when the Ukraine was faced with imminent Swedish invasion and the strong likelihood that the Russian army would retreat, leaving it to the mercy of the conqueror, Mazepa decided to save his neck and authority at whatever cost. Furthermore, he was personally dissatisfied with his

Russian masters: he had been insulted by the way the tsar and his close servitors, especially Alexander Menshikov, had addressed him, and he feared that as a result of the latter's intrigues he might be deprived of his hetman's mace altogether.*

On October 26, 1708, Mazepa openly declared his allegiance to the Swedes. Contrary to his expectations, his declaration elicited no great enthusiasm among the Cossacks, in consequence of which he could attract no more than fifteen hundred men to the king's standards. Peter, whom the news of Mazepa's treachery struck like lightning on a clear day, wasted no time in taking energetic measures, thanks to which the impact of the treachery was kept to a minimum. A decree was promptly issued that lifted wartime taxes and other obligations that previously had been imposed on the Ukrainian population. The decree proclaimed that Mazepa had pocketed these taxes for his own personal use in any case. Baturin, Mazepa's capital, was taken by storm and burned to the ground. By November 7, a new hetman had been selected, and the next day Mazepa was excommunicated by the Orthodox Church.

Mazepa's betrayal naturally weakened the Russian forces and caused Peter no end of concern; but it did not markedly strengthen the Swedish side. As a result, the winter of 1708–09, which proved unusually cold, passed without any notable activity on either side. As before, Peter was prepared to conclude peace, but at the same time, gradually acquiring faith in the military capability of the Russian army, he allowed for the possibility of a major pitched battle with the Swedes, an eventuality that until then he had studiously avoided. He was, by the way, so confident of victory that he put off decisive measures until spring, instead pressing ahead with his domestic agenda.

On December 18, 1708, Peter issued a decree laying the foundations for provincial reform. It divided the country into eight *gubernii,* or provinces, each to be administered by a governor appointed by the tsar

---

*In his biography of Menshikov, N.I. Pavlenko passes over this issue in silence (N.I. Pavlenko, *Poluderzhavnyi vlastelin* [Moscow, 1988], pp. 106–9), while in that of Peter, he merely notes that Menshikov lacked diplomatic tact and never suspected Mazepa's true feeling toward him (Pavlenko, *Petr Velikii,* p. 275). One cannot rule out the possibility that Menshikov actually was intriguing against him, as Mazepa was told, and possibly had concocted plans to remove him from the hetman's office. In any case, there can be no doubt that Menshikov's behavior in some measure provoked Mazepa's betrayal.

(normally chosen from among the highest dignitaries). They were to exercise vast administrative, military, and judicial authority, and in some cases would handle the finances of their provinces. The dating of the reform with this decree was accepted by Russian historians of the nineteenth century and reinforced by Soviet historiography. This historiography argued that the reform was motivated by the 1707–08 rebellion, which revealed the inability of local authorities "to administer quick and effective class justice."[23] Supporting this point of view, N.I. Pavlenko has suggested that the provincial reform "belongs to that group of Peter's administrative reforms that was most poorly thought out" because the issue of the relationship between local and central authorities had been left unresolved.[24]

However, not everyone would agree with such an interpretation. Evgenii Anisimov takes as his point of reference another tsarist decree, one that appeared a year earlier and assigned each of the nation's towns to one of six of its largest provinces [*gubernii*]. Anisimov observes that by the beginning of 1701, special administrative districts [*okrugi*], which enjoyed judicial and financial independence from the central apparatus, had already been created. The essence of the provincial reform, according to Anisimov, was to be found in the decentralization of government, in the transfer of some of the functions of the old offices to local authorities. The goal was to straighten out the fiscal situation. The reform designated the budget of each province, with priority being given to military needs.[25] In other words, the reform was called forth by the ever more acute need for fiscal means to prosecute the war. Subsequently, a specified number of army regiments was attached to each province, with the province being required to support them.

Another obvious cause for the reform lay in the inability of the old system to cope with new tasks: tasks related not to class struggle but to complications that had arisen in conjunction with the Petrine innovations as a whole. At the center, as we have already noted, we find a constant process of replacement of old institutions by new. By the same token, the administration of a huge country at the local level, from which the resources to wage war had to be drawn (and never sufficed), demanded the strengthening of authority and new principles of its organization. In this connection, the question of decentralization has to be raised. At first glance, authority was redistributed between the center and the provinces, with the tsar delegating to the governors some of his authority. Yet not only was central authority not weakened by this reform, but on the contrary, it was strengthened, as also happened during the later development of the system of *gubernii*.

While Peter was engaged in reform, the Swedish forces, having completed their maneuvers, drew up in the spring of 1709 around the walls of the town of Poltava, which Charles XII intended to make his stronghold in the Left-Bank Ukraine. The king assumed that the capture of this fortress would make a great impression on the Ukrainian Cossacks, not to mention the Turks, whom he hoped to entice into war with Russia. Here, around the walls of Poltava, the decisive battle of the war took place. It began the night of July 27, with an attack by the Swedes calculated to surprise their enemy. They succeeded, but only temporarily. Soon, the overwhelming superiority of the Russian artillery began to tell. Moreover, in the course of the first few hours, Peter, commanding the Russian troops, managed to hold his main forces out of combat. After fending off in person an attack by the Swedes on the heart of the Russian network of redoubts, he gave the order to attack.

Addressing his troops just before the attack, the tsar proclaimed: "Think not that you are fighting for Peter, but for the state entrusted to Peter, for the fatherland. . . . And as for Peter, you should know that his life is dear to him only if Russia lives in prosperity and glory for your benefit!"[26] The attack was successful: the Swedes could not withstand the charge, and fled, heedless of the commands of their king. With the remains of the Swedish army, Charles and Mazepa fled across the Dnieper, and thence to the Ottoman Empire. The indomitable Swedish army, considered the best in Europe, had all but ceased to exist. More than eight thousand dead Swedes were left on the battlefield; about sixteen thousand more surrendered to Alexander Menshikov, who had been sent in pursuit of them, at Perevolochna.

The victory of the Russian army at Poltava was first and foremost a result of the colossal resources the nation had poured into the recruiting, arming, and supplying of the new standing army after the defeat at Narva. But there can be no doubt as well that fortune did indeed favor Peter. The Swedes had committed numerous mistakes, primarily as a result of Charles XII's presumptuousness. The documents reveal that the tsar, while hoping for victory, was by no means certain of it, and pondered what steps to take in the event of defeat. But the outcome exceeded all his expectations. It is fitting that in a letter to Fedor Romodanovskii, Peter wrote of "the very great and unexpected victory." The address of the tsar to his troops, cited above, is also noteworthy. These are the words of a mature statesman, one who has endured numerous trials and tribulations and has now clearly formulated the principles on which he will base the rest of his reign. But no less serious trials still awaited the tsar.

* * *

"Perhaps no other military victory in the history of eighteenth-century Russia yielded such rich fruits as Poltava," noted Evgenii Anisimov. "Russia at that point became a significant player in Europe's political game."[27] A British historian has confirmed this view: "Poltava is an unmistakable turning point in Russia's relations with the rest of Europe. It enormously increased Peter's influence in Europe, besides endowing him with the prestige which military success alone could give."[28] And so it did. Hardly lingering at Poltava, the Russian forces pushed on into Poland, forced Stanislaw Leszczynski to take flight, and placed Augustus II back on the throne. Soon thereafter, Peter met with his former ally at Torun. There, on October 6, a new treaty of alliance was signed, in which Poland agreed to hand over Estonia to Russia. A Russo-Danish treaty also was signed, the agreement of Prussia not to allow Swedish forces to pass through its territory was obtained, and an alliance with Hanover was concluded.

From Poland the tsar set out for Petersburg, where he ordered the construction of palaces for his closest advisers, after which at the end of December he held a grandiose celebration in Moscow of the victory over the Swedes. Peter the victor, riding the same horse he had ridden at Poltava, was accompanied by his field marshals, Menshikov and Sheremetev. Behind them marched the Preobrazhenskii regiment, followed by a column of captured Swedish officers. Shortly before, Feofan Prokopovich, prefect of the Kiev Academy, who was destined to become one of the most celebrated publicists and church figures of Petrine times, bestowed upon the tsar in his "Victory Ode" the honorary title of the Roman emperors, "Father of the Fatherland." When at the beginning of 1710 the English ambassador Charles Whitworth carried with him to Moscow an official document from Queen Anne that identified Peter by his imperial title (the English apparently wanted to make amends for a diplomatic slight administered in London to Russian ambassador Andrei Artamonovich Matveev somewhat earlier),

Chancellor Gavrila Ivanovich Golovkin demanded that the title henceforth be used on all occasions. Golovkin himself became the first Russian count [*graf*] in 1709; prior to that time, only princely titles had been recognized in Russia. The following year, the title of count was bestowed on three more members of Peter's entourage, while Vice-Chancellor Peter Shafirov was named a baron.

In January 1710, Peter granted the new hetman a charter confirming the traditional rights of the Ukrainian people, after which he concentrated his forces in the Baltic region. In the course of this year, Vyborg, Riga, and Revel, the region's major fortresses, were seized from the Swedes. In August, Peter signed a manifesto on the annexation of Estonia to Russia. In the manifesto, it might be noted, Peter mentioned that Livonia had already taken the oath of allegiance to the tsar, although this fact did not deter him from promising the lands to the Polish Commonwealth. According to Russian historian S.F. Platonov, "Peter had established hegemony over Northern Europe, and felt that he was the most powerful and influential monarch in the North."[29]

As we know, every triumph usually has a down side to it. The victory and the obvious growing power and influence of Russia could not but alarm its allies in the anti-Swedish coalition as well as its neighbors, first and foremost the Ottoman Empire. In December 1710, Peter received a dispatch from the Russian ambassador in Constantinople, informing him that the Ottomans had decided to declare war on Russia. So much has been written in the historical literature devoted to these events about how Russia's enemies, and Charles XII in particular, incited the Turks to declare war, that one might be left with the impression that the Porte utterly lacked an independent foreign policy. Yet it was precisely at this time, according to those who specialize in Ottoman history, that in its European policy the Ottoman Empire began to abandon its habitual aggressiveness for the sake of a more temporizing approach, manifesting more flexibility and a desire to achieve its long-established goals by playing on the contradictions that existed among the European powers. The strengthening of Russia under Peter I "posed an impending danger to the Ottoman Empire, one consisting not only of a possible Austro-Russian alliance, but of the establishment of close ties between Petersburg and the Balkan peoples, who were under the rule of the Osmanis."[30] Taking this into account, it becomes clear why the Ottoman Empire refused to yield to the persuasion of the Swedes when the latter were at the peak of their power, but decided on war once Russia's potential threat had become more apparent. The Russo-Turkish hostilities that continued throughout the eighteenth century revealed that Ottoman fears were well-founded.

In 1711, however, Russia was not yet ready for hostilities, and Peter seemed to fear their outcome. As evidence we might cite two important preventive measures he took before setting off on his campaign. First, the tsar considered it necessary to secure the uninterrupted administration of the country in his absence. With this in mind, a Governing Senate was established by a decree of February 22. It was to be a collegially organized body composed of nine members. The decree made clear that this new higher institution was being created to govern "during our absences" [*dlia otluchek nashikh*], an assertion often interpreted by historians as an indication of the Senate's temporary character.[31] N.I. Pavlenko even suggests that it "was summoned forth by momentary needs," and that it "was to cease its existence as soon as the tsar returned from . . . the campaign."[32] In point of fact, however, another decree several days thereafter, on March 2, mentioned "our constant" absences "in these wars."* One would therefore have to grant that Evgenii Anisimov is correct in asserting that the Senate was created "as a permanent higher governing institution,"[33] for in reality the tsar was constantly absent. In other words, the Senate was to assume the function of the tsar, to fill in for him, to be, in V.O. Kliuchevskii's words, "the alter ego of the tsar in the eyes of the people." Another Russian historian, V.Ia. Ulanov, termed the Senate "the appointed collective steward of Peter's patrimonial estate."[34]

It is another matter entirely that the Senate was established in haste, and that the grab-bag of decrees associated with its creation, as was the case with most Petrine decrees, "can hardly be assigned to the pinnacle of the legal thought of the day."[35] The decree of March 2, nonetheless, assigned the Senate several well-defined objectives, the fulfillment of which was viewed from a long-range perspective: the search for new sources of revenue to meet military needs; the administration of jus-

---

*It should be noted that the word *dlia* in the eighteenth century had another meaning than the one that it subsequently acquired. If in place of the "during" one substitutes in the text of Petrine decrees the phrase "due to" [*po prichine*], it assumes another shading. Hence the English should be read not as "during our absences" (as in the English-language excerpt from M.M. Bogoslovskii's *Petr velikii i ego reforma,* in Cracraft, *Peter the Great Transforms Russia,* p. 88), but as "due to our absences."

tice; the filling out of the officers' ranks with those nobles who had thus far shunned state service; responsibility for the expansion and improvement of domestic and foreign trade (with China and Persia, in particular); and the regularization of the status of those economic enterprises that had been farmed out. All the Senators enjoyed equal rights, and were to take their decisions collectively. Unlike the Boyar Council and the Council of Ministers, the Senate promptly received its own chancellery, with sufficient personnel to staff it. From the very beginning, then, Peter intended that the Senate be a fundamentally new organ. Yet by April 1711, he was already expressing his unhappiness at the actions of the Senators, comparing them with "the old heads of chancelleries."[36]

Peter's second preventive measure appeared strictly personal in nature: on March 6, the tsar secretly married his longtime mistress, Marta Skavronskaia, who, ever since she had fallen into Russian hands in the Baltic in 1703, had been known as Catherine. At one time a washerwoman and servant in a Lutheran pastor's household, she had a lighthearted, undemanding nature, a lively spirit, and a determination to acquire the tsar's trust and to make herself indispensable to him. According to contemporary accounts, Catherine alone could calm Peter during his frequent attacks of uncontrollable rage, his convulsions, and his fierce headaches. By 1711, she had given birth to two of his daughters—Anna and Elizabeth. But tsars have no private life separate from the public. So it was that the secret marriage of March 6, 1711, bore important implications for subsequent Russian history, for descendants of this obscure "Finnish girl," as she was called, were destined to rule the nation, with the exception of an interlude after her death, right up to February 1917.

Also on March 6, 1711, Peter set off on his next campaign, this one against the Ottoman Porte. Many historians have described the Russians' inadequate preparations for the campaign, ascribing it to overconfidence. But the tsar himself recognized the complexity of the enterprise he was undertaking and foresaw the possibility of failure. His plan was to seize the initiative and, blocking the incursion of Turkish forces into Poland, where they might link up with the remains of the Swedish army, to strive for victory with the support of the Christians in Moldavia and Wallachia and the Balkan Slavs. It was for that reason that the tsar demanded that his generals advance without awaiting the delivery of supplies. The tsar's calculations were based on an underestimation of the enemy's forces and an overestimation of the military capacity of the Russian army, which badly needed a respite from battle and which, as time would reveal, would suffer from the terrible heat of the Moldavian steppe.

As a result of Peter's miscalculations, a Russian army of thirty-eight thousand, commanded personally by the tsar, discovered to its surprise that it was surrounded by a unified Turkish–Crimean force of at least twice that number on the banks of the Pruth River in July 1711. The Russian army found itself in a truly parlous position, one in which the fate of the army, and of Peter himself, seemed to hang in the balance. The tsar sued for peace with the Turks. His despair, apparently, was so great that he was prepared to hand back everything he had conquered with such effort in the previous ten years: the territory along the Sea of Azov as well as the Baltic region. The only concession he still refused to consider was the razing of St. Petersburg. In return for retaining Petersburg, he was even prepared to hand over the ancient Russian town of Pskov. Fortunately for the Russians, the Turks refused the concession and ended up signing a treaty according to which the Russians were obligated only to return the fortress of Azov and to raze the fortress of Taganrog on the Sea of Azov and that at Kamennyi Zaton, both built by Peter. In addition, Peter promised to withdraw his troops from Poland and to allow the Swedish king unhindered passage back to his homeland.

Thus, despite the efforts of Charles XII to convince the Turks to continue military activity and to demand from Peter the return of the Baltic lands he had conquered, the tsar got off relatively lightly. The Turks had their own objectives, which they had achieved, and they felt no desire to pull somebody else's chestnuts out of the fire. This proved to be a huge miscalculation on the part of the Porte for, had it completed the destruction of the Russian army on the Pruth, it might well have inhibited the emergence of a Russian empire in the first quarter of the eighteenth century. One can only hazard a guess at the consequences. But while Peter was prepared to accept any conditions except those of capitulation, the Russian troops were ready to fight on desperately. Moreover, the situation of the Turks was much more critical than the tsar could have imagined. Three attempts to attack the Russians had cost them eight thousand dead, as a result of which the Janissaries had refused to heed orders for still another attack. To make matters worse, a Russian corps commanded by General Karl Eward von Rönne was operating successfully in the rear of the Turks. After taking Braila, it had cut Turkish communications and was bidding fair to surround the Turkish army when peace was concluded.

On July 12, 1711, the Russian forces started to withdraw, and on August 2, they crossed the Dniester River. From there the tsar went on to Warsaw, to meet with the Polish king and then take the healing waters at Carlsbad. Along the way he stopped off at Torgau, where his son Alexei was married to the Princess Charlotte Christine Sophie of Brunswick-Wolfenbüttel. By February 1712, he was already back in Petersburg, where he festively celebrated his own marriage with Catherine. At first glance everything was as it had been, and the tsar's demeanor manifested at least external calmness. But it is no accident that most of the works on this time period describe the events taking place in the years immediately following the defeat on the Pruth in extremely compressed form. The dates flash by: 1712, 1713, 1714, 1715, and so on. One gains the impression that the tempo of events had slowed drastically and that the tsar was worn out. Both he and his country needed a breathing space.

After concluding peace on the Pruth, Russia delayed as long as it dared the return of Azov to the Turks and the withdrawal of its forces from Poland. As a result, the Porte twice declared war against Russia in 1712, but no military action took place, and peace was again concluded. At the same time, Peter and his allies warred in Pomerania, although without any particular success. The Danes and Poles, moreover, quarreled among themselves, and sought to enter into separate negotiations with the Swedes. All these activities came to a head in December, with the defeat of the Danish army at the battle of Gadebusch. The following year, Russian armies managed to achieve some success, with Menshikov seizing Stettin (Szczecin, in Polish), which for some reason was promptly handed over to Prussia.

In April 1713, the Russian navy moved to attack Finland. The campaign was successful; in May, Helsingfors (Helsinki) was captured, and in August, Åbo, which was then the capital of Finland. It is noteworthy that these conquests were achieved in the full realization that Finland would have to be returned at the final peace treaty. In 1714 and 1715, the tsar spent a substantial amount of time at sea, refusing to forsake his ship even when it was moored. "When one examines the contents of the tsar's 'Campaign Journals' for 1714 and 1715," notes N.I. Pavlenko in this context, "one gains the impression that they record the landmarks in the life not of the sovereign of a huge nation but of a naval officer who is completely immersed in such concerns as naval campaigns and naval exercises."[37] In July 1714, this same Russian fleet defeated the Swedish at the battle of Hangö. This was Peter's first major naval victory, and he even compared it with Poltava. To celebrate his victory the tsar returned to Petersburg, where in January of the next year one of those "jester marriages" so beloved by popular historians was arranged. In 1715, the irregular way of life the tsar had led for many years began to tell on his health. Peter's "Campaign Journals" take note of his ill health both in the summer and at the end of the year, when he spent an entire month in bed. At the beginning of 1716, the tsar headed abroad to take the waters.

Still in all, Peter could not bear to cut himself off from governmental affairs altogether. The tsar's thoughts remained occupied with familiar matters: the strengthening of the army, the reform of the administration, and the morals of his people. As was always the case, money and suitable people were in short supply. Another problem also grew more acute: malfeasance.

The Petrine reforms had moved to the forefront a whole pleiad of new, talented, fresh, energetic people, prepared to follow the example set by their sovereign by laboring unstintingly in his cause. But unlike Peter, who felt no inclination toward luxury and who over the course of many years demonstratively received from the treasury no more than the salary appropriate to his rank at the time—which the Prince-Caesar Romodanovskii granted him in return for actual service rendered—those who surrounded the tsar were far from disinterested in wealth. The Petrine reforms had opened up numerous opportunities for enrichment: new institutions with new responsibilities, increased manufacturing and trade, the supply of the army, the recruitment levy, foreign campaigns and journeys, and numerous other possibilities. Many people close to the seat of power had been drawn from social strata whose members previously could never have even dreamed of access to and participation in the distribution of the national wealth. Most of them, like their colleagues from distinguished aristocratic lines, were not known for their high moral standards. And where could they have acquired high moral standards? For the very methods of carrying out the reforms, the cynicism and brutality inherent in them, in no way encouraged the cultivation of such standards.

This was all the more the case since the reforms had discredited old moral values and norms of behavior without creating new ones. Time was required (centuries, according to Soloviev) before the idea of serving the state for "the common good," as propounded by the tsar, could penetrate the consciousness of his subjects. Meanwhile, the allure of power and easy profit proved irresistible. Furthermore, the chief cause of corruption in the Russian state apparatus both prior to and after Peter—and in fact, right up to the present day—lay in the shortage of revenues that prevented the state from paying its civil servants a decent salary. Hence, over the course of many centuries, Russians became accustomed to viewing state service as a means of personal "feeding," or enrichment.[38] As was the case earlier, the honest fulfillment of service obligations not only failed to bring a decent standard of living but often ruined a person. Thus, the diplomat A.A. Matveev complained to the tsar in 1719 that during his four-year stay abroad "in the name, and for the honor, of His Majesty he had to supplement his salary with his own funds, as a result of which he had become impoverished."[39] Bribery was something akin to a legitimate supplement to a functionary's salary, without which the functionary's existence would have become impossible.

Since judges received enough in the form of "gratuities," the revenue-seeker, Alexei Kurbatov, tried to convince the tsar to pay them no salary at all. Indeed, Kurbatov referred to his own experience, making no effort whatever to conceal the fact that he himself had accepted such "gratuities." The well-known Russian historian and leading state figure of the first half of the eighteenth century, Vasilii Nikitich Tatishchev, in effect lent theoretical justification to the assertion. In his "Testament," he related the gist of a conversation he had held with Tsar Peter in which he sought to prove to the sovereign that if he accepted gratuities from a petitioner not to render a decision contrary to the law but merely to speed it up, there was no criminality involved. Sergei Soloviev draws our attention to yet another peculiarity in the psychology of Peter's favorites: many of them began to identify with the state, and accordingly, to look upon state revenues as their own, arguing that their devoted services to the state gave them that right.[40]

In about 1713, Peter launched a merciless campaign against the looting of the state treasury, issuing a series of decrees, including one encouraging the denunciation of wrongdoers. Later, brutal forms of punishment for failure to denounce were introduced into law. It was at this time that the job of administrative watchdog [*fiskal*] was created. Among the holder's responsibilities was that of overseeing the activities of the state's civil functionaries, right up to the highest echelons. In the years that followed, many functionaries of various ranks were subjected to repression for "extortion," and publicly executed. Thus, in 1721 the governor of Siberia, Prince Matvei Petrovich Gagarin, was hanged in the presence of the tsar and his entire court. He had been convicted of taking numerous bribes in return for leasing out state resources, of tapping into state funds for personal needs, and of confiscating goods imported by merchants from China, even valuable gems purchased there for the tsaritsa. But Peter was unable to cure corruption as he had once dealt with the musketeers: the sickness had penetrated to the very heart of the state organism, infecting those people closest to the tsar, those who had enjoyed his unlimited trust for many years. Even those whose job it was to combat malfeasance and who were actually zealous in unmasking others, as a rule, sooner or later succumbed to this disease.

While struggling to combat the vices of those in service to the state, Peter constantly collided with the phenomenon of avoidance of service altogether. On this subject he received reports of dozens, and even hundreds, of nobles who had evaded service or education by taking refuge on their estates or even behind monastery walls. In the struggle against this evil, Peter was merciless. However, he resorted to legislation as well as punishment. In March 1714, a remarkable decree appeared "On the Order of Inheritance of Movable and Immovable Properties," better known as the "Decree on Single Inheritance."

In printed form, the decree itself took up only five pages; but due to its importance, a vast historical literature has been devoted to it. Composed by the tsar himself, this decree represents an important landmark in the history of the Russian nobility. In the first place, it legislated the equality of the service estate with the allodial estate in terms of form of property. In the second, the Russian autocrat introduced into Russian law the concept of unigeniture, a modified form of primogeniture. Henceforth, landed property was not to be subject to division among all the heirs of the deceased but rather was to pass to any one son of the father's choosing. It is apparent that the other sons, deprived of their source of regular income, as intended by the decree, would have to devote themselves to state service or else engage in private enterprise. Based on this assumption, most scholars maintain that the drawing of nobles into state service or into some other form of activity useful to the state was the decree's primary objective. There are others who suggest that the tsar wanted to transform a part of the nobility into a third estate, a juridical grouping situated between the nobility and the peasantry. Still others insist that the tsar was concerned primarily with the preservation of the nobility and that he even sought to transform it into something approximating a West European aristocracy. A remaining few are convinced of the antinobile thrust of the decree. Reinhard Wittram tried to resolve the conundrum by interpreting the decree as an expression of the tsar's "many-faceted thought."[41] But whether the tsar actually was pursuing several goals in drafting this decree is not as important as the fact that the consequences were multifaceted.

As we have seen, the old system of service rendered by state servitors assigned to provincial towns had fallen into decline by the end of the seventeenth century. The Petrine reforms—in particular, the reorganization and regularization of the army and the formation of the central state apparatus—had led to a situation whereby the old, pre-Petrine organization of service had ceased to exist. The new pattern of organization emerged only gradually. The assertion of the equality of the service estate with the allodial estate represented what might be termed the establishment of the first juridical norm after the elimination of *mestnichestvo* in 1682. It formally unified heterogeneous groups of service people into a uniform noble estate. The juridical distinction between provincial and capital nobles ceased to exist. Now the basic criterion for their classification became service. According to one of the decrees of this period, those nobles who had never served or entered trade—that is, those who were of no use to the state—were not allowed to purchase land. Several years later, in response to an inquiry from the War Collegium about how to distinguish the eminent nobility from the not-so-eminent, the tsar answered curtly: "Evaluate the eminence of the nobility by its usefulness."

The tsar considered the noble's professional preparation, his education, the most important evidence of his "usefulness." A royal decree forbad those nobles who were being sent abroad for study to marry, and Peter made certain that no indulgences were granted to even the most eminent of nobles. Thus, in 1709, the brother of Field Marshal Boris Sheremetev fell into disgrace because he had tried to circumvent the decree by arranging a marriage between his son and the daughter of Fedor Romodanovskii. In January 1714, a noble offspring who lacked any sort of education was forbidden to marry. This same offspring was also denied the right to occupy a command position in the army or an administrative post in the civil service. The tsar was persuaded that distinguished origins alone were no longer enough for a successful service career. In this same connection, we find in February 1712 a decree stipulating that no noble be promoted to officer rank who had not served as a soldier in a guards regiment and therefore had not received the necessary training.

Peter constantly concerned himself with the opening of new educational institutions (at the beginning of 1715 the Naval Academy was opened), with the dispatch of students abroad (in all, about one thousand people were sent abroad in the first quarter of the eighteenth century), and with the publication of a variety of useful books. Back in 1710, the tsar in his own hand had crossed out from a copy of a primer he had received a number of antiquated Slavic letters and ordered that the remaining be used "to print historical books and those on manufacturing."[42] This was the origin of the new "civil script," which has been used ever since in all secular publications.

While encouraging nobles to serve, Peter gradually reformed and regularized service to the state. In 1716, the tsar sent home from abroad his "Military Regulations," which established the arrangement and organization of the army, the obligations of the military servitors, the fundamentals of combat and field service, and military codes of justice. The regulations were destined for long life: they remained in effect for a century and a half. In 1712, a decree concerning the creation of a collegium [*kollegiia*] for foreign trade was promulgated. The very name of the institution was an innovation. But it was merely the first step in the radical reform of the central administration that was to follow. In 1715, modifications in local government, entailing a new, firmer division of the provinces based on statistical principles (the number of households), were introduced.

Around this time, the state's industrial policy also changed. By now it had become clear that the government by itself could not create an industrial base that would satisfy the needs of the army and navy. Thus the transfer of state-run enterprises to private hands began, with the new possessors receiving a variety of commercial privileges. But because the merchantry revealed little haste or desire to engage in industrial production, matters progressed slowly. Hence, for example, a decree was promulgated in 1715 that required the creation of joint-stock companies for the construction of textile mills, Peter's intent being that within five years woolen cloth for military uniforms would no longer have to be purchased abroad. When in 1720 the state-run Moscow Woolen Complex was transferred to private hands, however, he found it necessary to reiterate his intent.[43]

While industrialization had to be one of the nation's most urgent priorities if its technological backwardness was to be overcome, it was accomplished in a way completely at variance with that of other nations. As was already the case, the state retained full sovereignty over its subjects and their property. As Anisimov notes, "Everything that belonged to the subject could at any time 'be appropriated by the sovereign' and handed over to whomever he wished."[44] The rights of the enterprise's possessor, who had received it from the state or had constructed it at his own expense, were not the rights of a private owner but those of a leaseholder, one whose chief obligation was to fulfill state orders, primarily those of a military nature. On the one hand, this situation brought stability to production, serving the entrepreneur as a buffer against the unpredictability of the marketplace. But on the other, it rendered competition nugatory, and therefore deprived the industrialist of the stimulus to raise the quality and quantity of production. In the process, the industrialist himself became completely dependent on the state, and industry, by orienting itself toward the satisfaction of the state's demands rather than those of the nation at large, was threatened with ruination at the end of the war, with the accompanying slackening of the stream of military orders.

One of the most glaring peculiarities of the Russian industrialization process was the extremely restricted nature of the market for free hired labor. The possessor of the enterprise therefore depended on the state to supply him with labor power, for only the state could permit or forbid him to purchase agricultural serfs for factory work. Then there were those who hired themselves out to work in privately owned factories. They were for the most part peasants who had received permission from their masters to leave their villages temporarily to earn additional income on the side. In reality, their wages went chiefly to their landlords as payment of their quitrents. At state-owned factories, the chief form of labor power was ascribed peasants, who were usually state peasants who lived in the region around the factory and had to work off their state taxes and other obligations in this fashion.

With the transfer of state-owned factories to private hands, the situation of the ascribed peasants changed, as did the status of the possessors of the enterprises, who were making use of all these categories of labor power. Given the absence of any sort of legal basis for the existence of a "third estate," the possessors were "ensconced" in the serf-owning system, as a result of which, in Evgenii Anisimov's words, they "lacked a sense of their social uniqueness, and therefore failed to develop a sense of corporate identity." Based on such observations, Anisimov arrived at the significant conclusion that "in a system of industry based on serf labor there was no room for the development of capitalism (and consequently for the formation of a bourgeois class)."[45] In other words, while fostering industrialization by means of the creation of a network of industrial enterprises (for the most part in heavy industry), and thereby successfully eliminating much of Russia's technological backwardness, the state established industry on outmoded, serfdom-infused foundations, vesting it with irresolvable contradictions and impediments to further development.

Much the same was true of commerce. Like industry, it developed under the harsh control of the state. Moreover, the merchantry ended up with the extraordinarily heavy burden of military expenditures resting disproportionately on its shoulders, while the state dictated to it where, how, and in what to trade. In 1711, for example, the forced transfer of merchants to St. Petersburg from the nation's various towns was begun. In 1713, merchants were prohibited from shipping the fundamental items of Russian export through Archangel; they had to take them for sale to Petersburg, where the necessary infrastructure was still lacking. This policy—in effect, the state's exploitation of the merchantry and its capital for its own purposes—led to the ruination of many families that at the end of the seventeenth century had been among the merchant elite. The system of serfdom was to make its presence felt in the future as well: the stratum of the population from which new merchants with capital could be expected to emerge was extremely narrow.

The peculiarities of the Russian social structure, enmeshed as it was in the serf system, thus became a brake on economic modernization. Peter probably failed to recognize the significance of this fact, although he was attempting to copy the structures of European nations and, it would seem, could not but observe that those countries with which he wished to compare Russia no longer had serfdom. And if he failed to perceive this fact during his first trip abroad, when he was still quite young, why did it not strike him during the second, when he was already a mature political figure who knew only too well what he wanted?

As was the case with the first trip, the tsar's itinerary on the second trip took him first to Riga, which now belonged to Russia, and then to Danzig (Gdansk in Polish), where he had a meeting with King Augustus and attended the marriage of his niece Ekaterina Ivanovna to the Duke of Mecklenburg. This time Peter was no longer shy: he did not hide his face in his hands or stand around gaping. Rather, when he felt cold during a service in a Lutheran church, he snatched a wig off the head of the mayor standing next to him and planted it firmly on his own. From Danzig the tsar headed for Pyrmont, meeting with the king of Denmark along the way, and then for the United Provinces of the Netherlands. Once again he inspected the wharves, the manufactories, and the ships, rubbed shoulders with carpenters, bought pictures, and searched for ways to shorten the war. Seeking a mediator in his negotiations with Sweden, Peter headed for France in 1717. Passing through Dunkirk, Calais, Amiens, and Beauvais, the tsar once more studied fortresses, harbors, and military magazines. He expressed surprise at the poverty of the common people and revealed a certain modesty: upon arriving in Paris he declined to live in the Louvre, preferring instead to spend his first night in his own camp bed, set up in the cloakroom of a nearby hotel.

In the French capital the tsar visited an anatomical theater, the mint, and an observatory, met with famous scholars, dropped in on a session of the Academy of Sciences, was especially intrigued by public parks and the construction of fountains, and expressed regret at the extreme luxury of the court, which he believed would result in all sorts of problems for Paris. Although N.I. Pavlenko writes that "while in Paris, Peter manifested new intellectual interests,"[46] they were strictly utilitarian in nature, as they had been earlier. Nor did the tsar-reformer manifest any desire to learn more about the legal, political, or social systems of those governments on which his fate rested. But it may be that Peter considered serfdom an advantage for Russia because it enabled the authorities to mobilize nearly unlimited human and material resources when necessary. Without serfdom, his intentions would have been unrealizable.

After having spent about one and a half years abroad, the tsar was forced to return home in June 1717 because of "domestic circumstances." These circumstances were connected with Alexei, the tsar's son by his first marriage. Relations between the two men long been confrontational. Alexei, a rather passive and weak-willed person, had become a symbol of opposition to Peter, although he probably never actually participated in a conspiracy. He hated his father because of the energy, assertiveness, and violence with which he had carried out his reforms. What Alexei wanted most was a quiet life spent in the company of friends, especially his beloved Evfrosinia Fedorovna. A former serf, Evfrosinia had particularly endeared herself to the tsarevich after his wife, Charlotte of Brunswick-Wolfenbüttel, had died while giving birth to a son in 1715.

The tsarevich had received a threatening letter from his father, complaining that he lacked a worthy successor. Alexei hastened to respond, agreeing to renounce his claim to the throne. After going abroad, Peter summoned Alexei to him. The tsarevich went, but not to his father. Rather, he went to his in-laws in Vienna, where he sought political asylum, which he was granted. Disquieted by his son's disappearance, the tsar launched a search and finally located Alexei in Naples. He dispatched Peter Tolstoy, an experienced and utterly unprincipled diplomat, to fetch him back. After about a week, Tolstoy managed to convince the tsarevich to return to Russia, promising him freedom, permission to live with his beloved mistress, and the tsar's forgiveness.

At the end of January 1718, Alexei was brought back to Russia. Summoned before the tsar, he begged forgiveness in the presence of the court and officially renounced his claim to the throne in favor of his younger half brother, the tsarevich Peter, who had recently been born to Catherine. The tsar further demanded that his son name his confederates. Without hesitation, Alexei betrayed all those who had been faithful to him. An investigation was launched and several dozen people were implicated in a conspiracy. In order to conduct the investigation, the Secret Chancellery, an institution that would serve as the center of political investigation for several decades, was specially created. By the middle of March, the first executions were carried out.

The promises Peter had given his son notwithstanding, the tsarevich himself was among those who were drawn into the investigation. He was arrested and subjected to torture, in which his own father participated. By summer, when enough evidence against Alexei had been collected, the tsar handed the matter over to the examination of a court composed of people in the highest military and civil ranks as well as the church hierarchs. On June 24, the court condemned the tsarevich to death. Two days later, he died under unclarified circumstances. The next day, as was customary, the regular anniversary of the battle of

Peter I confronts his son, Tsarevich Alexei. From a painting by N.N. Ge.

Poltava was celebrated, and the tsar attended a festive dinner and ball. On June 29, he rejoiced on the occasion of the launching of a new ship, and on June 30, he buried his son.

"We shall never know what he felt in his soul," observes Evgenii Anisimov, "but . . . Peter was attempting to show that for him nothing was more important than the state's interests, in the name of which he had sacrificed everything, including his son."[47] Nikolai Pavlenko puts the case still more starkly: "The fate of the son or the fate of the state: this was the tsar's choice, and he made it." One can of course criticize the tsar, notes this last biographer, but only on the grounds of "abstract morality," and interests of state required that he transgress it.[48] But was this really the case? For even if he had to sacrifice his son to some higher goal, he did not have to torture him personally, much less demonstratively rejoice on the day following his death. On the contrary, even if we accept Peter's point of view, grief, however insincere it might have been, would have had a greater moral significance. By his conduct the tsar offended all the norms of Christian morality, thereby underlining the amorality of the policy he was pursuing.

We lack evidence to conclude whether or not Peter had any fatherly feeling for his son. But the tsar had consciously transformed himself into a cog in the machinery of state, and he demanded the same of others. The human personality and the value of human life meant nothing to him in comparison with the state and its interests. As a consequence, the state increasingly resembled a police state, acquiring features that would stay with it over the course of the next century and a half.

At the end of 1717, Peter turned to the reform of the central administrative apparatus. By a series of decrees he established a network of what were at the time termed collegia: institutions with clearly defined functions within their jurisdictions, with collegial organization, and with careful regulation of all the staff members' responsibilities. At first there were nine such collegia: the Collegium of Foreign Affairs, the Collegium of State Revenues, the Collegium of Justice, the Central Accounting Collegium, the War Collegium, the Admiralty, the Commerce Collegium, the Collegium of State Expenditures, and the Mining and Manufacturing Collegium. The number of collegia was subsequently increased to eleven, using the Swedish system as a model. This system was predicated on the principles of cameralism, a doctrine of bureaucratized state administration, which was popular in Central Europe in the sixteenth and seventeenth centuries. The daily work routine of the collegia was determined by a complex network of regulations, composed of individual regulations for each institution and a General Regulation for the entire bureaucratic system. The latter was promulgated in 1720. It established a regimen for the work of the institutions, their staffing, a common order for official procedures, a nomenclature for documents, and a protocol for drawing them up, certifying them, preserving them, and so on.

It is in these years that we find the origins of still another of Peter's grandiose reforms: that of the tax system. The very purpose of the reform—the imposition of taxes—meant that in one form or another it would affect the nation's entire population. Given the specific conditions of eighteenth-century Russia, its significance was unusually broad and multifaceted. The return from foreign campaigns of the huge standing army Peter had created provided the initial impetus for the reform. It was necessary to situate this army in the countryside in such a way that it could readily be maintained. It was decided to garrison the active military units directly in those regions that were required to maintain them, a calculation pegged to the size of the population and the type of unit involved (special calculations were carried out to figure out how many peasants it would take to maintain one infantryman or one cavalryman).

In conjunction with these calculations, a soul tax—that is, a tax on "the male soul"—was introduced as a replacement for the tax on households, which had hitherto been the dominant source of revenue. The state had yet to determine how many such souls there were. For this purpose, "registers" of the numbers of souls were to be compiled for each village. Once this task was carried out, it was decided to use special revisers to check the numbers submitted. In effect, their work took the form of a census of the population, or a "revision" of the male souls, a procedure that from then on was carried out regularly. During the course of the revision, a new problem was discovered: the large number of runaways. By resorting to extraordinarily harsh legislation, they were ordered apprehended and returned to their former places of residence. In the process, even those who had abandoned their place of birth years earlier and had long since settled in a new location, often having changed their occupation, were forcibly brought back. In order to deter future flight, a passport system was introduced. Henceforth the peasant could leave his place of residence only if he carried a passport that specified his destination and the period of time he would be away. Those who were caught without a passport, even if not runaways but simply inebriated or confused, were subject to arrest, punishment, and immediate return to their place of residence. All of this entailed a sharp escalation of police control over the population, and led to an increased harshness in the institution of serfdom itself.

An important consequence of the tax reform was an alteration in the social structure of Russian society. In order to carry out the reform, just who was and who was not to pay the soul tax first had to be determined. From the very beginning it was apparent that the nobility would not be subject to the tax, a decision that confirmed one of its most important privileges. But things, as it turned out, were not all that simple; for it was not always easy to distinguish a noble from a nonnoble. The very concept of "nobility" [*dvorianstvo*] as a cover term to identify a social stratum did not make its appearance until the end of

Peter's reign; until then the word *shliakhetstvo,* derived from the Polish, had briefly been employed. In pre-Petrine times, one's social status was defined by one's position in the service hierarchy, or one's rank. Then the service principle was replaced by lineage, by belonging to a noble line, which was defined by the ranks of one's ancestors. But that did not resolve the matter either. For it turned out that there were possessors of enserfed souls whose ancestors were not among those who, "thanks to their descent" [*po otechestvu*], had served with the upper service element in the Muscovite ranks, or with the middle service element assigned to the provincial towns. In particular, there were many such possessors of enserfed souls among those of the lower service element who served "by recruitment" [*po priboru*], whose obligation it was to guard the fortified defense lines along the nation's southern frontiers against nomadic incursion. From this category of people a special subcategory of state peasants was created when the soul-tax reform was implemented. It was composed of single homesteaders who, although now placed on the lists of tax-bearers, sometimes remained small-scale landlords.

One other category of the population was not subject to the soul tax: the clergy. However, legislation sharply curtailed both the total number of clergymen permitted by the state and the number who were free from taxation. According to Evgenii Anisimov, whose first monograph was devoted to Peter's taxation reform, it encouraged "the isolation of the clerical estate and the consolidation of social and juridical barriers that separated it from the tax-bearing estates."[49] The future was to reveal, however, that in reality the process of establishing the clergy as an estate was far from simple, and that the norms introduced by the soul-tax reform were practically the only attempt to define the clergy's status in this way.

The nobility and the clergy were the only two individual categories (excluding the military, of course) not to be incorporated into the larger soul-tax-bearing category. All the rest of the nation's population was subject to the soul tax. Its structure was, however, rendered more precise. Thus, a new category of state peasants was created, into which, in addition to the single homesteaders, the descendants of all the other numerous ranks of lower service people were integrated, as well as the black plough peasants of the Russian North, who had eluded serfdom, and the non-Russian peoples of the Volga region,

Siberia, and the Far East, who had earlier paid the Russian government a special tax in the form of furs, the *iasak.* The remainder of the rural population—the various categories of bonded people and servants living on landed estates who did not engage in their own independent economic activity but rather performed various jobs for the estates and their inhabitants, and thus remained outside the system of taxation on households—was now placed in the tax-bearing category alongside the tillers of the soil. The category of bondsman, which was gradually disappearing by the end of the seventeenth century, ceased to exist, as a result of which the enserfed peasantry was transformed into what was in essence a single social stratum.

Analogous measures were applied to the town. Here, too, the census of the population led to the forcible return of those who had left their places of residence. They were attached to the town in a way that reflected the pervasiveness of serfdom. In the process, the tsar-legislator did what he could to consolidate the urban population, regardless of the actual occupations of its members, defining them all as merchants. Strict limitations were placed on the ability of new inhabitants, those from the village in particular, to attach themselves to urban communities. On the whole, the soul-tax reform significantly increased the level of state "regulation." As a result, the social structure became more rigid, leaving only minimal opportunity for individuals to transfer from one social category to another. Thus, freedom of occupational choice became narrower and the possibility of geographic mobility more restricted.

It goes without saying that this did not happen all at once. The implementation of the reform took several years, continuing even after Peter's death. Its course depended on the international situation and was adjusted periodically in response to changes in it. In May 1718, Peter finally achieved the goal he had pursued so stubbornly: The Swedes at last agreed to initiate negotiations to end the war. A peace congress was opened on the Åland Islands. Negotiations started out slowly. Not until November, when Charles XII died unexpectedly in Norway, did it seem they would take a more harmonious turn. The new Swedish government, however, began to orient its foreign policy toward Great Britain, in the process losing interest in the cessation of war and the conclusion of peace on terms favorable to Russia. As a result, the Åland talks were broken off in September 1719 without yielding any results. In order to show the Swedes that their hopes for revenge were in vain, Peter ordered the resumption of military operations. In July 1720, off the island of Gränhamn, the Russian fleet seized four Swedish frigates carrying 104 cannons, which were brought to St. Petersburg in triumph in September.

Given the turn of events, the Swedes were forced to reconsider their decision. In May 1721, in the little Finnish town of Nystadt, negotiations were renewed, and after all sorts of delaying tactics and maneuverings, a peace treaty was finally signed in August. Estonia, Livonia, and Ingria, with the towns of Vyborg and Kexholm, passed into Russian hands. The war, which had lasted twenty-one years, cost thousands of lives, and exhausted the resources of both countries, was concluded, in the tsar's words, "as well as could be hoped for." Peter was delighted, and he and his people celebrated the victory for several months. Parades, banquets, masked balls, and huge theatrical presentations jostled each other for space first in Petersburg and then in Moscow. The whole court, those on the top four rungs of the Table of Ranks, the diplomatic corps, and the entire population of the two capitals participated in the festivities. In his great joy, the tsar even burned down the palace at Preobrazhenskoe, where he had announced the opening of the war.

Peter considered the Northern War a school for Russia and its population, although "students of science all usually graduate in seven years," while "our school lasted three times as long."[50] Russia required three times as long in order to overcome its domestic crisis by means of radical transformation and to move to a qualitatively new stage in its development. Peter himself rose to a new level of greatness as ruler and as autocrat: on October 22, 1721, at the Holy Trinity Cathedral in Petersburg, in the presence of the court, the upper nobility, and the high-ranking civil and military dignitaries, the Senate's decision to bestow upon the tsar the titles of "Emperor," "Father of the Fatherland," and "the Great" was announced. The Russian state had become an empire.

"By the beginning of the seventeen twenties," notes Evgenii Anisimov, "the ship of empire had been framed by the great carpenter, and amid the sounds of the last salvos of the Northern War she was already launched."[51] Details such as the ship's rigging were added in the period from 1720 to 1722. First the General Regulation mentioned above—the cornerstone of the bureaucratic system—was issued; and then in January 1721, the Regulation for the Main Magistracy appeared. Here we have the beginning of the renewed reform of urban administration. The Main Magistracy, which was in effect just another collegium, was subordinated directly to the Senate, while its president was appointed by the tsar. In their turn the town magistracies, elected by the townspeople, were subordinated to the Main Magistracy. The towns themselves were divided into as many as five sections, depending on the number of households in them, while the inhabitants were divided into two guilds [*gildii*]. The more prosperous merchants, town doctors, apothecaries, jewelers, icon painters, and artists were assigned to the first guild, while petty tradespeople, craftsmen, and hired workers were assigned to the second.

The Regulation for the Main Magistracy, moreover, called for the further subdivision of members of all occupations into trade corporations [*tsekha*], which resembled European guilds. All these innovations were introduced in tandem with a census of the urban population, with the purpose of imposing the soul tax on it. The census revealed that among the "merchantry" were numerous people who lacked any sort of financial means, any sort of property. They made their living by "day labor." Peter formulated the task of the reform as that of "reassembling the Russian merchantry, which like a house has fallen into ruin." But for all the verbiage, the objective was still purely fiscal, and as a consequence no stimulus was provided for the development of the Russian town as a trade and industrial center.

Also in January 1721, the regulation for yet another collegium, the Ecclesiastical Collegium, was approved. By this measure Peter resolved once and for all the issue of the relationship between church and monarchy in the Russian state system. The Ecclesiastical Regulation established on theoretical grounds the principle of the inadmissibility of any spiritual authority independent of the authority of the state itself, vested in the autocrat. Now, according to the regulation,

> The Fatherland need have no fear of revolts and disturbances from a collegially organized administration such as those that proceed from the personal rule of a single ecclesiastical administrator. For the common people do not understand how ecclesiastical authority is distinguishable from that of the autocrat. Instead, awed by the great dignity and glory of the Supreme Pastor [the Patriarch], they imagine that such an administrator must be a second sovereign, a ruler equal to or even greater than the autocrat, and that

the ecclesiastical rank is another, and superior, sovereign state.... Simple hearts are so misled by this notion that in certain affairs they look to the Supreme Pastor rather than to the autocrat.[52]

In keeping with the regulation, a Most Holy Synod, a collegially organized institution composed of church hierarchs appointed by the tsar, was created in February 1721 to replace the Ecclesiastical Collegium. Upon assuming their duties, the members took an oath of allegiance to the sovereign. About a year later, in May 1722, a Chief Procurator, a secular bureaucrat (and a military one at that), was assigned to supervise the activity of the Synod. James Cracraft justifiably refuses to see in the assignment of the Chief Procurator the reflection of any special attitude toward the church, noting that similar bureaucrats were assigned at the same time to other institutions (the function of Procurator-General, for example, was introduced into the Senate), and in general, "in the closing years of his reign Peter increasingly made use of officers and sometimes noncommissioned officers and even ordinary guardsmen in an attempt to enforce honest and efficient administration at every level of the government."[53] The point is that Peter made no distinction whatever between religious and secular institutions, viewing the church as simply another cog in the state's machinery, one of the mechanisms available to him to educate his subjects. In 1722, the state determined just how many clergymen there ought to be for a given number of inhabitants so that the excess could be incorporated into the soul-tax-bearing category. Those who remained were to preach sermons glorifying the achievements and principles of the government and dedicated to the anniversaries of battles and the capture of fortresses, and to the name days of the sovereign and members of his family.

In May 1722, a special synodal decree, violating the foundations of a basic church rite, obligated clergymen to denounce parishioners who had revealed to them during confession any evil designs against the sovereign or state authority. So that this peculiar means of investigating undesirables could achieve an all-encompassing character, attendance at church and confession was declared by a special joint decree of the Senate and Synod to be one of the obligations of all subjects. Supervision of attendance and, accordingly, the power to punish, was vested in the clergy. Over the course of his entire reign, moreover, Peter never lost sight of the monks, whom he considered little better than parasites. In 1723, the tsar ordered a census of them carried out, and forbad the tonsuring of new monks. His intent was to transform monasteries into military hospitals and almshouses. Although the great transformer did not manage to carry this project to completion, his intention is quite indicative of his attitude toward the church.

Nor did the tsar forget his nobles. In 1722, he introduced the remarkable Table of Ranks, with the objective of further regularizing their service by establishing a new hierarchy of military, civil, and court ranks, arranged in fourteen classes. At the table's foundation lay the principle of personal merit, according to which each civil and military servitor in his service career was to rise up through the entire ladder of ranks in sequence, from bottom to top. Moreover, it was not only nobles who could strive to attain the top "class of ranks." Anyone who had served in civil service up to a rank of the eighth class, or to the fourteenth in military service, had the right to receive hereditary nobility. In this fashion the table was designed to serve as a stimulus to attract large numbers of people into state service. It was extremely significant that civil service was put on the same table with military, for in pre-Petrine Rus service in the bureaucracy had been considered demeaning to those listed in the genealogical registers. To offset this bias, Peter had stipulated in his General Regulation that children of the nobility be trained in chancellery affairs.

Two weeks after the appearance of the Table of Ranks, Peter established the position of Heraldry Master and provided its holder with special instructions. The very name of the position pointed to the fact that the emperor intended to elevate the status of the Russian nobility, bestowing upon it certain European features, in particular supplying it with coats of arms. So it was that the designing of coats of arms (which, by the way, not only nobles but towns received) fell to the responsibility of the Heraldry Master. But his primary function, as that of the Heraldry Office that he headed, was the registration of the nobility, accompanied by the maintenance of special lists of nobles, the organization of reviews to determine suitability for service, the attestation of readiness for service, the assignment of noble youths to state service, and the clarification of the cases of those who refused to serve.

Study and then lifelong service became mandatory for nobles. Anisimov is correct in asserting that "Petrine policy with respect to the nobility was . . . extremely harsh"; for in comparison with the seventeenth century, the noble's freedom was sharply curtailed, thus raising the related question as to whether one can justifiably apply the term "ruling class" to the nobility of Petrine times.[54] Granted, even in the seventeenth century the noble was far from free, for his service was also obligatory. But since he served in an irregular army, he was of course much freer, and his entire life was less regulated, less subject to unremitting control by the state. As a result of Peter's reforms, the level of "unfreedom," if one may speak of it as such, sharply increased for the Russian nobility as well as for other social strata. Noble or non-noble, irrespective of the presence or absence of various sorts of privileges, each of the empire's inhabitants had to fulfill a strictly defined function in service to the state and to contribute to an increase in the state's wealth and power. Thus, the concept of "the good of the state" was fused with that of "the common good" to become the supreme value, in the face of which individual human life counted for naught.

The militarized, regimented Russian imperial state, created under wartime conditions by decrees issued in wartime, having become one of the great world powers, and sensing in full measure its new-found greatness and power, continued to look rapaciously about in search of new enemies even after the conclusion of the exhausting war with the Swedes. Only a few months elapsed after the end of the war before the Russian army set out on a new campaign, the Persian, which was intended to serve as the first step on Russia's road to Central Asia, the Caucasus, and eventually, to legendary India. The campaign proved successful, and as a result, the empire annexed the Dagestanian lands along the Caspian Sea, including the towns of Derbent and Baku. In 1724, a treaty was signed with the Ottoman Empire to partition the Persian possessions in the Caucasus region. The new acquisitions were to become the launching pad for the realization of Russia's vast offensive designs in the East. It was only the death of the emperor that thwarted their execution.

Peter the Great died on January 28, 1725, of a disease that he had battled for the previous few years. According to the descriptions of contemporaries, it took the form of uremia, a urinary tract blockage that Peter's physicians had difficulty diagnosing.[55] While we do not know whether Peter's entourage expected his death, the event obviously had a great effect on them all. As contemporaries inform us, none could refrain from crying. Feofan Prokopovich expressed the general mood best of all in a sermon preached at Peter's burial at the Peter and Paul Cathedral:

> What is this? What have we lived to see, oh Russians? What do we see? What are we doing? We are burying Peter the Great! ... He was the source of our innumerable good fortunes and joys, he who has raised Russia as if from the dead.

Feofan continued:

> He was, Russia, your Samson.... He was, Oh Russia, your first Japheth.... He was your Moses, Oh Russia!.... He was, Oh Russia, your Solomon.... And he was, Oh Russian church, your David and your Constantine.... As he has shaped his Russia, so shall it remain. He has made it beloved of good people, and beloved it shall remain. He has made it terrible to its enemies, and terrible it shall remain. He has made it glorified throughout the world, and it shall never cease to be glorified.[56]

* * *

The attentive reader will have noticed that in this book, unlike most works on Russia in the first quarter of the eighteenth century, the course of the Petrine transformation is presented in chronological order, without separating the reforms into administrative, military, church, and so forth. The latter pattern of organization has the advantage of allowing the reader to grasp in comprehensive form the changes in each of the spheres mentioned. On the other hand, because it sunders the links among Peter's individual measures, it seems to me that the broader picture is at least somewhat distorted. What emerges from it is a logic to the reforms—but a logic introduced by the scholar rather than that pursued by the tsar-transformer himself. By attempting to follow the history of the Petrine reforms as they developed, we may be better equipped to evaluate their results.

It was pointed out above that the radical reforms carried out by Peter the Great were a response to an all-encompassing domestic crisis, the crisis of traditionalism, which afflicted the Russian state in the second half of the seventeenth century. From this point of view, it is senseless to debate the question as to whether or not the Russian patient needed Peter's prescription, because it called for the only medicine that could save him. The patient recovered, grew stronger, got back up on his feet, and the crisis passed, demonstrating that the medicine had been properly administered. Just what sort of medicine was it? After all, the radicalism of the reform was merely its outer coating. The case can be made that this medicine was modernization or, put more precisely, the Europeanization of the nation's political, social, and economic institutions.* It was therefore Europeanization that had to be prescribed. From this point of view, it is similarly senseless to debate the question of whether Europeanization was beneficial to or harmful for Russia.

Another question that begs a response is that of whether or not the Petrine reforms were successful. In order to respond to the question, the criteria for evaluation must first be delineated. We can attempt to assume the position of the reformer himself. If we do so, we will have to acknowledge, despite reservations, that Peter managed to fulfill his plans almost completely. Russia became a great world power with a developed industrial base and with such authority vested in the absolute monarch, based on the regulation of the political structure, that, in David MacKenzie's words, "the great 'Sun King,' Louis XIV of France," might envy him.[57] The success of the reforms is indisputable also in terms of their scale and the extent of their impact on Russian society, culture, everyday life, and mentality. An enumeration (belonging to M.P. Pogodin) of those spheres of life, those "objects," that the hand of the reformer touched, is striking:

> A place in the European state system, the administration and its subdivisions, court procedures, the rights of estates, the Table of Ranks, the army, the navy, taxes, the censuses, the recruitment levies, the factories, the plants, the harbors, the canals, the highways, the postal service, agriculture, forestry, cattle raising, mining, horticulture, viticulture, domestic and foreign trade, clothing, external appearance, apothecaries, hospitals, medicines, calendar reform, language, the press, book publishing, military schools, academies—these are the monuments to his indefatigable activity and his genius.[58]

---

*The distinction between modernization and Europeanization about which Cyril Black writes is not particularly germane to Russia; but his "holistic definition" of modernization is quite useful: see C.E. Black's *The Dynamics of Modernization* (New York, 1966), pp. 6–7.

Indicative also are the facts cited by Anisimov concerning the longevity of the Petrine institutions: the collegia, the Senate and the Holy Synod, the system of taxation, the recruitment levies, and so forth.[59] Some survived for a century, others for almost two centuries.

But if modernization, understood as Europeanization, lay at the heart of the Petrine reforms, it is legitimate to pose still another question. To what degree did these reforms actually deliver Russia from the essence of the peculiarity of its historical development: the absence of a society based on genuine estates and the continued existence of serfdom? Here we come face to face with the most glaring contradiction in Peter the Great's reforms, one that allows for no simple verdict. On the one hand, the process of the creation of estates—at least one of them, the nobility—could begin thanks to Peter, whose reforms in principle simplified the social structure of Russian society, bringing it closer to that of Western Europe. On the other hand, as we have noted, Peter not only did not tackle the problem of serfdom but, on the contrary, in every way encouraged it by basing all of his innovations on the foundations of serfdom (to be understood not only in terms of the enserfed condition of the mass of the peasantry, but as a principle of organizing social relations as a whole). Peter made no attempt to abolish serfdom and, again as we have noted, did not think it possible to imitate in this respect those nations whose other political institutions he was so assiduously copying. Still, the historian has the right, exercised so avidly in Russia today, to engage in hypothetical history, or the purely theoretical discussion of the possibility of historical alternatives.

If a crisis afflicting society can only be overcome with the aid of radical reform, then the reforms themselves can only be carried out in crisis conditions; for only then are the conservative forces in society too weak to resist them. Such was the case in Russia at the beginning of the eighteenth century. It is apparent that neither the musketeers nor the Cossacks could serve as a focal point of resistance; only the nobility could. But by destroying the old organization of service people with its political and administrative institutions, Peter deprived it of the capability of uniting in opposition to him and his policies. The new organizational pattern of the nobility took shape only gradually; not until the end of Peter's reign did it acquire contours that were distinct enough to set it apart from the rest of society. It was during this relatively short time that an actual alternative to the serfdom-conditioned path of development existed for the Russian state. The nation did not yet harbor the political forces capable of resisting the reformer if he had thought of delivering the nation from its fundamental burden. But the alternative remained unrealized, and the nobility soon transformed itself into a powerful political force, one that saw in serfdom (and not without reason) its most important asset. While promoting the consolidation of the nobility into a unified estate and paving the way for the juridical formulation of its estate rights and privileges, Peter actually preserved and even strengthened the serf-like dependence of the nobility on the state. Within this contradiction we find concealed the guarantee of the future emancipation of the nobility and, at the same time, the strengthening of the "unfreedom" of the other social strata.

To a significant degree, as we have seen, all of these trends served to define the subsequent course of the nation's development. Henceforth all the processes in the social, political, economic, and spiritual spheres bore the imprint of serfdom, even if on the surface they seemed analogous to processes taking place in Western Europe. From this point of view, modernization to a significant degree proved superficial, even illusory. In reality, the greatest paradox of Petrine modernization consisted of the fact that the nation was transformed into a hyper-regimented state, a police empire, one in which the foundations for the emergence of a civil society were absent.

Such forms of modernization, according to Cyril Black, "might be called programs of limited or defensive modernization, designed to preserve the traditional society and protect it from the more intensive and thoroughgoing changes that might have resulted from the success of foreign or domestic modernizers."[60] One can hardly agree with the implication that Petrine modernization was designed to preserve traditional society; but there can be no debate whatever about the fact that in the final accounting it served to preserve the existing societal structure.* If, by the way, it had changed the structure of Russian society, we would be dealing here not with the reforms but with the revolution of Peter the Great.

---

*By societal structure I mean primarily the system of social relations existing in society, including mutual relations among all society's groups, and their relationship to the state and to the supreme authority, not the Marxist concept of the control of the state by a given class.

After Peter's death, a new, dynamic, secular society began to emerge in Russia. It consisted of people with a different outlook, with different intellectual and spiritual values and needs, customs, tastes, behavior, pastimes, and even external appearances. It was at this time that a new Russian secular culture began to take shape, one that with time would acquire worldwide significance. Another very important, related legacy of the Petrine epoch lies in the fact that this Europeanized culture became the exclusive property of a terribly narrow stratum of Russian society, one that had separated itself from the larger part of the population, thus contributing to the division of society into two unequal halves that understood each other poorly, if at all.

To compound the problem, the bearers of European cultural values, those whose cultural roots were not embedded in traditional Russian culture, were also the representatives of the politically most active segment of the population, whose hands had shaped the nation's history. Over the course of a quarter-century of reforms, with the tendency toward brutality that accompanied them, Russians managed to master European culture no more than superficially. In the Russian mind, European intellectual and spiritual values, which emerged from the humanism of the Renaissance and the rationalism of the seventeenth century, were superimposed on their traditional conceptions of the Russian people and their actual experience of social conditions. Thus, popular values were bizarrely deformed, creating a curious blend of what would seem to be incompatible elements. With the passage of time, as the incompatibility began to be realized, it spawned the Russian intelligentsia, a peculiar, purely Russian, phenomenon, one whose distinctive characteristic was the sense of guilt that educated Russians felt vis-à-vis the unenlightened masses.

Finally, one additional outcome of the Petrine epoch has to be mentioned: the position that the image of the great tsar-transformer occupied from then on in the Russian social consciousness. As Marc Raeff put it, "The figure of Peter the Great has dominated the development of Russian social and political thought, as well as Russian historical writing. As a matter of fact, the historiography of Peter the Great provides an almost perfect mirror for the Russian intelligentsia's views on the past and future of Russia, their relationship to the West, and the nature of the social and political problems confronting their country."[61] Whatever the opinions of Peter's contemporaries and posterity about his activities, he altered their very concept of the place and role of the sovereign in society. As Cynthia Whittaker pointed out, since Peter's time, reform has been "accepted as an intrinsic attribute, a principal legitimizing activity and a sign of sovereignty of the autocracy itself," while "each generation expected its own 'reforming tsar.'"[62] Were these expectations justified? Or did Russia face, after Peter's death, an "era of recidivism?"

Chapter 4

"The Era of Palace Revolutions"

This chapter's title is a phrase that has long been used by historians of eighteenth-century Russia to describe the period immediately following Peter I's death. Between 1725 and 1762 there were eight coups d'état, each of which raised a new sovereign to the throne, after which, as a rule, the composition of the ruling elite changed. As a contemporary scholar explains: "This period is known as 'the era of palace revolutions' not simply because the holders of power changed so often. Rather, just about every change of power was accompanied by disturbances, uprisings, arrests, and exiles. Thousands of people awaited the dawning of a new reign with terror; for they were uncertain about what the day would bring them."[1] It is difficult to disagree with this observation (although it should be noted that a change in power affected not thousands but, at most, hundreds of people). Nonetheless, by attaching such a label to a whole period of Russian history do we perhaps risk impoverishing it? Could it be that we are leading ourselves to believe that aside from palace revolutions nothing really significant happened?

If so, we would be wrong: V.O. Kliuchevskii suggested that "our palace revolutions of the eighteenth century bore very great political significance, which extended far beyond the boundaries of the court sphere, affecting the very foundations of the state order."[2] He had in mind first and foremost the role played in the coups by the guards regiments, which in effect disposed of the Russian throne as they saw fit. The historian V.Ia. Ulanov viewed the problem in a somewhat broader context. For him, the guardsmen were mere tools of the nobility which, as the most organized estate, and "compelled by its own estate interests, raised its authoritative voice there, where law did not

The Winter Palace in St. Petersburg in the first half of the eighteenth century. From an engraving by M.I. Makhaev.

prevail."[3] Back in the late eighteenth century, the ideologue of the Russian nobility, Prince M.M. Shcherbatov, was already writing of "the absence of fundamental law," referring to the legal situation with regard to the succession following Peter I's death.

In 1718, as mentioned in the previous chapter, the life of Peter's elder son, Tsarevich Alexei, was artificially cut short. At the time the answer to the question of who would succeed the tsar was obvious: Tsarevich Petr Petrovich, Peter's younger son by Catherine, who was proclaimed heir to the throne. But within a year, the child died. The sole remaining Romanov successor in the male line was now the son of Tsarevich Alexei, Grand Duke Petr Alekseevich. Peter was clearly disinclined to pass the throne on to him, however, so in 1722 he promulgated a decree whereby the reigning tsar acquired the right to name his own successor. This decree, many historians believe, violated an emerging tradition of succession in Russia, thus shaping the events that followed. A detailed elaboration of this position was recently offered by M.A. Boitsov:

> Inasmuch as there was no clear principle of inheritance . . . it happened that quite distant relatives of the deceased tsar could in principle claim as much right to the throne as, say, an elder son of the deceased, if only

an appropriate order from the monarch, or even a hint that could be interpreted as his will, could be found. Hence the number of possible pretenders to the throne increased significantly. Proponents of each of them hatched their intrigues and sought favor for him from influential dignitaries. Rivalry at court increased. . . . Even in cases where the successor had been chosen beforehand, and the appropriate document . . . had not been falsified, there could be no certainty that he would manage to rule the nation long and happily.[4]

V.O. Kliuchevskii was even more categorical: "By denying the supreme authority a legal basis . . . Peter with this law extinguished his own dynasty as an institution. There remained nothing more than individuals of royal blood without a clear-cut dynastic position."[5] Let us attempt to analyze the situation a bit more dispassionately.

In the first place, we should bear in mind that the Romanov dynasty did not come to power until 1613, and when it did it was not by inheriting the crown but by being elected by an Assembly of the Land. After Tsar Mikhail came his son Alexei, and then Alexei's son, Fedor. But Fedor Alekseevich died childless, and as a result an extraordinary situation arose in which the throne was occupied by two tsars at the same time, with their older sister serving as regent. After she was removed, effective power wound up in the hands of the younger brother, since the elder was incapacitated. At Peter the Great's death, his only heir in the male line, a grandson, was a mere ten years old. It is understandable, therefore, that a regent would have to be named if he were to ascend the throne. Only someone senior in the imperial family or one of the most important aristocrats could fill that role. The most senior member of the imperial family was Catherine, whom Peter had so festively crowned in 1724, making her his equal and sharing his throne with her. (Russians in fact took an oath of allegiance to Catherine.) Thus, actual power would have to end up in the hands of Catherine and her party. Some representative of this same party, since it was the dominant party, would emerge as regent, chosen from among the aristocrats closest to the throne.

So far as may be determined, Peter wavered between a testament naming his wife as successor and one naming his oldest daughter, Anna. He did draw up some sort of testament after 1722, but tore it up shortly before Catherine's coronation. Evgenii Anisimov believes that the testament named Anna to succeed him, but that Peter tore it up because he had changed his mind and decided to leave the throne to his wife.[6] Be that as it may, no new testament was ever drawn up. Shortly after her coronation the tsar suspected his wife of infidelity, executed her alleged lover, Villem Mons (who happened to be the brother of his own first mistress, Anna Mons), and put off the succession question to a more propitious occasion. That occasion never came.

While on his deathbed, asserts one of his contemporaries, Peter ordered a slate brought to him, and in a rapidly failing hand wrote: "Leave everything to. . . ." If the story is true, just what the tsar intended to do remains a mystery. In any case, given the situation, a decision as to the fate of the throne would necessarily have to reflect the outcome of the struggle among court cliques. Still, it should be noted that the outcome was all but predetermined: not so much by the decree of 1722 as by the individual fates of the dynasty's members. In January 1725, Russia crowned an empress to whom the oath of allegiance had already been taken rather than the ten-year-old grandson of the deceased tsar by his first wife, the son of a man who had officially been declared a traitor. Thus, the causative links in the chain assembled by Kliuchevskii and other historians—the decree of 1722, the legal vacuum, the role of the guards regiments, the palace revolutions—do not hold together. Those events that unfolded in the royal chambers in the last hours of Peter the Great's life were therefore unavoidable.

The memoirs that have come down to us put forward varying versions of the circumstances surrounding the struggle for the Russian throne in January 1725. All, however, agree that two parties stood face to face: the supporters of Tsarevich Peter and those of Catherine. Some try to identify the first party with the opponents of the Petrine reforms, associating it with representatives of the old elite, and the second with their proponents, among whom they number the tsar-transformer's closest followers. In reality, things were more complex than they might appear. In the first place, as has already been noted, there were more than a few descendants of elite families to be found among the proponents of reform; and, in the second, some of those that Peter the Great himself elevated were to be found among the supporters of his grandson. But somehow or other, relying on the bayonets of the guardsmen, Catherine's party, headed by Alexander Menshikov, won out. On February 8, 1725, the Senate officially proclaimed Catherine I's accession to the throne.

The fact that a woman had ascended the throne for the first time in

Russian history was quite significant. It mirrored as well as anything could the changes that had taken place in Russian society and the fundamental way in which they had altered the position of members of the so-called weaker sex. Guided by European norms of everyday behavior, Peter I had gradually taken the Russian woman out of her secluded quarters, first clothing her in West European–style dress, then incorporating her into court ceremony—allowing her to participate in a variety of festivities, balls, masquerades, and the like. In 1718, reflecting his desire to regiment the private lives of his subjects, the tsar issued a decree on public "assemblies," gatherings of people in private homes, where both men and women would come together, converse, exchange the latest news, play cards, and so forth. The decree prescribed in detail the rules of behavior in the assemblies, including fines for their violation.

The need to interact with others, to communicate and to carry on conversations with foreigners as well as other Russians, forced Russians to think about education. Members of both the old and the new elites had begun to hire tutors for their daughters, tutors who would teach them to conduct themselves properly, to dance, and to speak foreign languages. Without this minimal level of education, it had become difficult to find suitable husbands for them. The situation within the family of the tsar himself served as a case in point: Catherine was occupying an ever more visible position in society. Also important was the fact that many foreigners were now entering Russian society. Coming from various European countries, they brought with them their customs and outlooks, often becoming objects of imitation by the Russians.

One of Peter's means of carrying out his imperial policy (in keeping with the examples set by the other European nations of the time) was resort to matrimonial alliances. Peter gave two daughters of his older half brother Ivan—Anna and Catherine—in marriage to the Dukes of Courland and Mecklenburg respectively, while he married his own son to the Princess of Brunswick-Wolfenbüttel. Shortly before his death, he also decided to give his older daughter Anna in marriage to the Duke of Holstein. Peter linked all of these marriages with specific political projects. As we shall see, he succeeded: these projects really were fated to play an important role in eighteenth-century Russian history, not only in the pursuit of foreign-policy objectives but in the fate of the Russian throne.

"The Era of Palace Revolutions"

Catherine I. Engraving by A.-F. Dannemaker after a painting by Jean Marc Nattier.

The appearance of women on the Russian political scene, as should be clear from the foregoing, was linked inextricably with the Petrine reforms, with the very essence of modernization. It is therefore not surprising that several other female rulers followed Catherine I on the throne. Women as heads of state, it should be added, were not an uncommon occurrence in other European nations of the era, such as England, Austria, and Denmark.[7]

There is no way of knowing whether the former laundress Marta Skavronskaia, having become Russian empress by a twist of fate, had grown so ambitious that she cherished the dream of ruling by herself even before her husband's death. However accustomed she may have become to her new position during her years with Peter, however often she may have witnessed important government decisions being rendered by her husband, and however wise and useful her advice to the tsar may have been, she must have understood that she could never replace Peter the Great. But events had taken such a turn that any alternative to her own ascent to the throne posed a direct threat to her well-being, her freedom, and possibly even her life. That would be the case if the supporters of the son of the deceased Alexei and the grandson of Evdokia Lopukhina, who was still living in a nunnery, came to power. Whether Catherine wished to rule or not, she had no choice. To make matters worse, the problems she had to confront immediately after taking power were extremely complicated.

The identification of the post-Petrine period of Russian history as "the era of palace revolutions" has spawned yet another historiographic stereotype. If "the era of Peter the Great schooled Russia to receive strong impressions, which left contemporaries with their heads spinning and their minds agitated,"[8] then after Peter's death, as one historian would have us believe, "Russia sank into a half-forgotten state. It was as if everything had fallen asleep, had frozen. . . ."[9] In other words, a time of stagnation had set in. But for some historians, it was worse than stagnation. According to them, starting in February 1725, "a general tendency toward revision of the Petrine legacy begins to strengthen and pick up steam; doubts about the correctness of specific reforms resound more boldly and widely; and the rivulets of criticism begin to swell into torrents, which start to wash away the foundations of a Petrine policy that had seemed so unassailable only yesterday. The scent of counterreform fills the air."[10] The word is finally uttered: counterreform. But is not this verdict a bit too categorical?

If it is true that radical reform can be accomplished only when preceded by crisis, then it follows that the period of radical reform itself is always an exceptional period in a nation's history, one demanding maximum effort from all of society's forces. Once reform is accomplished, society needs a respite in order to take stock, in order to ascertain which of the reforms have taken hold and produced positive results and which have not; for the reforms' results do not always manifest themselves immediately. Time is necessary to accommodate to these results, to assimilate them, to acknowledge their significance, and to adjust them if necessary. Since the reforms touched just about every aspect of society; affected its social structure, system of government, and everyday life; created a new political-legal ideology; and fundamentally altered the nation's role in the world, such a need was especially acute in Russia after Peter I's death. For more than a quarter of a century, the nation had been subjected to the extremes of radical transformation, carried out, moreover, under wartime circumstances, and linked inextricably with war. The reforms were also carried out quite chaotically and inconsistently, without any preconceived plan.

Thus, the "breathing space" that followed Peter's death provided a very natural, and even necessary, respite after all the exhausting effort. And in fact the "breathing space" could be labeled such only by contrast to the stormy and extraordinary times that had preceded it. For the new government aggressively tackled the nation's growing domestic problems, which were numerous. The war had taxed the nation's resources, and the consequences were leading it into financial and economic crisis. The chief bearer of the taxes, the peasantry, which had shouldered the heaviest burden of the war and the reforms, faced ruination. It expressed its protest via mass flight. This flight, in turn, created acute dissatisfaction on the part of the nobility, since peasant flight undermined its source of income. The nobility accordingly demanded that the government take immediate measures to halt the flight, arguing that delay could have serious social and political repercussions. It is only by bearing this situation in mind that the initial measures undertaken by Catherine I's government can be judged.

Implementation of these measures began as early as February 1725, with a slight reduction in the soul tax. The measure was necessary and justified, although it was perhaps more for show than anything else, marking as it did the start of a new reign. Its initiator was Pavel Ivanovich Iaguzhinskii, Procurator-General of the Senate (a function created by Peter I in 1722). Several months after the start of Catherine's reign, Iaguzhinskii presented to the Senate a report entitled "On the maintenance of the army under the present peaceful conditions and how to render the peasants more prosperous." Thus, he linked the economic status of the peasantry with the quartering of the army, which he perceived to be the chief cause of its ruination. A debate was launched, and efforts were made to reexamine Peter I's soul tax reform. The soul tax, together with a series of bad harvests and the poor performance of local government agencies, was seen as the basic cause of the impending crisis in the countryside. Was this analysis correct?

Evgenii Anisimov has suggested that "the peasant burdens of the postreform period were the result not of the reform of the tax obligation but of the chronic strain on the tax-paying capacities of peasant agriculture over a whole quarter-century of wars and reforms." He nonetheless recognized that "the inflexibility of the basis of taxation . . . the obvious shortcomings of the new system of tax collection, some increase in taxation as a result of the reforms—all of this . . . contributed to the fact that tax arrears and the disappearance of taxpayers from the tax rolls were interpreted by contemporaries as a consequence of the soul tax's unsuccessful implementation." Anisimov also draws our attention to the fact that government officials of the post-Petrine period strived to prove that "Peter's reform activities resulted in the ruination of the nation and people." Such a claim was useful to them because "criticism of the Petrine reforms provided them with the political capital with which to consolidate their own rather insecure positions of power . . . by removing responsibility for the fate of the reforms and their results from their own shoulders."[11]

The significance of the political interests of one or another government official notwithstanding, the nation's dire economic situation was a more important factor in the crisis, and Catherine I's government was apparently justified in devoting its primary attention to the soul tax. Until spring 1727, concrete action was limited to the compilation of numerous reports, the authors of which were unanimous about the need for a fundamental break with certain practices associated with the collection of the soul tax. That spring, military units started to be withdrawn from the countryside, tax collection duties were transferred to the landlords, and local government was reorganized.

The desired results were not, however, forthcoming, because they were unattainable in such a short period of time. Peasant flight and tax arrears continued at their previous levels. Therefore, in 1728, fearing that the treasury would fall short of its needs, the soul tax was again collected with the help of the army. A special Commission on Taxation had been working ever since 1727. It studied the evolving situation for almost two years and then (only after Catherine I's death) issued a report in which it rejected the proposal to abolish the soul tax, limiting itself to the suggestion that the tax burden on the enserfed peasants be lightened. It is indicative that the commission was headed by Prince Dmitrii Mikhailovich Golitsyn, a representative of the old aristocracy.

Much more thoroughgoing were the changes in the central administration. The conflict between Alexander Menshikov, who was striving to concentrate power in his own hands, and the Senate led at the beginning of 1726 to the creation of the Supreme Privy Council, composed of six members. The council became the empire's highest administrative organ, deciding the most important questions of governance and establishing its political course. The three chief collegia—the War Collegium, the Admiralty, and the Collegium of Foreign Affairs—were subordinated to the council. Then the financial branch of the state administration was reorganized: the Collegium of State Revenues, now merged with that of State Expenditures, and the newly recreated Collegium of State Accounting and the Chancellery for [the Collection of] Tax Arrears were all subordinated to the council. The underlying idea of these reforms was that of centralization and concentration of power, a feature that was in complete harmony with the spirit of the Petrine reforms. As subsequent events were to reveal, the emergence of the council was far from accidental. It could be explained not only by the weakness of the person who held the orb and scepter in her hands but by the inadequacies of the political system Peter had fashioned.

From all that has been said, it follows that if Peter's successors actually harbored plans for counterreform, they never carried them out. Can one, moreover, even associate any preconceived critique of Peter I's reforms with actual counterreforms? After all, counterreform would have signified a return to the pre-Petrine past. Yet no traces of such an intention are to be found in the documents. As historian I.V. Kurukin has aptly observed, those who surrounded Catherine I, with Alexander Menshikov at their head, could not even conceive of it, for "the fundamentals of the Petrine reforms were irreversible. The decrees and regulations promulgated by Peter I remained in force, as did the Table of Ranks, measures to encourage trade and industry, the system of government, and innovations in everyday life. The army and navy created by Peter I were also preserved. . . ."[12] Moreover, a few of the projects conceived, but not carried out, by the deceased emperor were brought to fruition. (Thus, the Petersburg Academy of Sciences was officially opened later in 1725, and leading scholars were hired from all over Europe to staff it.) For these reasons, the measures carried out in the first two years after Peter's death do not in any way qualify as counterreform. Given the new conditions, they represented necessary adjustments in the nation's domestic political course. But in May 1727, a new shock wave shook the nation: Catherine I died, raising once more the question of the succession to the throne.

The death of the empress had been preceded by another round of intense court intrigue. It would appear at first glance that the arrangement of forces was what it had been in January 1725; but fate, in the person of Prince Menshikov, intervened. For many years prior to Peter I's death, Menshikov had been one of those closest to the empress. Once he managed to get her on the throne, he felt himself sovereign master of the nation, to the point where he lost touch with reality. The prince's unbridled greed and ambition led him to take unwarranted risks (as, for example, when he sought the crown of the Duchy of Courland). As a result, he drove other court dignitaries into opposition. Menshikov's influence on Catherine I was so great that prior to her death he managed to get her to agree to remove his main rivals from the court: Police-master General Anton Manuilovich Devier, Count Petr Andreevich Tolstoy, General Ivan Ivanovich Buturlin, Prince Ivan Dmitrievich Dolgorukii, and Andrei Ivanovich Ushakov.

It was logical to assume that after Catherine died, Menshikov, who had signed Tsarevich Alexei's death sentence, would attempt to obtain the throne for one of Peter I's daughters: either Anna, who by this time had already become the Duchess of Holstein,* or Elizabeth. But in the first case, Menshikov's relations with Anna's husband, Duke Karl Friedrich, had deteriorated badly, and in the second, he could not help but understand that with the coronation of a young, enthusiastic, energetic tsarevna he would cease to play a leading role in affairs of state.

So Menshikov banked on the eleven-year-old Petr Alekseevich, and

---

*One finds in the historical literature the assertion that having entered into marriage, Anna surrendered for herself and her posterity the claim to the Russian throne. This is incorrect: see E.V. Anisimov, "Smert' v kontorke," *Rodina,* 1993, no. 1, pp. 142–44.

in order to insure himself against all contingencies, managed to get the dying Catherine to sign a testament naming her husband's grandson her successor. The testament, moreover, contained the stipulations that the Supreme Privy Council would play the role of regent for the youthful emperor, and that the latter would marry one of Menshikov's daughters. By becoming head of the council and father-in-law to the emperor, the prince could count on acquiring more power than ever. There was, granted, one little juridical fine point that rendered Menshikov's position vulnerable: according to Peter's decree on the succession to the throne of 1722, the heir to the throne was to be proclaimed by the ruler himself or herself while he or she was still alive, while Catherine's testament was made public only after her death. But Menshikov's enemies had been vanquished for the time being, and on May, 7, 1727, the day after Catherine I's death, the prince presented the new emperor, Peter II, to the guards regiments.

Glancing at the character of the new Russian emperor, his passions and desires, it is not hard to espy numerous traits he had in common with his celebrated grandfather, traits that would reappear in other descendants of Peter the Great as well: for example, his love for everything concerning the military, his attraction to gross pleasures and amorous affairs, his restlessness, his willfulness, and his lack of fastidiousness in his attachments. The circumstances in which Peter II ascended the Russian throne differed significantly, however, from those that existed in 1689, when Peter I had rid himself of Tsarevna Sophia and could give himself over to his favorite pleasures for a time, without bothering to take any direct part in the governance of the realm. At that time Russia still had an established form of government, proven over time and based on tradition, and capable of functioning without the intervention of the tsar. Evidently, although the Petrine reforms were designed to create a more effective administrative mechanism, they created such a cult of the emperor's power that, given the absence of the guiding iron hand of the tsar-transformer himself and the fact that new traditions had yet to take shape, the wheels of this mechanism began to slow and eventually stopped turning altogether. In the absence of guidelines from the emperor as to the political course to pursue, top administrators, directors of agencies, and other high officials preferred inactivity to a show of initiative. They had grown accustomed to seeing the emperor in the forefront, providing an example by his own conduct and tireless labor. Under Catherine the imperial will had also been expressed in clearly defined fashion. So when rendering decisions on matters of state the members of the Supreme Privy Council were fully aware that they were empowered to do so by the empress herself. But Peter II had no desire to get involved in affairs of state, and he was unpredictable and stubborn to boot. Moreover, since he was still very young, it was feared that once he matured he might decide to change course abruptly, a step that would signify a change in governmental personnel as well. Until that point was reached, each government figure sought only to snatch a bit more, to stuff his pockets more fully.

Fate decreed that the young tsar would lack a worthy adviser capable of exerting a beneficial influence over him. During the first month of the new reign, Menshikov was, of course, the dominant state figure. He moved Peter into his own palace and attempted to keep him within eyesight at all times. He soon arranged Peter's betrothal to his oldest daughter, Maria, whose name the Synod ordered mentioned in all church ceremonies right after that of the sovereign. Menshikov himself received the rank of admiral and commander in chief, while his son received that of lieutenant general. But in June 1727, the prince took sick, and for five weeks had to relinquish the reins of power. His opponents at court, the most important of whom was Heinrich Johann Friedrich (Andrei Ivanovich) Ostermann, promptly took advantage of the circumstances.

An immigrant from Westphalia, and a dilettantish student at the University of Jena, Ostermann, thanks to his unquestionable capacity for governmental affairs, rose to become one of the highest-ranking officials in the Russian empire. Ostermann realized that because he was a foreigner he should avoid claiming the most visible posts for himself. He also knew when it was advantageous to remain in the background and avoid responsibility for decisions already taken, by feigning temporary illness if necessary. It was this same Ostermann who had helped Menshikov deal with his enemies. But less than two months later he was waging a struggle against Menshikov himself. To aid him in his plans, Ostermann put forward the two Dolgorukiis, father and son, whom he considered, not without reason, inept politicians who could be manipulated like puppets to promote his own policies.

The intrigue succeeded right from the start. When Menshikov fell ill, Ostermann managed to turn the young emperor, who was in any case dissatisfied with the brutal control "The Most Serene Prince" had

"The Era of Palace Revolutions"

D.A. Menshikov with his family in exile in Berezovo. From a painting by V.I. Surikov.

exercised over him, against Menshikov. As soon as the prince recovered, Peter made manifest his growing coolness toward him and toward his own bride-to-be. Menshikov made feeble efforts to defend himself, but without success. His biographers have claimed to detect a certain apathy on his part, as if he had reconciled himself to his fate. One gets the impression that he simply no longer had the strength for political struggle. On September 8, 1727, Menshikov was placed under house arrest, and on the following day sentenced to exile at one of his many estates. Within twenty-four hours a huge procession of thirty-three carriages set out, accompanied by a suite of one hundred and thirty-three people. Several months later, however, the place of exile was changed to Siberia, to which Menshikov, now stripped of his ranks, positions, and titles, was allowed to take with him a mere ten servants. There in Siberia, in the village of Berezovo, he died in November 1729.

The triumph over Menshikov, it would seem, should have made Ostermann the leading figure in government. But he failed to take into account one important factor: the character of his sovereign. Ostermann had hoped to become master of the emperor and his political affairs; but Peter, as already noted, expressed no interest in these affairs. He was far more attracted to wild revelries and other amusements offered up to him by his favorite, Prince Ivan Dolgorukii. Then, a little later, he started to spend his time at the hunt. From spring 1728 through fall 1729, according to contemporaries, he hunted down four thousand hares, fifty foxes, five lynx, and three bears in the forests around Moscow.[13] Peter II's court lived at a feverish pace that was to prove characteristic also of the courts of Peter III and Paul I. "The monarch speaks with everyone in the tone of a master and does whatever he wishes," noted a foreign diplomat. "He cannot abide contradiction, and is constantly busy traipsing around. All the cavaliers in his entourage are utterly exhausted."[14] Ostermann's admonitions all proved useless. From time to time Peter would comprehend the significance of Ostermann's words and promise to mend his ways and start paying attention to his studies, only to relapse, immediately forgetting his vows as soon as the favorite or his father thought up new amusements for him.

At the start of 1728, the emperor journeyed to Moscow for his coronation, expressing no desire to return to the empire's new capital, surrounded by swamps, where it seemed to him there was nothing interesting to do. While in the capital he had neglected to attend sessions of the Supreme Privy Council and the Senate, confining his participation to official ceremonies. The way in which he spent his time, incidentally, reminds one of the youth of another well-known figure of the time: Swedish King Charles XII, who with time, however, did shift his attention from games to serious matters. It is conceivable that Peter II simply lacked the time needed to make this transition. Sources attest to the fact that by fall 1729 there was a noticeable change in the tsar's conduct: he suddenly cooled toward his favorites, turned away from the hunt, and began to treat his studies more seriously. Whatever the case, there was not enough time left for Peter, for in January 1730 he suddenly came down with smallpox, and a week later, died. Russia once more faced the problem of succession to the throne, and again that problem would be resolved only after intense court intrigue. But before turning to the events of January 1730, the governmental policies that prevailed in the period from 1727 until 1730 must be elucidated; for the historical literature contains contradictory interpretations on this score.

Strange as it may seem, many of the historians who have written about the short reign of Peter II have fallen victim to the verdicts of contemporaries and the official propaganda of the following period. For that reason, the transfer of the court, and with it the government, to Moscow is often interpreted as a deliberate rejection of the Petrine reforms. The fact that the tsar's favorites—the princes Alexei and Ivan Dolgorukii, who with the disgrace of Menshikov had become the masters of the Supreme Privy Council—were members of the old Russian aristocracy is viewed one-sidedly as evidence that the nation was leaning toward counterreform. In reality, the transfer to Moscow bore symbolic significance only for critics of the regime. Peter II himself probably never gave a thought to the matter. What apparently mattered most to him was that the hunting was better in the forests around Moscow. As for the Dolgorukiis, they were too immersed in the pursuit of their own interests to think about counterreform. And it should be obvious that such thoughts would never even cross Ostermann's mind.

The government's inactivity and the absence of a thought-out and agreed-upon policy based on clear-cut principles was another matter entirely. It goes without saying that there could be no question of the continuation of radical reform. For the most part, the government concerned itself with nothing more than a resolution of the nation's most pressing matters. Nonetheless, one can still speak of ongoing adjustments in Peter I's institutions.

As before, the chief problem was financial. Unable to resolve the taxation issue, the nation's leadership turned its attention to trade, all the more readily since the merchantry had consistently complained about its oppression and ruination. The development of trade, it seemed, would yield results more quickly than that of industry, and therefore it was to trade that the Privy Councillors gave preference. Back in 1727, a Commission on Commerce, headed by Ostermann, had already been created. It had solicited the opinions of Russian and foreign merchants and, relying on them, had reopened the port of Archangel, which had been closed by Peter the Great; established free trade in a number of economic activities that had once been farmed out; eliminated some protective tariffs; and in general created more favorable conditions for foreign merchants.

These policies, which conflicted with the protectionist policies Peter I had pursued, were designed to provide a shot in the arm for the treasury. It should be added that Peter's policies had failed to produce the desired results, for while defending the Russian merchantry from its foreign counterparts, they at the same time placed it under rigid state control. Because they paved the way for open competition, the measures undertaken by the Privy Councillors were more beneficial. It is indicative that Ostermann's commission debated the question of the possible elimination of internal tariffs, a step that was not actually taken until a quarter-century later. On the whole, the Privy Councillors were inclined to remove the numerous inhibitions on trade and industry and to lessen state interference in the economy, both for administrative reasons and from a desire to assist entrepreneurs financially.

Local government likewise continued to undergo reorganization during Peter II's reign. First the Urban Magistracies and then the Main Magistracy were abolished and the towns subordinated to provincial organs of administration. In the provinces themselves, many lower-level and seemingly superfluous agencies were eliminated, a step that also saved money. The district [uezd] form of administrative organization, with its strict hierarchical system of subordination of district commanders to provincial ones, and provincial commanders in turn to governors, was resurrected. The jurisdiction of the latter was limited chiefly to the resolution of practical, everyday matters, although the judicial organs created by Peter I were eliminated and their functions transferred to the commanders and governors. Thus, as in the reorganization of the central government institutions, these measures were aimed at the further centralization of authority. The Supreme Privy Council also turned its attention to such matters as the codification of the laws, but again without producing any results, for the deputies elected by the provincial nobility proved incapable of dealing with matters as complex as legislation. On the whole it should be noted that a partial amelioration of the police regime took place under Peter II. There were no recruitment levies or wars, and arrears in the soul tax were "forgiven." Kurukin even discerns a certain stabilization of the regime, pointing out that "there was no large-scale popular discontent."[15]

In January 1730, the nation found itself yet again bereft of a monarch. This time, moreover, a true dynastic crisis unfolded, for the Romanovs had run out of direct descendants in the male line. True, there was Karl Peter Ulrich, the child born in 1728 from the union of Peter

I's eldest daughter Anna with Karl Friedrich, Duke of Holstein. Yet another claimant to the throne was Tsarevna Elizabeth (Elizaveta Petrovna), Peter the Great's second daughter. According to Catherine I's testament, it was to Anna and her descendants, or to Elizabeth, that the crown was to pass in the event that Peter II died childless. But the fact that this testament was made public only after the empress's death gave those who wished to do so cause to disregard it. While frivolous, Elizabeth, who had often accompanied her nephew Peter II on his trips to the forests and his estates around Moscow, was also considered ambitious, lacking in self-control, and therefore unpredictable. It was impossible to foresee, if and when she came to power, how she would deal with those who thus far had managed with such effort to retain the reins of authority in their own hands. As for Karl Peter Ulrich, an invitation to him to ascend the throne would have entailed an invitation to his father, Karl Friedrich (his mother, Anna Petrovna, had died shortly after his birth). Karl Friedrich was so well known and disliked at the court of St. Petersburg that no member of the Supreme Privy Council had any desire to see him as master. There is some evidence that the crown was offered to Peter I's first wife, Evdokia, and that she refused it.

Still another candidate was the Princess Ekaterina Dolgorukaia, the daughter of Prince Alexei and sister of Prince Ivan Dolgorukii, to whom Peter II's favorites managed to betroth the tsar in December 1729. When the tsar, who lay ill on the eve of his wedding day, was seized by death throes, the Dolgorukiis quickly drew up a testament for him, naming his bride-to-be his successor. But the tsar had already lost consciousness and never regained it to sign the document. At a session of the Supreme Privy Council, the Dolgorukiis quickly grasped the hopelessness of their intentions and abandoned plans to base their claims on a forged testament. It was at this juncture, as defeat stared the Dolgorukiis in the face, that the initiative was seized by Prince Dmitrii Mikhailovich Golitsyn. The senior member of the council and a representative of the old aristocracy, he was nonetheless a man who readily combined European education with a fondness for the Russian past, as well as an experienced statesman and diplomat. Golitsyn proposed that the throne pass to Peter the Great's niece, Anna Ioannovna (Ivanovna), the widowed Duchess of Courland.

There was a certain logic to Golitsyn's proposal. After all, Anna belonged to the senior branch of the Romanov line, which rendered her claim to the throne completely legitimate. But most importantly, this thirty-six-year-old woman appeared docile, and therefore easy to control. Widowed in 1711, a few months after her wedding, Anna had subsequently spent all of her years as a plaything in the hands of the Russian government, which used her for its own political purposes. It compelled her to live in Mitava (Mitau), the capital of Courland (present-day Jelgava in Latvia), where she was completely dependent on doles from St. Petersburg, and from which she wrote relatives and powerful ministers countless letters pleading for assistance. But Golitsyn understood only too well that once Anna ascended the throne her behavior might change. It therefore behooved him to forestall all eventualities, more especially since along with the new tsaritsa would come an all-powerful favorite who could dispose of the fate of Russian dignitaries as he saw fit.

While taking a criticial view of many innovations of the Petrine era, in particular of the way Russia had oriented itself so wholeheartedly toward the West, Golitsyn nonetheless considered the Swedish political system a model. In keeping with his views, he suggested that the time had come for the Russian nobility to acquire more freedom and to demand participation in the governance of the realm. Golitsyn proposed to the members of the council that the powers of the Russian autocracy be limited by compelling Anna to sign special "Conditions" [*konditsii*], according to which she would promise that without the consent of the Supreme Privy Council she would not declare war or conclude peace; levy new taxes; promote people to offices in the top four rungs of civil, military, or court service; deprive nobles of life or property without trial; distribute either allodial or service estates; or expend state funds.

This was the first attempt to impose significant limitations on the powers of the Russian autocracy by a collective government composed of representatives of the higher bureaucracy. At the time of the drafting of the "Conditions," the notion of higher bureaucracy coincided almost totally with that of "aristocracy," for the Supreme Privy Council was composed of four people, three of whom—Golitsyn and the two Dolgorukiis (Aleksei Grigorievich and Vasilii Lukich)—were of ancient lineage, and of course Ostermann. (The latter might well have arranged Anna's candidacy, for he enjoyed a relationship of mutual trust with her, while his older brother had once served as her tutor.) Two additional people participated in the session of the council that selected Anna: Field Marshal Princes Mikhail Mikhailovich Golitsyn and Vasilii Vladimirovich Dolgorukii.

The "Conditions" mentioned a council consisting of eight people. So it seems reasonable to assume that a further increase in its membership was planned by adding members of one or another aristocratic family. However, the "Conditions" mention nothing about the method of selecting members of the council, and therefore this right presumably was to reside with the empress. The "Conditions," moreover, foresaw legal guarantees for the entire nobility, not just its aristocratic element. The proposal thus entailed substantial alterations in the whole fabric of social relations, which might have facilitated the formation of full-fledged estates. The formation of these estates, in turn, could conceivably have hastened modernization and deliverance from those peculiar features of the nation's sociopolitical structure that were retarding its development.

We might note that neither in spirit nor in content did the "Conditions" contain even the hint of an attempt to return to pre-Petrine Rus. Viewed from another perspective, history had granted Russia one more chance, one more opportunity for an alternative path of historical development. It is in this vein that we should approach one of the most fascinating episodes in eighteenth-century Russian history, one vital to an understanding of the events of the century as a whole.

The "Conditions" prepared by the Privy Councillors were dispatched to Mitau, where Anna, desperate to escape from the town in any way she could, signed them without hesitation. Without dallying, the newly minted tsaritsa packed up her things, and arrived in Moscow February 10. But while she was en route, rumors of a "conspiracy of the Privy Councillors" (as the events were beginning to be known to contemporaries, and thus, subsequently, to historians) had spread throughout the city. The details at first remained murky. But on February 2, the signed "Conditions" were carried back to Moscow and announced to a session of members of the Senate, the Holy Synod, the holders of offices in the top four classes of state service, and other high dignitaries. The proposal to limit autocratic power for the benefit of a Supreme Privy Council composed of representatives of only a couple of families was viewed by many as an attempt on the part of those families to usurp power. "And thus," wrote one of the participants in the events with reference to the proposal's drafters, "they presented themselves as pretenders to the tsarist rank."[16] The consternation of the nobles (unfortunately for the Privy Councillors, an unusually large number of nobles had congregated in Moscow for what they assumed would be the forthcoming wedding of Peter II and Ekaterina Dolgorukaia) was so great that they had to be invited to participate in the discussion of methods to limit autocracy.

At this juncture, something quite unexpected happened. Energy that had been pent up over centuries, and to which Petrine times had lent a new quality, came bubbling to the surface. Within a matter of days, a number of projects had been drafted, in the discussions of which up to one thousand people took part. During the course of these discussions it was discovered that there were Russian nobles who were thinking about their estate rights and were familiar with the political structures of the Western nations, although for the most part they were not attempting to replicate them. Most of the projects proposed the creation of "upper" and "lower" governmental bodies, roughly along the lines of the upper and lower houses of the British Parliament. They were to be filled by election from office holders in the top four classes of state service and the "nobility" [shliakhetstvo] respectively,* with no more than one or two representatives to be drawn from a single family. All the projects foresaw the codification of specific estate rights for the nobility, a limitation on the period of obligatory state service, easier promotion of nobles to officer's rank, and the abolition of the principle of single inheritance. A number of projects mentioned the need to lighten the burden of taxation on the peasants.

Many historians who have written about the events of 1730 have viewed them as a struggle between the rank-and-file nobility and the aristocracy. For the reasons mentioned above, however, Russia had no aristocracy in the European sense of the term. If the plans of the Privy Councillors had come to fruition, it is possible that an aristocracy might have emerged. But the fact remains that these events coincided with the emergence of the nobility as a unified estate (in the historical literature this is generally referred to as the "consolidation of the nobility"[17]), a time when it was already being transformed into an independent political force. The acquisition by any segment of the nobility of special privileges (and D.M. Golitsyn was

---

*This division itself is remarkable inasmuch as it corresponded strikingly with the division into the boyardom and the service nobility that was evident in pre-Petrine Russia.

a proponent of this approach) ran counter to the interests of the estate as a whole. For given the specific Russian circumstances, that acquisition would have rendered the nobility dependent on a few families. "God preserve us from [the fate of] having ten despotic and powerful families instead of one autocratic sovereign," wrote Artemii Petrovich Volynskii, at the time governor of Kazan and destined to play an important role in the upcoming reign, in a private letter. "For we, the nobility, will be nothing but losers and will have to prostrate ourselves more bitterly than ever, and seek mercy from all of them."[18]

Arriving in Moscow and learning of the disagreements within the nobility, Anna Ioannovna, with the assistance of her relatives on her mother's side, the Saltykovs, prepared what might loosely be termed a coup d'état. On February 25, a deputation appeared before her from the nobility. Referring to the fact that the Privy Councillors had developed their plans in secret, its members begged her to convene an assembly of representatives to decide the question of reform of the state structure. After hesitating, Anna agreed and ordered that an appropriate decree be drawn up. But a great, prearranged clamor arose from those staunch defenders of autocracy, the officers of the guards regiments, who cried out that they would never allow anyone to dictate laws to the state. As a result, instead of a decree calling for the convocation of something similar to a constituent assembly, a petition calling for the reestablishment of autocracy was produced. At that point, Anna ostentatiously tore up the despised "Conditions." Limited monarchy, which had survived in Russia barely more than a month, had sputtered to an inglorious end.

The events of 1730 demonstrated the growing political independence of the nobility, its willingness to insist upon its estate interests, and its ever increasing influence on the nation's political life. These were all results of Petrine modernization. On the other hand, a lack of experience in political struggle, a low level of political culture, and—despite many years of propagating the notion of "the common good"—an inability to look beyond narrow estate interests, were also manifested. The conduct of the guardsmen was also noteworthy. While they were often considered mere mouthpieces of the nobility's interests, in the given situation they actually came out against those interests. Most important of all, of course, was the fact that Russia had passed up still one more window of opportunity granted it by history. Russia returned, this time consciously, to its "special path."

Anna I. Portrait by Louis Caravaque.

* * *

The significance of Anna Ioannovna's reign, which lasted a decade, lies first and foremost in the fact that it was in this period that the transition from the old Russia to the new was completed. As is usually the case in transitional periods, this stage in Russian history offers an odd admixture of what would appear to be incompatible elements, the coincidence of which would be considered impossible during a normal period in a nation's development. This period struck contemporaries, and via them posterity, as one of a change of generations. Peter I's old collaborators were passing from the scene, to be replaced by younger men, who were no less ambitious but perhaps even freer of moral inhibitions.

Those who exercised state authority directly had begun their careers under the great transformer. Much more important was the perception of events by the middle stratum of young civil servants and officers. It was to them, whose childhood and youth—traditionally recalled in rosy hues in our memories—fell within the Petrine era, that the new reign appeared as one of suffocating stagnation. It is no accident that they have left almost no memoirs. We have only those written by foreigners who happened to be in Russia. It seemed to the Russians that time was standing still and that nothing significant was taking place in their lives, nothing worth bringing to the attention of posterity.[19] This attitude toward the reign of Anna Ioannovna is also reflected in the historiography, and it has spawned a number of persistent historiographical stereotypes. The impressions of contemporaries, however, are not always accurate. Moreover, the life and history of a country, as is the case with its individual inhabitants, assume their form as a result not only of significant events but also of numerous mundane ones.

The empress's personal qualities also promoted the perception of Anna's time as one of stagnation. Anna Ioannovna was not pretty. In fact, she was rather masculine in appearance. She was tall and stout, and had a coarse voice and similarly coarse manners, habits, and tastes. Anna's court, which adored fancy clothes and jewels, combined elements of luxury that astounded foreigners with blatant signs of "Asiatickness," as it was termed by English-speaking visitors at the time. This court was full of jesters (some of them of distinguished origins), male and female dwarfs, and all sorts of freaks and soothsayers who

The wedding in the ice palace. From a painting by B.S. Iakobi.

grimaced, engaged in games, pummeled each other, eliciting roars of laughter from the empress and her entourage. In her quieter moments Anna loved to listen to Russian songs, folktales, and stories told by talkative old women. Her thoughts were constantly occupied with the rumors and gossip so characteristic of court life. She was especially interested in everything that concerned the domestic lives of her subjects. She often played the role of matchmaker and participated in marriage ceremonies. But Anna's particular passion was the hunt. She was a good markswoman and had no difficulty managing her weapon's strong recoil. At Peterhof, where she usually spent her summers, a menagerie was collected for her. It contained deer, tigers, buffalo, wild boar, bears, and other animals and birds.

Anna did have a sense of family loyalty: she served as guardian for several of the Saltykovs, and collected the family papers and portraits of her forebears. Her most recent biographer, I.A. Kurliandskii, has suggested that because she asked the governor-general of Moscow "to send her old government books with histories of 'previous rulers,'" the empress "was displaying an interest in Russian history."[20] The documents reveal, however, that this interest was quite singular. In her instructions to the Moscow archivists she asked to be sent those documents written "in the most antiquated manner, prior to the reign of His Majesty, Tsar Aleksei Mikhailovich, so that their composition and old mode of expression are curious and peculiar; but they are not to be long."[21] In other words, Anna was interested in history only insofar as it was "curious," that is, entertaining or odd. It is quite possible that the old documents she received were read aloud to her at bedtime.

The pinnacle, if such it be, of the empress's peculiar taste in entertainment was attained toward the end of her reign with the marriage of her court jester, Prince Mikhail Golitsyn, to a Kalmyk woman. A house fashioned out of huge blocks of ice, containing several rooms and galleries, and lighted at night by candles, was constructed for the grandiose spectacle. All of the furnishings were also made of ice and painted in various colors. Included in the wedding procession of several hundred were representatives of the various nationalities constituting the Russian empire, who rode to the festivities in sleighs pulled by dogs, pigs, and other animals. The bride and groom were placed in a cage on the back of an elephant. After the marriage feast, the "young couple" was escorted to a bed of ice, and a guard was placed at the door with orders not to allow anyone to leave the house of ice before morning. As the observant French minister, the Marquis de la Chétardie, noted:

> Such activities are designed to remind the notables of this realm from time to time that their lineage, their fortunes, their qualities, and the ranks with which their sovereign has honored them will in no way protect them from the least bit of arbitrariness on the part of their potentate, and that she ... has the right to plunge her subjects into an insignificance the likes of which they have never known before.[22]

The assertion of the absolute power of the Russian monarch noted by the foreigner, and expressed by Anna herself in one of her private letters as "I am free to reward whomever I wish,"[23] was put into practice in the form of growing police terror. By 1731 the Secret Chancellery, which had been abolished four years earlier, was reestablished. Headed for many years by Andrei Ushakov, it dealt with everything that could even remotely be considered treason, conspiracy, or an attempt on the life or honor of the sovereign. Into this last category fell any careless words, even those uttered in the heat of the moment or under the influence of alcohol, or even accidental slips of the pen in listing the name or titles of the sovereign in written documents. According to a decree of 1730, one could be sentenced to death for such violations, although in practice the sentence was usually commuted to corporal punishment and exile to Siberia. A refusal to drink to the health of the sovereign, the narration of an unseemly dream from the night before, or even worse, conversion to another religion (especially to Judaism) would be treated as a crime.

Now more than ever, denunciation flourished. Household servants and peasants denounced their landlords, wives their husbands and vice versa, children their parents, and so forth. During the investigation, both the person denounced and the person who did the denouncing were subjected to torture, after which most of them emerged crippled. If the denouncer was unable to prove the veracity of his denunciation, he was punished as a criminal. In all, about ten thousand people fell victim to the Secret Chancellery in the 1730s.[24] Nor were the victims confined to any one particular social stratum. The most notorious political trials of Anna's reign were Artemii Volynskii's and the trials of those who had attempted to impose the "Conditions" on her.

At first, the empress appeared to hold no grudge against the Dolgorukiis. But a few months into her reign, she had them exiled, first to their estates and then to Berezovo, where Menshikov had recently died. In 1738, the investigation into the events of 1730 was reopened, and within the next year four of the Dolgorukii princes were executed and several other members of the family were sentenced to prison. D.M. Golitsyn ended his days locked up in a fortress. As for the Volynskii affair, it can only be understood within the context of the court and political circumstances of the day.

The unhappy private life of the empress, who had been widowed at such a young age, could not but tell on the manner in which she was to administer the Russian state. Back in Mitau, the person closest to Anna was the Courland noble Ernst-Johann Biron (Bühren). He made his appearance in Moscow shortly after the empress's coronation. Anna felt such constant need of his company that she tried never to let him out of her sight. She shared with him all her joys and sorrows. Biron with his wife and children and the empress composed what was in essence a single family unit. Anna was quite attached to her favorite's children, leading some historians, apparently not without justification, to speculate that at least one of his sons was her own child. The sovereign's love for Biron was so great that if he was overtaken by a bad mood, she suffered from the same bad mood. Biron's hold over her was truly unlimited, and as was completely predictable under such circumstances, she would take no important decision without consulting him.

Biron was an ambitious and imperious man but also calculating and rather cautious. He therefore tried not to flaunt his role in government, accepting no key posts, a situation that subsequently confused some historians. Biron's role was, however, apparently clear to contemporaries. And while the Russian people were willing to excuse their legitimate monarch's bad intentions, the influence of any favorite acting in a governmental capacity, whether officially or unofficially, competently or incompetently, struck them as illegitimate. So in their minds they naturally associated everything bad in Anna's reign with Biron. Hence, the concept of the "era of Biron" [the *Bironovshchina*] was linked to his name, and has taken firm hold in the historical literature.

In general, the term "Bironovshchina" is employed to identify the wave of police terror discussed above, the foundations for which were laid by Peter I and, linked with this terror, the so-called "era of foreign domination." Here we come face to face with one of the touchiest issues in Russian history, one not confined to the interpretation of events taking place in Anna Ioannovna's reign but bearing substantially broader significance. As we have already noted, the Petrine reforms put an end to the policy of isolationism and transformed Russia, in reality as well as in outlook, into a part of Europe. Yet Russia's backwardness, formerly unrecognized but now acknowledged, and the need to learn from the foreigners who were flocking to Russia in pursuit of their fortunes but who were not always paragons of good behavior, gave rise to a sense of wounded national self-esteem. In turn, the latter collided on the one hand with a sense of national superiority that had been fostered for centuries, and on the other with the perception of everything foreign as hostile. The haste with which the reforms had been carried out in the first quarter of the eighteenth century left no time to ponder properly what was taking place, as a result of which unhappiness with "the Germans" [*Nemtsy*] (for thus the Russians labeled all West Europeans) manifested itself on the everyday level, although it was more prevalent among the lower strata of society than the upper.

The breathing space that followed Peter I's death brought with it a qualitative step forward in society's outlook. The process of creating a national consciousness based on new values began slowly to pick up momentum. Pride in the most recent national achievements, old prejudices, and imperial vanity mingled in an extraordinarily odd fashion in this new Russian consciousness. Such an unusual development can largely be attributed to the fact that the formation of a new Russian national consciousness coincided in time with the creation of an empire, and a continental empire at that. This empire was contiguous in nature: that is, in the process of expansion, colonial territory was annexed directly to that of the mother country. This process in its turn produced a Russian imperial mindset that extended beyond the nation's traditional frontiers, while at the same time Russians refused to come to grips with the implications of the changes taking place within the newly expanded frontiers.

Take for example the active participation of Baltic nobles (or, as they were termed, "Baltic-Sea Germans" [*Ostzeiskie Nemtsy*]) in the governance of the realm. This was a phenomenon that increased steadily over the course of the eighteenth century and became especially prevalent at the beginning of the nineteenth. The prominence of Baltic nobles was frequently viewed, especially in the latter period, as an insult to Russian national dignity. This was so despite the fact that formally the "Germans" were full-fledged subjects of the Russian sovereign and as such enjoyed rights equal to those of the Russian nobles proper.

It was toward the middle of the nineteenth century, when Russian national consciousness had acquired its distinct characteristics and debates about the legacy of Peter I grew especially pronounced, that the historiographic myth of the "Bironovshchina" as the period of the "domination of foreigners" took shape, to be enshrined in the history books produced by Sergei Soloviev and Vasilii Kliuchevskii. In reality, things were not quite so simple.

In addition to Biron, we find Ostermann, Count Karl von Löwenwolde (born in Livonia), Field Marshal Burchard Christoph von Münnich (born in Oldenburg), and a number of other foreigners among those holding high office in this period. Some of them occupied positions that Russian dignitaries craved, thus creating an understandable discontent among the latter. An analysis of the court struggle, however, clearly reveals that the division among the various cliques was not based on national identity but, as was common in such situations, reflected a struggle for power between older and younger generations of those close to the throne. The "Germans" did not predominate in the ruling administrative organs. Rather, a statistical analysis reveals that no "domination of foreigners" whatever existed in either the army or the state apparatus. Moreover, while under Peter I foreigners were shown preference in state service, the terms of service for foreign specialists in Russia had changed to the point where they were now similar to those for Russians. An analysis of the case files of the Secret Chancellery likewise refutes the myth of the "Bironovshchina." In those affairs, instances of national or ethnic resentment are almost never mentioned.[25]

When we turn to Anna's domestic policy, we find almost no change from that of her immediate predecessors. Right at the beginning of her reign, the empress announced the elimination of the Supreme Privy Council and the reestablishment of the role of the Senate, which had been trampled on by the Privy Councillors. In the process the number of Senators was increased to twenty-one. The variety of functions assigned to the Senate and the manner in which its deliberations were organized, however, still inhibited expeditious decisionmaking on important questions. As a consequence, the Cabinet of Her Imperial Majesty was created in 1731 to replace the council. It was assigned the function of administering the country directly, dealing with foreign as well as domestic policy.* Within a few years, the signatures of the cabinet ministers were formally equated with that of the empress. Ostermann remained the most influential member of the Cabinet, although his relations with Biron were those of two people jockeying for power. Despite the competition, Ostermann managed to retain his authority.

A blatant catering to the nobility's interests was an important feature of the domestic policy of the time. In the first year of Anna's reign Peter's decree on single inheritance was already rescinded, and in 1736 the mandatory service requirement was reduced to twenty-five years, at the end of which the noble had the right to retire. Also speaking to the interests of the nobility was policy in the area of industrial entrepreneurship, which continued the trend toward limiting government intervention in the economy. Under the guidance of Biron's protégé Baron A.K. Schemberg—a name associated with large-scale financial manipulation—a review of legislation dealing with metallurgy was carried out in the 1730s. This industry flourished in Anna's reign to

---

*The term "cabinet" in the sense of the sovereign's private chancellery had been used under Peter I and would again under Catherine II.

such an extent that by 1740 Russia produced more cast iron than any other country in the world. In 1739, a new mining regulation was adopted that led to the privatization of state enterprises. At first glance, this was a reasonable measure, one that should have served to stimulate production. But given Russia's specific conditions, the majority of enterprises ended up in the hands of powerful dignitaries who lacked the experience and the expertise necessary to run them. Concerned only with making the quickest and largest possible profit, they gave little thought to the long term.

Measures to encourage the development of trade that had been undertaken earlier were having a noticeable effect by the time of Anna's reign. The Russian export of grain and other agricultural produce increased substantially, assisted greatly by the reopening of the port of Archangel. Still, one must treat with care the data cited by some scholars[26] concerning a general increase in trade, expressed in rubles, inasmuch as they fail to take into account the rise in prices and the fall in the value of the ruble. The latter phenomena in their turn were caused by Peter I and his immediate successors, who manipulated the minting of state coinage in order to produce quick profits. Thus, in the period from 1727 until 1730 alone—that is, just prior to Anna's accession to the throne—four million rubles' worth of underweight copper coinage was struck.[27] Starting in 1730, when a special Commission on Monetary Matters was created, governmental monetary policy underwent review. The striking of small-value copper coins all but ceased, the optimal relationship of copper to silver money was established, the value of the copper that went into copper coins was set, and so forth. As a result, the nation's financial situation could be stabilized.

Nonetheless, state revenues increased very slowly, failing to keep pace with expenditures. Nor was the state able to cope with the problem of arrears in the soul-tax payments, which remained the basic source of revenue for the state budget. In 1732 the amount of arrears equaled all the money collected from direct taxation for the year. In response, Anna's government wisely decided not to require the full soul-tax payment in 1730, a measure it repeated in 1735, when the nation was beset by bad harvests. At the time, an imperial decree was issued requiring landlords to feed their peasants and to supply them with seed grain for planting. This last measure was of course motivated not by any humanitarian impulse but by the state's concern for its revenues and for keeping tax arrears to a minimum,* since the size of those revenues affected the maintenance of the army and navy, which in turn were critical to the pursuit of an active imperial foreign policy.

Under Catherine I, Russian foreign policy, pursuing on the whole the line laid out by Peter I, followed what was in essence a policy of "small deeds" that was dynastic in orientation. The nation's foreign policy interests focused primarily on Schleswig, to be taken from Denmark, which was promised to the empress's son-in-law, the Duke of Holstein, and on Courland, where Russian influence was to be preserved. In the first case, the intent to undertake military action against Denmark led to an exacerbation of relations with Great Britain, as a result of which Russia had to back off from its plans for Schleswig. In the case of Courland, Russian policy managed to head off the marriage of Anna, at that time still Duchess of Courland, to the illegitimate son of Polish king Augustus II, Maurice of Saxony, whom Courland's nobles supported. It did not, however, manage to achieve the election of Alexander Menshikov as Duke of Courland.

Under Peter II there was a discernible pause in foreign policy, and foreign diplomats went so far as to predict that if matters were allowed to continue in that fashion for long, Russia would sacrifice its significance in the international arena and slip back into the condition that prevailed in pre-Petrine times. With the accession of Anna Ioannovna to the throne, foreign policy became more active, although its orientation remained the same. The first concern was the struggle for Courland, which was crowned with success in 1737 with the election of Biron as Duke, an event that secured the inclusion of Courland in Russia's sphere of influence, and its eventual annexation. In this struggle Russia collided with Poland, with regard to which Peter I had already laid out Russia's basic approach. The Turks represented the second major concern of Russian foreign policy.

The conclusion of an alliance treaty with Austria in 1726 was of prime importance in relations with both Poland and the Ottoman Empire. The commonality of interests between Russia and Austria in both

---

*It should be noted that Anna's government was quite aware of the fact that the peasants were not to blame for the arrears. Rather, the fault lay with the nobles, who were depriving their peasants of their livelihood. The state accordingly issued several decrees threatening with dire punishment those nobles who did not pay taxes for their peasants. Possible punishments included the confiscation of estates. Thus, while catering to the nobility's interests, the state never lost sight of its own.

instances guaranteed the firmness and longevity of the alliance. Thanks to it, Austria gradually began to acquire the decisive role of swing power in any coalition of European powers, a role it was destined to play throughout the eighteenth century.*

In 1733, Russia and Austria undertook joint military action in Poland and managed to achieve the removal of the French-sponsored Stanislaw Leszczynski and the election of Augustus III as Polish king. In 1735, the two allies entered into war against the Ottoman Empire, during which Russian troops under the command of Münnich seized and ravaged the Crimea and won a number of striking victories along the Sea of Azov and in Moldavia. Austria's lack of success, however, reduced to a minimum Russia's gains from these victories, which cost so many lives. As a consequence, Russia achieved nothing more than the return of Azov at the Peace of Belgrade in 1739, and even then it was denied permission to reconstruct its fortifications there.

Historians view Münnich's military abilities in conflicting ways. Some term him a "remarkable commander" and a "talented engineer,"[28] while others, on the contrary, describe him as a mediocrity and observe that because of him the army suffered from "poorly conceived strategic plans, a low level of operational thinking, an overemphasis on military routine, weak organization of supplies for the troops, and colossal human losses."[29] Contemporaries apparently thought more highly of the field marshal, and his personal courage was widely respected. When the fortress of Ochakov was stormed, for example, Münnich led the charge at the head of a battalion of the Preobrazhenskii regiment, and he himself planted its standard on the fortress's walls.

Passing judgment on Münnich as commander would not be so important if it did not involve an evaluation of the condition of the Russian army. The fact is that when Münnich directed the War Collegium in 1732, a number of new regulations and instructions were drawn up. These, unlike their Petrine counterparts, as the military historian L.G. Beskrovnyi has observed, "directed the military preparation of the troops along a completely new path, one in the spirit of the Prussian system."[30] According to P.P. Epifanov, "the state's military mecha-

---

*The uniqueness of Austria's situation over several decades was related to the fact that both before and after the death in 1740 of Habsburg Emperor Charles VI, who left no male heir, its foreign policy revolved around the recognition or lack of recognition of his daughter Maria Theresa's claim to the throne by various other governments.

nism" was deranged by "the implantation of Prussianism." Moreover, the "embezzlement of state property" and the extravagance perpetrated by the favorites "were reflected in the most pernicious way in the condition of the nation's armed forces, and were accompanied by such retreats from the founding principles elaborated in the heat of battle over the course of the twenty-year Northern War that they often bordered on betrayal of Russia's national interests."[31] When leveling such serious accusations, the author, whose anti-German bias is clear, apparently did not consider it necessary to substantiate them in any way.

It should be noted that the Ottoman Empire was Russia's primary enemy not only in the 1730s but also in later decades of the eighteenth century. In military action against that power, as Beskrovnyi concedes, Münnich's innovations proved quite effective. True, he doubts that they were as effective against the regular standing armies of Europe.[32] But Russia's successes in the war with Sweden from 1741 until 1743, which had been sparked by Swedish dreams of revenge and concluded with the occupation of Finland by Russian forces, speak to the contrary. Looking ahead, it should be noted that when Petrine regulations were reinstituted in the army after 1741, no one gave a thought to the question as to whether they might be outmoded some twenty years after the signing of the peace of Nystadt.

In summarizing our discussion of Russian foreign policy under Anna Ioannovna, it should be emphasized that by orienting it along the same lines followed by Peter I and by plainly pursuing the same imperial goals, Anna solidified this policy for decades to come. At the heart of her policy lay the alliance with Austria to combat the Porte and to transform Poland into nothing more than a marionette, an ongoing rivalry with France for influence in Central and Eastern Europe, particularly in the German states, and a determination to resolve the fate of the Crimea as she saw fit. If the results of this policy were not as apparent early on as they would become in the second half of the century, this was not due to any betrayal of Russian national interests on the part of Anna or her government, as some have claimed.* Rather, one has to look to thoroughly objective causes. In any case, the Russian national consciousness that was taking shape was inclined to recognize these results as successes.

---

*It will readily be noted that such an interpretation depends upon an identification of national interests with imperial.

It is no coincidence that it was precisely at this time that the creative activity of the poet Vasilii Trediakovskii began. In 1734 he in effect created the new genre of the classical triumphal ode in the Russian language, composing his *Triumphal Ode on the Surrender of the City of Danzig,* accompanied by his theoretical "Considerations on the Ode in General." A few years later, in his 1739 ode *On the Victory over the Turks and Tatars and on the Capture of Khotin,* the first to be composed in iambic tetrameter, Mikhail Lomonosov made his debut in Russian poetry, declaiming:

> Russia, how fortunate thou art
> Under Anna's mighty protection!
> What beauties do thine eyes behold,
> On the occasion of this new triumph!

Still, the younger generation of Russians (those who might have looked nostalgically back to pre-Petrine times had by now finally departed the scene), when comparing the great tsar-transformer Peter I with those who were now ruling Russia, could not but experience a certain sense of dissatisfaction, which we find reflected in the Artemii Volynskii affair. A member of the younger generation of "fledglings of Peter's nest," Volynskii became a protégé of Biron's and advanced in state service at mind-boggling speed, first being named to the position of Master of the Hunt, and then in 1738, to that of cabinet minister. Not noted for his high moral standards, shrinking at nothing in order to achieve his ends, vain to a fault, greedy, coarse, and arrogant, Volynskii now decided to take on Biron himself, attempting to encroach on his influence with the empress. But he failed to appreciate her loyalty to the person who had stood by her in the most difficult moments of her life. After some hesitation, Anna agreed to Volynskii's arrest.

Investigation revealed that a group of his friends had gathered regularly at the home of the cabinet minister in the evenings, and that together with them he had composed a "General Consideration on the Rectification of Domestic State Affairs." The document, replete with Volynskii's ill-advised remarks on Anna, was interpreted as a conspiracy against the empress. After terrible torture, Volynskii and his friends were judged and condemned by a special court composed of Senators and other high-ranking dignitaries. In June 1740, they were publicly beheaded. The execution made a dreadful impression on contemporaries, among whom the former cabinet minister enjoyed a certain degree of popularity. They began to think of Volynskii as a patriot who perished because he had challenged the hated Biron. When in October of the same year Anna Ioannovna died, as Evgenii Anisimov stresses, "everyone understood that sooner or later the favorite's authority was bound to dissipate."[33]

* * *

In 1731, soon after ascending the throne, Anna Ioannovna started to concern herself with identifying a successor. The as yet unborn son of her niece, Anna Leopoldovna—the daughter of her sister Catherine and the Duke of Mecklenburg-Schwerin—was declared the heir to the throne. At the time, Anna Leopoldovna was a mere thirteen years old. Shortly thereafter, a fiancé was selected for her: Prince Anton-Ulrich of Brunswick-Lüneburg. Three years older than his bride, he was still small in stature, shy, and socially ill at ease. In order to offset the initial, rather unfavorable impression he had created, it was suggested that he win his princess's hand by military deeds. So he was sent off to war against the Turks under Münnich's command. The prince showed himself a brave and honorable officer. Participating in the capture of Ochakov, he earned the rank of major general. Having grown up to be a man, tall and broad-shouldered, Anton-Ulrich returned to Petersburg. In his absence, Anna Leopoldovna had managed to fall hopelessly in love with a handsome foreigner, Count Moritz Carl zu Lynar; but the empress insisted that she marry Anton-Ulrich, so in July 1739 the wedding at last took place. In August 1740, Anna Leopoldovna gave birth to a boy, who was destined to rule, if only briefly, as Russian emperor Ivan VI.

Historians believe that the empress, who was on her deathbed at the time, wavered and, possibly, pondered the possibility of leaving the throne to Anna Leopoldovna herself. But the niece's inattentiveness to her aunt during the latter's illness decided the matter, and Ivan Antonovich was declared the successor. That decision raised the question of a regency for the two-month-old baby. There were three possibilities. First of all, the role of regent could be assigned to his parents, or to Anna Leopoldovna alone. But the empress apparently feared that in the latter case, real power would reside in the hands of Leopold, Duke of Mecklenburg, Anna's father, who was notorious for his bad character and not particularly welcome in Russia. The reins of power could also be handed over to a collegially organized body, the Cabinet of Ministers. But this would signify a return to the very model of power that Anna Ioannovna had rejected at the start of her reign. Finally, the third claimant to the regency was Biron, who hatched a complex intrigue in order to achieve his ends. In addition to a simple love of power, he was apparently motivated by the recognition that the empress herself had hitherto served as the sole guarantor of his good fortune, and that with a change in rule his chances of preserving it were problematic. By getting the empress to name him regent, Biron would not only retain power in his own hands but increase it, and by legal means. He managed to attract influential members of the cabinet to his cause and to convince the empress to sign the desired decree. According to a story that cannot be verified, the empress, as she signed the decree, which was to be made public only after her death, exclaimed: "I feel sorry for you, Duke; you are seeking your own destruction!"

Among those who actively helped Biron get his hands on the regency was Münnich, who according to some historians was already laying plans to overthrow the regent if he refused to share power with him. In view of the short period of time in which the field marshal had to operate before the empress died, he could do no more than convince her to favor Biron. If no decree whatever on the regency had been signed before she died, disorder might well have ensued. In that case, given the general discontent with the favorites, the one person both Münnich and Biron feared most of all—Tsarevna Elizaveta Petrovna—would have had a real shot at gaining the throne.

The government was fully informed of the widespread sympathy for Elizabeth, especially among the guardsmen in the capital. During the 1730s, numerous cases passed through the Secret Chancellery in which Elizabeth's name figured prominently. Those who were arrested had frequently sworn allegiance to her. After Anna Ioannovna's death in October 1740, when people were required to take the oath of allegiance to the emperor Ivan Antonovich, and in essence to Biron, the stream of such occurrences increased. Thus, for example, a sailor by the name of Tolstoy metaphorically announced, when interrogated in the presence of Andrei Ushakov, that "the eagle has flown, and has looked to secure the benefit of his children. But his daughter was left out." When subsequently explaining himself, he claimed that he was speaking of the sovereign emperor, Peter the First. He, the sovereign, during his reign, had looked after, and accomplished everything for, the benefit of his children. But a daughter was left out, the Sovereign Tsesarevna Elisavet Petrovna, and now we are to take the oath of allegiance to her, the sovereign tsesarevna, [a situation] about which all the soldiers in the regiments are talking.[34]

Old Believer prisoners likewise refused to take the oath, pointing out that "the father of his majesty is a foreigner, does not go to [our] church, and does not worship the holy icons."[35]

Whatever the case, there were no massive demonstrations against the infant emperor and his regent in October 1740, although the struggle for power within the ruling elite by no means subsided. Within several days of the declaration of his regency, Biron was informed of hostile comments directed his way by Prince Anton-Ulrich in conversation with close friends. The episode led to heated explanations, followed by public repentance by the prince, after which he refused to leave his chambers for two weeks. The easy victory turned Biron's head, and he apparently decided that the controversy had not signified anything particularly important. On November 7 he quarreled with Anna Leopoldovna, said a number of coarse things to her, and threatened to send her packing back to Germany, together with her husband. This conversation proved fatal to Biron, for on that very night a coup d'état put an end to his rule.

The chief organizer of the coup was Münnich, who assumed that by delivering the Brunswick family from Biron he would render it such a signal service that he would easily acquire for himself the coveted rank of commander in chief, thus securing for his lifetime the leading role at the Russian court. Not that he claimed the role of regent; he intended to present that to Anna Leopoldovna. Calling upon the guardsmen to arrest Biron, he cleverly threw out the name of Elizabeth, thanks to which they were prepared to pass through hell and high water for him. The coup was accomplished without complications, and on November 9, a manifesto appeared, issued in the name of the baby emperor, announcing the removal of the Duke of Courland from the regency. Biron was packed off to Siberian exile.

According to contemporaries, the coup d'état was greeted with joy. "There has never been an example," the French minister Chétardie informed Versailles, "of so many people gathered in front of the palace as there were today, and all of them displayed such unfeigned happiness."[36] After the oath of allegiance was administered to Anna Leopoldovna in her capacity as regent, she brought the baby Ivan Antonovich to a window of the palace to show to the mass of people, who greeted him with cries of joy. Thus began the rule of the Duchess of Brunswick.

Two contrasting opinions concerning Anna Leopoldovna have emerged, as the historian S.F. Librovich observed at the beginning of the present century. "Some contemporaries considered her quite intelligent, kind, humane, disdainful of pretense, indulgent, magnanimous, and pleasant in disposition. Others, on the contrary, reproached her for her arrogance, bluntness, secretiveness, and contempt for those who surrounded her, asserting that she had a mediocre mind and was capricious, hot-tempered, indecisive, and lazy."[37] To all appearances, the evaluations of Anna Leopoldovna contained in memoir literature depended upon how she herself related to the authors. For the historian, the most important criterion is the nature of the regent's actual performance.

The first decrees of the new regime were quite traditional for such instances: participants in the coup received rewards, although Münnich's was not exactly what he had in mind. The rank of commander in chief went not to him but to Prince Anton-Ulrich. The field marshal had to content himself with orders, money, and a position as cabinet minister. This fact alone indicates that Ivan Antonovich's parents intended to rule by themselves. Mikhail Golovkin was also named a member of the cabinet, as a result of which half of the members of the government were Russian and the other half foreigners. The situation was the same with regard to court service, where Löwenwolde, a Livonian, was named grand marshal of the court, while Dmitrii Andreevich Shepelev, a Russian, was named marshal of the court. Six of the eight chamberlains were Russian. Thus, there are no grounds for asserting that the regent gave preference to foreigners. Anna Leopoldovna was, moreover, pious and punctually observed all the rites of the Orthodox church.

In the *Complete Collection of Laws of the Russian Empire,* compiled in the eighteen twenties and thirties, 185 legislative acts can be dated to the period between November 1740 and November 1741: that is, we find 15.4 acts promulgated per month, which closely approximates the legislative activity for the eighteenth century as a whole. The actual number of decrees was quite possibly twice that figure. So far as the content of Anna Leopoldovna's legislation is concerned, it does not manifest any desire for major innovation. In October 1740, Biron had declared an amnesty for a number of categories of prisoners, and in December those categories were broadened. On November 12, a decree was promulgated defining the procedure for the submission of petitions to the appropriate institutions, by now traditional for all the governments of the eighteenth century, "and on rendering decisions concerning them without any bureaucratic delays."[38] A decree followed in December, forbidding everyone aside from those in the first three classes of ranks to wear expensive clothing adorned with gold or silver. In February 1741, the special privileges claimed by Livonia and Estonia were confirmed. In March the cabinet agreed with the Senate, which had suggested that Peter I's desires be ignored, and that all who wished to construct houses of stone in any town in the empire be permitted to do so, while in June the Senate forbad the entry of poor people into St. Petersburg. Finally, in September the descendants of Ivan Susanin (the peasant who, according to tradition, had saved the future Tsar Mikhail Romanov from the Poles in 1613) were granted a charter confirming their exemption from the recruitment levy.

This brief review of Anna Leopoldovna's legislation indicates that if her regime had any sort of program, it was to continue the policies of preceding rulers. The regent herself felt no great attraction to affairs of state, and often spoke, sighing, about how she hoped that her son would soon grow up to rule. In this situation, if the government had had energetic and decisive servitors available to it, it might possibly have accomplished quite a bit. But Anna Leopoldovna had retained basically the same people who had surrounded her aunt. Prince Anton-Ulrich was equally ill suited to governmental activity. "He was kind, brave, and honorable," noted a historian of the last century, "and would have made a fine officer of the guards, or even a regimental commander—but no more than that."[39] The description was quite apt: Anton-Ulrich would reveal both his kindliness and his nobility in full measure in the upcoming years, as he looked after his family in exile. But the life of a statesman was not for him.

Ivan Antonovich meanwhile continued to grow under the watchful eye of one of his mother's favorites, Maid of Honor Julie Mengden. He was seldom displayed to strangers, even when etiquette would seem to demand it. The documents preserve evidence of the toys found in the emperor's room, and of the celebration of his first birthday on August 12, 1741. On that day a lavish banquet was staged, while in the evening fireworks and illumination displays were arranged. The balls, masquerades, hunts, and theatrical presentations that followed one after the other were the most common forms of entertainment at Anna Leopoldovna's court, which is understandable if one bears in mind that the regent was but twenty-two years old at the time. Within their narrow circle of courtiers, she and her husband played chess, billiards, badminton, and tennis, but most often cards. The previous menagerie was kept, and ten elephants were added. In October 1741, they got out of control, "started fighting over a female," and after destroying their cage, broke out. One of the elephants "smashed up the Senate and a Finnish village."[40]

The government's blatant disinclination to treat the governance of the realm seriously elicited more and more dissatisfaction. The legitimacy of Anna Leopoldovna's authority began to be questioned, while the prospect of seventeen more years of the status quo hardly inspired anyone to lend her active support. Tension within society grew, and the prospect of the overthrow of the regent seemed more and more likely. She alone, it seemed, did not want to take notice of the mood. Back in March 1741 Münnich, despairing of changing anything, went into retirement, and Ostermann threatened to do the same. Experienced politicians fully realized the nature of the situation that was developing in Petersburg, being aware that the disaffected were gathering ever more tightly around Tsarevna Elizabeth, and deemed it necessary to take the requisite security measures. Some suggested that Elizabeth be sent to a nunnery, others that she be immediately married off. Elizabeth was well aware of these proposals. Perhaps more than anything else, the dangers they posed drove her, no less a lover of the gay and carefree life than her niece, down the road to conspiracy.

Word of the conspiracy, in which several foreigners were involved, inevitably reached the ears of Cabinet members. On November 11, Ostermann, brought into the regent's chambers on a stretcher, begged her to arrest immediately one of the main conspirators, Elizabeth's French physician Armand Lestocq, and also to isolate the *tsesarevna* herself.* The regent responded that she did not believe the tsesarevna

---

*Tsesarevna was the title bestowed on wives of heirs to the throne [tsesarevichi] as well as (in the cases of Anna and Elizaveta Petrovna) daughters of tsars who were in the line of succession.

guilty, and in any case would talk with her herself. On November 23, Anna had a conversation with Elizabeth, the gist of which has been recorded in various versions. It is, however, clear that the tsesarevna categorically denied her participation in any conspiracy and readily managed to convince the gullible regent of her innocence. Neither Prince Anton-Ulrich nor the members of the Cabinet could convince Anna of the impending danger. The only measure to which she would consent was to have herself proclaimed empress, which was to be done on her birthday, December 18. But time had run out. The conversation of November 23 had served to hasten the course of events. On the night of November 24–25, 1741, another government coup put an end to the infant Ivan Antonovich's brief reign.

The coup that brought Elizaveta Petrovna to the throne has been thoroughly described in the historical literature,[41] although there is disagreement about specific details. According to one version, Elizabeth herself, at the head of the guardsmen, appeared at the Winter Palace to arrest Anna Leopoldovna and her husband, awakening the regent with the words: "Little sister, it's time to get up!" According to another version, she awaited the outcome of events in a sleigh parked alongside the palace. Anisimov is probably correct in crediting the second variant, because Elizabeth's presence in the palace was not required. Moreover, she "might fear that a coup d'état carried out for the sake of emancipating Russia from foreigners, as it was subsequently proclaimed, would degenerate into an ordinary family squabble."[42] As for Ivan Antonovich, the grenadiers participating in the coup let him remain sleeping quietly in his cradle. Waiting until he awakened, they carried him downstairs and handed him to Elizabeth, who allegedly exclaimed: "Poor child! You are innocent, but your parents bear a heavy guilt."[43]

Overthrowing the one-year-old emperor proved a relatively easy matter. Avoiding mistakes when deciding the fate of the Brunswick family was more complicated. The manner in which the problem was finally resolved mingled purely medieval notions with more modern approaches in a fantastic fashion. Had the scenario occurred a hundred or so years earlier, the child as well as his parents doubtless would have perished at the hands of the executioner. But Elizabeth understood only too well that such treatment of the family would injure her in the eyes of her subjects and the entire world. Immediately after ascending the throne, moreover, she had publicly vowed that no one would be executed during her reign. To add to that, the new empress was sentimental and never bore any particular animosity toward Ivan Antonovich and his parents. She may even have felt conscience-stricken. It may well have been because she wished to erase Ivan Antonovich and Anna Leopoldovna from her memory, that she ordered collected and destroyed all manifestoes, official lists of those who had sworn allegiance to Ivan Antonovich, and other documents in which their names were mentioned.

First it was decided to send the disgraced family abroad. But its members got no farther than Riga, where they were detained for a year. Then they were held for another year in Dünamünde (now part of Riga). By this time, Anna Leopoldovna had given birth to two daughters, Ekaterina and Elizaveta. After this, they were all returned to Russia proper, first to Raneburg and then to Kholmogory, where in 1744, Ivan Antonovich was taken from his parents. In 1745 and 1746, Anna Leopoldovna gave birth to two more sons, Peter and Alexei, after which she died. Her body was brought back to Petersburg and buried with all the honors due her. The persistent rumors surrounding the fate of the overthrown emperor forced the government to confine him in the Shlisselburg fortress in 1756. There he was fated to die in 1764 at the hands of his jailers, who were determined to keep him from being freed by Vasilii Mirovich, an impoverished army lieutenant attempting to improve his own economic prospects.

Meanwhile, Ivan Antonovich's father, brothers, and sisters remained in Kholmogory. There the children grew up and learned to speak Russian with traces of a northern accent. As the documents attest, both sisters and the two brothers suffered from various physical disabilities and were in addition emotionally and mentally underdeveloped. In 1774, Prince Anton-Ulrich died. Finally, in 1780, his unfortunate children were packed off to their aunt, Dowager Queen Juliana Maria of Denmark. The Princess Elizaveta died in 1782, Alexei in 1787, and Peter in 1798. The only one still alive, the elderly and deaf Princess Ekaterina, petitioned Emperor Alexander I unsuccessfully in 1803 for permission to return to Kholmogory.

But let us return to November 1741, as the new empress, Elizaveta Petrovna, ascended the Russian throne.

Chapter 5

"*You Know Whose Daughter I Am*"

The palace coup of November 1741 closed one chapter in Russia's history and opened another. The new chapter was to last for twenty years, for that was how long the reign of the Empress Elizaveta Petrovna lasted. During her reign, the empire made the transition from its childhood and adolescence in the first half of the century to its full maturity in the second. Herein, perhaps, resides its primary significance, and for that reason alone it is worthwhile paying close attention to how this transition happened, to those trends and processes, people and ideas, that shaped its development.

Our attention is drawn first of all to the specific features of the coup itself. Like its predecessor, it was carried out at the tips of guardsmen's bayonets. But while earlier the guardsmen were supernumeraries cleverly manipulated by court cliques, they were now the leading actors. For several years before the coup, Tsesarevna Elizabeth had spent extensive time in the company of the guardsmen, had served as godmother to their children, and on various festive occasions had distributed money among them. By 1741 she was no mere abstraction to them, familiar by name only, but rather an acknowledged favorite, benefactress and patroness, as well as the daughter of a man whose name was inextricably linked in their minds with the fabled achievements accomplished on Russia's behalf. According to Evgenii Anisimov's calculations, roughly one-third of those who sided with Elizabeth on the night of the coup had begun their service careers under Peter I. "One can imagine," writes the historian, "how the griz-

Elizabeth I. Engraving by Johann Stenglin from a portrait by Louis Caravaque.

zled veterans recounted for their listeners stories about their years spent on campaigns with the great emperor, and about Elizabeth growing up before their very eyes."[1]

Another unique feature of the November 1741 coup was that representatives of the ruling elite were almost totally absent from the conspiracy, while foreign diplomats, hoping by means of a coup to accomplish their own nations' foreign policy objectives, actively participated. The French ambassador, Joachim Jacques Trotti, Marquis de la Chétardie, and the Swedish envoy, Erik Mattias, Baron von Nolcken, persuaded Elizabeth to undertake the coup, supplying her with money and demanding in return various concessions, including the return of the Baltic provinces to Sweden. The money proved useful to Elizabeth, and their arguments influenced her to a degree, although she made no promises and refused to sign her name to any obligations. Sweden, hoping to avenge the losses inflicted on it by Peter I, declared war on Russia, and published an absurd manifesto claiming that it was merely trying to defend the rights of Peter's descendants to the throne. Given the rise in patriotic fervor, it would have been tantamount to suicide for Elizabeth to come out in support of the Swedes. Resolving to act independently, she showed up in person at the barracks, and with the words "Lads! You know whose daughter I am; follow me!" she called upon the guardsmen to seize the Winter Palace.

These few words—"whose daughter I am"—were vitally important; indeed, they exerted a truly magical force. It was no accident that the new empress, who usually signed her name in the French manner—"Elisabeth"—was to go down in Russian history not as Elizabeth I, but as *Elizaveta Petrovna,* or the daughter of Peter. It was the prospect of reestablishing the Petrine legacy that energized the guardsmen on the night of the coup, and to the degree that there was any programmatic content at all to the coup, represented one of its specific features. Further, the sense of national humiliation that was evident in the 1730s arose not as a result of actual oppression of Russians by foreigners but because of the specificity of the conditions in which the new national consciousness was being formed. Complaints about the alleged abandonment of Petrine principles during the 1730s transformed Elizabeth into a symbol of sorts, while her secondary position at court was seen by many as an insult to the memory of the great emperor inflicted by foreigners, a usurpation of authority.

The tsesarevna obviously knew how to exploit these feelings and to stir them up in order to utilize them when necessary. Remarkably, she found support not necessarily in the officer's ranks but among the common soldiers, where the majority stemmed from the peasantry. They best expressed the prevailing mood of the capital's population and composed what was in essence the public opinion of the time. "It would be a big mistake to think that there is no public opinion in Russia. Because there are no proper channels for its expression in Russia, it reveals itself in improper forms, by leaps and fits and starts, and only at crucial historical junctures. But it reveals itself with all the more vigor and in forms all the more peculiar," wrote the historian Vasilii Bilbasov in the last century,[2] with the events of 1762 in mind. These words can be applied with equal justification, however, to the coup of 1741. The patriotic coloration to the coup of November 25, 1741, argues Evgenii Anisimov, distinguished it from other palace coups in eighteenth-century Russia, and allows us to view it, in a certain sense, as something more than fortuitous. Rather, it was characterized by a high level of public consciousness, if not on the part of all Russian society then at least in wide circles in the capital city.[3]

The "patriotic coloration," however, represented merely the coup's veneer. Paradoxically, everyone seemed to forget that it was none other than Peter I, and not his mediocre successors, who first opened to foreigners the pathway to power in Russia. There were also many foreigners in the tsesarevna's entourage: indeed, they prepared the coup together with her and participated actively in it. This was the first instance in which the national sensibilities of the Russian people were skillfully manipulated by political figures for their own purposes.

Contemporaries attest to the fact that national sentiment was so strong in the coup that foreigners actually anticipated xenophobic riots. Elizabeth was forced to declare that she was taking them under her personal protection, a step that was not enough to forestall all excesses. It is difficult to say just how sensitive Elizabeth herself was to the national issue. But, to resort to the observation of the popular historian Konstantin Waliszewski, "the Russian banner had been raised, and the new regime had to accommodate itself to its colors."[4] Throughout her reign Elizabeth gave marked preference to Russians over foreigners when handing out high government posts. But although there was no longer anyone comparable to Biron, Münnich, or Ostermann running the country, Germans, Englishmen, Italians, and others continued to play important roles in the army and navy as well as in scientific and cultural institutions. As we will see, the cultural influence of the West, particularly of France, in particular, grew more perceptible. On the other hand, the nationalist character of the coup became fundamental to the ideology of the new reign for, unlike the previous fifteen years, Elizabeth's regime had its own distinct intellectual foundations. An official ideology, reflecting the mood of those on whom the stability of the regime depended, supported the regime and preserved it from the unexpected. This was true even when the government's inactivity became glaring. Just what sort of ideology was it?

Evgenii Anisimov espies two fundamental ideas, or conceptions, originating in the period, noting their pivotal influence on the subsequent historiographic tradition. Both were direct offspring of the coup's ideology. One was "the political canonization of Peter the Great" and the enunciation of a course to perpetuate his legacy. The second was a negative evaluation of the period stretching from Catherine I's death until Elizabeth's accession.[5] The significance of both of these conceptions extends far beyond the bounds of Elizabeth's reign. The first of them retained its significance throughout the entire life span of the Russian autocracy. The second offered a convenient precedent for those who attempted to fashion their policy on the basis of contrasts. Thus, Peter III attempted to blacken the reign of Elizabeth; Catherine II, that of Peter III; Paul I, that of Catherine II; and Alexander I, that of Paul I. It was extremely important to Elizabeth that the emphasis on fidelity to the Petrine tradition be garbed in patriotic dress. This emphasis created favorable conditions for the direction of the forces building up in society, which were leading to the formation of a national literature, science, and culture, all of which received a powerful impulse.

All that has been said about the uniqueness of the 1741 coup, and about how it was reflected in the following period, is to a certain degree pertinent also to Elizaveta Petrovna as a person and as a political figure. Let us examine her personality in a bit more detail. The first thing that strikes one when describing Elizabeth—and this was agreed upon by all who left memoirs—was her stunning beauty. This feature defined her character, inclinations, habits, and passions as nothing else did. From her earliest youth, Elizabeth had loved gaiety and every sort of amusement: balls, masquerades, feasts, the hunt, and theater. The young tsesarevna sparkled at court festivities, attracted the enraptured glances of foreign diplomats, and was reputed to be unsurpassed in the art of dancing. She adored fancy dress and jewels, and often brought Anna Ioannovna's wrath down upon herself when she appeared at court in clothes that were more luxurious than the empress's.

When she herself became empress and had unlimited resources available to her, she never wore the same costume twice. Occasionally she even changed costumes two or three times in the course of a ball. Thus it was that her clothes closet bulged with several thousand dresses. Over time, the need to retain her status as the leading beauty of the realm grew into what was in effect an obsession for Elizabeth. She was jealous of all women who might rival her, and responded to them as only an autocratic Russian tsaritsa could. Several times she publicly cut off the hair of women at court she considered too lavishly adorned, for example, and once she even ordered that their heads be shaved. When foreign merchants brought new stocks of cloth to St. Petersburg, they were first shown to the empress, and if she liked some of them, she bought them up so that others could not make dresses from the material. In the last years of her life, as Elizabeth began to notice that her beauty was fading, she turned into a recluse, spending countless hours in front of her mirror and hardly ever leaving her chambers.

Elizabeth's character also played a role in the 1741 coup. In the years following the deaths of her father and mother, the tsesarevna had been forced to accept the stringent limits within which each new regime compelled her to live. At first, during Peter II's reign, she still wielded great influence, spending time in the company of the young emperor, who, only five years younger than his aunt, actually fell in love with her. But with the accession of Anna Ioannovna to the throne, she was forced to play a subordinate role. She was constantly reprimanded for her frivolous behavior and gaudy dress and threatened with being married off and sent out of the country.

There were numerous claimants for Elizabeth's hand in marriage. But for one reason or another, no marriage agreement was ever concluded. To aggravate matters, while Peter I had intended to give his daughter in marriage to the king of France, the standing of her potential suitors declined steadily with time, as a result of which the tsesarevna faced the threat of becoming the spouse of some insignificant prince from some second-rate European court. During Anna Leopoldovna's reign, Elizabeth's ill-wishers even suggested that the regent dispatch her to a nunnery. To make matters worse, Elizabeth's personal life was subject to constant surveillance.

It was to be expected that by the time she was thirty-two, her age at the time of the coup, she had come to know love and affection. But she was not free to relish them. To take but one example, Alexei Shubin, a second lieutenant in the Semenovskii guards regiment, was arrested in 1731, deprived of his nobility, and sent off to hard labor in Siberia for the crime of having fallen in love with the tsesarevna. Another important irritant was the need for sums of money to support her lifestyle. To meet her needs she required piles of money. Thus it was that this vital, merry, frivolous woman, seeking nothing more than pleasure in this world, and not thirsting after power for its own sake, understood that the only way she could achieve independence and freedom of action, the only chance to live life the way she wanted to and satisfy all her wishes, was to seize power.

The purely feminine aspects of Elizabeth's character affected the nature of her reign in two ways. She seized the throne not to establish her own favorite of the Biron or Münnich variety. Moreover, it was precisely her unwillingness to resort to such forms that attracted the guardsmen to her. Rather, she strived never to permit the reins of government to slip from her own hands, and to distribute authority evenly among her ministers. In her relations with them, and when taking decisions in general, she was extremely cautious, and as her most recent biographer, V.P. Naumov, has stressed, she never took a single hasty or precipitous step throughout her life.[6] This caution was reflected first of all in the fact that the empress never acted on first impressions and never made decisions after hearing but one opinion. On the contrary, she solicited the opinions of various people, who often contradicted each other, and only then did she come to some sort of resolution. S.M. Soloviev suggested that Elizabeth's chief merit was her dispassionate and patient relations with people. He noted that she knew of their mutual animosity and intrigues, paying no attention to them as long as they did not impinge on state interests. She treated them all evenhandedly, not allowing them to undermine each other.[7]

Such traits were doubtless useful in organizing her reign, but they did have their down side. If when turning to her subjects for advice the empress had held her own opinion, one that was based on specific principles she simply wished to check, the result would have been positive. But the problem was that, as a rule, Elizabeth did not have her own opinion because she lacked firmly held political principles. Her declared adherence to the Petrine legacy represented an appeal to the past. Elizabeth did not have a concrete political program. As a result, she often found herself in no position to choose among the views offered her, and so she continually put off decision making.

Immediately after ascending the throne, the empress still expressed an interest in government and even dropped in on sessions of the Senate, whose authority she had so solemnly promised to restore (as she had also promised to eliminate the Cabinet of Ministers). But her interest soon began to flag, and, as she was indolent by nature, she lacked any inclination for systematic work, preferring relaxation instead. All of this became visible in her indecisiveness and her reluctance to examine important issues. Memoir literature and other documentary evidence of the era uniformly complain of her failure to render decisions on the most important state matters for months on end and of her lack of availability, especially in the last years of her reign, even to her own ministers or to foreign ambassadors. As was the trend at the time, Elizabeth took foreign policy under her own personal supervision, and carried on a direct correspondence with the king of France, for example, the content of which was occasionally unbeknownst even to Russian diplomats. But she sometimes failed to answer her royal correspondent for several years on end.

By rejecting a system of government headed by a powerful first minister, on the other hand, Elizabeth was ardently defending the autocratic nature of her authority. With the elimination of the Cabinet of Ministers, a cabinet serving as the empress's private chancellery was recreated. The cabinet drafted all her decrees and instructions, including those directed to the Senate. Researchers note that although nominally the Senate's significance grew, in reality the extent of its dependence on the autocrat's will was substantially greater than her father had intended. And inasmuch as the empress made no decisions independently, the direction policies took depended, in the final analysis, on those she selected as her advisers. Elizabeth convened meetings of those advisers, or "conferences," as they were termed, as circumstances demanded. In March 1756, however, the conferences were made a formal institution when the empress ordered that they convene regularly and with permanent participation. The new institution received the name the Conference at the Imperial Court, and it assumed many of the functions once performed by the Supreme Privy Council and the Cabinet of Ministers, although officially the extent of its authority and functions was never defined. It is fully apparent that given Elizabeth's unwillingness to take the burden of responsibility for decision making on her own shoulders, it was impossible to do without such an organ; yet she was determined not to limit her own authority in any way.

There was still another facet to Elizaveta Petrovna's personality, one noted by all her contemporaries: a deep religiosity. The empress prayed often and at great length, strictly observed fasts, and performed frequent pilgrimages to holy places of the Orthodox Church. Yet despite all these actions, her piety was bereft of toleration, a trait she held in common with her father. A comparison of Elizabeth with Austrian Empress-Queen Maria Theresa reveals that both were religious fanatics who also saw uniformity of religion as a means of strengthening the state. But with Maria Theresa it was the Greek Orthodox and Protestants who suffered, whereas Elizabeth did not worry about Catholics or Protestants but dissenters from the Russian Church and peoples of completely different faiths. Indeed, as early as 1742 Elizabeth ordered that all Jews be expelled from the empire, and measures were likewise taken to demolish Armenian churches and Muslim mosques during her reign.

The conversion to Orthodoxy of members of other religions gave the empress particular pleasure, and she herself often stood as their godmother. The Old Believers—Russians by nationality and moreover Orthodox—were again subjected to terrible persecution at her orders. How could such religious intolerance coexist with the concept of "enlightened absolutism," features of which some historians are prone to ascribe to Elizabeth's reign?[8] As James Brennan has justly remarked, the "enlightened" Voltaire with his skeptical view of religion was also anti-Semitic, and it could be argued that since his form of anti-Semitism was based on race rather than religion, it was far worse.[9]

The significance of Elizabeth's religiosity matched fully the national coloration that the 1741 coup bore and that her entire reign acquired. Orthodoxy occupied an exceptionally important place in the emerging Russian national consciousness, being generally recognized as a special treasure. But Orthodoxy did not draw the Russian people closer to other Europeans as Protestantism and Catholicism might have done. On the contrary, it separated them. As a consequence, the antinomy of Russia–the West—became a stumbling block of sorts in the sociopolitical consciousness of the Russian people, who proved unable to either reject the West completely or accept it wholeheartedly.

The imposition of selected elements of European civilization on Russian customs and traditions, and the impossibility of reconciling them, would give rise to an unusual duality of consciousness later on, when it would become a subject of reflection and eventually become the nourishing milieu of the Russian intelligentsia. This duality clearly manifested itself in Elizabeth and her tastes. Thus, the empress admired French gallantry and attempted to follow French styles in her dress and imitate Versailles in the splendor of her court. At her order, French and Italian architects built huge palaces in the baroque style. In their luxuriousness they astounded even foreign diplomats who thought they had seen everything. In them hung great works of European art, to which Elizabeth was obviously attracted. The baroque of Elizabeth's time, as Anisimov notes, "suited as nothing else did the empress's tastes, and to a great extent contributed to that exterior brilliance that marked court life under Elizabeth."[10] The great nobles attempted to imitate her, and it was at this point in Russian history that they began to hire French tutors and governesses for their children. It is indicative that naive Russian nobles at first were persuaded that just being French was enough to guarantee the quality of one's upbringing. This ardor for everything French would prevail in Russia for several decades.

Yet at the same time Elizabeth adored Russian and Ukrainian cuisine and Russian folk tales and songs, although her love for the latter did not hinder her from loving Italian opera as well. It was here in Elizabeth's time as well that a trend later referred to as "protective" began to take shape in Russian social thought. Mikhail Lomonosov, a man justly considered the founder of Russian science and poetry, and one who brought glory to Elizabeth's reign, served as its spokesman. He argued that only those facts and those pages in Russian history that contributed to the nation's greater glory should be incorporated into historical works, while silence should be maintained on all else. It followed, according to Lomonosov, that only well-intentioned people—either those who were native-born Russians or else had sworn their allegiance to Russia—could be entrusted with writing the empire's history.[11]

The contradictions in Empress Elizabeth's nature revealed themselves in yet another area. Upon ascending the throne, she promised never to subject anyone to capital punishment. And in actuality no death sentences were confirmed by her, although they continued to be passed. The punishments with which she replaced execution (life at hard labor, slitting of the nostrils, branding) were hardly exemplars of humane treatment. On the whole, however, the officially proclaimed doctrine of monarchic clemency, when taken in conjunction with French aesthetic and behavioral ideals, played an essential role in the amelioration of morals, without which the culture of the baroque could not have taken root. Nonetheless, Elizabeth's reign witnessed several sensational political trials, the victims of which suffered brutal punishment.

Immediately after the coup, Ostermann, Münnich, and a number of other high dignitaries aligned with Anna Leopoldovna were arrested and handed over for trial. Unlike her father, Elizabeth quite naturally did not participate in torture; but she did follow the interrogations from behind curtains. Five people were condemned to death, a sentence that was commuted on the scaffold to exile in Siberia. In 1744, catastrophe struck French minister Chétardie. One of his letters, containing unflattering remarks about the empress, was intercepted and shown to her by his enemies. Chétardie was immediately expelled from the country, but only after his knightly order and portrait of the empress set in jewels, presented to him by Elizabeth, had been confiscated. Several years later another organizer of the 1741 coup, Dr. Armand Lestocq, fell into disgrace. He was sentenced to several years in the Peter and Paul Fortress, after which he was exiled and his property confiscated.

The most celebrated of all the trials, the one that gained the most notoriety throughout Europe, was that known as "the Lopukhina Affair," named for the chief defendant of a whole group of "conspirators." (It is worth noting that Natalia Fedorovna Lopukhina was Anna and Villem Mons's niece, while her husband was a relative of Peter the Great's first wife.) Within the Lopukhin family and among those close to it, as the investigation revealed, Elizabeth's origins and behavior were spoken of with disdain, and the name of the toppled Ivan Antonovich was mentioned reverently. Although matters did not go beyond loose talk, all of those arrested, including several women (one of whom was pregnant), were nonetheless cruelly tortured and condemned to have their tongues cut out and to be executed, the latter sentence commuted to exile. Before they were banished to Siberia, the women were publicly stripped and knouted, and their tongues "shortened."

Any enumeration of the facets of Elizabeth's personality that became features of her reign would be incomplete without mention of the men who managed to gain the favor of this fascinating woman. Mention must be made in particular of those whose proximity to the throne enabled them, intentionally or not, to have an impact on Russian history. Foremost among them was Alexei Razumovskii. The handsome son of a Ukrainian Cossack, a singer in a chapel choir who had a beautiful voice, he had appeared among the courtiers at Tsesarevna Elizabeth's court by mere happenstance at the beginning of the 1730s. Once there he won her heart and, after Shubin had been removed, he became, in Anisimov's words, "the undisputed master of Elizabeth's court," a fact mirrored in the numerous letters and petitions sent to Razumovskii by supplicants of various ranks.[12] Rumors concerning a secret marriage between the tsesarevna and her beloved began to circulate at the time.

Despite the controversy, Razumovskii managed to avoid the fate of his predecessors. Since he took no interest at all in political affairs, was good-natured and indolent by nature, treated his own "favor" with irony, was none too clever and, to all appearances, even illiterate, he was considered harmless and therefore not to be taken seriously. After the coup the former chorister promptly was named a lieutenant general, and then knight of the order of Saint Andrew the Apostle and Grand-Master of the Hunt. A few years later he was promoted to field marshal general. The bestowal of all these ranks and titles, as was customary for the time, was accompanied by the grant of villages with thousands of enserfed peasants, to the point that with time he became one of the richest men in Russia. Razumovskii's influence on Elizabeth, and at court in general, was of course very great. Formally, however, he never occupied any posts in the central administration, and was never, for example, a member of the Conference at the Imperial Court. Still, his presence altered Russian policy toward the Ukraine for a time.

Back in 1734, during the reign of Anna Ioannovna, the hetman's directorate had been replaced, if only de facto, after the death of Hetman Danilo Apostol by a collegially organized body composed primarily of Russians and subordinated to the Senate. In 1742, soon after her coronation, Elizabeth received a deputation of Ukrainian Cossacks, who were promised that some former Ukrainian privileges would be reinstituted. In 1744 the empress herself journeyed to Kiev, where she promised to reestablish the hetmanate. A few years passed before Kirill Razumovskii, the favorite's brother, was selected as the new hetman. At the time of his selection in 1750, he was only twenty-one years old. Several years prior to this, the former shepherd had been summoned to St. Petersburg and from there sent abroad to study, spending time in both Tübingen and Paris. Upon his return, he was named president of the Academy of Sciences. The selection of Razumovskii as hetman had beneficial consequences for the Ukraine. The Russian regiments that had been stationed there were withdrawn; several tax advantages were granted; and supervision by the Collegium of Foreign Affairs, a sign of political autonomy, was reestablished. Although he was intelligent and more educated than his older brother, the young Razumovskii was also lazy. Not envisioning himself as a statesman, he soon became bored with the hetman's responsibilities and spent most of his time in St. Petersburg.

Alexei Razumovskii preserved his position at court right up to Elizabeth's death. His position in her heart, however, was reassigned to another by the end of the 1740s. That other was Ivan Ivanovich Shuvalov, who was named gentleman-of-the-bedchamber to the empress, and in this fashion assumed the status of official favorite, which he retained to the end of her reign. Shuvalov had been educated in the European manner, loved serious reading, appreciated art, was familiar with Enlightenment ideas, and corresponded with Voltaire. His influence was reflected in the love of everything French that was so widespread in the 1750s.

Like Razumovskii, Shuvalov occupied no official posts and was never a member of the Conference at the Imperial Court. Instead, he conducted himself extremely modestly, rejecting all honors, titles, and rewards. As Anisimov accurately noted, Shuvalov's "modesty, which he readily acknowledged and even cultivated ... was not so much a facet of his character as it was a posture, a rather unusual type of behavior for the time.... Such extraordinary behavior distinguished Shuvalov from the general run of the titled dignitaries and underscored his singular character still more strikingly than orders and ranks could have." Shuvalov was undoubtedly more intelligent, and far more capable, than Razumovskii, and his actual power was quite considerable, particularly in the last years of the empress's life, when he was just about the only one to have direct access to her chambers. The formal insignificance of his place in the bureaucratic hierarchy proved convenient to Shuvalov because it relieved him of any responsibility for the success of affairs to which he was privy, and often even allowed him to avoid resolving them.[13]

Count P.I. Shuvalov. From an engraving by Johann Stenglin.

Shuvalov's outlook and frame of mind were quite typical of the time. An admirer of the Enlightenment and of French culture in general, he was nonetheless an ardent Russian patriot, one who considered it his responsibility to strive for the development of his fatherland's science and culture. Over the years, he sponsored Lomonosov, helping and defending him during his numerous conflicts with the administrators of the Academy of Sciences and even with the Orthodox Church. It would not be amiss to label Shuvalov the first Russian Maecenas, the founder of a tradition that survived up until the October Revolution. Also associated with the name Shuvalov is the establishment of two very important cultural institutions, the Moscow Imperial University and the Academy of Arts, the openings of which launched a new stage in the history of Russian education.

Finally, it is worth mentioning that Shuvalov's special role at court secured for his cousins Peter and Alexander Shuvalov dominant roles in the administrative apparatus. Most of the important domestic political measures and reforms of Elizabeth's reign, some of which were put into practice while others remained on paper, are linked with these two, especially with Peter.

* * *

Peter and Alexander Shuvalov had participated in the 1741 coup. Still, they owed their elevation primarily to their family ties. Not only was Ivan Shuvalov their cousin, but in 1742 Peter Shuvalov married the empress's closest friend, Mavra Egorovna Shepeleva, who exerted great influence on Elizabeth. Mavra was no longer young, was unattractive, and had a nasty disposition, according to those who have left memoir descriptions. But she was intelligent and lighthearted. She and her spouse apparently were well suited to each other, for Peter Shuvalov was also intelligent and capable, and at the same time vain, greedy, and indiscriminate in his choice of means to achieve his goals. By the mid-1740s he had already accumulated a general's rank, a count's title, and a chamberlain's post. For all practical purposes, he had gained complete control of the nation's civil administration by the end of the decade.

Contemporaries unanimously condemned his moral qualities, which among other things helped create an atmosphere of constant intrigue at court. Despite the fact that everything he did was designed primarily to cater to his own self-interest, much of his activity proved in the end to be beneficial to his country, for by nature he possessed a quality rather rare in his contemporaries: an appreciation for innovation. "After the death of Peter the Great," notes Anisimov, "there was perhaps no other statesman in Russia who responded as avidly as Peter Shuvalov to every proposal or new idea, or encouraged his subordinates in this same direction."[14]

It is no coincidence that Peter Shuvalov's authority increased at the end of the 1740s, for by that time, most scholars agree, Elizabeth had finally become convinced that Russia could no longer continue to be governed solely on the basis of laws and institutions inherited from her father. Until then, the empress, according to A.E. Presniakov, "out of deep admiration for the aims of her great father considered his work on the governmental structure to be so accomplished and complete that consistent and conscientious implementation of his legislation alone would suffice to provide for the state's complete well-being."[15] In addition to the reestablishment of the role of the Senate and the elimination of the Cabinet of Ministers mentioned above, the Mining and Manufacturing Collegium, the Main Magistracy, and a number of other institutions and agencies abolished by Peter I's successors were recreated in the first months of the new reign.

In the period from 1744 until 1746, an attempt was made to restore the Petrine system of local government institutions. But the plan proposed by the Senate was not approved by the empress, whose desire to reestablish the structures of her father, according to Iurii Gote, had cooled by the mid-1740s. So the members of the Senate laid the unsuccessful project aside for good.[16] The reason for the failure to accept the plan to restore Peter's local government institutions was, however, more serious than that. Indeed, the plan revealed in all its starkness the unwieldiness and ineffectiveness of the Petrine institutions.

The attempt to return to the Petrine order was also observable in a more mundane sphere. The requirements to wear European dress and to shave beards and mustaches, for example, were confirmed by special decrees. The spirit of petty regulation of the subject's everyday life was resurrected in other ways. In December 1742, Elizabeth forbad the wearing of expensive costumes adorned with silver and gold filigree and also more than a set amount of lace. Those expensive costumes that had already been sewn could be worn; but they had to be marked with a special wax seal in order to prevent deception. It was forbidden to keep bears in the home, stage boxing matches out of doors, or use curse words in public in the two capitals.

Still, it should be noted that some retreat from Petrine policy actually did take place from the very beginning of Elizabeth's reign. In 1742, seigniorial peasants were forbidden to enlist voluntarily for military service, while five years later, landlords were given the right to sell their serfs as recruits. Both of these measures, of course, catered to the interests of the increasingly independent and powerful nobility, on whom the sovereign was ever more dependent. On the other hand, the need to impose order on the system of military recruitment was recognized. Toward this end the nation was divided into five districts, from which recruits were drafted ad seriatim: that is to say, no more frequently than once every five years.

The problem of the army and its composition, as before, was linked in the most intimate fashion with the state's finances and its tax policy. Upon ascending the throne, Elizabeth in a grand gesture forgave all tax arrears for the period 1719–30 and even eliminated the Chancellery for [the Collection of] Tax Arrears. In another ten years, tax arrears were forgiven for the period up to 1747, and on top of that the soul tax was lowered, first in 1742–43, and then again in the mid-1750s. Concurrently, a new census, or revision, of the tax-paying population was carried out starting in 1743. It proved advantageous to both the state and the taxpayers. The former unearthed a significantly larger number of tax-bearers (6,643,335 male "souls") than had previously been identified, while the latter were now freed from the necessity of having to pay for those who had either died or run away.

At the start of the 1760s, still another revision of the census was conducted, which revealed that the number of tax-liable subjects had increased by more than 700,000.[17] In the second half of the 1750s, preparations were begun for a land survey, with the goal of obtaining more precise measurements. It was to be known as the "Elizabethan survey." Even more importantly, under the influence of Peter Shuvalov a start was made on revising the state's tax policy, with preference now to be given to indirect taxation. Specifically, Shuvalov proposed that the prices of salt and alcohol (which were state monopolies) be raised, a recommendation that increased state revenues approximately three hundred percent in the period from the end of the 1740s until the beginning of the 1760s. Anisimov aptly notes that the notion of substituting indirect taxes for direct was without doubt progressive for the mid-eighteenth century, and that it was precisely in this same direction that the financial policies of the most advanced countries of Europe were headed.[18]

Still more important was the reform of the domestic tariff system proposed by Peter Shuvalov. In keeping with the proposal, internal customs duties were eliminated at the end of 1753, with the loss in revenue offset by an increase in import duties. In this regard Russia was not only on a par with most of the European nations, but even ahead of them. The attempts of Jean-Baptiste Colbert to enact an analogous reform in France had failed, for example, and internal duties continued to be collected right up to the outbreak of revolution in 1789 (and this despite the fact that Russia was a far larger country). Shuvalov's tariff reform led to the creation of a duty-free domestic market that stretched from the Russian–Polish border to the northwest coast of North America.

The new tariff policy was mirrored in the customs duties schedule introduced in 1757, which was openly protectionist in nature and was designed to discourage the import into the country of manufactured products that might compete with Russian goods. Such a tariff policy proved profitable for the state, which roughly doubled its revenues. Yet because expenditures on the imperial court constantly increased, because conspicuous consumption had by now become a symbol of social prestige for the Russian nobility, and because in 1756 Russia became involved in a costly war, money proved to be in catastrophically short supply. Hence, the Russian government tried to borrow money abroad for the first time. Much to its chagrin, its applications were turned down. Then, on Peter Shuvalov's initiative, the treasury resorted to the manipulation of the currency by minting huge amounts of copper coinage of reduced weight, as a result of which the debased coinage began to depreciate, with its value in weight failing to correspond with its nominal value. Since the copper coinage began to depreciate, prices to rise, the exchange rate to fall, and the balance of payments to suffer, the policy on the whole exerted a negative influence on the nation's economy.[19] These were problems with which succeeding regimes would have to grapple. Such problems notwithstanding, scholars have perceived in Elizabeth's reign "a peculiar sort of industrial boom."[20]

This boom was the consequence of two very important factors. The first was the privatization of industry, a process that had already been initiated in the preceding reign. The second was an increase in demand on both the domestic and international markets for Russian metallurgical products. Still another positive circumstance was created by the orientation of Elizabeth's policy as a whole, which favored the nobility. Select members of the ruling circle—the Shuvalov brothers, the Vorontsov brothers (Mikhail Vorontsov, who was married to the empress's cousin, was first named Vice-Chancellor and then Grand Chancellor), the powerful magnate Count Ivan Chernyshev, and others—acquired ownership of most of the factories. These aristocratic owners, who already enjoyed unlimited opportunities to exploit the wealth of the earth, the waters, and the forests on their own vast estates, also gained substantial advantages in the form of state credits, tax benefits, and the like.

While encouraging an increase in production in the short run, this privileged position at the same time rendered competition from others almost impossible, a situation that could not but negatively affect the development of industry in the long run. But there was a still more negative impact: investment capital accumulated not in the hands of members of an emerging bourgeoisie but in those of a nobility whose interest was confined to the acquisition of the most immediate super profits, which were not then reinvested in production. As a rule, such factory owners paid little heed to increasing production and, if it did increase, it was usually as the result of expanding facilities rather than raising productivity. The credits they received from the state, moreover, seldom were expended in the manner intended by the donor. As a result, most of these entrepreneurs not only failed to turn a profit on their enterprises but ended up in debt, up to their ears, to the state and to private creditors.

When discussing Russian industry it is also extremely important to point out that for the most part the enterprises employed enserfed peasants, whose labor could not be productive because it was unfree, as the factory owners sought to squeeze as much work from them as they could. In 1744 Elizaveta Petrovna's government confirmed a Petrine decree permitting non-noble entrepreneurs to purchase serfs for work in their factories. Thus the nation's industrial development continued along the same dead-end path that Peter I had laid out for it. As a result, the industrial boom proved merely ephemeral.

The ongoing search for new sources of income for the nobility led to yet another innovation in the economic-financial realm: loan banks, which were first proposed by Peter Shuvalov. The first of them was the State Loan Bank, established in 1754,* which in reality composed two separate banks, one for the nobility and the other for the merchantry. The first of these two banks loaned money on collateral such

---

*It is interesting to note that a uniform interest rate of six percent was established for all forms of loans. Moneylenders who demanded a higher rate were subject to criminal prosecution.

as jewels and precious metals or even inhabited estates—that is, enserfed peasants. In the latter case, the size of the loan granted would depend on the number of serfs being mortgaged, with the value of a serf being formally established. The bank's original declared capital permitted the mortgaging at any given time of up to two percent of all the enserfed peasants in Russia. It was only to be expected that a nobility in dire need of money would figure out how to take advantage of the bank's largesse. And it did, with the result that by 1860, when the bank's doors were finally closed, it and similar institutions held mortgages on the overwhelming majority of seigniorial estates.

In 1758, during the course of the financial reform, which was closely linked with the reminting of copper money, the Copper Bank was established. It gave out loans in copper money, which were then to be repaid in silver. It, too, accepted enserfed peasants as collateral. High officials were its chief clients. They quickly absorbed the bank's entire capital fund, leaving the state with little hope of ever recovering it. The founder of the bank himself, Peter Shuvalov, who died in 1762, left his heirs a debt to the Copper Bank of about 470,000 rubles; and this despite the fact that formally no once-only loan was to exceed 180,000 rubles. In 1763, in Catherine II's reign, this bank's doors were finally closed.

If there was another measure undertaken in Elizabeth's reign that starkly characterized the government's industrial policy, it was that of granting the nobility a monopoly on the distillation of alcohol. According to a decree of 1755, only nobles were allowed to own enterprises in this most profitable branch of economic activity. Enterprises owned by non-nobles were to be liquidated or sold. Unlike metallurgical works, which were located primarily in areas where the corresponding ore was to be found, distilleries became associated exclusively with landed estates. That is, they were located directly on the landlord's estate, and exploited unfree labor.

At first glance at least, the abolition of domestic customs duties, the growth of indirect taxation, and the creation of banks should all have stimulated economic growth and propelled the nation along the path of modernization. But to the extent that the system of serf relations created by Peter I remained unchanged at the base of the economy, Russia's potential for development was minimized. Even after the leap forward, it was doomed to lag behind the leading European nations. Negative processes also continued to develop in the social sphere. Thus the possibilities for economic aggrandizement that opened up for the nobles distorted the formation of their estate consciousness. Approaching the matter from another perspective, the possibility offered the merchants to become owners of serfs, associated with their need to utilize unfree labor, led to the formation of a psychology and outlook that were remote from those of their West European counterparts.

Not even the institution of serfdom was vouchsafed to remain unchanged: it continued along the path of consolidation. It was under Elizabeth that the practice of selling individual serfs without land, apart from their families, was first engaged in on a large scale. The practice was to become especially widespread in the decades to follow. Then a well-known decree appeared in 1760 permitting landlords to exile to Siberia remiss or culpable peasants, and to count them toward their recruitment quotas. Only those peasants who were capable of working were to be exiled. Once in Siberia, they would become free and be utilized by the state to settle the region. Still further deprivation of the serfs' remaining freedom was at hand. The case could not have been otherwise for, after all, the serf foundations of social relations and the uneven development of the individual juridical estates had led to a situation whereby the "emancipation" of the nobility could only be accomplished at the expense of the serfs. In effect, the freer the nobles became, the more firmly the serfs were transformed into slaves.

* * *

The innovations in the financial and economic realms instituted primarily at Peter Shuvalov's initiative were but part of a broader program of reform of Russian society put forward during Elizaveta Petrovna's reign. The atmosphere of the time and the ideology of Elizabeth's reign contributed to the fact that the potential for reform that had been pent up over the decades following Peter's death acquired a new quality. It became incarnated in a complex of ideas, the majority of which were to be realized in the future, but which ripened, were debated, and were popularized under Elizabeth. The groundwork for reform laid during her reign rendered all the easier its painless future realization. This was perhaps the most important contribution of this stage of Russian history, which had become a bridge, as it were, over which the Russian Empire was to cross into the next stage in its development.

Soon after ascending the throne, the empress ordered the Senate to review all the laws promulgated since the death of Peter I, with the

The punishment of criminals: slitting the nostrils and branding. From a painting by G. Geïssler.

intention of eliminating the contradictory principles embedded in the legislation. The task proved so difficult that over the course of the next eight years the Senate managed to review the laws only up to 1729. By 1754, Shuvalov managed to persuade Elizabeth of the senselessness of reviewing old decrees and the necessity of elaborating a new code of laws, an *Ulozhenie*. For that purpose, a special Codification Commission was created under the jurisdiction of the Senate. It received broad powers and displayed great activity. In addition to the commission itself the empress established thirty-five so-called particular [*chastnye*] commissions, or subcommissions, which were to prepare materials on specific matters. Responsibility for the preparation of the necessary materials was also laid upon administrative organs at the local level. Their views were sought on the most effective means of organizing local government administering justice. Following an enumeration of all civil servants holding offices on the Table of Ranks measures were also taken to strengthen and regularize the central administrative apparatus. For all practical purposes, according to the historian S.M. Troitskii, the enumeration constituted at the same time an evaluation of their performances, being accompanied by the promotion in rank of some and the retirement of others. In reality this proved the last all-encompassing review of what he terms the "gentry-bureaucrats."[21]

The product of the commission's activities was a draft law code consisting of three parts. The first two dealt with civil and criminal law, and the third—entitled "On the Status of Subjects in General"—was to become the foundation for Russian society's estate structure. The concentration of the commission's efforts on this last issue is noteworthy, revealing as it does that the need to establish a legislative framework for the estate structure was perceived as acute. However, the composition of the commission, which was made up of top state servitors, could not but tell on the nature of the document produced, which was infused with a pro-noble spirit. In compressed form it responded to just about all the noble estate's wishes and hopes. For example, it transformed the nobility into a closed corporation by abolishing the provisions of the Petrine Table of Ranks that allowed for entry into its ranks by non-nobles who achieved a certain grade in state service. Eliminated altogether was the principle of obligatory state service that had been strengthened in Petrine legislation.

The project also foresaw the elimination of torture, corporal punishment, and exile to hard labor as they applied to the nobility. It also abolished the state's practice of confiscating the estates of nobles who had committed criminal acts. In this fashion, private property in landed estates, and the serfs inhabiting them, was juridically guaranteed. Such property, moreover, was to become inalienable. Even more strikingly, the possession of landed property was to become the monopoly of the privileged nobility. Correspondingly, the right of non-nobles to purchase peasants for work in factories was to be eliminated. The nobility's monopoly on the distillation of alcohol was to be extended to other branches of industry: to metallurgy and glass making. Finally, a special article in the draft declared outright and in unambiguous fashion the right of the nobility to possess peasant "souls" and the right to complete freedom of action in its dealings with them.

The nobility's estate rights and privileges, that were incorporated in the draft of the law code dealt primarily with property and hence were economic in nature. The nobility's pretensions in the political realm were far more modest, focusing primarily on the demand to create organs of noble self-government at the local level and, in general, to hand over local administrative organs to landlords at the local level. It is indicative that there is not a trace in the proposed legislation of any effort to resurrect the conditions of 1730, which attempted to impose limitations on the autocracy. On the whole, however, these ideas had not died out in Russian society but rather were garbed in the dress of the concept of enlightened absolutism.

The activity of the Codification Commission stimulated the elaboration of various projects, which became a fashionable undertaking. Indeed, the second half of the eighteenth century provides the scholar with numerous and varied projects for governmental restructuring. One of them, carefully analyzed by Anisimov, flowed from the pen of Elizabeth's favorite, Ivan Shuvalov. In his project Shuvalov emerges as the proponent of the well-regulated state based upon the principle of mutual observation by the monarch and his or her subjects of "fundamental and unchanging" laws, a principle traceable to the ideas of Montesquieu. It was Shuvalov's intention that the empress even take a special oath binding herself and her successors to observe these laws. The laws, however, were not to be mere plagiarisms of Montesquieu's theories but rather were to take Russian conditions into account. Thus, the project called for a specific quota on the number of foreigners occupying important governmental posts, while key positions were to be filled exclusively by Russians. It was stated explicitly that the Russian throne could only be occupied by someone of the Orthodox faith. On the whole, though, Shuvalov's project lacked any clearly elaborated estate rights, foreseeing nothing more than the introduction of specific privileges for the nobility.[22]

The hopes of the drafters of the projects were not destined to be fulfilled. Elizaveta Petrovna devoted less and less attention to governmental affairs as time went on, and by the same token was less and less inclined to contemplate any serious reforms. To compound the problem, the period coincided with the Seven Years' War, which proved so debilitating for Russia.

* * *

The foreign policy problems Elizaveta Petrovna confronted immediately upon ascending the throne were complex and quite delicate. On the one hand, Russia was at war with Sweden, which had proclaimed as its objective the reestablishment on the Russian throne of

Peter I's posterity, to which Elizabeth belonged. To complicate matters, the empress's closest adviser was the French ambassador, to whom his government had sent instructions to obtain concessions for Sweden. On the other hand, the empress's proclamation of her determination to defend Petrine principles would not permit any concessions whatever to the Swedes. Indeed, concessions would have represented a direct betrayal of these principles. The facts that Europe was engaged in a war at the time over the Austrian succession, and that the two warring coalitions were vying to secure Russia's support, which might under the given conditions prove decisive, was a circumstance favorable to Russia. The chief "instigator" of the war was Prussia, which was just launching its long struggle to create a "greater Germany" and would henceforth act as the disturber of the peace in Europe. The foreign policy options with which Elizabeth's government was confronted boiled down to either taking Prussia's side in the struggle or else attempting to halt its expansion. The decision was to become historical in the true meaning of the term, and would long define the nature of Russo-German relations and the correlation of political forces on the continent.

From a purely theoretical point of view, one might have concluded at the time that a firm alliance of Russia with Prussia would lead to the immediate partition of Poland,* and subsequently all of Europe, between the two powers. It was, however, so obvious a possibility that Great Britain, France, Austria, and the Ottoman Empire, whatever the contradictions that might have divided them, would not have stood idly by and watched as Russia and Prussia asserted themselves as the masters of Europe. In the face of such a threat they might well have united. That step would have put an end to all of the projects, which in turn would have signified a serious defeat for Russia, one that could have long relegated it to the ranks of the second-rate powers. But all of this lies in the realm of speculation. In reality, Russia was confronted with the necessity, as before, of resolving two fundamental problems, the Polish and the Turkish, a conflict with the Turks being unavoidable.

---

*This is fundamentally V.P. Naumov's contention: "At that time the nation had to choose between two alternatives: to strengthen and enlarge its holdings along the Baltic Sea coast in struggle against Prussia, or else to resolve the 'Polish question' (the annexation of the Right-Bank Ukraine and Belorussia), which would have been possible only with the aid of a Russo-Prussian alliance" (Naumov, "Elizaveta Petrovna," *Voprosy istorii,* 1993, no. 5, p. 68).

Given the predictable Austrian opposition, this conflict would prove extremely hazardous.

The first steps Elizabeth took in the international arena were cautious but firm. In peace negotiations with Sweden, with France serving as mediator, Russia refused to consider any territorial concessions whatsoever. In 1742, Swedish intractability led to a renewal of military activity, as a result of which the Russian army occupied almost all of Finland. In 1743, Sweden was forced to sign a peace treaty at Åbo. All the while the "French party" at the Russian court actively intrigued in favor of Prussia, with its efforts leading in the same year to a treaty of alliance, by the terms of which France and Russia agreed to assist each other in the event of an attack by a third party. Meanwhile, Frederick II's agents were doing everything they could to exacerbate relations between Russia and Austria, hoping in the process to exploit the "Lopukhina Affair," in which the Austrian minister was enmeshed. But the "French party" bumped up against a powerful opponent in the person of Vice-Chancellor Aleksei Petrovich Bestuzhev-Riumin, a talented diplomat and firm proponent of the Petrine principles of Russian foreign policy.

Bestuzhev proposed that Russian foreign policy be based on three very important alliances: with the maritime powers of Britain and the United Provinces of the Netherlands, with Saxony, and with Austria. The goal of his policy was to forestall an accretion in strength by any power whatsoever, which was understood to mean chiefly Prussia, but Sweden, Poland, and the Ottoman Porte as well. Thus, Bestuzhev's foreign policy doctrine bore a clearly expressed anti-Prussian character. Frederick II spent a great deal of effort trying to dislodge the Vice-Chancellor from power, but in vain. Even the "Lopukhina Affair," in which the wife of Bestuzhev's brother was also enmeshed, failed to affect the empress's relationship with him. The apologies offered by Maria Theresa in conjunction with this affair even contributed to a rapprochement between Russia and Austria. A major role in all of this intrigue was obviously played by Elizabeth's hostility toward Frederick II, whose malignant gossip at Elizabeth's expense was common knowledge in Petersburg. In 1744, Bestuzhev, as already mentioned, managed to gain the removal of Chétardie from court. This was a major victory for the experienced statesman, who had no qualms whatever about resorting to the most sensitive intrigue—the interception and deciphering of the dispatches of foreign diplomats, bribery, and other weapons available in the arsenal of the diplomacy of the time—in order to achieve his ends.

That same year, Russia concluded an alliance with Saxony, and Bestuzhev was named Chancellor. When in the fall of 1744 war over Silesia between Prussia on the one hand and Austria and Saxony on the other broke out, the court of St. Petersburg chose to interpret Prussia's actions as aggressive. The empress decided to enter on the Saxon side, and Russian forces in the Baltic region were ordered to prepare for the forthcoming military campaign. As a result, Prussia was compelled to make peace with its enemies. In 1746, Bestuzhev's years of effort were crowned with the signing of a defensive alliance with Austria. The treaty contained secret articles obligating the two sides to act jointly against Prussia and the Ottoman Empire. Soon thereafter, Russia did in fact intervene in the War of Austrian Succession by signing an agreement with Great Britain stipulating that a Russian force of thirty thousand troops be moved toward the Rhine River. This step had a substantial impact on the negotiations at Aachen, hastening the signing of a peace treaty.

These events, coupled with Russia's efforts to counter attempts to reestablish an absolutist regime in Sweden, led to a break in relations with France and Prussia. Within a few years, however, a dramatic regrouping of the major powers took place, one linked with the worsening of relations between France and Britain. In its search for new allies, France drew closer to Austria and Russia. For a time, the latter attempted to maintain good relations with both Britain and France; but the signing in London in 1755 of a British treaty with the Prussian king finally tipped the scales in favor of a Russian alliance with France and Austria. Russia began to push for renewed war, willing to use all means at its disposal to prevent Prussia from growing stronger. Frederick II resolved to get the jump on his opponents, and in August 1756 again marched his troops into Silesia. The attack marked the start of the Seven Years' War, into which Russia entered on the first day of September.

The clash with Prussia was unquestionably the product of the application of Bestuzhev's foreign policy doctrine over the course of time. But the war was to reveal the doctrine's shortcomings. Bestuzhev had assumed that the powerful alliance of Russia with Austria would frighten Frederick II into inactivity, while the permanent presence of a small Russian corps in Europe would head off full-scale war. The victim of his own illusions, the Chancellor had overlooked Prussia's military preparations. Taking advantage of several years of peace, that nation had managed to mobilize, equip, and train the best army in Europe. Even when war broke out, Bestuzhev's illusions did not immediately dissipate.

Not until January 1757 was a Russian plan for the forthcoming campaign in place, and only in May did the Russian army under the command of Field Marshal Stepan Fedorovich Apraksin march off from its headquarters in Riga for East Prussia, with the objective of seizing Königsberg. Apraksin showed no inclination to hurry. In the middle of July he crossed the frontier, and a month later, on August 15, 1757, he engaged a Prussian army in battle at Grossjägersdorf. The Russian army, which enjoyed a substantial superiority in numbers over the Prussian, suffered twice as many casualties as the Prussian but nonetheless gained the victory. For reasons that still remain unclear, Apraksin failed to take full advantage of the victory. He opted not to pursue the enemy, deciding instead to carry out meaningless maneuvers that exhausted his troops without contributing to the realization of the campaign's objectives.

Most historians, echoing Apraksin's contemporaries, suggest that Apraksin feared for the rapidly deteriorating health of the empress, being fully aware that the heir to the throne, Grand Duke Petr Fedorovich, wholeheartedly opposed the war with Prussia. In October 1757, Apraksin was replaced. In his stead the empress assigned General Villim Villimovich Fermor, son of an English immigrant. The removal of Apraksin, who was accused of high treason, led to Bestuzhev's downfall. In February 1758, the Chancellor was arrested at a session of the Conference at the Imperial Court and handed over for trial. He was condemned to death, but Elizabeth commuted the sentence to banishment to his estate. As her new Chancellor she named Count Mikhail Vorontsov, a proponent of Russo-French rapprochement.

Meanwhile, the war continued unabated. In January 1758, the Russian army took Königsberg and then pressed deeper into Brandenburg. In August it engaged Frederick II's forces at Zorndorf. After a battle that proved bloody and exhausting for both sides, Fermor gave the order to retreat, a measure that was generally interpreted as evidence of a Russian defeat. The first year or so of war had revealed serious shortcomings in the Russian army; so during the second half of 1758 and the beginning of 1759, it was reinforced and reequipped. In the spring of 1759, it received still another commander-in-chief. Peter Saltykov was named Fermor's replacement. Linking up with an Austrian corps, Saltykov won a huge victory at Kunersdorf in the spring. The victory did not, however, usher in an immediate end to hostilities, although in September 1760, a Russian cavalry unit occupied Berlin for a brief period of time. Not until 1761, when the two allies, Russia and Austria, had exhausted their enemy, did they seem to be on the verge of crushing Prussia decisively. But it was not to be: for on December 25, 1761, Empress Elizaveta Petrovna died. Peter III, who succeeded his aunt, ordered an immediate cessation of hostilities.

Grand Duke Petr Fedorovich, who was born Karl Peter Ulrich, Duke of Holstein, and who now became emperor Peter III, was the son of Elizabeth's older sister, Anna Petrovna, via her marriage to Karl Friedrich, Duke of Holstein. Anna herself had died in 1728, soon after giving birth to Peter. Her orphaned son (he lost his father in 1739) was hastily summoned to Russia at the beginning of 1742, proclaimed heir to the Russian throne, baptized in the Orthodox faith, and given the name of Petr Fedorovich. In 1745, he was married to Sophie Auguste Friederike, Princess of Anhalt-Zerbst. The marriage would prove unsuccessful, to put it mildly. The prince's character was so unbearable, if contemporary accounts are to be believed, that Elizaveta Petrovna often wept when contemplating her nephew's demeanor, foreseeing as she did that his reign would prove disastrous for Russia. The empress could not, however, bring herself to deprive Peter of his right to the throne.

On December 25, 1761, at a time when all of the churches in Russia were conducting festive Christmas services, and the priests, who knew nothing of what had just happened, were leading prayers for Elizaveta Petrovna's health, the nation lurched into a new period in its history. The middle of the century had come to an end; its second half was beginning.

Chapter 6

The Age of Catherine the Great

The death of Empress Elizaveta Petrovna at the very end of 1761 heralded the start of the shortest reign in Russian history, that of Peter III, which lasted a grand total of six months. Contemporaries and historians are all but unanimous in their evaluation of this ruler. "Nervous," "overly sensitive," "impatient," "stubborn," "capricious," and "cowardly" are some of the adjectives they use to describe Peter the Great's grandson. Such adjectives, and others of a similar sort, leap out at us from the pages of memoir literature and historical works.

Despite his years in Russia, where he landed as a thirteen-year-old, Peter never managed to become attached to the homeland of his ancestors, much less take a liking to it. Russia's traditions and customs, its interests and its people, remained alien to him. It is hard to say just what was responsible for this state of affairs: natural inclinations, a faulty upbringing, the "golden cage" in which Elizabeth kept him, or perhaps a combination of all three. The historian V.P. Naumov is quite possibly correct in suggesting that if fate had placed Peter not on the Russian throne but the Swedish, to which he also had a claim, he might well have managed "to live a long and happy life, to marry successfully, and to acquire glory by his great deeds."[1] But fate decreed that he become heir to the Russian throne.

Peter's pro-Prussian sympathies, his proclivity for hollering out during church services, and his love for beer and tobacco and military games, were all well known to Petersburg society. The emperor's lack of statesman-like qualities, his capriciousness and unpredictability rendered him dangerous to his court retinue as well as to the nation's future as a whole. Despite the passage of time, moreover, he never managed to establish a satisfactory relationship with his wife, who was far more developed intellectually and spiritually, and who, cleverly playing on the contrast, garnered significantly more sympathy than her husband both at court and among the population at large. As a consequence, dissatisfaction began to grow from the very first days of Peter's accession to the throne. Just as predictably, conspiracies aimed at his overthrow began to be hatched.

Peter himself appeared to neither understand nor notice any of this. Like a child who has eluded the supervision of grownups, he took great delight in being able to do whatever came into his head and to live however he wanted. As was his habit, he continued to offend the public during religious ceremonies; drill his soldiers endlessly; arrange boisterous evening feasts with friends; and appear in public with his mistress, Elizaveta Romanovna Vorontsova. Nonetheless, during his brief six-month rule he managed to implement several important domestic political reforms as well as alterations in the nation's foreign policy. In February 1762, the emperor promptly signed three very important decrees: on the elimination of the Secret Chancellery, on the freedom of the nobility, and on the secularization of church estates.

The Secret Chancellery had served the regime assiduously throughout Elizabeth's reign, striking fear in the hearts of her subjects, who understood only too well that since the authorities were prepared to deal so ruthlessly with important court figures and aristocrats, the life of an ordinary subject was not worth a plugged nickel. Given the ubiquitousness of denunciation, any word blurted out in anger could instantly transform its speaker into a traitor or rebel. Peter III's decree forbad the utterance of that infamous phrase "the Sovereign's word and deed" [*slovo i delo gosudarevo*], by which subjects were to alert the authorities to lèse-majesté, while the very name of the Secret Chancellery, which had elicited such fear and terror, was to be consigned to oblivion. Political investigation was not of course eliminated altogether; but it was now more open; responsibility for it was distributed among several agencies; and the role of denunciation in Russian life was, if not eliminated entirely, at least curtailed.

The promulgation of the manifesto on the freedom of the nobility, signed by Peter III on February 18, 1762, represented a new stage in the consolidation of the Russian nobility as a juridical estate. The most important of the manifesto's stipulations freed the nobles from obligatory service to the state. Henceforth, they could choose to serve or not

Peter III. From a portrait by Johann Stenglin.

to serve, and could even travel abroad freely and enter the service of friendly foreign governments, a step that formerly was considered treasonous. Here we have a change in the very foundations of the relationship between state and nobility. The nobility was now emancipated from the fetters of serfdom to the state and had acquired personal freedom. The case can be made that it was only from this time on that the term "ruling class" may legitimately be applied to the Russian nobility.

One concrete manifestation of the measure's consequences that has been noted by scholars was the stream of nobles abandoning state service in the first few years after its promulgation. The phenomenon had extremely important societal, cultural, and moral repercussions. Thousands of nobles returned to their manorial estates to live, thus significantly enlivening the cultural life of Russia's provincial towns and the architecture of manor houses in the second half of the eighteenth century.[2] It was also at this time that we find emerging the provincial noble so familiar to us in the classical Russian literature of the nineteenth century. As Isabel de Madariaga has observed, "The manifesto did open the way to the creation of a totally new class in Russia, what one might call 'private man' as distinct from service man, society as distinct from and opposed to the state.... [T]he Russian noble was at last on a par with the gentry and nobility of other countries."[3]

Another aspect of the February 18 manifesto has attracted the attention of scholars, one linked with its influence on the development of the Russian bureaucracy. The concentration of a large number of nobles in the provinces reinforced their desire to take control of local administrative organs. Related to this phenomenon, the historian S.M. Troitskii believes that the massive retirement of nobles from state service encouraged a flow of members from other, nonprivileged social groups into the bureaucracy.[4] The recent research of I.V. Faizova indicates, however, that the massive retirements of the first few years of the manifesto's existence took place chiefly in the military sector. Moreover, many of those who left military service subsequently transferred into civil service. As a result, within three years the state, faced with a surplus of civil servants, was forced to limit the freedom of such transfers.[5] Faizova's findings underscore the substantial changes that had taken place in the consciousness and value system of the Russian nobles, who but a few decades earlier had considered civil service "degrading" to their dignity and honor: in short, ignoble. This change can no doubt be traced back to the nation's Europeanization, to the penetration into Russian society of the ideas of rationalism and enlightenment. Then there was the fact that civil service in Russia, directly associated with access to limitless state revenues, was economically far more lucrative than military service. Leaving aside the economic aspects, the manifesto on the freedom of the nobility took into account the estate's most important concerns, which had been formulated in the draft produced by Elizabeth's Legislative Commission.

The decree on the secularization of ecclesiastical estates—that is, the transfer to state control of the landed possessions of monasteries and other church institutions, together with the serfs who inhabited them—had been awaited just as long. This measure too had long since been prepared by Elizabeth's ministers. It was only the empress's indecisiveness that had prevented its implementation. Secularization represented still one more step in the direction of undermining the authority of the Russian Orthodox Church, of transforming it into just another state agency. From this time forth, the church was deprived of its primary source of revenue, which had permitted it to retain a degree of independence from the state. The state, in its turn, was always in great need of resources, and thanks to secularization it could put its hands on a new and very substantial source of revenue.

All three of Peter III's domestic political reforms were unquestionably in keeping with the modernizing direction of the nation's development and, it would seem, should have garnered the emperor popularity and support. But this was not the case. In the first place, it was well known that the reforms' real author was not Peter himself but his ministers, who had already prepared them under Elizaveta Petrovna. In the second, Peter displayed unseemly haste in implementing them, signing three decrees within three days, thus making it clear that he lacked any coherent and cohesive political reform program. And while in February he had heeded the wise counsel of those surrounding him, it was impossible to predict what his next steps would be. Offsetting the potential advantages Peter might have derived from his reforms was his attitude toward Orthodoxy, which generated nothing but unhappiness and frustration. Rumors abounded that he intended to alter Orthodox ritual, remove icons from the churches, and force Russian clergymen to shave their beards and wear Lutheran-style frock coats instead of cassocks.[6]

The emperor heaped insult on injury by the measures he undertook in the military and foreign policy spheres. Distrusting with good reason the loyalty of the guards regiments that were quartered in St. Petersburg, Peter as his first official step disbanded the Life Guards Company, the privileged unit of the Preobrazhenskii Regiment that had raised Elizaveta Petrovna to the throne in 1741. His foreign policy changes compounded his problems. Refusing to postpone the matter for further deliberation, the new emperor hastily concluded peace, and then arranged an alliance, with Prussia. In keeping with its terms, he handed back all the territory the Russian army had conquered at such great cost in the course of the Seven Years' War. Then, decked out in a Prussian-style military uniform, he proceeded to praise the achievements of the Prussian army.

Peter's prime foreign-policy objective was to claim back from Denmark the Duchy of Schleswig, which had once belonged to his Holstein ancestors in his father's line. Fatuously considering himself a great military leader, he declared war on Denmark and announced his intention of launching a campaign at the head of his guards regiments. The plan elicited no enthusiasm whatsoever from the guardsmen, who had no desire to abandon their comfortable St. Petersburg quarters for the sake of a senseless war that could not possibly bring Russia any benefit.

Given this unacceptable state of affairs, Peter III's overthrow was foreordained. On June 28, 1762, a coup d'état took place that led to the enthronement of Peter's wife, Ekaterina Alekseevna, known to history as Empress Catherine II. Several days thereafter Peter perished under mysterious circumstances at the Ropsha Palace, not far from Petersburg, where he was being kept under guard. According to one version, he died as the result of an unfortunate altercation that no one had planned, while according to another he was deliberately murdered by the very guardsmen who had been assigned to protect him.[7]

As was the case with preceding coups, that of June 1762 was the result of a sedulously prepared conspiracy. It was carried out by Catherine with, once more, the support of guards regiments. Still, it displayed its own specific characteristics. However paradoxical it might appear, this technically illegitimate action bore witness to Russian society's advance to a higher level in its intellectual and spiritual development. As events showed, Peter III was in essence a political figure without ties to the people, one who acted unrealistically and lacked the support of any concrete political or social force. For all practical purposes he was a petty tyrant, a despot. He seemed to have much in common with his grandfather, Peter I. But this was only at first glance, for the latter's measures were, when all was said and done, based on a specific outlook and, therefore, far more justified. Peter the Great also created a system that, as he himself acknowledged, entailed the notion of his own responsibilities toward his subjects (see Chapter 3), who could anticipate certain modes of behavior from the monarch.

In pre-Petrine times, the very existence of royal authority, regardless of who sat on the throne as long as he was the legitimate sovereign, was what was crucial to Russians. Now the mere legitimacy of authority was no longer in and of itself sufficient. More important now was the sovereign's political personality. A petty tyrant who took unjustifiable measures could not be accommodated in this system. In other words, Russian society, or at least its politically active component, had "matured" into a nonacceptance of petty tyranny.

Still one more observation remains to be made. Recently, works have appeared by several authors desperately anxious to prove that the image of Peter III that has taken shape in the historiography of the period has been distorted, thanks in large part to the efforts of his wife and other authors of tendentious memoirs. The most serious of the works on the subject stem from the pens of the Russian historian A.S. Mylnikov and his American counterpart Carol Leonard.[8] Although worthy of consideration, it seems to me, the material they present is still insufficient to warrant a fundamental reexamination of Peter III's historical role. It stands to reason that one ought not to allow an understandable sympathy, or even pity, for Peter as a person to influence one's judgment of Peter as an emperor. Eighteenth-century Russia, unfortunately, lacked the legal mechanisms capable of defending the nation and its people in instances in which someone incapable of ruling assumed power. The only available mechanism of self-regulation in such situations was the coup d'état.

* * *

No one else who has ever sat on the Russian throne has had as little legal claim to it as Catherine II. She could be compared with the first False Dmitrii, the pretender who occupied the throne by deceit at the beginning of the seventeenth century. But he had held power for less than a year when, cursed by the population and the church, he perished

The Age of Catherine the Great

at the hands of assassins. Catherine's reign, which lasted almost thirty-four years, proved to be one of the most felicitous in Russian history. In the 1830s, the philosopher Peter Chaadaev, declared insane by Emperor Nicholas I because he dared to subject Russia's past to merciless criticism and to question its future, suggested that "it is unnecessary to speak of Catherine II's reign, which bore such a national character. It was [a reign] in which perhaps no other people could identify so completely with their government as the Russian people did with theirs in those years of victories and felicity."[9] Her subjects called Catherine, a German, "Little Mother," and bestowed upon her the title of "The Great." And when she died, according to P.A. Viazemskii, "The English minister to Catherine's court, who was present at the burial, observed: 'On enterre la Russie'" [They are burying Russia].[10] The phenomenon of Catherine II was both unique and simultaneously characteristic of eighteenth-century Russia. It was she who was destined to complete many of Peter I's projects and to put forward new principles of governance, greatly altering the nation's visage and the relationship between state power and the public.

The new empress was born April 21, 1729, in Stettin, in what was then Prussia but is now Poland, into the family of Prince Christian August of Anhalt-Zerbst and his wife, Princess Johanna Elisabeth. At her birth the baby was given the name of Sophie Auguste Friederike, receiving the name of Catherine [Ekaterina] in Russia in 1744 when she formally converted to Orthodoxy. From the very beginning, Catherine's character, her desires, and her spiritual quests and needs differed dramatically from those of her husband. She was intelligent, clever, and ambitious, and she understood perfectly well that in the person of her husband, Peter, fate had smiled upon her, and so she was prepared to fight for her fortune with all her might. In the eighteen years that separated her arrival in Russia from her accession to the throne she sought to comprehend as best she could the nation, its history, its traditions, and its customs. She herself subsequently admitted that she had seized any occasion she could to win over the sympathies of her future subjects. She was demonstratively pious, generous in her gift-giving, and not at all reluctant to flatter shamelessly. As a result, she was enormously successful in achieving her objectives.

Life with an unloved husband was of course no bed of roses for the young and attractive wife. It is therefore hardly surprising that in the early 1750s she took three lovers, one after the other. In the following

Catherine II. Engraving from a portrait by L.M. Bonne.

decades, they would be replaced by still others, giving rise to numerous rumors and legends, and presenting fertile ground for the authors of historical novels and film scenarios.[11] In reality, however, Catherine was neither a nymphomaniac nor a Messalina. Her private life for all practical purposes was screened from outside view. If her favorites received ranks and awards, as they did, it was because that was the natural way for the empress to express her benevolence toward them. Real power always remained in her own hands.

Rather early in life Catherine took a liking to reading, and she soon graduated from fluffy French novels to serious works on history, jurisprudence, and philosophy. By the mid-1750s the works of Voltaire and other Enlightenment figures—those who at the time shaped the thinking of educated Europeans—graced her table. Once on the throne, she herself turned to writing. Plays, articles, fairy tales, memoirs, and works on history and linguistics all flowed from her pen. And all of this was in addition to the extensive correspondence she carried on over many years with numerous Russian and foreign correspondents as well as her work on broad legislative projects, only a portion of which she managed to carry to fruition. Catherine II stands apart from all the other Russian tsars and tsaritsas by dint of her education, the quality of her mind, and her ability to pose key questions, making her a true intellectual on the throne.

While attracted to "elevated" ideas, Catherine II was by no means removed from down-to-earth concerns. One of the most important of her human qualities, and that which helped determine her conduct, was her love of power. For the sake of preserving that power she was prepared to sacrifice any of her principles and philosophical ideas. She was, moreover, an experienced courtier, one who was able to judge people, understand their psychological profile, take advantage of their strengths and weaknesses, and yet make herself pleasant and likable to them. Many authors of memoir literature have noted that Catherine was a wonderful conversationalist, capable of listening to and grasping others' ideas and adapting them to her own purposes. While she was not indifferent to flattery, she assigned the most important state posts to those who possessed the requisite knowledge and capacity. Those whom she considered useful she was prepared to tolerate around her as long as they performed their duties. Associated with Catherine II's reign are the names of a whole pleiad of such talented state figures as A.G. Orlov,

A.A. Viazemskii, N.I. Panin, A.R. Vorontsov, G.A. Potemkin, A.A. Bezborodko, and I.I. Betskoi. Earning glory by their military exploits were A.V. Suvorov, P.A. Rumiantsev, F.A. Ushakov, and G.A. Spiridov. They were first and foremost the empress's loyal servitors; she never shared her power with any of them. The principles of selection used to fill the top ranks did not exclude court intrigue, struggles among court cliques, and other features normally associated with sovereignty, especially with absolute sovereignty. But the role they played at Catherine's court was less prominent that it had been during her predecessors' reigns.

Constantly occupied with affairs of state; faced with deciding major and minor issues on a daily basis; and relaxing by engaging in writing, reading, and corresponding with prominent figures, Catherine was a true workaholic. Here is how she herself described her working day to one of her correspondents in 1774:

> My health does not worry me in the least. I get up at six o'clock at the latest, and sit until eleven in my office, where I receive not he who is in favor but he who has business to discuss with me. I often receive people whose names I hardly even know. Those who enjoy my favor have been trained to leave if they are not there on business. After lunch there is nothing [scheduled], while in the evening I meet with whomever wants to come, and head off to bed at ten thirty at the very latest.[12]

At the time of her accession to the throne Catherine was well versed in the most recent achievements of European philosophy and political and economic thought, on the basis of which she formed her ideas about what was necessary for the state's well-being. When combined with her knowledge of Russian reality, these ideas contributed a number of principles to the empress's political program. Several of them, as well as the tactics for their realization, were adjusted over time, but the basic objectives and principles remained unchanged. In view of the fact that the ideological underpinnings of this program and, therefore, of the domestic politics of the era, were based on Enlightenment ideas, this period of Russian history itself has been labeled in the historical literature the period of "enlightened absolutism."

It should be noted that the assertions just made are far from universally accepted. Based on their evaluations of Catherine's domestic policies, historians can be grouped into several competing camps. Many suggest, for example, that the empress made attempts at liberal reform only in the first years of her reign, and then shifted to a political course openly favoring the nobility. Others refuse to recognize two periods in her reign, claiming that Catherine adhered to a pronoble policy consistently from beginning to end. Widespread in Soviet historical literature was the thesis that the ideals enunciated by Catherine were impossible to harmonize with the reality of serfdom that defined Russia in the second half of the eighteenth century. Historians of this school maintained that assertions of enlightenment, and the liberal phraseology employed by Catherine II in general, were nothing more than a smoke screen behind which a hypocritical empress managed to hide her vanity and ambition and masked what were in actuality her reactionary views. Alexander Pushkin's oft-quoted observation, drawing upon Molière, that Catherine was "a Tartuffe in a skirt and a crown" served as their point of departure. Bound up with such debates was the question of the legitimacy of applying the label "enlightened absolutism" to her reign. It is no accident that a number of Western scholars substitute for it the term "enlightened despotism." The question "Was Catherine II an enlightened despot?" has truly become a staple in the scholarly literature and on midterm exams.[13]

The most recent attempt to resolve this question was undertaken by Russian legal historian Oleg Omelchenko, who examined in great detail Catherine's reform projects, unpromulgated as well as promulgated. He concluded that the strivings and hopes of "enlightened absolutism" in no way impinged upon the nobility's social position, the monarchic form of state organization, or the feudal bureaucracy. But at the same time, according to Omelchenko, the goal of "enlightened absolutism" was to "create exclusively by means of legislative policy a renovated state and legal structure that embodied the ideal of 'legal monarchy,' one in which public stability would be based upon social consensus and a policy of state liberalism."[14] One can easily discern the numerous contradictions in the passage cited, for "social consensus" could be achieved only by concession on the part of the nobility as well as other estates. May one moreover reproach "enlightened *absolutism*" for failure to struggle with absolutism? More importantly, when all is said and done, the term "enlightened absolutism" is but one of a number of labels historians are prone to attach to phenomena of the past, which once attached, often overshadow the actual substance of those phenomena. Let us therefore attempt simply to examine the facts, discovering just what ideas formed the basis of Catherine's policies, how she converted them into reality, and also what the most important events were that occurred over the course of her thirty-four year reign.

The ideas of the French Enlightenment philosophes (chiefly Montesquieu) concerning the well-regulated state, which was to be erected on an estate structure based on fundamental law, and the mutual obligations of the monarch and his subjects, formed the core of the empress's theoretical views. She superimposed them on her own notions of Russia's national interests and needs. First and foremost, Catherine considered herself the inheritor and perpetuator of the legacy of Peter the Great, with whom she would contend for praise throughout her life. Catherine saw his chief attainment as the Europeanization of Russia, as his transformation of the nation into a mighty empire capable of playing a leading role in international affairs. She was convinced that the very success of the Petrine reforms offered the most convincing proof for Russia's claim to membership in European civilization. At the same time, the empress viewed contemporaneous Europe rather critically, and by no means considered it necessary to borrow from it wholesale. Moreover, with the passage of time, as she became a true Russian patriot, she persuaded herself that in many respects Europe should look to Russia as an example rather than vice versa. But Catherine viewed critically the haste and ferocity with which Peter I had carried out his reforms. For her the principle of gradualness was one of the most important. Nicholas Riasanovsky had described Catherine's attitude toward Peter the Great's legacy in the following fashion:

> Catherine's close attention to the first emperor led also to criticisms, which, apparently, deepened with the passage of years.... [M]ost of her observations were, no doubt, her own, based on her constant rethinking of the role of the reformer.... Concerned especially with the ideal of the just legislator ... Catherine II found Peter the Great sadly wanting. His laws ... were essentially the old, backward and cruel *Ulozhenie* of 1649, and he failed to make them more modern and humane. In fact, he tended to emphasize punishment and to rule by fear rather than through love and approbation of his subjects. Although the

enlightened German empress approved the direction of the Russian ruler's reforms, his desire that the old world be replaced by the new, he himself, in her perspective . . . belonged too much to that old world.[15]

Catherine II elaborated her own "rules for administration" in the form of "Five Subjects." This is how she adumbrated them:

1. One must complete the civilizing of the nation one has been called upon to govern.
2. One must introduce good order into the state, uphold [civil] society, and see that it obeys the laws.
3. One must institute good and effective regulatory power in the state.
4. One must facilitate the flourishing of the state and render it prosperous.
5. One must render the state feared in and of itself and respected by its neighbors.

Each citizen must be taught to recognize his obligations toward the Supreme Being, toward himself, and toward society; and one must teach that citizen certain skills, without which he will barely get along in everyday life.[16]

* * *

Having ascended the throne, Catherine proceeded from the very first months of her reign to mark out new approaches toward resolving existing problems. Reluctant to implement her ideas immediately, she first attempted to familiarize herself with the state of affairs. To deal with a number of vital questions, she created commissions composed of upper-level civil servants, who were assigned the task of examining given problems and proposing solutions to the empress. In that way Catherine seemed to be giving her subjects the chance to tackle these problems in their own fashion. It was not possible, however, to postpone all decision making. So in the first years of Catherine II's reign, which in general were devoted to preparation for reform, important reforms were actually implemented in several areas. The first dealt with the central administrative apparatus, the most important being the Senate reform of 1763.

As the reader will have noted from previous chapters, the functions of the Senate changed constantly in the post-Petrine period. These functions depended on the emergence of other institutions that were from time to time elevated above it in the bureaucratic hierarchy. To a significant degree, the emergence of other institutions was mandated by the structural inadequacies of the Senate itself as it had been created by Peter I. His grandson Peter III abolished Elizabeth's Conference at the Imperial Court and replaced it with his Imperial Council, which in its turn was eliminated by his widow Catherine. True, the project for an institution similar to her husband's had been proposed to her, and she even seemed disposed to sign the corresponding decree. In this instance, the project had been proposed by Nikita Ivanovich Panin, one of the most talented state dignitaries of Catherine's reign. He suggested to the empress the creation of an executive institution whose rights would be juridically recognized, and although they would not be as extensive as those of the Supreme Privy Council as outlined in the "Conditions" originally signed by Anna Ioannovna, would nonetheless represent a concrete limitation on the powers of the monarch. But perceiving that Panin's intentions did not enjoy broad public support, Catherine declined to sign the project. Only later, in 1769, did she create a council, which was assigned advisory rather than executive powers.

The need for the Senate's reorganization was clear-cut. Its decrees were poorly implemented and matters took months, and at times even years, to resolve, while the Senators themselves were not particularly competent. As Catherine herself discovered when she attended several of its sessions, the members did not even have any idea how many towns there were in the Russian Empire. The plan for the reorganization of the Senate, also prepared by Panin, but in this case confirmed by the empress, called for its division into six departments with clearly defined functions and spheres of competence. The Senate was deprived of its legislative function but preserved its supervisory one intact, remaining the highest court of appeal. The linkage of these last two functions in one institution constituted its chief weakness, although it did for a time enable the central administrative apparatus to operate more precisely and more efficiently.

Another important reform dating from the first years of Catherine II's reign was also associated with Peter III's legacy. Upon ascending the throne, the empress promptly declared null and void the secularization of church estates, a measure of her husband's that had aroused much antipathy among the clergy. The problem of what to do with those estates, however, remained, and in the first year of her reign the empress formed a special commission to study the matter. Over a period of a year and a half, the commission drew up another variant of the secularization reform and gradually prepared society for it. In February 1764, Catherine II signed the corresponding decree. All monastery and other church estates, together with the serfs living on them, were placed under the jurisdiction of the Collegium of Economy, an institution specially created for that purpose. Accordingly, the erstwhile church peasants now became known as economic peasants, while their legal position approximated that of state peasants. All their taxes they now paid directly to the state, a measure that for them entailed a significant lessening of their burden.

About two million peasants benefited from the reform. They were relieved of their labor obligations to the religious institutions, saw an increase in the size of their landed allotments, and now found it easier to engage in trade and handicraft. In the broader picture, the significance of this reform lay in the fact that the number of privately owned serfs diminished, thus narrowing the scope of serfdom as an institution. It should be noted that, over the course of her reign, when distributing lands with tens of thousands of enserfed peasants on them as rewards to those close to her, Catherine II refused to touch the economic peasants, preferring instead to pass out inhabited lands acquired specifically for that purpose or else escheated manorial estates.

Another consequence of the secularization reform was associated with the condition of the Russian Orthodox Church. Because the state now maintained the monasteries and the monks in them from its own funds, it took it upon itself to decide from this time forth how many of each the nation needed. The clergy was in effect transformed into just another component of the state bureaucracy, while the state expanded its capacity to interfere in the spiritual life of its subjects. In attempting to implement her ideas for the creation of a juridically defined estate-based society in Russia, Catherine never tried to transform the clergy into a full-fledged estate.

A third reform of the first years of Catherine II's reign, and one that exerted just as long-range an impact on the fate of the nation and its population, also dealt with the administrative system. Catherine found intolerable a situation in which a number of the nation's regions had preserved their traditional forms of administration, forms that usually dated back prior to the territories' integration into the Russian Empire. The empress was persuaded that the entire nation ought to be governed by a uniform set of laws and principles. Especially intolerable from her point of view was the situation in the Ukraine, which had preserved its autonomous status, thus hindering the full exploitation of its colonial dependence on Russia. In particular, Ukrainian peasants had preserved the right to move freely from one landlord to another, a right that from the Russian perspective complicated the collection of taxes from them. Early in 1764, in a secret directive to Prince A.A. Viazemskii appointing him Procurator-General of the Senate, Catherine II wrote:

> Little Russia [the Ukraine], Livonia, and Finland are provinces governed by privileges that they have had confirmed. To abolish them all at once would be quite unseemly. But to label [these provinces] foreign countries, and to deal with them on such a basis, would be more than a mistake, it would be truly stupid. These provinces, as well as Smolensk, should by the gentlest of means be brought to the point where they russify, and stop looking around like wolves to the forest.... Once Little Russia has no more hetmen, an attempt must be made to see that the very title of "hetman" disappears forever.[17]

In autumn 1764, Catherine accepted the resignation of the last Ukrainian hetman, Count Kirill Razumovskii. She then proceeded to name Count Peter Rumiantsev governor-general of the Ukraine. Over the next couple of years the last vestiges of the former Cossack "freedom" were gradually eliminated, as were the Ukraine's separate system of administrative-territorial division and its municipal freedoms. A May 1783 decree forbad all peasant movement permanently in any part of the empire, an act that signified the consolidation of the system of serf relations in the Ukraine. A policy directed at the unification of the nation's administrative system continued to be pursued persistently in the following years, facilitating the formation of the Russian Empire as a unified state, which in turn may have helped prolong its life.

When describing Catherine II's nationality policy, mention must be made of one of its innovations: the invitation to Europeans to settle in Russia. In contrast with policy of the preceding decades, it was not merely a limited group of foreign specialists that was being invited in. To begin with, Catherine was quite familiar with the widespread economic doctrine of populationism, or the utility to be derived by the state from increasing the nation's population. As British historian Roger P. Bartlett notes, "her reign was in fact the first in Russia to show systematic concern with population."[18] Moreover, she invited to Russia simple peasants, and not for a specified period of time but permanently. Her primary objective was to settle the vacant lands along the lower Volga River and in the vicinity of the Ural Mountains and, eventually, the Crimea and the Northern Caucasus. It is worth pointing out that Catherine had no fear that free foreign peasants would set a dangerous example for Russian serfs. By the mid-1760s, more than thirty thousand colonists had arrived in Russia. They were granted extensive privileges, including credits to get established, large plots of land to farm, generous exemptions from taxation and conscription, and religious freedom.

A propos of religious freedom, it should be noted that although Catherine was always demonstratively pious and at every turn paraded her adherence to Orthodoxy, she manifested a tolerance toward other religions that one did not find in Elizaveta Petrovna. This toleration extended not only to other Christians such as Russian Old Believers, Catholics, and Protestants, but also to Muslims. Nor did she appear to bear an animus against Jews. When in the second half of her reign she found herself with a rather substantial Jewish population as a result of the first partition of Poland, she initially extended the same rights to it as to the rest of the population. Pressure, however, from the Orthodox clergy and the Russian merchantry, which feared competition from Jewish traders, forced Catherine in 1791 to establish the infamous pale of settlement, which limited the right of Jews to settle in specified parts of the country, live in the two capitals, study at institutions of higher learning, and so forth.

To return to the commissions established by Catherine in the early 1760s, the results of their deliberations apparently failed to satisfy her. She persuaded herself that their members were simply looking out for their own narrow estate interests. Yet she did study in detail the materials these commissions produced, and she eventually made use of them in her own legislative efforts. It was at this stage that she decided to enlarge the circle of those who were involved in the fate of the reforms. Her method was to convene a legislative commission made up of representatives from the nation's various social and ethnic groups and regions. This new institution received the old designation of the Commission to Compile a Draft for a New Law Code, or Legislative

Commission. It was to be composed of elected deputies who were to bring with them mandates, or instructions [*nakazy*], from their constituents. Having no intention of abdicating the role of enlightened lawgiver, Catherine compiled for the Commission's deputies her own instructions, in which she outlined her notions of the proper content and character of the laws to be codified.

The empress launched work on her Grand Instructions [*Bolshoi nakaz*] early in 1765, attempting to incorporate into them the basic ideas of Montesquieu and other prominent Enlightenment philosophers and legal experts of the time. After completing work on the Instructions, Catherine felt compelled to show them to those in her immediate entourage, on whom her hold on the throne to a certain degree depended. Thus the Instructions were in a sense subjected to censorship, as a result of which some of the boldest political passages were excised. The documents that have been preserved enable us to ascertain that the issue of serfdom, which the empress considered economically harmful as well as contrary to the first principles of humanity and justice, proved the real bone of contention. For all practical purposes, Catherine II was the first Russian monarch to ponder the possibility of relieving the Russian social structure of this great evil. Yet the issue is not raised in the Instructions.

The Grand Instructions, published in July 1767, open with a consideration of the necessary nature of the laws, which are to correspond to the historical character of the people for whom they are being instituted. The salient characteristic of the Russian people, asserts Catherine, is that they are European. Yet for a nation as large as Russia the autocratic form of government is necessary, for any other form would prove destructive. The goal of absolute rule is the well-being of all the citizens. The autocratic sovereign rules in harmony with the laws, the observation of which the Senate oversees. All citizens are equal before the law, and are free to do whatever the laws allow. The laws therefore have to encompass all spheres of activity, and for that reason special chapters of the Instructions are devoted to trade, the population, the upbringing of children, and so forth. Based as they should be on the principle of private property, trade and production are essential to the state's well-being, which also depends on the proper upbringing of citizens consonant with the laws and the moral ideals of Christianity.

As one of its most important tasks, the Legislative Commission was to elaborate a set of laws for each of the individual, juridically defined estates. For that reason, special chapters of the Grand Instructions are devoted to the nobility and the townspeople, or "middle sort of people," as Catherine termed the third estate. The empress of course realized that a nobility already existed in Russia, and that it only remained to grant it the appropriate laws, whereas the third estate had to be created from scratch by means of legislation. There are no chapters on the peasantry in the Instructions, and it is not known whether they were in the original draft.

A substantial section of the document, based for the most part on the teachings of the Italian legal scholar Cesare Beccaria, is devoted to crime, investigation, trial, and punishment. The laws, wrote Catherine, had not been instituted to frighten but to help educate citizens. And punishment, whatever form it may take, must not be directed at torturing the criminal but rather at eliciting shame and repentance, for punishment is above all dishonor. That is all the more reason to have the punishment strictly fit the crime, for otherwise it would lose its meaning. Before a defendant is to be judged, the crime must be carefully investigated, and the accused must have the right to defend him- or herself. Only a court can pronounce a person guilty, while that person cannot be considered a criminal until the moment sentence is passed. Torture is inadmissible during the investigation, and there is little need for capital punishment. Such punishment should be reserved for those criminals who threaten the very existence of the state, its tranquility and well-being. As long as domestic and foreign stability prevails, the state is capable of defending itself without resorting to the death penalty.*

Such is the basic content of the Grand Instructions, one of the most significant documents of Catherine's reign. Many authors who deal with them complain that their maxims remained mere empty verbiage, never to be put into effect, or so it seems to them. One must bear in mind, however, that the Instructions were nothing more than guidelines for the deputies to the Legislative Commission, and it was they who

---

*This reservation deserves further elucidation. Unlike Elizabeth, Catherine II did not consider it necessary to abolish capital punishment altogether. Indeed, the first public execution in Catherine's reign took place as early as 1764, when Junior Lieutenant Vasilii Mirovich attempted to liberate the unfortunate Ivan Antonovich from Shlisselburg Fortress. In keeping with their orders, the former baby tsar's guards murdered him before he could be set free. Bereft of a purpose, Mirovich surrendered and was handed over for trial and executed.

were to draft and put into effect laws based on the principles the empress had elaborated. The very distribution of the Instructions exerted more than a little significance, all the more so since they bore the empress's imprimatur. Published in Russian and a number of other European languages, the Instructions were made available for sale to the general public. It is worth noting that they became popular in a number of European nations and were even banned from Louis XV's France because they were considered so revolutionary.

The Grand Instructions are written in simple, accessible language and the presentation of the ideas is rather commonplace. Most of those ideas were, however, completely new to eighteenth-century Russians. Of extraordinary importance in the Instructions was the enunciation of such concepts, hitherto unknown in Russian law, as the presumption of innocence and private property as the cornerstone for the development of an effective national economy. It is also indicative that the Instructions attributed such great significance to the formation of juridically defined estates, an objective posited as one of the basic goals of the intended reforms. The empress apparently had not yet fully comprehended that the resolution to this problem was bound up tightly with that of another—serfdom. If she did recognize the problem, she misled herself about the degree of "enlightenment" of her subjects. It is important to emphasize, however, that Catherine did accurately suspect that this was the most critical problem confronting the Russian political system, and that without a resolution to it modernization was headed down a dead-end path. It is evident, moreover, that she was satisfied with neither the draft project "On the Condition of Subjects in General" produced by Elizabeth's commission nor the draft on nobles' rights compiled in 1763 by a special commission on the rights of the nobility. The elevation of one estate at the expense of the others was obviously not to her liking.

One finds in the specialized literature the assertion that so far as Catherine was concerned, the Legislative Commission was nothing but a farce, and that she never held out any hopes for its activities. The existing documentation supports the contrary view. The empress truly believed that the commission would prove able to draft a system of laws, which she planned to cap with a new law on the succession to the throne, providing for succession in the male line. In her draft of this last law she noted that "in keeping with its nature, the first and most basic law of this autocratic empire must be drafted and bestowed by

The Age of Catherine the Great

our own Imperial hand. That law concerns the unshakability of the throne and regularity in the succession to it."[19] But the empress's larger hopes were not destined to be fulfilled, and she would have to compose more than one law in her own hand.

The commission convened in Moscow in July 1767. Here we have the first attempt in Russian history to create something akin to a parliamentary institution. It comprised 572 deputies elected by the nobles, townspeople, Cossacks, economic peasants, black plough peasants, one-court peasants, and non-Russian peoples of the Volga region and Siberia. Their assignment was to formulate new laws. This was the limit of their authority, which was far narrower than that of members of European parliaments. But to the extent that the laws were to deal with practically every aspect of life, the deputies had the opportunity to express themselves openly on the most vital questions of the day. As a result, the commission's sessions witnessed the eruption of sharp debates touching on the rights of the nobility and merchantry and their mutual relations, on the condition of the peasantry, on trade and the construction of factories, and on the judicial system. Subcommissions were established for the actual elaboration of legislative projects dealing with specific matters.

Soon after the Legislative Commission opened, it became clear that its members were poorly prepared for their legislative assignment. Among the problems evident from the very beginning were the low level of education manifested by the majority of the deputies and the utter absence of a political culture, parliamentary experience, and juridical awareness. Most important of all, the deputies for the most part proved to be extremely conservative. Concerned chiefly with the preservation of their own narrow estate and group interests, the nobles feared penetration into their ranks by members of other social groups. They also proved unwilling to listen to any talk about the abolition of serfdom, or even its amelioration. The townspeople, on the other hand, wanted to acquire some of the nobility's privileges, primarily the right to buy enserfed peasants in order to put them to work in their factories.* The Baltic nobles demanded the preservation of their special status, while their Ukrainian counterparts wanted the same rights as the Russian nobles. The situation that emerged in the commission was

---

*Back in 1762, Peter III had forbidden the purchase by non-nobles of peasants without land for work in factories.

quite peculiar. The maxims contained in Catherine's Instructions were handed down to the deputies from on high, and were reinforced by the authority of Imperial power, and therefore not open to debate. But the influence of the Instructions on those questions that were debated was practically nonexistent, although the deputies were required to reread them every month.

It would seem that the maxims abstracted from the Instructions had nothing in common with the reality of Russian life. It was also no small factor that the deputies were for all practical purposes deprived of the right to make decisions. They could do nothing more than approve or disapprove of any given project submitted to them. But the elaboration of these projects dragged on and on, and the only one that was actually presented to the deputies for their consideration was the draft of a law on the nobility. The draft proved to be too unpolished, so it was sent back to the subcommission for reworking. Months passed, and discussions in the Legislative Commission yielded no results. In December 1768, citing the outbreak of the (first) Russo-Turkish War, a disenchanted empress signed a decree adjourning the commission. The subcommissions continued to function for a number of years, transforming themselves into what were in effect regular state institutions. The materials they gathered, as well as the results they produced, were subsequently utilized by Catherine when drawing up new laws.*

Thus ended the first stage of Catherinean reform, one that was marked by the empress's effort to carry out reform with the assistance of representatives from various social and ethnic groups. The most important conclusion Catherine derived from the experience was that the overwhelming majority of her subjects were deeply conservative and that radical reform was therefore impossible. Still, she was made aware of their deep-seated desires, and from then on had to adapt her legislative activities to those desires. Such conclusions exerted decisive influence on the tempo and tactics of her further reform efforts. It took

---

*One finds in the historical literature various explanations for the disbanding of the commission. The majority of Soviet historians maintained that Catherine closed down the commission because she feared the overly bold speeches of the deputies. Oleg Omelchenko recently came up with an original point of view when he argued that the commission had simply fulfilled its objective. It is hard to agree with either of these perspectives. The views of the empress herself were considerably more radical than those of the majority of the deputies, while the commission had not fulfilled its objective, which was to draft legislation.

several years to work out these new tactics, years that were filled with serious domestic and foreign policy convulsions.

The first half of the 1770s was the most threatening period of Catherine II's entire reign. First the nation was shaken by the Plague Riot in Moscow in 1771, and then by the uprising in 1773–74, headed by Emelian Pugachev. The epidemic of bubonic plague that broke out in Moscow was apparently brought up from the military front of the Russo-Turkish War. At the epidemic's peak, up to seven hundred people per day died in the city. Shops, factories, and government offices were closed, hundreds of people were left without any means of subsistence, and the streets were filled with people with nowhere to go. Since there was no known cure for bubonic plague at the time, the quarantine measures undertaken by the doctors were designed merely to limit its spread. Even more tragically, healthy people frequently made their way into pesthouses, promptly became infected, and died. All of this elicited frustration on the part of the population, a lack of confidence in the authorities, and a distrust of the medical profession. The icon of the Mother of God, affixed to St. Barbara's Gate in Kitaigorod,* became the focus of the populace's attention. This icon was reputed to have curative powers. A crowd of people continually gathered around it to pray, and by kissing it infected each other. Peter Eropkin, the commandant of Moscow, and Amvrosii, the archbishop of the city, decided to remove the icon in order not to abet the spread of the infection. This measure incited the desperate populace to revolt. A mob, armed with whatever it could lay its hands on, beat the archbishop's emissaries unmercifully, and then broke into the Kremlin. There, at the Chudov Monastery, it located Amvrosii's residence. It failed to find Amvrosii himself at home, but looted the monastery. On the next day the crowd broke into another Moscow monastery, the Donskoi, where the archbishop was hiding, and tore him to pieces.

As a full-scale uprising, the riot lasted three days, until Eropkin managed to assemble a small military detachment, which proved able to disperse the rioters with grapeshot. After a brief investigation, four of the most active participants were hanged, while another two hundred or so were knouted, birched, or whipped. The subsequent investigation revealed that the riot had begun without any instigation

---

*Kitaigorod was a district of Moscow located not far from the Kremlin, which used to be surrounded by a fortified wall with gates.

whatsoever, and that its participants were acting purely on the spur of the moment: the rioters demanded nothing more than a closing of the pesthouses, burial of the dead, and a cessation of the doctors' efforts. The very fact that the uprising took place, however, bore testimony to the fundamental lack of confidence of the mass of people in the agents of authority, a distrust magnified by the extreme nature of the situation.

Far more serious, and on a far broader scale, was the Pugachev uprising, the largest social upheaval in the eighteenth century. It was distinguishable from previous uprisings by its scale, by its greater degree of organization, and by its more clearly defined objectives. Nevertheless, as was the case with similar events dating back to the early and mid-seventeenth century, the instigators and chief actors were Cossacks. Their primary goal was to destroy the existing nobility in order to take its place in the Russian social hierarchy. This was to be the Cossacks' last attempt at such a goal. Other groups of the population participated in the uprising alongside the Cossacks, with each of them pursuing its own objectives. There were peasants, who were struggling against serfdom. Then there were the non-Russian peoples of the Volga region, who were fighting for national liberation. Finally, there were the metallurgical workers in the Ural Mountains, whose aspirations were for all practical purposes no different from those of the peasants. Nor should one overlook the participation of the Polish Confederates, who had been exiled to the Urals after their rebellion had been put down and their nation partitioned for the first time in 1773. Given such diverse objectives, it seems obvious that if the rebels had won, dissension would soon have broken out in their own camp.

Proclaiming himself Emperor Peter III, who had miraculously been saved from the hands of assassins, the Don Cossack Emelian Pugachev signed decrees, composed in the traditional tsarist manner, granting his followers noble titles and creating organs of administration similar to those that existed in official Russia at the time. In order to attract the great mass of enserfed peasants to his banner, he had no qualms about granting them freedom and land. But it is quite obvious that if he had come to power, he would have done nothing more than recreate the existing system, for that was the only one he knew. Two elements found in the Pugachev documents, in fact, suggest that any state structure he might have established would have been even more archaic than that of Catherine's Russia. In the first place, an Old Believer influence can be detected in these documents, as Pugachev promised to adhere to the old faith, to forbid the shaving of beards, and to compel the wearing of Russian-style clothing. In the second, he promised "the common people" Cossack-style "freedoms": that is, a militarized form of organization of the population into units governed by archaic forms of democracy. Thus, on the whole, the political framework and goals of those who were rebelling were quite conservative.

Nevertheless, it is apparent that Pugachev's appeals and slogans struck a responsive chord, for they represented just what the peasants were longing for from a good "father-tsar." Still, the obvious contradiction between the promises of freedom and liberty he made, on the one hand, and the summonses in his manifestos to remain loyal slaves [*raby*], on the other, is striking. It should be noted that right up to Catherine's time, in keeping with the decree of Peter I mentioned above, all subjects, regardless of their social position, termed themselves "slaves" when addressing the tsar. Nourished on the works of the Enlightenment, Catherine found the word "slave" repugnant and eventually prohibited its usage.

Like other uprisings of this magnitude, the Pugachev rebellion was accompanied by copious bloodshed and incidences of barbarity and vandalism. Thousands of nobles, officials, clergymen, townspeople, and ordinary soldiers who refused to recognize the pretender's authority fell victim to the uprising. In pitched battles between the rebels and regular army units, no fewer than ten thousand people perished, with some sources claiming even twice that number. Roughly four times as many were wounded and maimed. When occupying towns and villages, the rebels plundered and laid waste to churches and monasteries, destroyed icons and church plate, and killed monks and priests. But death and destruction were by no means the exclusive monopoly of the rebels. After the suppression of the Pugachev uprising, the state subjected its participants to massive repression. Many of Pugachev's followers were knouted or forced to run the gauntlet, while others were branded with hot irons, had their nostrils slit, and were exiled to hard labor. The most prominent of the uprising's leaders were executed.

A review of the course of the Pugachev uprising, however brief, jars the imagination by the extent of the movement, the number of social elements drawn into it, and the ease with which the rebels managed to seize great expanses of territory and attract to their banners large segments of the population. The uprising began on the Iaik River in September 1773, and by October, Pugachev's troops, three thousand strong, were besieging Orenburg. The military detachment sent to relieve the town was defeated, with part of it going over to the rebels. The town was captured. Leaving a unit of his army at Orenburg, Pugachev set off to seize the town of Iaitsk, but failed to accomplish his objective completely: the town was taken, but the fortress continued to offer resistance. Meanwhile, in January 1774, Pugachev's commanders, Ivan Zarubin-Chika and Ivan Griaznov, besieged Ufa and Cheliabinsk, while Bashkir leader Salavat Iulaev attempted to take Kungur.

By March, regular army units had reached the region of military activity, and on March 22, they defeated the rebels at Fort Tatishchev. In the days that followed, other rebel detachments suffered defeats at Chesnokovka and Ekaterinburg. With a detachment of five hundred men, Pugachev headed for the Urals, where he again collected an army of several thousand. On May 8, 1774, he launched a new campaign, managing to capture several forts in the course of ten days. But on May 21, his main forces were defeated at Troitsk. Burning everything in his path, Pugachev moved northward, to Krasnoufimsk, and then to Osa. On June 21, the latter surrendered, opening the way to Kazan for the rebels. Taking the Votkinsk and Izhevsk metallurgical works along the way, as well as Elabugu, Sarapul, Menzelinsk, and other towns and fortresses, Pugachev approached Kazan in early July. On July 12–13, the town was seized, but the fortress continued to hold out. Regular troops under the command of Colonel Ivan Mikhelson rushed to the aid of the besieged fortress, and on July 15, Pugachev's army was once again defeated.

The remainder of the self-styled emperor's main army crossed the Volga River. Again, a detachment of three to four hundred men was transformed into an army thousands strong within a matter of weeks. In fact, the road to Moscow now lay open before Pugachev. Moreover, the region in front of him was inhabited by serfs, on whose support he could certainly count. It was at this point, however, that the Cossack leader's attitude toward the peasantry revealed itself: he decided not to lead them to Moscow. Instead he turned to the south, to the Don region, where he hoped for the support of the Don Cossacks. On July 23, Pugachev seized Alatyr and moved on to Saransk. On July 27, he entered the latter town to the peal of church bells. But within three days he was forced to abandon it, when he received word that regular troops were on their way. On August 2, Pugachev's forces took pos-

Pugachev delivers his judgment. From a painting by V.G. Perov.

session of Penza, and by August 6 they were approaching Saratov, where on the next day the inhabitants took the oath to "Emperor Peter III." Three days later, Pugachev abandoned Saratov, and on August 21, after achieving several small victories over army units, Kalmyks, and Kazakhs, he approached Tsaritsyn. Negotiations with the Don Cossacks defending the town yielded no results. A battle ensued, during which word of Colonel Mikhelson's approach was received. Pugachev retreated, but on August 25 was overtaken and decisively defeated at the Salnikov metallurgical works. Soon thereafter, he was seized by his own followers, bound, and handed over to government forces.

* * *

The Pugachev uprising, which terrorized the nobility-oriented Russian state, had drastic repercussions for Catherine's subsequent domestic policy. For one thing, the empress became convinced of the deep-seated conservatism within the lower as well as the upper strata of the empire's population. For another, she now also believed that only the nobility could serve as a reliable pillar of the throne. Finally, the uprising made it glaringly obvious that the country was in deep social crisis, and therefore, that it was no longer possible to postpone reforms, which had to be implemented gradually, by means of slow, everyday work. By 1775, the first fruits appeared in the form of one of the most significant legislative acts of Catherine's reign, the "Fundamental Law for the Administration of the Provinces of the All-Russian Empire."

The publication and implementation of the "Fundamental Law" signified the beginning of provincial reform, at the core of which lay the reorganization of the system of local government. The need for such a reform was dictated by the very logic of the development of the Russian state. This logic demanded the creation of a tightly centralized and unified system, one in which each square meter of territory and each inhabitant would be placed under the unremitting control of the state. But it was necessary to link this requirement with the estate interests expressed by the Legislative Commission. Moreover, Catherine had not lost sight of her plans to create a third estate.

The provincial reform introduced a new administrative-territorial delineation, by which the country was divided into twenty-five provinces, which were broken up into forty-one smaller units at the end of Catherine's reign. In other words, taking the Petrine system as her point of departure, Catherine honed it to produce further centralization, although in the guise of dispersing authority. The new provinces encompassed territory containing from three to four hundred thousand people, which was then further divided into districts containing twenty to thirty thousand each. Whatever unique national-historical or economic features the regions might have had were ignored when drafting the reform. Executive authority in the province was vested in the Governor or Governor-General, for whom a special office, the Provincial Board, was created. Primary executive authority in the district resided with the Police Chief, who was given a chancellery to assist him. A Provincial Magistracy was created to administer all the towns of the province, while the individual towns were governed by Town Magistracies headed by Burgomasters.

The Provincial Reform Law separated judicial organs from the executive, thus taking a step forward in implementation of the principle of separation of powers. Moreover, for the first time in Russian judicial practice, criminal proceedings were separated from civil. On the other hand, the estate principle was retained in the creation of the courts. People were to be judged in courts composed solely of their peers: that is, members of their own estate. The separation of powers also remained incomplete, for the governor was granted the right to intervene in the judicial process. He was assigned the task of combating judicial red tape, and was even permitted to suspend judicial proceedings. Completely new to Russian judicial practice was the so-called Court of Conscience, which was a supra-estate organ that combined the functions of court of petty claims and prosecutor's office. Borrowed by Catherine from English judicial practice, the court was charged with reconciling disputants and putting an end to quarrels and discord. To a significant degree the inadequacies of the empress's judicial reform may be explained by the absence in Russia of professional lawyers and the lack of development of law and legal thought.

The "Fundamental Law" of 1775 called for the creation of Boards of Public Welfare at the local level. These were the first institutions in Russia with specifically designated social functions. They were to assume responsibility for the establishment of public schools, orphanages, hospitals, almshouses, and the like. As was characteristic of eighteenth-century legislation, the law stipulated meticulously what and how to teach children, how to maintain hospital and school premises, and how to feed and sustain the sick.

The law transferred to elected representatives of the local nobility a number of responsibilities in the newly created offices. In this way, the state managed to fill posts that otherwise might have remained vacant, while it satisfied the wishes of the nobility to have authority at the local level transferred into its hands. In reality, however, the independence of the local offices was more apparent than real, for the noble who was elected to a post in local government was transformed into nothing more than a state functionary drawing a state salary. This little detail alone is enough to refute the claims of those historians who argue for the profoundly pro-noble nature of the 1775 Provincial Reform. Given the realities of eighteenth-century Russia, it goes without saying that the promulgation of a legislative act that ran counter to the interests of the nobility was not to be anticipated. But it should be apparent that Catherine was concerned not so much with the satisfaction of the interests of a given estate as with those of the state as a whole, as she understood them.

The "Fundamental Law" of 1775 was a complex, multifaceted and self-contradictory document, for the components of society's life and the state apparatus it touched upon were themselves varied and contradictory. But on the whole it remained within the framework of the political program that Catherine II had laid out at the very beginning of her reign. Her measures in the economic sphere likewise remained within the mainstream of this program. The empress recognized perfectly clearly that a flourishing trade and a powerful industry were necessary prerequisites for the successful implementation of any domestic or foreign projects. The principle of free enterprise, based on private property, she believed, should serve as the foundation stone of trade and industry. The development of this principle and its introduction into Russian life took place gradually. In the 1760s, monopolies in some branches of industry were eliminated, while those large factories that thanks to the generosity of the Copper Bank had fallen into private hands in the last years of Elizabeth's reign, were transferred back to the state. This last measure proved to be a mixed blessing, for the state lacked the means to develop heavy industry. As a result, Russia lagged still further behind the advanced European nations. On the positive side, the procedure for organizing and registering new enterprises was simplified.

In 1775, privileges for merchants of the first, second, and third guilds were introduced. At the same time, the property qualification for entry into the guilds was increased: that is, the right to register in a merchant guild was made available only to the richest, those who were in a position to "declare" a given amount of capital for tax purposes. The empress intended this measure to stimulate entrepreneurial activity. The right to establish industrial enterprises without any sort of special permission from the government was granted that same year. In 1780, a special decree strengthened private property in factories and mills. All these measures had a beneficial impact on the development of industry, especially light industry: silk weaving and textile mills, tanneries, hat making, and the like. The case was somewhat different in heavy industry. Although new metallurgical industries were constructed in the Ural Mountains and new blast furnaces brought on line, the pace of development of this important branch of industry was too slow, as was the rate of capital turnover. In addition to the causes mentioned above, the fact that Ural metallurgical industries employed primarily the labor power of enserfed, or so-called "ascribed" peasants, who proved quite unproductive, helps explain this lag.

A number of measures undertaken by Catherine II contributed to the development of Russian foreign trade. The monopolies enjoyed by some trading companies were eliminated, free navigation of the high seas in wartime was stipulated in conventions arranged with foreign nations, and Russian consulates were opened in their ports. Manufactured items such as cast iron, cloth, and sailcloth assumed an ever larger role on Russia's export list. In 1763, the ban on the export of grain was lifted, a step that subsequently led to Russia's becoming one of the chief suppliers of grain to the international market. All the while, Russia continued to export such traditional items as timber, furs, and hemp. All of these were simply raw materials or else semiprocessed goods, while Russia imported items intended for immediate personal consumption: wine, furniture, jewelry, china, textiles, art objects, and so on. It was at precisely this time, some historians maintain, that Russia fell into the role of colonial supplier of raw materials to a more economically developed Europe.

Fundamental changes also took place in the nation's financial policy during Catherine's reign. As was always the case, the state found itself chronically short of money and thought up a variety of means to obtain more. At first it followed a well-traveled path by recasting silver and bronze coins, minting from them coins with lower metallic content. But in 1769, the state began to print money, the so-called assignats, which served as Russia's first paper money. At the outset, the population proved hesitant to accept paper money in lieu of "real" money. While these assignats gradually gained acceptance, the government proceeded to print so many of them that their value fell, and the excess had to be withdrawn from circulation and burned.

The banking industry also continued to develop, although it was still completely controlled by the state. In 1769, noble and commercial banks were opened, the latter providing loans to merchants. Starting in 1770, the banks began to accept money for deposit, and in 1772, the first savings and loan banks opened to provide short-term credit. Finally, in 1786, the already existing banks were merged into a State Loan Bank. The availability of credit on favorable terms had a beneficial impact on trade and other forms of entrepreneurial activity. The state itself, however, was the first to resort to loans in Catherine's reign. In 1769, in the midst of the first Turkish War, it took out a loan in Amsterdam, and in the following year took out another in Genoa. The repayment of the foreign debt took up to five percent of the national budget. This figure and the budget deficit that Russia ran were not unusual for the time. Despite measures introduced to eliminate it, the deficit became chronic, even increasing over time.

Agriculture underwent far less change in this period. Whatever increase in output was registered in this sector was achieved thanks largely to extensive rather than intensive changes: that is, output was increased by bringing new land under cultivation. Agricultural technology, the level of efficiency, and therefore labor productivity, remained practically unchanged. True, we find in this period the first Russian enthusiasts for a scientific approach to agriculture, an approach that was encouraged by the state. In 1765, a Free Economic Society was created whose mission was to spread scientific knowledge in the economic sphere, chiefly in agronomy. The "Works" [*Trudy*] published by the society were no less popular with the reading public than the French Enlightenment writers. None of this, however, led to major improvements in agriculture, nor could it have led to them, because enserfed labor remained the cornerstone of Russian agricultural production.

Despite its many complexities and shortcomings, the Russian economy continued to develop in the second half of the eighteenth century. State decrees directed at stimulating production and trade on the basis of free enterprise opened the last remaining floodgates, as it were, permitting the exploitation of the full potential harbored by a system still shaped by serfdom. This potential, however, was far from limitless, as serfdom continued to pose an insuperable obstacle to the normal path of development. Just what was the empress's attitude toward serfdom? And what happened with regard to serfdom during her reign?

In her memoirs Catherine expressed her thoughts on this subject in unequivocal terms. She wrote that a predisposition to despotism manifested itself

> in [noble] children from earliest childhood because they see how cruelly their parents treat their servants. There is not a home to be found in which there are no pillories, fetters, or various other instruments of torture [designed to punish] for the least offense those whom nature has placed in this unhappy class. And they cannot smash their fetters without violating the law. One hardly dares to suggest that they are people just as we are. And when I say it myself, I run the risk of having stones thrown at me. What indeed did I not have to endure from the criticism of an unreasonable and cruel public when the Commission for the Compilation of a New Law Code began to debate certain matters relating to this subject, and when unenlightened members of the nobility, whose number was infinitely greater than I could ever have imagined (because I esteemed too highly those who surrounded me on a daily basis), began

to surmise that these matters could lead to some amelioration of the present condition of the tillers of the soil?[20]

In another document written in the empress's hand we read:

> The great motivator of agriculture is freedom and private property. When each peasant is assured that what belongs to him does not also belong to another, he will improve it. State taxes are not burdensome to him because they are quite moderate. And if the state has no need of increasing its revenues, the tillers of the soil can dispose of their resources as they see fit, if only they have their freedom and private property.[21]

Catherine was not far from the truth when she asserted that she would be stoned at the least attempt on her part to raise the possibility of the abolition of serfdom. For the nobility was prepared to go to any extreme in its defense of its chief privilege, which represented the cornerstone of its economic prosperity. Had she pressed on, the empress might well have put her crown at risk. This does not suggest, however, that Catherine II was adamantly opposed to serfdom. The rejection of serfdom as an inhumane institution that contradicted the principles of the Enlightenment and was harmful to the economy was coupled in her mind with a conviction concerning the lack of intellectual and spiritual development of the common people and the need to educate them, and what she saw as the generally beneficial relations between serfs and their masters. Such a view was characteristic not only of the empress but of many enlightened people of the time.

Catherine was in no position to take on the serf owners directly, even though, as we shall see, she harbored specific plans for the serfs. Meanwhile, serfdom itself, as in preceding reigns, continued to develop. The lifestyle of the nobles, both in the provinces and in the capitals, was increasingly based on the European way of life. This required more and more money, which could only be obtained from the serfs. As a result, their obligations to their landlords increased by twelve times over the course of the century. Legislation dealing with serfdom mirrored this trend. Two truly odious decrees, marking the pinnacle of serfdom's development, appeared in Catherine II's reign. The first was that of January 17, 1765, which allowed landlords to hand over those serfs guilty of legal transgressions for hard labor.

The decree had a rather lengthy prior history, extending all the way back to Peter I, when the tsar ordered that those who had failed to pay their taxes be sent off to hard labor. The landlords seized on the decree, seeing in it the opportunity to dispose in the same manner of those serfs who were guilty of other transgressions. The Admiralty suggested that the landlords' request be met and asked the Senate for permission to put the serfs to work, promising even to pay the landlords a ruble a month for each of them. The Senate did decide to meet the Admiralty's request, but only halfway, wisely concluding that if landlords were paid for their serfs who were sent off to hard labor, they would start sending off those serfs who were not guilty of anything. The use of convict labor for work in the galleys helped the state immensely, and thus one can conclude that the motivation for the decree was purely economic.

The second of the decrees that bears mention appeared August 22, 1767. It forbad peasants to submit complaints against their landlords directly to the empress. This decree was by no means Catherine's creation, for it simply reiterated a norm that had prevailed since the seventeenth century. Its specific timing was determined by the empress's reaction to the six hundred peasant petitions that were submitted to her during her trip down the Volga River in the spring of 1767. Even Catherine II, despite her diligence, was unable to work her way through all of them. Her decree therefore reaffirmed that all petitions, regardless of their origin, henceforth be submitted not to her but to those institutions expressly assigned to examine them. As a rule, however, it was difficult if not impossible to obtain justice from these institutions.

To illustrate this point, mention should be made of the infamous Saltychikha affair. Daria Saltykova was a Moscow landowner with a sadist disposition, who, over the years, tortured her house servants, killing a number of them. Complaints lodged against her brought no results because the wealthy estate owner had no trouble bribing the officials responsible for enforcing the law. When the affair finally came to light, Catherine ordered that Saltykova be deprived of her noble status and her property and be imprisoned in a cell in one of Moscow's nunneries. It is obvious that Saltykova was mentally ill, for a normal landowner capable of reasoning would not have killed her servants, if only because they comprised the basis of her prosperity.

Having described the nation's economic situation and the problem of serfdom, we are now in a better position to understand the thrust of Catherine II's legislative program, which was pursued so actively throughout the second half of the 1770s and on into the 1780s that historians term this period in her life the period of "legislomania." In 1782, seven years after launching her provincial reform, the empress promulgated a "Statute on Decorum or Police [Statute]," which propagates the idea of a well-regulated state, Petrine-style. The core content of the document deals with municipal self-administration, which is organized along the same lines as the provincial. The town is divided into sections of 200–700 households, and the sections, into wards of 50–100 households. Each section is assigned its own police officer, and each ward, its own watchman. Supervising them all is the municipal board of decorum, which also exercises control over trade, the apprehension of runaways, the maintenance of roads, streets, and bridges, the suppression of games of chance, the construction of municipal baths, the dispersal of groups and mobs not permitted by the law, and other administrative and policing functions.

The statute devotes particular attention to matters of faith. On the one hand, the new law proclaims a policy of religious toleration, while on the other it firmly defends Orthodoxy, forbidding its followers to convert to other religions and banning all propaganda that challenges Orthodoxy. Rules of conduct in church are specifically emphasized. Included in the Statute on Decorum is a set of instructions entitled "Mirror of the Board of Decorum," a moral code of sorts for the average citizen as well as a guide for the police, which are to enforce the law. In and of themselves, the statute's maxims differ hardly at all from those that Russians were accustomed to hearing from the pulpit. Because they were now enshrined in legislation, however, they acquired the force of law. The "Mirror," it is worth noting, bears a decisively supra-class character, with its teachings considered uniformly applicable. Each prohibition in the statute stipulates a specific punishment in the event of violation.*

Having completed the reorganization of the administrative system, Catherine threw herself into her chief project, the elaboration of legislation for her estates. On April 21, 1785, which happened to be her

---

*As the historian Grigor'ev has pointed out, the text of the "Mirror of the Board of Decorum" stems directly from a French work entitled "Traité de la police" by Nicolas de la Mare: see V. Grigor'ev, "Zertsalo Upravy blagochiniia," in *Russkii istoricheskii zhurnal,* 1917, nos. 3–4.

birthday, she promulgated two sweeping documents. They have come to be known as the Charter to the Nobility and the Charter to the Towns. The first incorporates just about every privilege the nobility had acquired over the course of the century, thus climaxing the long process of the juridical formulation of its rights and privileges. The charter establishes that henceforth, "for all times and unalterably," noblemen may be deprived of their noble status only after they have been convicted by a court of such crimes as treason, brigandage, thievery, and violation of an oath. Moreover, they may only be judged by their fellow nobles. These same noblemen are not to be subjected to corporal punishment without having first been deprived of their noble status. The charter confirms the right of these noblemen to serve or not to serve, as they wish, as granted by the 1762 Manifesto on the Freedom of the Nobility, and to take service with friendly foreign governments. This last right is not unlimited, for in times of emergency they are to return home at the first summons of the sovereign to serve the fatherland, sparing neither effort nor life itself.

Also confirmed are all the noblemen's rights to their inherited and acquired property, with the former not being subjected to confiscation, even in the case of the most egregious crimes. In such instances their property is to be transferred to their heirs. In other words, landed estates have finally become the private, inalienable property of the nobility. A special article of the charter permits nobles to build factories and mills on their estates. Manor houses are freed from the quartering of troops, and the nobles themselves, from all forms of taxation. Provincial assemblies of the nobility are created in the provinces. Among other tasks they are made responsible for the maintenance of provincial Heraldry Books of the Nobility, in which the names of all the local nobles are to be registered.

As outlined in the 1785 charter, the nobility's estate privileges finally served to distinguish it from all other elements of the population. They confirmed its ruling position, thereby hastening the creation of a noble self-consciousness and a sense of noble dignity. In the minds of Russian nobles the empress remained a true benefactress and protectress. All of this led to the identification of the Catherinean epoch as a "golden age" of the Russian nobility. It would, however, be inaccurate to assume that while drawing up her charter the empress ignored the state's interests. While the title of the charter emphasizes its permanent nature, at the same time it emphasizes the dependence of the nobility on the monarch's will. The nobleman who has never served the state is denied the right to vote in the noble assembly or to be chosen for elective office. On the whole, the charter offers the nobility no new privileges but merely codifies and confirms those it had already acquired. Moreover, the charter says nothing at all about the right to own enserfed souls, which signals the empress's intention to keep the question of serfdom open.

The Charter to the Towns is of an entirely different nature. In the first place, it is addressed not to an estate but to a physical entity, the town, and deals not only with the personal and estate rights of the urban population but with questions of the organization and activities of merchants' and artisans' guilds and organs of municipal self-administration. The unusually multifaceted nature of the document is again linked to the lack of development of the third estate. The first chapter of the Charter to the Towns is devoted to the structure of the town, its population, schools, and so on. The second deals with the residents themselves, the "urban inhabitants" or *meshchane*.* The catalog of rights and privileges it bestows parallels that of the nobles' charter. Just as the noblemen of the province are to form a provincial assembly of the nobility, the urban inhabitants are to form an urban corporation, which is to maintain the Book of Town Inhabitants, the equivalent to the Heraldry Book of the Nobility.

According to the charter, the urban inhabitants are to constitute a separate estate, with their rank to be hereditary, like the nobility's. They are to be deprived of their rank for the same crimes as the nobles are, with the verdict to be rendered by an estate-based court, this time the Urban Inhabitants' Court. The charter confirms the right of each townsman to engage freely in entrepreneurial activity and holds out special privileges to those merchants wealthy enough to belong to guilds. All of them are freed from paying the soul tax and meeting the recruitment levy. The extent of the rights granted, however, depends on the guild to which they belong, and by implication, on their declared wealth. Thus, for example, merchants of the first and second

---

*It should, however, be noted that in the same document Catherine II also resorts to the term *meshchane* to identify those urban dwellers too poor to claim membership in one of the merchants' or artisans' guilds, a usage that only serves to confuse matters: see Hugh Hudson, "Urban Estate Engineering in Eighteenth-Century Russia: Catherine the Great and the Elusive 'Meshchanstvo'," *Canadian-American Slavic Studies,* vol. XVIII, no. 4 (1984), pp. 393–410.

guild are freed from corporal punishment. To take another example, merchants of the first guild may ride in a coach pulled by a pair of horses; merchants of the second guild, in a two-horse carriage only, and merchants of the third, in a cart pulled by a single horse. The "eminent citizens" [*imenitye grazhdane*] represent a special category of urban inhabitant: they enjoy the right to hitch four horses to their coaches. Eminent citizens in the third generation are granted the right to petition for noble status.

The urban inhabitants are to form new organs of municipal self-administration: town councils, headed by town heads. The town council is to guarantee proper order in the town, enforce the observation of rules of trade, and so forth. In addition to the merchants' guilds, the charter foresees the creation of artisans' guilds similar to those of medieval Western Europe. The manner of the work of the artisans, their relations with other guild members, and so on. are thoroughly detailed in the document. Catherine realized that artisans' guilds were already antiquated in Europe, serving only to hinder the development of the economy. But, she believed that Russia had yet to achieve an analogous stage of development and that therefore, artisans' guilds would, on the contrary, stimulate development.

Such was the basic content of the two charters of 1785. But it goes without saying that to bring her program of estate creation to fruition, Catherine would have to deal with the most numerous estate, the peasantry. The available documentation makes clear that a charter was also prepared for the peasantry. Yet it never saw the light of day. The unpromulgated charter is addressed not to all peasants but only to the state peasants, who are referred to as "free rural inhabitants." It bestows on them rights equivalent to those of townsmen and nobles. According to the draft of the charter, which has survived, new organs of self-administration and administrators are to make their appearance in the village: the Village Foreman, the Village Elder, and the Chamber of Administrative Affairs, a body similar in function to the Provincial Assembly of the Nobility and the Urban Corporation. As were the other estates, the peasants are divided into six categories, with the first two being freed from corporal punishment.

Viewing all three charters together, David Griffiths has concluded that in their totality they form "a constitution, to employ the term as it was understood in the pre-Revolutionary context." Such a term "connoted the principles, permanent laws, and institutions that provided the framework for orderly governance, whether that form be monarchy, aristocracy, republic, or a mixture thereof." Griffiths pointed out that "when the charters are treated as a package, as they should be, one discovers a unified political program reflecting a coherent and consistent vision of the form the empress thought society ought to take."[22]

As has already been noted, however, the third of the charters was never promulgated. The reason for this is transparent: resistance from the nobility, which Catherine was unable to surmount. Given the situation in which she was operating, the empress was able to accomplish only that part of her program that she could carry out without fear of calling forth serious social unrest. From this perspective, her attempts at reform have to be recognized as successful. It is from Catherine's times, according to historians, that one can speak of the appearance of full-fledged estates in Russia. Yet the empress continued to work on her legislation even after 1785. As the documents preserved in the archives attest, she refused to abandon her idea of creating an estate structure in its totality. For example, she intended to establish a special institution with the functions of a supreme court, to be composed of elected representatives of the three estates: the nobility, urban dwellers, and the state peasantry. Her drafts in the areas of family, property, and criminal law have also been preserved. A new reform of the Senate was designated for 1797. Among the projects one can find her thoughts on ways to eliminate serfdom. In one set of notes, we read: "Here is a convenient way: establish that henceforth when someone sells his land, all the serfs on it will be declared free from the moment of purchase by the new landowner. Over the course of a hundred years, all, or at least most, of the land will change hands, and the people will be free."[23]

As we see, Catherine had no hopes for the immediate emancipation of the serfs, and moreover considered a "sharp turn" on this matter dangerous. According to other sources, she prepared a decree by which all children of serfs who were born after 1785 would be declared emancipated. In one way or another, it is apparent that the fulfillment of Catherine's broadscale program of reform, which might have created the preconditions necessary for the emergence of a civil society in Russia, collided with major contradictions inherent in the Petrine transformation. Given the conditions of the times, these contradictions could not have been overcome without social upheaval. The empress accurately perceived the boundaries up against which she could press without fear of calling forth such upheaval, and halted when she got there, thus rendering her reforms among the most successful in Russian history.

Catherine II's reforms were not confined to domestic administration, estate organization, and the economy. One of her most important concerns was education. As a diligent student of the French philosophes, Catherine understood that the success of any social transformation depended on the level of enlightenment of the people, on their ability to accept new ways. It was clear that it was insufficient merely to give a person a specific assortment of knowledge. His psychology, his value system, and even his moral foundations had to be changed. Among the commissions established by Catherine in 1763 was one on public education. But the fate of the project it elaborated was the same as those of the other commissions of the time.

Ivan Ivanovich Betskoi, who himself had received a relatively good education abroad, became the major proponent of Catherine's policies in the educational sphere in the early part of her reign. In 1763, he was named director of the Cadet Corps and president of the Academy of Fine Arts. A year later the empress confirmed his exegesis entitled "General Statute on the Education of Youth of Both Sexes," at the heart of which lay an idea popular at the time: that of "educating a new sort of person." The author intended to found a network of schools where children between the ages of 5 to 6 and 18 to 20 would be educated in isolation from the corrupting influence of the surrounding society. The schools were to be estate based, although Betskoi devoted particular attention to the education of people between the ranks: that is, those who failed to fit comfortably into any of the existing estates.

In keeping with Betskoi's intentions, a school attached to the Academy of Fine Arts was opened, and an educational institution bearing the name The Society for [the Education of] Two Hundred Well-Born Young Women was established in St. Petersburg. The following year, a division for young urban women was opened at the society. Subsequently, reform of the various Cadet Corps was carried out, and foundling homes for orphans and others were established in Moscow and St. Petersburg, as well as a commercial school in the latter city. For all of these new academic institutions Betskoi elaborated special statutes in which enlightened ideas were embodied in mandatory procedures. Children were not to be beaten and hollered at. Instead, the development of their natural qualities and inclinations was to be encouraged, and their interest in study cultivated by means of praise and persuasion. The statutes were periodically republished in order to foster broad circulation of the ideas pervading them.

The Society for [the Education of] Two Hundred Well-Born Young Women in St. Petersburg, otherwise known as the Smolnyi Institute, was the first female academic institution in Russia. As such it enjoyed the personal sponsorship of both Betskoi and the empress. Catherine often visited the institute, and even corresponded with some of its pupils. The foundling homes, maintained by charitable contributions, also enjoyed a special status. The very encouragement of such financial contributions, and the example set in this respect by the empress, were to assist in creating within society a new atmosphere and a new orientation in relations among people. It is to this time that Russian philanthropy can be dated. Later it was to make an essential contribution to the development of Russian culture and education.

By the end of the 1770s, however, it had become apparent that Betskoi's system was not producing the desired results. It had proved impossible to isolate pupils from their surroundings, if only because those who taught them had been reared under the old conditions. To compound the problem, the institutions that had been established did not, and could not, constitute a system of public education. So, in 1782, Catherine created a Commission on the Establishment of Educational Institutions, in which Theodor Janković, a well-known pedagogue specifically recruited from the Habsburg Empire for the purpose, played a leading role. The commission elaborated a plan for the creation of a two-tiered system of two-year primary schools in the district towns and both primary and four-year high schools in the provincial capitals. These schools were to teach mathematics, history, geography, physics, architecture, Russian, and foreign languages. It was for these schools that Betskoi and Catherine brought out a book entitled *On the Duties of Man and Citizen*. It elaborated for the student the concept of the soul and the benefactor, one's duties to God and to society, to the state and to those dear to one, information on health and hygiene, and advice on household management. For all practical purposes, the book represented a popular exposition of the ideas of the enlighteners.[24] In subsequent years, a number of aids for teachers, manuals, instructions, and textbooks were developed to supplement this primary text.

The product of all this effort was the emergence of Russia's first unified system of public education, with a common pedagogic methodology and structure to the academic process, one based on a system of separate classes and lessons. The public schools theoretically encompassed all estates, although the fact that they were only established in towns meant that most peasant children in reality had no access to them. Herein lay the reform's chief shortcoming, although fairness requires one to note that the state at this point was simply unable to create a network of schools that would extend to the village level, if only because there were not enough teachers to staff them. This said, the fact remains that the significance of what was accomplished, in terms of extent as well as permanence, was truly immense.

The example set by the empress, who enjoyed reading and writing, exerted a beneficial impact on contemporary Russian culture. Here was a fleeting moment in Russian history in which an alliance, so to speak, was reached between state and culture, a moment when culture had great need of the state's sponsorship. The penetration of the state into the life of society had not yet become all-inclusive, while culture had not yet taken firm hold, had not yet carved out for itself an independent role in society, had not yet arrived at a sense of its own worth. The ideology of "enlightened absolutism" acknowledged the legitimacy of the freedom of word, thought, and self-expression, for the autocracy did not yet perceive a threat in them: that was to come later. In Catherine's time we find the formation of that cultural milieu that was to exist in Russia up to the October of 1917 Revolution. No small role was played by this empress, who elevated its formation to the level of state policy.

The era of Catherine II was a golden age of Russian architecture, painting, music, literature, and theater. Active during this time were architects R. Nikitin, Iu. Felten, J. Vallin de la Mothe, I. Starov, and V. Bazhenov, artists A. Antropov, I. Argunov, F. Rokotov, D. Levitskii, V. Borovikovskii, and A. Losenko, composers D. Bortnianskii, I. Fomin, and V. Pashkevich, and the writers, poets, and dramatists A. Sumarokov, M. Kheraskov, D. Fonvizin, G. Derzhavin, Ia. Kniazhnin, and others. Catherine followed the literary scene closely, encouraged its authors, participated in the creation of projects for the construction of new towns and the reconstruction of the old, and collected those works of art that now make up the core collection of St. Petersburg's Hermitage Museum. The empress deserves special mention for her role in the development of Russian journalism, which flourished in the 1760s and 1770s.

In 1769 the empress founded a satirical journal, entitled "A Little Bit of Everything" [*Vsiakaia vsiachina*], whose official editor was her state secretary, G.V. Kozitskii. Catherine needed the journal in order to express her point of view on socially significant issues. In it she published several articles that in indirect fashion attempted to explain the reasons for the failure of her Legislative Commission. Another of the journal's themes was the exposure and satirizing of a variety of human vices. It gave rise to lively polemics on the nature of satire. The question posed was whether one should seek merely to combat the abstract vices themselves, or attack the specific bearers of those vices. Opposing the empress in this debate was the literary figure Nikolai Ivanovich Novikov, who himself brought out a number of satirical journals in this era.

In the literature devoted to analyzing the polemics between Catherine II and Novikov, one frequently comes across the assertion that they were ideological in nature, and as a result Novikov ended up being censored by the state. The available documentation does not support such a claim. In fact, the difference in their outlooks was at the time quite insignificant. Viewed from another perspective, the open polemics in the press engaged in by the empress with one of her subjects were unprecedented in Russian history. The press, and literature in general, were not yet robust enough to make her feel that she had to defend herself. The other authors, for that matter, were not yet all that bold. Hence it was that the censor's wrath fell only on those works that were considered heretical, atheistic, or immoral. Moreover, the development of science and culture was contributing to the formation of a Russian national consciousness, accompanied by a growth in interest in Russia's historical past and by consideration of the place of the Russian people in world history. It is indicative that Novikov's satirical journals published caustic satires on the blind imitation of French manners and morals.

The shaping of the basic tendencies of Russian social and political thought continued apace in this era. The overly optimistic view of Russian history propounded by the empress inevitably collided with conflicting perspectives. A contrary view was enunciated by Prince Mikhail Mikhailovich Shcherbatov, a government figure, historian, and author of the multivolume *History of Russia* as well as a number of publicistic works. A deputy to the Legislative Commission, Shcherbatov headed what might be termed the aristocratic opposition, being most consistent in defending the interests of the nobility. He best expressed his attitude toward the reality around him in his essay entitled "On the Corruption of Morals in Russia" [*O povrezhdenii nravov v Rossii*], which was not published until the mid-nineteenth century, and even then only in the émigré press. Insofar as Shcherbatov was concerned, the eighteenth century was a period of general decline in morals, which he juxtaposed to the ideals he assumed had prevailed in pre-Petrine Russia. It might be argued that Shcherbatov was a predecessor to the Slavophiles, who represented one of the major currents in nineteenth-century Russian social thought. Like them, he was broadly educated in the European manner, had a sense of wounded national pride, tended to look down on other peoples, and grieved for the erosion of the moral values of Muscovite Rus. By so doing he was expressing what was in essence a conservative point of view.

Another current in Russian social thought at the time was associated with freemasonry. The penetration of masonic ideas into Russia can be traced back to the turn of the century. It was not, however, until mid-century that they truly flourished, when highly visible state dignitaries—the Chernyshev brothers, the Panin brothers, Roman Vorontsov, and others—joined the organization. According to some sources, masonic meetings took place in the presence of Peter III at Oranienbaum while he was still grand duke. Later, Catherine's close collaborator, I.P. Elagin, became a masonic leader. Among other freemasons were the poets Sumarokov, Kheraskov, Maikov, Popov, and Derzhavin, the architect Bazhenov, and the actor Dmitrievskii. Also attracted to freemasonry in their youth were Shcherbatov and Alexander Radishchev, with whom we will deal below. The Freemasons proclaimed emancipation from all estate and national limitations and the construction of a society of free people based on moral purification and self-perfection. For the thinking Russian of the eighteenth century, freemasonry represented a viable alternative to both official state ideology and an equally unacceptable blind imitation of French or British culture. It would seem that in freemasonry the eighteenth-century Russian, already alienated from national tradition, recognizing this alienation, and suffering because of it, assumed he had discovered some sort of "third way." The practical activity of Russian freemasonry was still confined at this time to purely Enlightenment activities.

A new stage in Russian, and in European, freemasonry began in the 1780s. It stemmed from a general disillusionment with Enlightenment ideas. Mystical knowledge now became the key to the Freemasons' spiritual search. We begin to see a belief in the existence of some sort of mystical secret to the universe, one that, if discovered, would lead to humanity's perfection, something that the resort to reason had failed to accomplish. Given this outlook, combined with its secret rituals, freemasonry seemed attractive, even alluring. But with this transformation, it became dangerous in the eyes of the authorities. For they were now dealing with something that appeared to be a new ideology with religious overtones. Catherine II at first viewed freemasonry relatively tolerantly, as nothing more than the misguided product of stupidity and light-headedness. Subsequently, however, she began to sense in it a dangerous attempt to formulate an alternative ideology in which there was no place for her, or, indeed, any autocratic power. In one of the empress's letters from the 1780s, addressed to her close adviser Aleksandr Andreevich Bezborodko, we read:

> I consider it my duty to warn my faithful and gentle people about the temptations dreamed up as teachings outside our borders by all sorts of masonic lodges and . . . other mystical heresies. They incline toward the destruction of Christian Orthodoxy and every beneficent government, introducing in their stead disorganization under the guise of an imaginary and unattainable equality that does not even exist in nature.[25]

The fate of Nikolai Novikov served as a warning to others. In addition to books bearing an Enlightenment character, Novikov began to publish in the late 1770s, on a press leased from Moscow University, a large number of purely masonic works whose distribution in Russia was prohibited. Novikov's masonic activities had long since alarmed the empress, and so when in 1792 a search of his storage facilities uncovered hundreds of copies of forbidden masonic works, the publisher was arrested and handed over for trial. His punishment would not have been as severe had it not been discovered in the course of the investigation that the Freemasons, Novikov included, were maintaining close links with foreign Masons, Prussians in particular, and had attempted to establish contact with the heir to the throne, Grand Duke Pavel Petrovich. So negatively and seriously did Catherine treat any outside effort to influence her son that Novikov was imprisoned in Shlisselburg Fortress for the rest of her reign.

There was yet another direction to Russian social thought of the time, this one represented by Aleksandr Nikolaevich Radishchev. The conventional wisdom is that the formation of a Russian revolutionary ideology began with him. Having received his education abroad, Radishchev became an advocate of the ideas of the enlighteners. But as those ideas were refracted in his outlook, they acquired a radical, nihilistic character, leading him to reject decisively the existing order in Russia, and serfdom first and foremost. A similarly critical attitude toward existing reality was also emerging in Europe; but there, the bourgeoisie became the collective spokesman for revolutionary ideology, as it struggled for its rights. Radishchev and his supporters failed to recognize the distinctions between Russia and Europe in terms of historical development and current situation. Nor had the negative aspects of the French Revolution revealed themselves with sufficient clarity. It seemed to Radishchev, therefore, that revolutionary transformation would resolve all of society's problems and provide the people with genuine freedom. These ideas were propounded by him in a book bearing the title *A Journey from Petersburg to Moscow* [*Puteshestvie iz Peterburga v Moskvu*], which he published on his own printing press in 1790.

In the margins of Radishchev's book Catherine noted: "He is a rebel worse than Pugachev." Just what was it that so upset the empress? It was apparently not the criticism of serfdom but rather an apparent rebellion against what she considered properly constituted authority: indeed, against her own rule. The *Journey*'s author was trying to show that conditions in the state were bad and that the people were living in worse circumstances than she had realized. But Catherine was convinced that this was a lie, a calumny, and that however bad serfdom might be as an institution, her subjects could not possibly be so unhappy. The empress's reaction—confiscation of the book's entire run and the exile of its author—was understandable and natural. The great Russian writer Pushkin subsequently observed that Radishchev's book contained a strange amalgam of all the progressive French ideas current at the time. In half-digested form, he noted, they were superimposed on a distorted perception of the Russian past and present. The sum reflected "ignorant scorn for the entire past, weak-minded amazement at his own age, blind reverence for innovation, bits of superficial knowledge, [and] random accommodation to everything."[26]

Whatever one's reaction to the works and activities of Novikov and Radishchev, it should be borne in mind that the two became the first victims of the state's struggle to repress free thought. Their fate signaled that the alliance between state and culture had come to an end and the long period of opposition between the two had begun.

* * *

Having completed our review of the most important components of Russia's domestic situation in Catherine II's reign, we should note that on the whole it was an era of domestic political stability, although not one of stagnation. It was a time of important governmental initiatives, of legislate activity that affected just about every aspect of state and society and that for the most part had long-term significance. Owing to objective causes and numerous subjective factors associated with her own personality and those of many of her aides, Catherine was not able to implement fully her plans. Still, she proved one of Russia's most successful reformers, and her reforms exhibited a creative rather than a destructive character. The state grew wealthier, and the lives of its subjects more prosperous.

The history of the Catherinean reforms offers an object lesson in the value of gradual reform of society, one eschewing "sharp turns." It is apparent that in their basic content the Catherinean reforms reflected a continuation of the modernization process, one that in this instance concerned not only the external Europeanization of political institutions but the creation of a new social structure. Given the right set of circumstances, this structure might have developed into a civil society. At the same time, the Russian state, the empire, grew in strength, while the political significance of its administrative and policing apparatus increased. The conflict between state and society became for all practical purposes unavoidable. At the center of the controversy lay serfdom, which rendered inevitable the victory of the state principle over the societal.

The era of Catherine II was also a time of intellectual and spiritual fermentation, the formation of national consciousness, and the introduction into society of the concepts of honor and dignity. It was a time of the development of free thought and the encouragement of literature and the fine arts. Despite all, it would be inaccurate to conclude that Catherine's reign comprised some sort of "golden age" in Russian history. Behind the prosperous facade lurked the horrors of serfdom, the prevalence of favoritism, and the flourishing of corruption. The negative tendencies grew especially powerful in the last few years of

Doodles by Catherine II in the margins of a draft legislative project.
Courtesy of the Russian State Archive for Ancient Acts, Moscow (fond 10, opis' 1, delo 22, list 76).

Catherine's reign, when her delusions of grandeur, it would appear, overrode her sober view of the nation's true state of affairs. As Vasilii Kliuchevskii wrote, "To judge on the basis of legal structure and general impression, the empire appeared in the last years of her reign to be a well-proportioned and majestic building. Yet on closer examination there was chaos and disorder, a picture painted with broad and careless strokes, designed to be viewed from afar," but "the general mood smoothed out the rough spots."[27]

Worthy of remark, as already noted, was Catherine's attempt to implement domestic political reform, thus proving in principle the possibility of reform in Russia. Let me cite in conclusion the gist of a letter from Catherine's former state secretary, V.S. Popov, to Emperor Alexander I, in which the former narrates a conversation he had with the empress. He mentioned to her with surprise the blind acceptance with which her wishes had apparently been received by the public, and the eagerness with which everyone had sought to please her. Her response was that it had not been as easy as one might think. With regard to the apparent eagerness of people to please her, the empress insisted that on the contrary, it was she who made the effort to please others according to their merits. This was because it was easier for her to please others than for others to please her. Devoid of whims, caprices, and uneven temper, she found that people tended to enjoy her company. As for the public's willingness to accept her decrees, she claimed that they were observed only if they were suitable for implementation. And they were suitable because she took great pains in their drafting. "I select the circumstances, I get advice, I explore the ideas of the enlightened part of the public, and conclude therefrom what impact my decree will have." Only when she was certain of general approbation did she issue her decrees and have the satisfaction of seeing them obeyed. Herein, according to the empress, lay the secret of what seemed to outsiders to be her unlimited power.[28]

Chapter 7

The Empire Advances

It is time to examine how Catherine II carried out Peter the Great's legacy in the realm of foreign policy. This legacy, first and foremost, involved the strengthening and expansion of the empire by means of new conquests. Viewed from this perspective, Catherine was indeed a worthy heir to the Great Transformer.

As we have seen, particularly in the case of the Ukraine, the imperial perspective altered the Russian attitude toward recently annexed peoples and territories. With the creation of the empire, those territories lost their autonomous status, becoming nothing more than provinces of an empire. This process, begun under Peter I, was revived and given new impetus under Catherine II. In her reign the imperial idea and the imperial consciousness underlying it flourished as never before. At its base lay the conviction that Russia, as Byzantium's successor, had the right to deal with the fate of other peoples as it saw fit. Nationalism, which had appeared in Anna Ioannovna's reign and gained impetus in Elizabeth's, now emerged as a full-fledged ideology, although it had yet to acquire xenophobic overtones or hinder the spread of West European cultural influence, be it German mystical philosophy or French fashion.

Nationalism, with the imperial idea at its base and engendered by the specific nature of eighteenth-century Russian historical development, was not, however, unique to Russia. Rather, its emergence coincided with the birth of nationalism, of attachment to one's native land as a current of social thought, in Western Europe. The empress herself, as already noted, became over time a pronounced Russian patriot. She took great pride, and not without reason, in the fact that she, a foreigner, had managed to become empress of Russia. For foreigners, she wrote, Russia was "a touchstone of their worth." According to her, "He who succeeds in Russia can be certain of succeeding everywhere in Europe.... In Russia, like nowhere else, there are masters at discerning weaknesses, the ridiculous, and shortcomings in a foreigner. One may rest assured that they will miss nothing, because, naturally, no Russian deep in his heart likes any foreigner."[1] At the end of her life Catherine expressed the same idea more pointedly: "There was a time when we were ordered to copy everything from the Danes, then the Dutch, then the Swedes, and then the Germans. But the caftans were too narrow. Designed for small bodies, they did not fit our expanse and were destined to disappear, which is just what happened."[2]

Catherine took justifiable pride in the economic potential, the size of the population, and the territorial expanse of the nation under her scepter. Also impressed with her role as successor to the Byzantine emperors, she believed in the special historical mission of the Russian people, and considered it necessary to carry out this mission in the foreign policy arena. The empress's personal ambition played no small role in this endeavor, for she dreamed of seeing herself not only in the role of great lawgiver and reformer but also basking in the glory of military success. And she had yet another consideration: success in the foreign policy arena would bring great personal prestige to the ruler, thus strengthening her authority with her subjects and therefore her hold on the throne.

From the foregoing it should be apparent that there were a number of motives driving an active foreign policy which, given the practice of international relations in the eighteenth century, could be carried out only at the expense of other, non-Russian peoples. To a great extent, similar motives also drove the foreign policies of other European states. Russia's political, economic, and geographic position in the second half of the eighteenth century, however, determined that its policy would be crowned with success. It was significant that such powerful European nations as Great Britain, France, the United Provinces, and Spain had already largely expended their aggressive ardor on the acquisition of overseas colonies, while a few, such as Britain, even began to lose some of theirs during Catherine's reign. But in contrast, Russia focused its activity not somewhere on the other side of the ocean but along its borders, close to the spheres of interest of other European nations. The emergence of such a powerful competitor could not but alarm its European neighbors.

This brief discussion should not be concluded without noting that certain new traits began to appear in the realm of foreign policy. The spread of the ideas of the Enlightenment, and their acceptance by a number of European monarchs in an effort to buttress the theory of enlightened absolutism, signified that, if only in words, these monarchs would have to proclaim their adherence to the need for peace if the state were to prosper. It was at this time that the art of diplomacy took its place alongside that of warfare, presenting nations with the possibility of obtaining their objectives by peaceful means. The concepts and norms of international law developed and became more complex. For the first time, one had to take account of public opinion, which passed verdict on the actions of sovereigns and states on the basis of "natural reason."

* * *

The Russian Empire's international situation at the moment of Catherine II's accession to the throne was far from simple. The diplomatic successes of Elizabeth's reign, reinforced by the bravery exhibited by the Russian soldiers on the field of battle in the Seven Years' War, had been nullified by the impulsive Peter III. The old foreign policy system had been destroyed, but the new one was unsuitable. Nor was the financial situation any better: the army had not received its pay for seven months. The other nations were no less weakened as a result of the war, however, and they too had to establish anew the direction of their foreign policy. In other words, Catherine was presented with the rare opportunity to elaborate her own foreign policy course without reference to the past. Moreover, inasmuch as Russia had been victorious in the war and its armies were still stationed in Europe, it enjoyed certain advantages over the other nations. So it was predictable that news of the June 28 coup in Petersburg would send shock waves through the courts of Europe, especially the Prussian. The weakness of others lent Catherine strength, so much so that foreign diplomats noted that she treated them in a proud, and even haughty, manner from the very start of her reign. This independent tone when addressing foreigners impressed her court retinue, presenting as it did a sharp contrast with that of Peter III, who tended to fawn before Prussia.

The fundamental problems confronting Russian foreign policy, those that Catherine II had inherited from Petrine times, remained the Turkish and Polish. Poland by now had in effect become a plaything in

Russian hands, a reality Catherine fully recognized. While still grand duchess she had written: "Is a despotic neighbor really more useful to Russia than that happy Polish anarchy that we are imposing?"[3]

Catherine II launched her foreign policy by recalling the Russian troops stationed abroad and confirming peace with Prussia, although she rejected the military alliance Peter III had concluded with Frederick the Great. The Russian government then turned its attention to Courland, which formally recognized Polish suzerainty. Catherine was determined to annex Courland to Russia, and therefore considered it necessary to place on the duchy's throne her own candidate, one who was not tied in any manner to the Polish king. Her candidate was Ernst-Johann Biron, who had been allowed by Peter III to return from exile. In order to achieve her goal, Catherine resorted to firmness, and even brutality, demonstrating to the world, as it were, that her foreign policy would continue along the same path as her predecessors'. In order to acquire the crown for Biron, Russian troops were dispatched to Courland. The international situation favored Russia so strongly that if the troops had been ordered to remain, Courland could have been integrated into the empire already in 1762. But Catherine also wanted to present herself as a just ruler. To that end, she satisfied herself with what she had achieved to date, making Biron her vassal and paving the way for the duchy's absorption into the empire in 1795.

Also in 1762, Catherine had the idea of putting her own candidate on the Polish throne as well. In response to the long-awaited death of King Augustus III in October 1763, she undertook decisive measures. Her new objective was, however, more complex than the Courland venture. In order to achieve it she had to secure the nonintervention of the other European powers. To that end, in March 1764, she signed a new treaty of alliance with Prussia, by which the two sides agreed on joint measures to preserve Poland in its current politically weak state, presenting the two powers with the possibility of shaping Polish politics to their own desires. The Prussian alliance guaranteed the nonintervention of France and Austria, which had their own candidates to propose for the Polish throne. Russia's program was again fortified by the introduction of Russian troops into Poland. In August 1764, as a result, Catherine's erstwhile lover, and in effect her puppet, Stanislaw Poniatowski, was elected king of Poland. At first glance, the election appeared to have been a great victory for Russia; but in fact, Russia would find itself bogged down in the Polish quagmire for years to come.

A powerful party centered on Prince Adam Czartoryski, whose nephew was the newly elected king, sought to reform the Polish governmental structure. With Russian support, its members hoped to introduce hereditary monarchy to Poland, promising in return to improve the legal position of Orthodox Poles, who together with Protestants were categorized as dissidents. Russia found itself in a complicated situation. Public opinion had long insisted on support for the dissidents. But agreement with Czartoryski's plans would require an alteration in the fundamental principles of Russian policy toward Poland. After much agonizing, Catherine demanded full rights for the dissidents but refused to permit political reform of the state. In consequence, Russia sacrificed the support of a pivotal political force. Catherine's policy collapsed in 1768, when the so-called Confederation of Bar, comprised of important Polish magnates, armed itself in opposition to Russian demands. Once again Russian troops had to be dispatched to Poland, this time under the command of Alexander Suvorov. Although Suvorov was on the whole successful, the resolution to the Polish problem was put off.

In the meantime, Russian high-handedness in Poland had disquieted Austria and France. Their alarm was increased by the Russian attempt to form a "Northern System," a network of alliances propounded by Nikita Panin, the director of Russian foreign policy at the time. It called for the creation of a set of alliances with the Protestant states of Northern Europe, designed to provide Russia with a leading role in world politics. France and Austria thought it necessary to divert Russia's attention and to channel its energies elsewhere. As the result of complicated intrigues, they managed to arouse the Ottoman Empire to declare war on Russia in the fall of 1768.

Although more than five years had elapsed since Catherine II had ascended the throne, Russia was still inadequately prepared for war. It entered hostilities without any particular enthusiasm, all the more so because military conflict with the Turks elicited unpleasant associations. Still, the empress herself was full of enthusiasm, and she became utterly absorbed with this field of activity, which was entirely new to her. One of her letters from this time reads:

> . . . thus I found it necessary to order our forces to gather in the designated places, and assigned the commands to two experienced generals: the main army to Prince Golitsyn and the other to Count Rumiantsev. May God grant the first the same good fortune his father enjoyed, and the

second the same good luck! If I had feared the Turks, I would have called upon Field Marshal Saltykov, who has already covered himself with glory. But, taking into account the great complexities of this war, I decided to protect that distinguished warrior of many years, who in any case has earned enough glory. I am absolutely confident that regardless of which generals I might choose, each will be more than a match for his opponent, the vizier whom the enemy appoints. God will punish those who have started this war! God sees that it was not I who did the instigating. But it will not be the first time that Russia confounds its enemies, for it has conquered [enemies] in more dangerous circumstances than the present. Hence it is that, thanks to God's mercy and the bravery of His people, we await the same favorable outcome in the current circumstances.[4]

Upon entering into war with the Ottoman Empire, the Russian government concluded that its primary objectives would be recognition of its right to the free navigation of the Black Sea, the acquisition of a suitable port along the Black Sea coast, and the establishment of secure borders with Poland. The course of the war at first favored Russia. By spring 1769, Russian troops had already occupied the towns of Azov and Taganrog, and at the end of April they defeated two powerful detachments of Turks at Khotin, although the fortress itself was not seized until September. Then, in September and October, they chased the Turks from Moldavia, leading Catherine to begin to call herself princess of Moldavia. In November, Russian troops took Bucharest. A Russian corps sent to Georgia also met with success. Finally, on June 24–26, 1770, a Russian fleet commanded by Alexei Orlov gained a remarkable victory over a Turkish fleet almost twice its size in the harbor at Chesme. The Turks lost fifteen ships, six frigates, and almost fifty smaller ships: in sum, just about all its fleet.

A short time later, the Russian infantry achieved equally remarkable victories. In early July, a Russian army commanded by Peter Rumiantsev defeated the combined forces of the Turks and Crimean Tatars at the Larga River, close to where it joins the Pruth. The Turks left more than a thousand men on the field of battle, while the Russians suffered only twenty-nine dead. On July 21, a celebrated battle took place at the Kagul River, where Rumiantsev's twenty-seven-thousand-man detachment managed to defeat an enemy force of 150,000, about 100,000 of whom actually participated in the battle.

From July through October 1770, the Russians seized the fortresses of Izmail, Kilia, and Akkerman. In September, General Peter Panin took Bender. In 1771, Russian troops under the command of Prince Vasilii Dolgorukii entered the Crimea, and within several months seized its major fortified points.

It would seem that everything was going smoothly; but in reality, the situation was more complex. For one thing, simultaneous war in Poland (against the Confederation of Bar), Moldavia, the Crimea, the Caucasus, and Central Asia was imposing an almost unbearable strain on Russia's forces. For another, it was clear that the European powers would not tolerate a major accretion of Russian strength at the expense of the Ottoman Empire. Therefore, Russia could not count on retaining all the conquests it had made in the course of the war. Back in 1770, Russia had already made peace overtures, but the Porte, actively supported by Austria, showed no interest in ending hostilities. Nothing but participation in the first partition of Poland in 1772 could dissuade Austria from supporting the Turks.

The idea of profiting from the war at the expense of Poland first arose at the court of Petersburg in the early years of Catherine's reign. Prussia repeatedly put forward similar proposals throughout the 1760s. For a time, the empress hoped to acquire the Polish-held territories of Lithuania and Belorussia, which she considered historically Russian, while preserving a smaller, nominally independent Poland to serve as a buffer between Russia and Prussia. The war with the Confederates, whom Austria supported, dragged on, however, and Russian policymakers realized that they would have to come to some sort of agreement with Austria if Russia was to free itself to deal with the Polish and Turkish wars.

These circumstances produced an agreement to partition Poland, which was signed July 25, 1772. According to the document, Russia obtained the Polish portion of Livonia (the territory of present-day Lithuania and southern Latvia), as well as the counties of Polotsk, Vitebsk, Mstislav, and part of Minsk. Austria got Galicia (present-day Western Ukraine), while Prussia got the counties of Pomorze, Chelm, and Malbork, part of Great Poland, and Bazmilia.

At first glance, Russia appeared to have acquired the most significant share. In all, it annexed 92,000 square kilometers of territory with a population of one million three hundred thousand people. But in reality, its plunder was rather modest in both strategic and economic terms, for Austria obtained the very important economic and commercial center of Lvov, while Prussia got the most highly developed agricultural regions. It is true that Russia asserted its own sphere of influence over what remained of the Polish-Lithuanian Commonwealth. For all practical purposes, the Polish king could do nothing without the approval of the Russian ambassador to Warsaw until 1788. With Russia's consent, King Stanislaw August Poniatowski in 1776 implemented reforms designed to strengthen the Polish state system, thus permitting Russia to withdraw its troops from Poland in 1780.

In 1774, after long negotiations, Russia finally managed to conclude peace with the Ottoman Empire. According to the Treaty of Kuchuk-Kainardji (named after the village where the treaty was signed), Russia finally obtained free passage for its merchant ships through the Bosphorus and Dardanelles, the fortresses of Kerch and Yenikale, and a substantial financial indemnity. The Turks were obligated to grant autonomy to Moldavia and Wallachia, to cease oppressing the Orthodox in the Caucasus, and also to recognize the independence of the Crimea—an independence that, from the perspective of Russia's policymakers, would secure its integration into the Russian empire at a future date.

The Treaty of Kuchuk-Kainardji brought to an end the first phase of Catherine II's foreign policy activity. The next, encompassing the 1770s through the mid-1790s, was also marked by major successes in the diplomatic and military spheres. But they were to be achieved under differing circumstances, for the correlation of forces in the foreign policy arena would shift somewhat in this later period.

The lands Russia acquired by dint of the Treaty of Kuchuk-Kainardji were wedged in between the possessions of the Ottoman Empire, Poland, and the Crimean khanate, a situation that served to guarantee future confrontations. It was clear, moreover, that Russia would seek to strengthen its position along the northern Black Sea coast, and that the Ottoman Empire would resist any such move. In reality, heartened by internal disorders in Russia, the Turks substantially reinforced the garrisons of their fortresses on the northern coast of the Black Sea and inundated the Crimea and the Kuban with their agents, while the Turkish fleet carried out naval demonstrations close to the Crimean coast. In so doing, the Ottoman Empire was counting on the support of the European powers, primarily England. By 1775, however, England's attention was deflected for the immediate future by war with its rebellious North American colonies. It would even find it necessary to turn to Russia with an appeal for a corps of twenty thousand soldiers to aid it in its struggle with the American rebels. As diplomatically as she could, Catherine refused, but she watched the developing conflict attentively, hoping to take advantage of it for her own purposes.

Meanwhile, in December 1774 a revolution had taken place in the Crimea. It brought to the throne a new khan, Devlet Giray, who attempted to court both the Ottoman Empire and Russia. The Russian government would have nothing to do with him, as it wanted a khan whose loyalty would be exclusively to Russia. Russia's candidate was Shahin Giray, and in order to achieve his elevation to the throne, Russian troops prepared to invade the Crimea in the spring of 1776.

Russia obtained support for its activities in the Crimea by strengthening its alliance with Prussia. A new agreement between the two was signed in August 1776, and by November Russian forces had entered the Crimea. In March of the next year, the old treaty of friendship with Prussia was extended, and in April, Shahin Giray was placed on the khanate's throne. When a revolt was raised against him less than a year later, it was suppressed with the assistance of Russian troops.

While these maneuvers were in progress, a new conflict between Austria and Prussia broke out in Central Europe. The point of contention was Bavaria, a part of which Austrian Emperor Joseph II had attempted to annex to his domains. Unwilling to tolerate a radical shift in the balance of power, Prussia immediately turned to Russia for assistance, which it had every right to expect thanks to the treaty it had just renewed, while Austria turned to France for help. But the latter was on the eve of war with England, and therefore had no interest in fanning the fires of war on the European continent. When in spring 1778 war between Austria and Prussia nonetheless broke out, and the Ottoman Empire at just about the same time undertook an unsuccessful attempt to land troops in the Crimea, France offered its services to mediate both conflicts. Prussia agreed to France's proposal, but with the proviso that Russia be added as comediator. Suddenly, the Russian government was faced with the pleasant prospect of significantly strengthening its presence in the international arena.

In March 1779, a peace congress opened at Teschen (in present-day Poland), to all practical purposes under the aegis of Russian minister Prince N.V. Repnin. The congress concluded in May with the signing of the Teschen peace agreement, which represented a substantial victory for Russian diplomacy. In keeping with the terms of the treaty, Russia became not only mediator of the final treaty but guarantor of the peace, which gave it the possibility of intervening directly in German affairs. Equally important was the mutual understanding that Russia achieved with France, with which relations had been strained for years, since Elizaveta Petrovna's reign. With France's mediation, a Russo-Turkish agreement, an "explanatory convention," also was signed, which confirmed Crimean independence and Shahin Giray's rights to the khanate's throne.

The year 1780 witnessed still another success for Russian diplomacy, when the empress produced an important international initiative: the celebrated Declaration of Armed Neutrality. According to its stipulations, the ships of nations that were not party to a military conflict had the right to trade freely with all nations, even belligerents, without fear of interruption. It also propounded a narrow definition of contraband, one that excluded naval stores, an important Russian export. The declaration was directed primarily against Great Britain, which was attempting to cut off Russian seagoing commerce with British enemies. Soon Sweden, Denmark, the United Provinces, and others had joined the league that was created to enforce the principle of free ships, free goods.[5] In effect, an anti-English coalition was formed. Although it remained neutral, to the extent that it limited the freedom of action of the Royal Navy on the high seas it aided the American cause. It was at this time also that the idea of the so-called "Greek Project" arose within Russian governing circles.

At the heart of the "Greek project" lay the intention of reestablishing the Greek empire, with its capital at Constantinople, and with Catherine's second grandson, Konstantin Pavlovich, as its emperor. Indeed, the tsarevich, who was born in 1779, was given the name Konstantin (Constantine) with the "Greek project" in mind. At the celebrations marking his birth, Greek poems were read and a medal was struck with a representation of the cathedral of St. Sophia (by then transformed into a mosque) in Constantinople. Such a development in Russian foreign policy doctrine was dictated by the very logic of events. For, as the historian Alexander Brückner, one of Catherine's first scholarly biographers, has noted: "Each acquisition by Russia at the expense of the Turks and Tatars impelled the Russian government to extend its aggressive activities still farther."[6]

Russia's newly acquired status in the international arena, attained in consequence of its successes at the Congress of Teschen, instilled it with confidence in its ability to execute the project. But in order to bring the plan to fruition, Russia would have to revert to the Austrian alliance. It was not particularly difficult to decide to carry out the switch, because all the possible benefits of the Prussian alliance had been exhausted. The first step toward a rapprochement with Austria was taken in the spring of 1780, when, during Catherine's tour of her newly acquired western provinces, she arranged a meeting with Habsburg emperor Joseph II. It was then that agreement on an anti-Turkish alliance was reached, much to the satisfaction of both rulers. This agreement made provision, at least in general terms, for the execution of the "Greek project." A year later, Catherine II and Joseph II exchanged official, although private, letters outlining their mutual obligations in the event of war with the Ottoman Empire, and calling for the preservation of the Polish political system in its existing weak form. The exchange of letters, dreamed up by Catherine, represented an innovation in international relations, one that increased the likelihood of the agreement remaining secret. This was followed by an exchange of letters that dealt directly with the reestablishment of the Greek empire. It should be noted that no official agreement concerning the "Greek project" was ever concluded because the plan was too bold to be permitted to become widely known. In essence, the "Greek project" was a long-range goal, a dream of the empress and the basis of her foreign policy doctrine.*

By the early 1780s, the situation in the Crimea had once again deteriorated. Shahin Giray's hold on the throne had weakened noticeably, and in the spring of 1782 he had to flee to Kerch in search of Russian protection. The Ottoman Empire was preparing to place its own candidate on the khanate's throne when Catherine gave Grigorii Potemkin the order to dispatch Russian troops to the Crimea. These troops placed Shahin Giray back on the throne. But having done so, this time they did not leave. After several months of hesitation, Catherine received assurances of total support from Austria, and on April 8, 1783, she signed a manifesto "On the Acceptance of the Crimean Peninsula, the Island of Taman, and the Entire Kuban Side into the Russian State."

The annexation of the Crimea was rendered possible by strong Austrian diplomatic support and the nonintervention of the other European

---

*As Isabel de Madariaga has described it, the Greek Project "was an aim, a direction, a dream" (Madariaga, *Russia in the Age of Catherine the Great,* p. 384).

powers, which, disinclined to rush to the defense of the Turks, convinced them to accept the inevitable. Yet the annexation itself did not proceed without complications. In summer 1783, Nogay Tatars who inhabited the Kuban's coast rose up against Russian domination. In August, a Russian detachment of a thousand men crushed an uprising of Nogays, who greatly outnumbered it. The Russian forces were commanded by Alexander Suvorov, whose secret maneuvers took the Nogays completely by surprise. Finally, on August 1, 1783, the Nogays were soundly defeated at the mouth of the Laba River, and the Kuban was integrated into the Russian Empire.

By now the borders of the Russian Empire pressed up against the Caucasus Mountains. The people who lived there were squeezed between Russia, the Ottoman Empire, and Iran, a situation that rendered the survival of the small independent states highly questionable. It was clear that in the growing military collision between Russia and the Ottoman Empire, the Caucasus could well become a theater of military operations, and that before war broke out the mountain people would have to choose one or the other side. Since events of recent years had demonstrated that Russia was becoming the dominant power in the region, it would be wisest to ally with it. It was also no small matter that the peoples of Georgia and Armenia adhered to Eastern Orthodoxy, and so unification with Russia would at least guarantee that there would be no religious oppression. After negotiations between the Russian government and representatives of the Kartlo-Kakheti ruler Heraclius II, the Treaty of Georgievsk was signed on July 24, 1783. By the terms of the treaty, the Kartlo-Kakheti kingdom accepted Russian protectorship, which guaranteed its inviolability and territorial integrity. In keeping with the treaty's secret provisions, two battalions of Russian troops were stationed in Tiflis (present-day Tbilisi).

The following years of Catherine's foreign policy were marked by diplomatic activity designed to secure Russia's position in the international arena by establishing closer relations with Austria, and to a lesser extent France. As a consequence, Russia's relations with Prussia and England became strained. In January 1787, Catherine, accompanied by the court and selected foreign diplomats, set off on her fabled trip through the Crimea. The journey was important primarily for its international implications. While in the Crimea, Catherine was to meet with the Austrian emperor and the Polish king, and to display to them Russia's growing military might. The chief objective of this grandiose

Prince G.A. Potemkin. From an engraving by G.T. Kharitonov.

undertaking, whose main architect was Grigorii Potemkin, was to frighten the Ottoman Empire into submission. It is from Catherine II's trip to the Crimea that the well-known term "Potemkin village" stems. It is alleged that Potemkin constructed lavish sets intended to represent nonexistent settlements along the route. Such staging was in fact fairly typical of all court celebrations of the time. Moreover, Potemkin decorated actual settlements; but he decorated them so extravagantly that viewers began to doubt the genuineness of those settlements that actually existed.

All of this extravagant staging, in conjunction with the demonstrations carried out by Russian army regiments, Tatar and Kalmyk cavalry, and the Black Sea fleet, created an indelible impression on foreigners. The French minister to Russia, Count Ségur, recalled his conversation with Emperor Joseph II, who exclaimed to him: "What a singular journey! Who would have dreamed that, together with Catherine the Second and the ministers of France and England, I would be wandering in the Tatar steppes! This is altogether a new page in history!" "It seems to me instead," responded Ségur, "like a page from *A Thousand and One Nights,* that my name is Gaafar, and I am walking with the Caliph Haroun al-Rashid, who, according to his custom is in disguise."[7]

The imperial theme pervaded the entire organization of Catherine's journey to the Crimea and dominated all of Potemkin's grandiose staging. Thus, the gates set up at the entrance to Kherson were designated the road to Byzantium, while the newly built towns in New Russia were given Greek names. Joseph II's presence underscored the common intentions shared by Vienna and St. Petersburg.

The opportunity to seek to carry out these intentions came sooner than anticipated. In mid-July 1787, the Russian ambassador to Constantinople was presented with an ultimatum containing demands designed to be unacceptable. It was then announced that all hitherto existing treaties between the two governments were abrogated, and the return of the Crimea was demanded. This ultimatum heralded the start of the second Russo-Turkish war.

Russia entered the war without having completed preparations for it. Army units were not yet at full strength, the construction of the Black Sea fleet was still unfinished, and stores of supplies and munitions were lacking. On September 7, however, Catherine signed a declaration of war. Potemkin was named commander in chief of the Russian army. He himself took control of the main, or Ekaterinoslav, army, which numbered up to eighty-two thousand men. Command of the second army, about half that size, was given to Rumiantsev. A twelve-thousand-man detachment was to operate in the Caucasus, while the Don Cossacks were to cover the Kuban.

Turkish plans called for large-scale landings in the Crimea and at the mouth of the Dnieper River at the start of the war, while the major offensive would be conducted in Moldavia. In October 1787, a Turkish fleet blockaded the mouth of the Dnieper and disembarked a six-thousand-man detachment on the Kinburn spit. But it was awaited by a detachment of Russian troops commanded by Suvorov, who gained a spectacular victory over the Turks. This victory on the Kinburn spit at the very beginning of the war proved extremely important to the Russian army. But not every undertaking went so smoothly. Back in September, Russia's Sevastopol fleet had been battered by a storm. As a result, the siege of the Ochakov Fortress was long delayed, with the Russian army unable to capture it until December 1788. The measures undertaken by Austria, which had by now entered the war on the Russian side, proved ineffective, and there was no reason to count on any particular assistance from that quarter. The slow response of the allies and their indecisiveness were interpreted by some as weakness, and in summer 1788, spurred on by Britain and Prussia, Sweden attacked Russia. Still smarting from the terms of the peace of Nystadt of 1721, the Swedes were dreaming of revenge.

The decisive naval battle with the Swedes took place off the island of Hogland on July 6. Both fleets were badly battered. Russian sailors under the command of Admiral Samuel Greig seized the Swedish seventy-gun ship *Prince Gustavus,* and the Swedes—the *Vladislav,* a Russian ship of comparable size. The Swedes, however, were the first to veer off, allowing the Russians to claim victory. Deprived of naval support, Swedish infantry units enjoyed little success in 1789, and so Sweden had to make peace the following year.

The year 1789 proved to be a decisive one in the Russo-Turkish war as well, marked as it was by additional Suvorov victories. On July 21, an army of five thousand Russians and twelve thousand Austrians placed under his command took by storm the Turks' fortified camp near Fokshany, destroying in the process a thirty-thousand-man Turkish corps commanded by Mustapha Pasha. A month and a half later, after completing in two and one half days a strenuous forced march of one hundred versts, or roughly sixty-six miles, Suvorov inflicted a crushing defeat on the Turks at the Rymnik River.

In the last few months of 1789, Russian forces took Akkerman and Bender while their Austrian counterparts seized Belgrade and Bucharest. The international situation as a whole, however, was shaping up unfavorably for Russia and Austria. Sweden was waging war against Russia, while Prussia opposed Austria. Nor was there any reason to count on the support of France, where revolution had broken out in July. Prussia in the meanwhile had activated its diplomacy, concluding treaties with Poland and the Ottoman Empire. When Emperor Joseph II died in March 1790 and his successor, Leopold II, fearing war with Prussia, was forced to conclude a cease-fire with the Ottomans, Russia was left to face its enemies alone.

There was disagreement at the court of St. Petersburg about the wisdom of pursuing the war. Catherine, however, accurately concluded that when push came to shove, Prussia would avoid an open conflict with Russia, while Britain's attention would be diverted by the events occurring across the channel in France. At the end of 1790, the Russian army gained a number of convincing victories over the Turks, the most stunning being the capture of Izmail, a fortress the Turks had considered impregnable.

Turkish forces also suffered defeat in the Northern Caucasus. Finally, on July 31, 1791, the Russian fleet under the command of Fedor Ushakov defeated the Turkish fleet south of Cape Kaliakra. On the very same day, an armistice was concluded with the Turks, who had sued for peace. At the end of December, the long-awaited peace treaty was signed at Jassy. By the terms of the treaty, the Ottoman Empire was finally forced to recognize the Russian annexation of the Crimea, and the Dniester River was designated the border between the two powers.

While the Russo-Turkish war was being waged, the Polish problem was growing more and more acute. In 1787, King Stanislaw August had undertaken another attempt to strengthen the Polish state system by means of domestic political reform. To Russia he proposed Polish military assistance in its struggle with the Ottoman Empire in return for Russia's support of reform in Poland. Prussia, however, opposed the conclusion of the agreement, which had already been drawn up. Meanwhile, the Polish Diet, later to be known as the Four-Year Diet, was convened. It was Stanislaw August's plan that the Diet would approve the strengthening of royal authority. Strong antimonarchic opposition within the Diet, however, led to a reorientation of Polish politics away from Russia and toward Prussia, resulting in the Polish-Prussian treaty of 1790 mentioned above. The Diet adopted a number of important measures, the most important of which was promulgation of the constitution of May 3, 1791.

Claiming that it upset the established international order, Catherine II expressed alarm and anger at news of the Polish constitution. She made it clear that a strong, independent Poland was not at all to her liking. Once Austro-Prussian and Russo-Turkish tensions were resolved, she moved her troops into Poland.

The Russian campaign in Poland did not last long, and by the summer of 1792, the Russian army controlled all of the Polish-Lithuanian Commonwealth. In December, Petersburg responded positively to Prussia's proposal for another partition of Poland, which was officially announced in April of the following year. Thanks to this second partition, Prussia acquired 58,000 square kilometers of territory, encompassing the cities of Danzig, Thorn, and Poznan. The Russian empire increased its holdings by 250,000 square kilometers, and it now included Eastern Belorussia and the Right-Bank Ukraine. The Austrians did not participate in this partition.

In the aftermath of the second partition of Poland, a broad-scale Polish patriotic movement erupted, headed by Tadeusz Kosciuszko. At first, the rebels enjoyed success. But their hopes were dashed when Suvorov assumed command of the Russian troops. After Kosciuszko's uprising was crushed, the Central European powers carried out the third and final partition of Poland in October 1795. Austria received 47,000 square kilometers of Polish land, including the city of Lublin, and Prussia acquired 48,000 square kilometers, including Warsaw, while Russia got 120,000 square kilometers, including Western Volhynia, Lithuania, and Courland. The third partition of Poland put a temporary end to Polish statehood, which did not reemerge until 1918.

Catherine's activities in the foreign-policy arena in the last years of her reign were by and large conditioned by the revolutionary events taking place in France. At first, those events elicited from the empress something approaching malignant joy, reflecting the critical attitude she had always maintained toward the political regime in France. News of the events in France, including the enunciation of the Declaration of the Rights of Man and Citizen, the basic ideas of which corresponded with the ideas set forth in the empress's Grand Instructions, was regularly published in the Russian press. By 1792, however, the empress was interpreting the events more and more as a rebellion against constituted authority, and therefore as a threat to all the monarchs of Europe. Catherine actively aided the French émigrés and participated in the formation of an anti-French coalition, especially once news was received in Russia at the beginning of 1793 of the execution of the French king and queen. As long as she lived, however, Catherine never sent the Russian army into action against the French. The empress counted on enmeshing Austria and Prussia in French affairs, thus freeing herself to pursue the execution of her own plans.

When offering an overall evaluation of Catherine's foreign policy, it has to be acknowledged that in keeping with the spirit of the times, with contemporaneous ideas, and with the concrete circumstances of the international situation, the policy bore a markedly imperial character, one distinguished by expansionism; a lack of regard for the interests of other peoples; and, to a certain degree, aggressiveness. Catherine II successfully continued, and triumphantly completed, the process begun by Peter I, transforming the Russian empire into a great world power. The impressive foreign policy achievements of Catherine's thirty-four years on the Russian throne, reflected in substantial territorial acquisitions and a clear-cut solidification of Russia's claim to a leading role in world politics, permitted it to act in its own interests in resolving almost any international issue. For better or for worse, they also gave her nineteenth-century successors the chance to expand the empire's frontiers still farther.

It might be argued that the "one and indivisible" empire (to resort to an official formulation widespread in prerevolutionary Russia and now again enjoying popularity), with its seemingly inexhaustible human and economic resources and endless spaces that swallowed up any invader, was created in the Catherinean era. It was a multinational state with a unique ethnic, economic, cultural, and social makeup. The victories achieved by Catherine's commanders on land and on sea caused the hearts of the Russian people to swell with pride. But they also contributed to the formation of an imperial ideology. We see this ideology reflected in the boast of A.A. Bezborodko, the leading member of Catherine's Collegium of Foreign Affairs, that no cannon could be fired in Europe during the empress's lifetime without her permission.

The foreign-policy successes of Catherine's reign were of course impressive, and were evaluated as such by her contemporaries as well as by several generations of Russian posterity. From the longer historical perspective, however, many of these apparent successes eventually posed serious problems for Russia and its people. For one thing, the empire took shape as a unified state with a strong, centralized authority, features which helped it survive for many years; for only strong centralized authority could maintain this huge nation in subservience. But at the same time, the empire gradually came to view itself as the highest form of organization and its preservation as a vitally important patriotic duty. It is evident that given such a vision, the interests of individuals as well as whole peoples were secondary in the best of cases, and usually simply ignored. The national interests of all the peoples inhabiting the empire were infringed on, including the Russian people, the people of the metropolis, who not only failed to derive any benefit from this situation but were forced to shoulder the primary burden for the nation's viability. Even worse, the empire's minorities associated the government's colonialist policies with the Russian people, a perspective that in turn encouraged the inflammation of national discord.

In addition, Russia's active participation in the partitions of Poland defined the character of Russo-Polish relations for the next two centuries, transforming them into a central factor in Russian foreign policy. To a great extent, international stability came to depend upon relations among those powers that had participated in the partitions. Because the Polish people could not accept the destruction of their statehood, over the course of the nineteenth century the Russian government repeatedly had to resort to military force to suppress uprisings in Poland. Since the force was applied by Russian soldiers, it naturally gave rise to strong anti-Russian sentiment. "The specter of the Polish-Lithuanian Commonwealth arising from its historical grave," noted V.O. Kliuchevskii, "created the impression of living, popular strength. It may well be that in order to avoid the hatred of the people, their statehood should have been preserved."[8]

On a closing note, the appearance in Russia of the Jewish question (just how it was "resolved" was treated in the preceding chapter) was also linked with the partitions of Poland, for it was from partitioned Polish territory that Russia acquired most of its Jews.

* * *

Catherine II's reign, one of the longest in Russian history, came to an end with her death in November 1796. She died unexpectedly, without having completed her intended reforms, or having implemented even those projects that were already down on paper. Among the latter was the draft of a manifesto on the order of succession to the throne, drawn up in 1785. It was intended to be part of a larger complex of laws. The fact that the empress did not manage to carry out her intentions, coupled with her complicated relationship with her son Paul, gave rise to rumors, which have made their way into the historical literature, to the effect that she intended to deprive her son of the throne, passing it on instead to her grandson Alexander. The available evidence, however, lends no credence to this assertion. To leave the throne to her grandson, bypassing her son, would have signified to Catherine a rejection of those very principles of legality that she had so adamantly propounded throughout her lifetime. Consequently, she could not bring herself to take the step, although she undoubtedly realized that after her death many of her reforms might well be consigned to oblivion. In one of those revealing notes she wrote for herself, she commented: "I am not sure for whom I am laboring, or if my work, my concern, and my ardent effort on behalf of the empire will prove to be in vain, for I see that I cannot render my way of thinking hereditary."[9]

With the death of Catherine II, an epoch in Russian history came to a close, an epoch that mirrored all the most important themes that spanned the eighteenth century and that had their origins in the Petrine reforms. Russia had become a powerful police-bureaucratic state with a strong army and navy and a leading role in international relations. An important stage in the formation of a new Russian culture, a national science, and the arts had been concluded. In almost three and one half decades on the Russian throne, Catherine herself had become a symbol of Russia, its wealth and its power. During this period, two generations had grown up without knowing another sovereign, without experiencing massive repression, and accustomed to foreign policy successes and stability in political life. It was to be the children of those who composed the "unflogged generations" of nobles, to resort to Natan Eidelman's felicitous expression, who would play such a defining role in the nation's fate in the following century.

With Catherine II's departure from the scene, eighteenth-century Russia expired, although, according to the calendar, it still had four years of life remaining.

Paul I in his youth. Engraving from a portrait by L.M. Bonne.

Chapter 8

"He Wanted to Be an Ivan IV"

Following Catherine II's death in November 1796, her son, Emperor Paul I, ascended the throne. In order to understand and properly assess the short but exceptionally important and event-filled reign of one of the most puzzling and contradictory figures in Russian history, one must bear in mind that the new ruler was already forty-two years old when he ascended the throne. So he was a mature person, with his character, political convictions, and notions of Russia's needs and the best methods of meeting them already formed. The emperor's character and political views had taken shape under very unstable and unusual circumstances.

Because the empress was extremely concerned about perpetuating the dynasty, Paul's birth in 1754 was greeted at Elizaveta Petrovna's court as a long-anticipated and welcome event. Immediately after birth, the child was taken into Elizabeth's chambers, to which his parents were admitted only by special permission. Until the coup d'état of 1762, Paul was raised for all practical purposes without parental affection, knowing neither his mother nor his father well. The latter cared little for him: in his manifesto on his accession to the throne, in fact, neither Paul nor Catherine was even mentioned. In 1761, Nikita Ivanovich Panin was named his chief mentor, and over the years, he grew genuinely fond of his charge. Himself an advocate of the enlightenment, he dreamed of raising Paul to be an ideal sovereign for Russia. In reality, according to contemporaries, the young Paul was a well-educated, romantic youth, one who believed in the ideals of enlightened absolutism. He was well prepared for governmental affairs and grew up with the realization that he would one day rule Russia. Aware of this future, he compared the theory he had learned with existing reality, espied a lack of correspondence between the two, and gradually began to criticize his mother's policies. Catherine, however, had no intention of yielding the throne to her son, or even of sharing power with him. She nonetheless knew that both at court and in the nation at large there were more than a few people who preferred the son to the mother.

If Paul's ambition had not been played upon by various intriguers, who constantly reminded him of his rights to the throne, his relations with his mother might have turned out differently. But over the course of Catherine's reign, the grand duke's name constantly cropped up in testimony at various political trials, while rumors of his accession to the throne spread throughout the country. Pugachev even referred to him as his "son." All of this compelled the empress to treat Paul gingerly, and even with suspicion. She accordingly did everything she could to keep him from meddling in politics. In turn, Paul grew irritated and disenchanted. As a reasonably intelligent and energetic person, he fretted over his lack of involvement in affairs of state, as with the passage of the years he was forced to observe from the sidelines matters he considered his by right. He viewed as an insult and degradation the fact that the empress's favorites enjoyed more authority than he, the legitimate heir to the throne. To this must be added the mockery and caustic comments of his mother, who considered the young Paul too naive and sensitive, thereby unwittingly embittering him. Paul's character gradually changed for the worse: he grew more nervous, quick-tempered, suspicious, bitter, and despotic.

In 1773, Paul married Princess Wilhelmine of Hesse-Darmstadt who upon her conversion to Orthodoxy took the name of Natalia Alekseevna. Having just outgrown the supervision of his mentors and teachers, the young man fell madly in love with his equally young wife. Sadly, that love did not last long; for in 1776, Natalia Alekseevna died in childbirth. Seeking to console her son, who was devastated with grief, Catherine tried to prove to him that his wife had been unfaithful. She apparently succeeded; for, a few months later, Paul was married again, this time to Princess Sophie Dorothea of Württemberg, who upon her conversion to Orthodoxy was given the name of Mariia Fedorovna. In 1777, they had a son, the future Emperor Alexander I, and in 1779, another son, Constantine. Both grandsons were taken from their parents and raised under their grandmother's direct supervision.

In 1781–1782, Paul and Mariia Fedorovna toured Europe, where they created positive impressions at major European courts. But toward the end of the journey, Paul acted carelessly, openly criticizing Catherine's policies and her favorites. His lack of discretion became known to the empress who, upon his return, attempted to remove him from court by presenting him with the country estate of Gatchina, where henceforth Paul would spend much of his time.

As Peter I had once done at Preobrazhenskoe, and Peter III at Oranienbaum, Paul now created his own little army at Gatchina, spending his time drilling his troops, taking as his model the Prussian military system. To the luxury and disorderly life of the Petersburg court he juxtaposed the discipline, order, and asceticism (of a certain sort) maintained at his estate. He took delight in the unconditional subordination of his soldiers, dreaming of the time when all of Russia would be similarly subordinated to him. Catherine, it seemed to him, was too lax and liberal, qualities inappropriate for a true autocrat, and associated in his mind with the shortcomings of female rule. All of this, he believed, had a detrimental impact on the condition of the nation which, especially after the revolutionary events in France, was faced with a serious revolutionary threat of its own. The danger could be avoided only by recourse to strong authority. The historian N.K. Shilder, who was Paul's first scholarly biographer, narrates an episode relating to the French Revolution:

> Once when Pavel Petrovich was reading newspapers in the empress's office, he became furious. "What are they talking about there!" he cried out. "I would immediately put an end to it all with cannons." Catherine responded to her son: "You are a wild beast, or don't you understand that cannons cannot combat ideas? If you rule in such a fashion, your reign will not last long."[1]

Paul's inclination to deal with the French rebels with the aid of cannons was not, however, merely a reflection of his mercilessness or political myopia. Behind it lay a specific worldview, one according to which the existing regime had to be preserved at all costs in order to avoid revolution. This was to be accomplished by resorting to military discipline and policing measures and by purging the nation of all its harmful elements, embodied, according to Paul, in various manifestations of individual and social liberty. These manifestations Paul claimed to see in the behavior and way of life of the nobles, in their neglect of state service, in the Catherinean elements of self-government, in the excessive luxury of the court, and in the relative freedom of thought and expression, viewing them all as consequences of the mistaken nature of Catherine's policies. As Roderick McGrew, the author of a recent biography of Paul I, notes, by the time Catherine died, he was completely blind to her achievements and totally out of sympathy with her objectives. Given the nation's parlous situation, he was persuaded that he would have to carry out a revolution in order to forestall a worse revolution.[2]

To the Enlightenment ideals of civil liberty Paul juxtaposed those of medieval knighthood, with its concepts of nobility, faithfulness, honor, bravery, and service to the sovereign. This was, wrote historian Natan Eidelman, "a knightly, conservative ideal that was intended to combat 'liberty, equality, fraternity'.... Knighthood against Jacobinism ... that is, ennobled inequality against 'wicked equality.' "[3]

Paul's dreams were partially realized on November 6, 1796, when Catherine died. Eyewitnesses to the events are unanimous in their descriptions of what followed. "Everything immediately assumed another aspect at court," recalled the poet and statesman Gavriil Derzhavin. "Spurs clattered, as did jackboots and cutlasses and, as if conquering a town, military people broke into rooms everywhere, creating a great din."[4] The martial spirit altered the profile of court and capital. As the author of another memoir recollected:

> In the era of Catherine's death and Paul's accession to the throne, Petersburg was, without a doubt, one of the most beautiful capitals in all of Europe.... Because policing measures had to be carried out with all possible splendor, the metamorphosis was accomplished extremely quickly, and Petersburg ceased to resemble a contemporary capital, adopting instead the boring profile of a petty eighteenth-century German town.[5]

The very first steps Paul took as emperor demonstrated his determination to countermand all of his mother's policies. This intention colored his entire reign, as a result of which, in Kliuchevskii's words, what were his "very best undertakings in concept were spoiled by the stamp of personal hostility he placed on them."[6] Hence it was by no means Paul's liberal sympathies that explain his freeing of Nikolai

Novikov, Alexander Radishchev, and Tadeusz Kosciuszko and other Poles, or his removal of many high state officials on charges of corruption. The new emperor simply sought to wipe away, as it were, the previous thirty-four years of Russian history, to declare them nothing but a mistake.

In Paul's domestic policy, several related trends are discernible in his reforms of the state administration, estate policy, and the military. At first glance, the reform of the state apparatus carried out by Paul exhibited the same tendency as Catherine's policy—that of the further centralization of authority. Paul achieved the same goal by different means, however—although several of his measures did continue policies laid out by the empress. Thus, under Catherine, we see a great increase in the significance of the procurator-general of the Senate, under whose jurisdiction fell numerous state matters, including all financial policy. Under Paul, this same procurator-general was transformed into something approximating a prime minister, performing the functions of minister of internal affairs, of justice, and, to some degree, of finance. It is no accident that Paul once announced to his own procurator-general, A.A. Bekleshov: "You and I, and I and you; together we will run affairs."[7] Further alterations in the functions of the Senate as a whole, which in her late drafts Catherine was preparing for what was in essence the role of organ of supreme judicial review, were linked with the reorganization of central and local administration.

Back in the 1780s, a number of collegia had been eliminated, leaving only three: the military, the Admiralty, and foreign affairs. Declaring the freedom of private initiative, Catherine had decided to transfer the minimal control necessary for the development of the economy to local authorities.[8] Paul reestablished several collegia, thinking it necessary, however, to transform them into ministries: that is, substituting the principle of individual for collegial directorship. Thus, in 1797, the completely new Ministry of State Domains was created to oversee the lands belonging directly to the royal family, and in 1800, the Ministry of Commerce was founded. In still more decisive ways, Paul broke with the entire system of local government created by the Provincial Reform Law of 1775.

In the first place, the position of lord lieutenant [*namestnik*] which, the new emperor believed, enjoyed too much independence, was eliminated. In the second, the boards of public welfare and boards of decorum were closed, municipal estate administration was merged with police organs, and the town dumas were abolished. The judicial system created by Catherine also underwent reform. A number of judicial instances were eliminated entirely, while the civil and criminal court chambers were merged. Related to these changes, the Senate's role as a judicial organ was again expanded. Paul also changed the administrative-territorial division of the country as well as the principles of administration on the empire's outer reaches. Thus, Catherine's fifty provinces were transformed into forty-one provinces plus the Don [Cossack] Host Region. Certain traditional organs of administration were returned to the Baltic provinces, the Ukraine, and several other border territories.

In all of these reforms a contradiction is evident: on the one hand, one finds centralization,* the concentration of all the threads of administration in the tsar's hands, and the elimination of elements of self-administration, and on the other, the return to a variety of forms of administration on the empire's borderlands. Behind this contradiction lay first and foremost the weakness of the new regime, its fear of not being able to maintain control over the entire nation, and its desire to acquire popularity in regions fraught with national liberation sentiment. But of course there was also the wish to undo everything inherited from the previous regime. Paul's judicial reform and his elimination of the organs of estate self-administration, which concerned not only the urban population but also the nobility, signified a step backward for Russia.

The attack on the nobility's privileges, which had been codified in the 1785 Charter to the Nobility, began for all practical purposes in the first days of Paul's reign. Then, in 1797, a review was announced of all those entered in the registers of regimental officers who, while not on active duty, had not been granted retirement. This measure was presumably called forth by the practice in Catherine's reign of enlisting young boys in regiments so that by the time they entered active duty

---

*To treat Catherinean reform, associated with the elimination of certain collegia, as reflective of decentralization would be incorrect. As O.A. Omel′chenko has aptly noted, "The notion and goal of centralism remained unchanged." Further, "The difference consisted in the fact that in the first variant—the old collegial system—the bearer of centralism was a network of agencies strictly controlled by and subordinated to the monarch, while in the second it was ostensibly independent bureaucrats of agencies and institutions, who were regulated almost absolutely in all their administrative activity and who acted strictly according to state regulation" (Omel′chenko, *"Zakonnaia monarkhiia" Ekateriny II,* p. 264).

they could already claim officer's rank on the basis of their seniority. In point of fact the number of such "officers" was insignificant, especially when compared with those who were listed as sick, on leave, and so forth. Moreover, many high-level civil servants not only held posts in the state apparatus but had been awarded the rank of general; and were enrolled in various (often guards) regiments. Paul was obviously determined to see that those who were enrolled in the regiments were actually serving.

At first glance, Paul's measure seems quite reasonable and just; but it was followed by limitations on the privileges of those nobles who were no longer serving. After asking for lists of such nobles in August 1800, Paul demanded that most of them be called back into military service. Moreover, starting in October 1799, transfer from military to civil service required the Senate's express permission. Another decree barred those nobles who were not serving from participating in noble elections and from filling elective office. In addition, the noble assemblies at the provincial level were abolished, the rights of those at the district level were restricted and, attacking the perceived problem from the other direction, the authority of the governors to meddle in the nobility's elections was strengthened. In 1797, nobles were required to pay a special tax for the maintenance of provincial administration, and in 1799, the sum was increased. Corporal punishment was occasionally applied to members of the nobility (as was true of other categories of the population), who had been freed from the threat by Catherine.

Yet it would be a mistake to view Paul's policy as hostile to the nobility. Rather, one sees in it a clear desire to transform the nobility into a knightly estate: disciplined, organized, serving to a man, and devoted to its sovereign. Not coincidentally, Paul made an attempt to restrict the flow of non-noble elements into the ranks of the nobility, forbidding the promotion of non-nobles to the rank of junior officer, which brought with it automatic nobility.

Viewed from this same perspective, the emperor's policy with respect to the peasantry also becomes clearer. Much more than its predecessor, Paul's reign was marked by the large-scale distribution of peasants as rewards for service. In a little over four years Paul managed to pass out almost as many peasants as his mother had in her thirty-four (about 600,000, in all). The difference was not, however, just in the numbers. While Catherine rewarded her favorites with either escheated estates that had reverted to the state or else those confiscated from recalcitrant nobles in newly conquered lands, Paul handed out state peasants for the most part, thereby significantly worsening their lot. Other peasants were adversely affected by Paul's decrees as well. In December 1796, a decree was promulgated that bound the peasants to private landlords in the Don Cossack Host Region and in New Russia, while in March 1798, another permitted factory owners who were merchants by birth to purchase peasants for work in their enterprises, with or without land, thus reversing Catherine's policy. Then there were decrees that affected all the peasants. After declaring at the start of his reign that every subject had the right to submit petitions to him personally, Paul proceeded brutally to stop all such attempts on the part of the peasants.

On the other hand, a number of Paul's legislative acts helped ease the yoke of serfdom. In February 1797, the sale of house servants and landless peasants at auction was banned, and in October 1798, the sale of Ukrainian peasants without land was also prohibited. For the first time in many years, enserfed peasants were ordered at the accession of Paul to take the oath of allegiance to the new emperor along with those who were free. In December 1797, peasants and townsmen were excused their soul tax arrears, while the recruitment levy announced under Catherine was dropped. The most famous of the acts was the so-called "Manifesto on the Three-Day Labor Requirement," promulgated by Paul together with a number of other enactments on his coronation day, April 5, 1797. The basic intent of the manifesto was to reaffirm the prohibition of work on Sundays, a juridical norm since the 1649 Law Code. The manifesto treated the restriction of labor obligations to three days per week as a desirable, more rational distribution of the peasants' work time.

The lack of clarity to the manifesto, however, gave rise to varying interpretations by contemporaries as well as subsequent historians. The serfs welcomed it as a lightening of their burden and attempted to initiate complaints against those landlords who refused to live up to its terms. Indeed, there were instances in which landlords were actually subjected to reprimand, and even punishment, for failure to do so. In this regard the historian V.I. Semevskii wrote: "The manifesto of 1797 bore great significance. It represented the first attempt to limit the obligations of enserfed peasants, and our government viewed it as positive law, despite the fact that it was not enforced."[9]

Nonetheless, one ought not to leave out of the reckoning the fact that the manifesto was not enforced. Moreover, in certain regions of the country, as for example the Ukraine, where labor obligations were traditionally limited to two days per week, the manifesto, on the contrary, aggravated the peasants' condition. However strange it may seem, the manifesto's lack of clarity was probably intentional. On the one hand, fearing peasant uprisings, Paul was attempting to forestall them by taking such populist measures. By so doing, he was acquiring another instrument to wield in applying pressure on the nobles. On the other hand, because the throne's dependence on the nobles was so great and Paul had no intention of attempting to pressure them, he was unable openly to ease the yoke of serfdom.

More transparent were Paul's intentions to impose on the army the Prussian military traditions he had so adamantly applied at Gatchina. The reforms began with the introduction of new uniforms, copied lock, stock, and barrel from the Prussian: long coat, stockings, and black lacquered shoes, as well as powdered hair cut to a specified length. In December 1796, a new regulation was issued that emphasized the training of soldiers for parade. Since its archetype was the Prussian regulation of 1760, none of the innovations in Russian military thought that had been tested on the field of battle during Catherine's reign were taken into account. Soon, several more regulations were issued for the separate branches of service. Underlying them all was the assumption that the most important thing to achieve with the army was mechanical coordination of the various forces and the automatic execution of orders. Individual initiative and independence were considered harmful and therefore impermissible. According to a contemporary historian, in his attempt to rectify the shortcomings of the Russian army, Paul I was unable to distinguish the sensible from the wrongheaded. Military reality proved incompatible with the operatic quality of the new uniforms, which failed to withstand the elements. The ballet-like military exercises performed on the parade ground proved useless in repulsing the attacks of enraged Janissaries, in storming fortress walls, or in engaging the decisive French infantry in battle. Paul in effect threw the baby out with the bath water. The best military qualities of the Russian army, so carefully cultivated in Catherine's time, were discarded along with the lack of discipline and other abuses.[10]

When taken in conjunction with the endless parading, the dismissals, the exiles, and even the arrest of many officers, Paul's measures aroused tremendous discontent within the army: not only in the capital but in the provinces as well. For example, an antimonarchist circle could be found in Smolensk province already in the period from 1796 to 1798. Among its members were officers from several regiments stationed there, local officials, and even some retired military personnel.

When discussing Paul I's domestic policies, mention should be made of several new measures associated with the status of the sovereign and the royal family. On his coronation day, the emperor promulgated a decree on the succession to the throne, establishing the transfer strictly in the male line. The decree remained in effect right up to 1917. Also new was the Ministry of State Domains, mentioned above, which in effect signified the incorporation of the royal family's economic resources within state jurisdiction. Convinced of the divine origins of royal authority, Paul did what he could to organize the external manifestations of the apotheosis of autocracy. A great aficionado of the various court ceremonies and rituals, he saw to it that they were performed punctiliously, down to the observance of the minutest detail. They were distinguished by unusual splendor and often lasted many hours.

Court life was totally devoted to the observance of strictly regulated rites, which increased in intensity in 1798, when Paul was proclaimed Grand Master of the Order of Malta. It should be noted, however, that all this Europeanized ritual was not traditional for Russia. Indeed, it was already viewed as archaic in Europe, and therefore elicited only smirks from most contemporaries. In no way did it achieve the goal the emperor set for it. Rather, it merely served to discredit him in the eyes of society. Contemporaries on the whole experienced the dual sensations of fear and contempt for Paul's pettiness and outmoded concept of nobility, his outbursts of uncontrolled rage, and his ostentatious pretense of justice. In his youth his fate was compared to that of Hamlet, a reflection of his troubled relationship with his mother. Now that he had acquired power, there was something of Don Quixote about him.

Behind Paul's back there always loomed the image of his mother, whose authority stood so high that every attempt on his part to alter things appeared pathetic and even comical. In comparison with the Great Catherine, Paul was too petty. Foreordained to failure were all of his attempts to apotheosize imperial authority. The Petrine reforms had already taught Russians to view the sovereign as a mortal being who fulfilled specific responsibilities with respect to his or her subjects. Catherine had openly proclaimed that the sovereign was an unavoidable evil. There could be no turning back.

Paul extended his petty regimentation of the everyday life of his subjects to the area of dress. Thus, special decrees prescribed the specific style and fit of clothes, forbad the wearing of round hats and shoes with laces (instead of buckles), and so on. Special bans were extended to personal appearance (it was forbidden to wear whiskers and large curls) and leisure activity (it was forbidden to dance the waltz). All of these restrictions extended not only to Russian subjects but to foreigners as well. So it was that the Sardinian chargé d'affaires in Petersburg had to be recalled because he had worn a round hat.

All of Paul's measures obviously pursued the goals of restriction of his subjects' individual freedom, consolidation of all spheres of life under his supervision, and struggle with diversity of opinion and with the right to choose one's style of life, mode of behavior, clothes, and so forth. In fact, Paul espied a revolutionary threat in the very possibility of allowing such freedom. In order to combat the penetration of revolutionary ideas into the country, he introduced censorship and forbad the importation of books from abroad.

It is quite possible that if Paul's reforms had dealt only with administrative and policing matters and had been introduced cautiously and consistently, his fate might have been different. But society, which had already tasted the fruits of "enlightened absolutism," had no desire to part with even the minimal portion of freedom that it had acquired in Catherine's reign. To compound the problem, the emperor's impetuous, quick-tempered, changeable, and unpredictable character created a state of instability and of uncertainty about the future, just as his father's had. In such circumstances, the fate of the Russian nobility seemed to depend on the incidental caprice or change of mood of a person whom its members saw as no more than a petty tyrant on the throne, someone dangerous and at the same time comical. Moreover, while in previous coups d'état the guards alone had played the decisive role, now dissatisfaction had spread to just about the entire army. Paul had failed to gain the support of any social stratum. As the outstanding Russian historian of the early nineteenth century, N.M. Karamzin, noted:

> What the Jacobins had done to the republican system Paul did to the autocratic: he induced hatred for the abuse of it.... He wanted to be an Ivan IV. But the Russians had already had a Catherine II, and understood that the sovereign, no less than his subjects, should fulfill his sacred responsibilities. If he failed to do so, the ancient covenant be-

tween authority and obedience would be destroyed, and the people plunged from the level of civilized existence into the chaos of private natural law.[11]

Thus was Paul's fate sealed. The conspiracy against him began to mature from the very beginning of his reign. Numerous high officials, court dignitaries, high-ranking military officers, and even the heir to the throne, Grand Duke Aleksandr Pavlovich, were involved in it, or at least informed of it. March 11, 1801, proved the fatal date for Paul. On that night, several dozen conspirators broke into the emperor's chamber in the recently built Mikhailovskii Palace and killed him. Alexander I was promptly proclaimed Emperor of All the Russias.

As we have already observed, historians are prone to evaluate Paul's reign in divergent ways. Some have labeled it a period of "unenlightened absolutism" (N.Ia. Eidelman), and others—"a military-police dictatorship" (M. Safonov), although they agree that a prolongation of Paul's regime would have retarded Russia's sociopolitical development. Iu. Sorokin has demurred, expressing the view that Paul's policies corresponded with the interests of absolute monarchy, while the methods he chose corresponded with the goals he set.

American historian Roderick McGrew has claimed that "Peter and, more subtly, Catherine were innovators determined to change Russia, to make her different than she was, and better. Paul, confronted by an era of profoundly unsettling changes, used his powers to preserve, ultimately to perfect, what already existed." McGrew saw the historical significance of Paul's reign in the fact that while many Russians, especially those at court and in the army, had every reason to push Paul out of their memories, the measures the emperor undertook in his brief reign were fundamental to what Russia was to become in the first half of the nineteenth century. His reforms created a highly centralized governing system centered around the ruler. They also introduced military principles into the emerging bureaucracy, restructured the army and the military establishment, created an orderly line of succession, institutionalized the royal family, and permanently cut off Catherine's experiments with local government.[12]

In trying to choose among these views, we are immediately confronted with the question as to whether Paul's innovations really were counterreforms with respect to Catherine's reforms. At first glance there can be no doubt that they were. The term "counterreform," however, implies a return to the prereform situation. Yet we have already seen that Catherine's reforms represented a logical continuation of those processes in Russian society's development that were launched by Peter I's reforms. As Catherine understood them, they merely intensified these processes and modernized them to take into account the passage of time. Her intention was to create a civil society, but she intended to do so by resorting to the administrative and police apparatuses. From Paul's point of view, Russia was not yet prepared for the emergence of a civil society: the very prospect struck him as threatening. Therefore, the regulated, policed state became for him an end in itself. What he was trying to do was to slow down, if not halt altogether, those processes that were taking place in Russian society. To this extent, his measures did actually constitute an attempt at counterreform.

The storehouse of means available to Paul, however, was not unlimited. In practice, neither further centralization of the administration nor solidification of the royal family's status nor attempts to whittle away at estate rights contravened the course laid out by his predecessor. The paucity of available means indicates that the room for maneuver with respect to potential reform had by this time been narrowed considerably. The attempt at counterreform, representing not a return to the past but a slowing down or halting of progress, was doomed to failure. The processes launched by the Petrine reforms could be adjusted, and their direction altered a bit, as Catherine II had done; but they could not be reversed.

The qualitatively new stage of development of social consciousness about which Karamzin wrote made its impact felt in another respect. Paul mourned the fact that there had been no age of knighthood in the history of the Russian nobility. But he failed to understand that, having skipped this stage, the nobility had gone on to attain a higher stage. It could not, and had no wish to, return to a misty past. As had already happened several times over the course of the century, the nobility responded to an attack on its rights with desperate resistance. The very concept of knighthood, moreover, was distorted by the emperor. He saw in it no more than the principles of discipline and faithful service to the sovereign, failing to note that the concepts of knightly honor and personal dignity that were also involved were incompatible with his attempts to impose a military-policing system on society and thereby limit the civil rights of the members of Russia's only free estate. The very concept of civil rights, however confused, inadequately thought out, and juridically unformulated it may have been, had been spawned in Catherine's era. Associated with it were the notion of the obligations of the sovereign, the principle of his mutual relations with his subjects, and limitations that he dare not violate, leaving him as the autocratic defender of national interests. The coup d'état of 1801 was therefore not simply the product of the conspiracy of a small clique of officers in guards regiments. Rather, it was the predictable reaction of Russian society to a monarch who had failed to live up to its standards, and whose conduct overstepped the boundaries of the permissible.

Let us turn our attention to one more way in which the new stage of social consciousness made its impact felt. The concept of the obligations of the monarch, which emerged in Petrine times and was strengthened in Catherinean, was not only in harmony with new ideas of the state but represented a peculiar reaction to the fact that, beginning with the first Romanovs, Russian society's relationship to the royal family was different from what it had been earlier. After all, the Romanovs had been but *one of many* prominent families laying claim to the throne. They were *elected* to this throne, and therefore those who had elected them instinctively felt they had the right to evaluate their performance. The authority wielded by tsarist power was also undermined by dynastic crises and the fact that over the course of the eighteenth century the throne was occupied by relatively "incidental" people. This lack of authority is vividly attested to, for example, by investigations conducted by the Secret Chancellery in the 1730s, in which the notion that the empress (in this case Anna Ioannovna) was little more than an "old hag" [*baba*], with nothing royal or divine about her, runs like a red thread through the proceedings. Also deserving of mention is the fact that the glaring contrast between Catherine and Paul's reigns invited contemporaries to draw even sharper distinctions between the two, giving rise to the myth that Catherine's era was a "golden age" for the Russian nobility. The myth proved to be quite tenacious, taking root in foreign as well as Russian historiography.

Another important question raised by Professor McGrew, and before him by the Russian historian Iurii Alekseevich Sorokin,[13] is that of the impact of Paul's reforms on the nation's subsequent history. In

St. Petersburg in the time of Catherine II. From a painting by Benjamin Pattersen.

fact, once he came to power, Alexander I continued to create ministries (that is, to introduce the administrative principle of individual directorship and responsibility), undertook measures to further strengthen the army, also relied on officialdom, and left intact Paul's succession law. The history of the reign of Alexander I (1801–1825), however, is in reality the history of still another reformer on the throne, one whose ideas were doubtless much closer to Catherine II's than they were to those of his father, although more radical in character. Faced with tasks that were global in nature, and planning for the restructuring of the entire administrative system, Alexander was reluctant to waste time on such "petty concerns" as the restoration of his grandmother's institutions of local government. Nor did he deem it worthwhile to alter the system of succession to the throne, for he was thinking of changing the entire role of the autocrat in the power structure. Moreover, Paul's law on succession merely repeated Catherine's unpromulgated projects. With respect to the bureaucratization of government, and of society as a whole, the prize here goes to Peter I rather than to Paul.

The only way to offset the processes already under way was to create a civil society. Administrative means would not do. But here we confront a constraint placed upon the potential reformer's range of activities, one that his father sensed, and that young Emperor Alexander felt in even greater measure. In point of fact, a solution to all of Russia's fundamental problems was directly contingent upon a resolution of the problem of serfdom. At this stage in Russia's development, it was a problem that was not amenable to solution by peaceful means. The historical opportunity that had been passed up in the late seventeenth and early eighteenth centuries continued to extract its cost.

Conclusion

With the coup d'état of 1801, Russia entered another phase in its history. Lying ahead were the failed attempts at reform undertaken by Alexander I and the victories over Napoleon, the Decembrist uprising and the disgrace of the Crimean War, new radical reforms that changed the face of society and revolutionary terror, the wonderful literature of Pushkin and Tolstoy, and the anti-Jewish pogroms. Russia was headed toward the most critical date in its history: October 1917. Just what role did the eighteenth century play in this history? What contribution did it make to it and with what results? To such questions there can be no easy answers. After all, a veritable kaleidoscope of people, circumstances, and events has passed before the eyes of the reader of this modest book. A simple evaluation of each of them is impossible; for all of them, firmly intertwined, constitute the Russian history of the eighteenth century, and contribute to that indivisible unity the nation could claim as it crossed the threshold of the next.

We have seen how its rulers, attempting to overcome the crisis of traditionalism by adopting a program of modernization, transformed Russia into an empire, without whose consent, as Chancellor A.A. Bezborodko boasted at the end of the century, not a cannon could be fired in Europe. Dressed in a European frock coat, the European-educated Russian, an advocate of the latest philosophical ideas and a connoisseur of the decorative arts, became a full-fledged member of the family of European peoples, making his contribution to the development of its civilization. The structure of Russian state institutions, innumerable laws, the organization of trade and artisan guilds, and the lifestyle of elite society all reflected to a great degree, and were often simply copies of, analogous West European models. But at the same time, the dead weight of Russian historical tradition made itself felt at all levels. Thus, the European traveler arriving in Russia, who was often entranced by his first contact with Russian high society and failed to espy any particular difference between the aristocratic salons of Paris and Petersburg, suddenly discovered to his surprise that the salon itself could exist only because its patroness owned several hundred enserfed slaves, while her husband, with whom he had so pleasantly conversed about the latest philosophical ideas, occasionally gambled away some of those slaves in card games.

The French historian Jacques Le Goff relatively recently put forward the conception of "an extended Middle Ages." According to him, the Middle Ages began in late antiquity and ended only in the eighteenth century, or even the beginning of the nineteenth.[1] Le Goff based his assertion upon the assumption that the peasant village foundations of the West European Middle Ages, and therefore the corresponding mentalité, survived this time period almost unchanged. But those harbingers of modernity that had attracted the attention of Le Goff's predecessors emerged from the womb of that very same agrarian society, and therefore European society's transition to a qualitatively new stage in its development took place relatively smoothly and gradually.*

The same could not be said of Russia. Since the era of the Petrine reforms, Russian society had achieved unity only nominally, and only insofar as its population was incorporated into one nation. But the two parts of this society, separated by an ever-widening cultural chasm, existed in differing historical times, as it were, and even in differing historical time frames. For one part, time had stood still, had been frozen, as the Middle Ages lingered on for many decades.** For the other part, a new era had begun, the time for which was kept on European clocks. Living in differing time frames and adhering to differing values, the members of these two components of Russian society spoke different languages, understood each other more and more poorly, and in general grew increasingly remote from each other.

Yet despite these incompatibilities, they were linked by innumerable

---

*Although clearly not painlessly, as the French Revolution that broke out in 1789 reminds us.

**Just how long these "long" Middle Ages actually lasted in Russia is a topic for specialized research. Still, it seems apparent to me that they did not end completely until the emancipation of the serfs in 1861.

inseparable threads. Mutually dependent, they found themselves more and more affected by this dependence. It is within this context, as has already been noted, that the roots of the Russian intelligentsia are to be sought. It is also within this context, it seems to me, that we have to search for an explanation for the special "spirituality" of Russian culture, and of the intelligentsia's exaggerated love for "the people." Here, too, we will find the source of a revolutionary radicalism that was based on poorly understood social theories imported from the West, faith in which led the intelligentsia into irreconcilable conflict with its own government. It is here that we must look for the most important contradictions, and therefore the inevitability of future social convulsions.

From what we have already discussed, it becomes clear that when seeking to elucidate the significance of the eighteenth century in Russian history we must once again turn our attention primarily to the Petrine transformation. For it was then that the irreversible changes took place that were to determine the course of the nation's development well into the future. The most important question is not whether modernization was unnecessary or even harmful for Russia, for modernization was simply unavoidable; it alone could preserve the country as a unified and independent state.

Yet at the same time, modernization was carried out by resorting to governmental coercion and force in an effort to combat Russian tradition. This modernization itself became the means of preserving, and even strengthening, the significance of the state, which alone could command the submission of this huge multinational nation that harbored such a fractured society. Serfdom was necessary to the state, for it strengthened the state's authority over its subjects. But serfdom also gradually became the state's chief nemesis, sapping its strength and retarding further modernization, while at the same time it rendered the nobility ever stronger and more independent of the state. This last process, too, contributed to the phenomenon we know as the Petrine reforms. For it was precisely in Petrine times that the nobility began to transform itself into a full-fledged estate, which for Peter was of course the means to modernization, not an end in itself. Given its economic dependence on the enserfed peasantry, the estate development of the nobility inevitably brought with it the consolidation of serfdom. The nobility, therefore, not only failed to contribute to the formation of a civil society but, on the contrary, actually hindered it. The state, in turn, came to depend all the more on the nobility. So its policy of catering to the nobility's demands represented what was in effect a policy of compromise, thanks to which the state managed to preserve its authority. Nor should one ignore the moral aspect, for serfdom corrupted the nobility morally, creating a deformed style of life and pattern of consciousness. Deformed as well were the nobility's relations with society's remaining groups, for which serfdom also served as a barrier to social growth and transformation into full-fledged estates.

Peter I's successors, Catherine II in particular, continued to push Russia along the path of modernization. Resorting to more "civilized" methods, she corrected to some degree the negative consequences of the Petrine reforms. Her methods, however, failed to eliminate completely the internal contradictions inherent in this transformation. A new structural crisis became unavoidable, and it would extend well beyond the social and political realms. While in the second half of the seventeenth century the crisis in the economy manifested itself first and foremost in an ever-growing lag behind other European nations, in the following century neither the construction of new factories and the appearance of new branches of industry nor the expansion of trade and merchant capital could fundamentally alter the situation. For, as was the case earlier, unproductive serf labor lay at the base of the economy's development. A huge state, striving to identify the means to keep itself viable, was able to support only those branches of industry that in turn supported the military effort. The probability of correcting the situation, by means of radical reform if necessary, became more and more unlikely until the catastrophe of the Crimean War finally untied this truly Gordian knot.

It is not the purpose of this study to enter into a discussion of why the reforms of the eighteen-sixties and seventies failed to lead to development along Western lines, and to forestall still another cataclysm, that of October 1917. Let me merely note here that perhaps one of the explanations lies in the fact that the processes that had emerged at the beginning of the eighteenth century had been allowed to progress too far and consequently were no longer amenable to rectification, even by radical means. These processes had a considerable influence on the formation of Russian culture and on the mentality of the Russian people of the modern era.

Some of the processes' more unusual features have already been discussed above. Still, it would be useful to dwell a bit on the problem of interethnic relations within the empire and the aspects of imperial ideology that were bound up with them, for they manifested themselves in domestic as well as foreign policy. As we have already mentioned, the state itself stood at the center of official ideology, as its ultimate value, beginning in Petrine times. Over time, this state became a multinational empire that allotted a leading role to the Russian people, and to Eastern Orthodoxy as a state religion. In this context, the notion of the special role of the Russian people not only in the international arena but within the state's borders, with respect to the non-Russian peoples who had settled the land, took root in the public consciousness. The integration of these peoples into the empire was looked upon exclusively as a benefit to them, and as a form of sacrifice borne by the Russian people for the sake of others, giving them therefore the right to a ruling position within the empire.

The concept of the Russian people as benefactors, and hence deserving to dominate others, was fertile soil indeed for the most aggressive forms of Russian chauvinism. It cannot be doubted that for some peoples, in the Caucasus for example, annexation to Russia actually offered salvation from what was possibly even physical annihilation. In a number of cases, the peoples who were being annexed lagged behind Russia in their social, economic, and political development. But at the same time, integration into the empire also raised the specter of forced russification: that is, a threat to national cultural traditions. Still, even this represented only one aspect of the problem.

Given the uneven social and economic development of the nation's various regions and the fact that the Russian people inhabited the metropolis of a continental empire, Russians—and primarily those Russians who were anything but privileged—would have to shoulder responsibility for creating and maintaining cadres for a huge army, a police apparatus, a bureaucracy, and industry. In other words, basic responsibility for the maintenance of the viability of this huge nation rested with the Russian people. Hence the ruling position of the Russian people was in reality chimerical, and they themselves, although the ruling people of the metropolis, derived no benefit from their situation. The course chosen by Catherine II—to consolidate governance within the confines of the empire (although altered somewhat in the first quarter of the nineteenth century)—theoretically called for equality among all subjects, or at least all Christian subjects. When, however, starting in the middle of the century, members of the Baltic nobility, many of whom had been assimilated into the Russian elite and accepted Orthodoxy, began to play an increasing role in the nation's governance, the situation irritated Russian nationalists and evoked their protest. It might be noted that the attitudes they expressed are reflected in the historical literature up to the present day.

The consequence of such a situation was a growth in Russian nationalism, chauvinism, and xenophobia as well as anti-Russian sentiments, movements, and uprisings, which were once again suppressed by recourse to Russian bayonets. Interethnic relations were, thus, yet another "time bomb" planted under the imperial edifice, one that sooner or later, but inevitably, would explode.

The list of contradictions engendered by Petrine modernization and its course of development, or else preserved in the traditions of pre-Petrine Rus, could be extended indefinitely. But the chief conclusions to be drawn are perhaps that Russia continued to traverse its own "peculiar" path, and that the events taking place in the eighteenth century in significant measure determined that path.

Notes

Introduction

1. Sidney Monas, foreword to *The Origins of Autocracy: Ivan the Terrible in Russian History,* by Alexander Yanov, translated by Stephen Dunn (Berkeley, 1981), p. xiii.
2. Aleksandr Solzhenitsyn, *Arkhipelag GULAG, 1918–1956: Opyt khudozhestvennogo issledovaniia,* vol. 1 (Moscow, 1989), p. 292.
3. See *Literaturnaia gazeta,* 26 October 1988.

Chapter 1

1. S.M. Solov'ev, *Publichnye chteniia o Petre velikom,* reprint edition (Moscow, 1984), p. 38.
2. George Vernadsky, *The Mongols and Russia* (New Haven, Conn., 1953).
3. L.N. Gumilev, *Drevniaia Rus' i Velikaia Step'* (Moscow, 1989), p. 519.
4. See for example the pertinent comments in the widely used American textbook authored by David McKenzie and Michael W. Curran, *A History of Russia, the Soviet Union, and Beyond,* 4th ed. (Belmont, Calif., 1993), p. 92.
5. Gumilev, *Drevniaia Rus',* p. 466.
6. I.Ia. Froianov, *Kievskaia Rus'* (Leningrad, 1980), pp. 107 and 115.
7. V.B. Kobrin and A.L. Iurganov, "Stanovlenie despoticheskogo samoderzhaviia v srednevekovoi Rusi," *Istoriia SSSR,* 1991, no. 4, p. 58.
8. Froianov, *Kievskaia Rus',* p. 68.
9. See B.D. Grekov et al., eds., *Ocherki istorii SSSR: Period feodalizma, IX–XV vv., v dvukh chastiakh,* pt. 2 (Moscow, 1953), p. 38.
10. L.V. Danilova, "Stanovlenie sistemy gosudarstvennogo feodalizma v Rossii: Prichiny, sledstviia." *Sistema gosudarstvennogo feodalizma v Rossii: Sbornik statei* I (Moscow, 1993), pp. 59–61.
11. Gumilev, *Drevniaia Rus',* p. 492.
12. Iu.G. Alekseev, *Osvobozhdenie Rusi ot Ordynskogo iga* (Moscow, 1989), p. 4.
13. Richard Pipes, *Russia under the Old Regime,* (New York, 1974), p. 106.

14. G.B. Gal'perin, *Forma pravleniia Russkogo tsentralizovannogo gosudarstva XV–XVI vv.* (Leningrad, 1964), p. 41.

15. A.A. Zimin, *Rossiia na poroge novogo vremeni* (Moscow, 1972), pp. 409 and 411.

16. On the complicated issue of mestnichestvo see Iu.M. Eskin, "Mestnichestvo v sotsial'noi strukture feodal'nogo obshchestva," *Otechestvennaia istoriia,* 1993, no. 5, pp. 39–53.

17. K.N. Leont'ev, *Izbrannoe* (Moscow, 1993), pp. 32 and 34.

18. N.F. Demidova, *Sluzhilaia biurokratiia v Rossii XVII v. i ee rol' v formirovanii absoliutizma* (Moscow, 1987), pp. 22–35.

19. See Richard Hellie, *Slavery in Russia* (Chicago, 1982).

20. L.V. Cherepnin, *Zemskie sobory Russkogo gosudarstva XVI–XVII vv.* (Moscow, 1978), pp. 61–62 and 77–78.

21. Pipes, *Russia under the Old Regime,* pp. 70–71.

22. X.-I. [Hans-Joachim] Torke, "Tak nazyvaemye 'Zemskie sobory' (k voprosu o soslovno-predstavitel'noi monarkhii v Rossii)," in *Sbornye voprosy otechestvennoi istorii XI–XVIII vv. Chteniia pamiati A.A. Zimina* (Moscow, 1990), pp. 263–66.

23. Cherepnin, *Zemskie sobory,* p. 390.

24. See Gal'perin, *Forma pravleniia Russkogo tsentralizovannogo gosudarstva,* p. 55; N.E. Nosov, *Stanovlenie soslovno-predstavitel'nykh uchrezhdenii v Rossii* (Leningrad, 1969), and other works.

25. See Brokgauz and Efron, *Entsiklopedicheskii slovar',* vol. 30 (St. Petersburg, 1900), p. 911; *Sovetskaia istoricheskaia entsiklopediia,* vol. 13 (Moscow, 1971), col. 347; *The New Encyclopedia Britannica. Micropedia,* 15th edition, vol. 8 (London, 1975), p. 968.

26. Zhak [Jacques] Le Goff, *Tsivilizatsiia srednevekovogo Zapada* (Moscow, 1992), p. 80.

27. *Razvitie russkogo prava v XV–pervoi polovine XVII v.* (Moscow, 1986), p. 46.

28. See for instance Janet Martin, "A Consideration of Theoretical Approaches to the Study of Economic Developments in 17th Century Muscovy: 'If It Ain't Broke, Don't Fix It'," paper presented at the Second Workshop in Early East Slavic Culture, Stanford University, 19–24 June 1993.

29. See *Nashe otechestvo: Opyt politicheskoi istorii,* vol. 1 (Moscow, 1991), p. 56 (chapter authored by A.N. Medushevskii).

30. See A.L. Stanislavskii, *Grazhdanskaia voina v Rossii XVII v.: Kazachestvo na perelome istorii* (Moscow, 1990).

31. L.E. Morozova, "Mikhail Fedorovich," *Voprosy istorii,* 1992, no. 1, p. 39.

32. A most interesting, although debatable, perspective on this problem has recently been put forward by V.M. Zhivov: see his "Religious Reform and the Emergence of the Individual in Russian Seventeenth-Century Literature," paper presented for the Second Workshop in Early East Slavic Culture, Stanford University, 19–24 June 1993.

33. M.S. Anderson, *Peter the Great* (London, 1978), pp. 13–14.

34. A.P. Bogdanov, "Zapiski svidetelei preobrazovanii," in *Rossiia pri tsarevne Sof'e i Petre I: Zapiski russkikh liudei* (Moscow, 1990), pp. 13–14.

35. N.S. Kollmann, "Ritual and Social Drama at the Moscovite Court," *Slavic Review,* vol. 45, no. 3 (1986), p. 493.

36. See the introduction to Robert O. Crummey, ed., *Reform in Russia and the USSR* (Urbana, Ill., 1989), p. 2.
37. A.M. Panchenko, *Russkaia kul'tura v kanun petrovskikh reform* (Leningrad, 1975), p. 35.

Chapter 2

1. The words are Evgenii Anisimov's: see his *Vremia petrovskikh reform* (Leningrad, 1989), p. 18. For an English translation of a condensed and modified version of Anisimov's book, see *The Reforms of Peter the Great: Progress Through Coercion in Russia,* translated and with an introduction by John T. Alexander (Armonk, N.Y., 1993).
2. S.M. Solov'ev, *Sochineniia v vosemnadtsati knigakh,* reprint edition, book 7 (Moscow, 1991), p. 29.
3. A.K. Nartov, *Rasskazy Nartova o Petre Velikom* (St. Petersburg, 1891), p. 29.
4. Cited in V.I. Buganov, *Stranitsy letopisi Moskvy: Narodnye vosstaniia XIV–XVIII vekov* (Moscow, 1986), p. 149.
5. V.O. Kliuchevskii, *Kurs russkoi istorii,* pt. 4, in his *Sochineniia v deviati tomakh,* reprint edition, vol. 4 (Moscow, 1989), p. 352.
6. M.I. Semevskii and V.N. Smolianinov, eds., *Arkhiv kniazia F.A. Kurakina,* vol. 1 (Saratov, 1890), p. 50.
7. Lindsey A.J. Hughes, *Sophia, Regent of Russia, 1657–1704* (New Haven, 1990).
8. See A.P. Bogdanov, "Zapiski svidetelei preobrazovanii," in *Rossiia pri tsarevne Sof'e i Petre I: Zapiski russkikh liudei* (Moscow, 1990), pp. 13–14 and 354.
9. V.I. Buganov, *Petr Velikii i ego vremia* (Moscow, 1989), p. 11; A.P. Bogdanov, "Zapiski svidetelei preobrazovanii," p. 8.
10. Cited in N.I. Pavlenko, *Petr Velikii* (Moscow, 1990), p. 24.
11. Anisimov, *Vremia petrovskikh reform,* p. 19.
12. Pavlenko, *Petr Velikii,* p. 31.
13. Anisimov, *Vremia petrovskikh reform,* pp. 34–35.
14. See Edward J. Phillips, *The Founding of Russia's Navy: Peter the Great and the Azov Fleet, 1688–1714* (Westport, Conn., 1995), pp. 61–64.
15. Solov'ev, *Sochineniia,* book 7, p. 523.
16. Cited in Anisimov, *Vremia petrovskikh reform,* pp. 25–26 and Pavlenko, *Petr Velikii,* pp. 66–67.
17. See Valentin Boss, *Newton & Russia: The Early Influence, 1698–1796* (Cambridge, Mass., 1972), pp. 9–14.
18. *Pis'ma i bumagi Imperatora Petra Velikogo,* vol. 1 (St. Petersburg, 1887), p. 266.
19. Pavlenko, *Petr Velikii,* p. 81.
20. Solov'ev, *Sochineniia,* book 7, p. 548.
21. Johan Huizinga, *Homo ludens. A Study of the Play-element in Culture* (London, 1948), p. 186.
22. V.E. Vozgrin, *Rossiia i evropeiskie strany v gody Severnoi voiny* (Leningrad, 1986), p. 70.

23. Pavlenko, *Petr Velikii*, p. 65; Anisimov, *Vremia petrovskikh reform*, p. 82.
24. Ibid.
25. See A.V. Ignat'ev, I.S. Rybachenok, and G.A. Sanin, eds., *Rossiiskaia diplomatiia v portretakh* (Moscow, 1992), p. 28.
26. P.N. Miliukov, *Gosudarstvennoe khoziaistvo Rossii v pervoi chetverti XVIII stoletiia i reforma Petra Velikogo,* second edition (St. Petersburg, 1905), pp. 543–46.
27. See Khans [Hans] Bagger, *Reformy Petra Velikogo: Obzor issledovanii*, trans. V.E. Vozgrin (Moscow, 1985), pp. 152–55.
28. Kliuchevskii, *Kurs russkoi istorii*, vol. 4, p. 25.
29. Marc Raeff, "Peter's Domestic Legacy: Transformation or Revolution?" in James Cracraft, ed., *Peter the Great Transforms Russia,* third edition (Lexington, Mass., 1991), p. 287.
30. Anisimov, *Vremia petrovskikh reform*, pp. 40–41.
31. Solov'ev, *Sochineniia,* book 7, pp. 549–50.
32. "Ivan Afanas'evich Zheliabuzhskii. Zapiski," in *Rossiia pri tsarevne Sof'e i Petre I,* p. 265.
33. Robert O. Crummey, *Aristocrats and Servitors: The Boyar Elite in Russia, 1613–1689* (Princeton, 1983), p. 163.
34. Anisimov, *Vremia petrovskikh reform*, p. 89.
35. Cited in L.A. Chernaia, "Ot idei 'sluzheniia gosudariu' k idee 'sluzheniia otechestvu' v russkoi obshchestvennoi mysli vtoroi poloviny XVII–nachala XVIII v.," in *Obshchestvennaia mysl': issledovaniia i publikatsii,* vyp. 1 (Moscow, 1989), p. 36.
36. Solov'ev, *Sochineniia,* book 7, p. 600.
37. *Istoriia Severnoi voiny, 1700–1721 gg.* (Moscow, 1987), p. 46; Buganov, *Petr Velikii i ego vremia,* p. 72.
38. Anisimov, *Vremia petrovskikh reform*, p. 94.
39. Kliuchevskii, *Kurs russkoi istorii*, vol. 4, p. 50.
40. Pavlenko, *Petr Velikil,* p. 142.

Chapter 3

1. Cited in Pavlenko, *Petr Velikii,* p. 145.
2. Solov'ev, *Sochineniia,* book 7, p. 605.
3. Ibid., book 8, pp. 85–86.
4. M.I. Pyliaev, *Staryi Peterburg* (St. Petersburg, 1889), p. 10.
5. A. Sharymov, "Byl li Petr I osnovatelem Sankt-Peterburga?" *Avrora,* 1993, nos. 7–8, pp. 106–65.
6. E.V. Anisimov, "Linii zhizni," in *Peterburgskii mirazh* (St. Petersburg, 1991), p. 8.
7. A. Blair Ruble, *Leningrad: Shaping a Soviet City* (Berkeley, Cal., 1990), pp. xxvi and 23.
8. Iu.M. Lotman and B.A. Uspenskii, "Otzvuki kontseptii 'Moskva–Tretii Rim' v ideologii Petra Pervogo," in *Khudozhestvennyi iazyk srednevekov'ia* (Moscow, 1982), p. 241.
9. Ibid., pp. 239–41.
10. Pavlenko, *Petr Velikii,* p. 164.

11. Cited in Solov'ev, *Sochineniia,* book 8, p. 73.
12. Ibid., pp. 74 and 158.
13. Anisimov, *Vremia petrovskikh reform,* p. 104.
14. Solov'ev, *Sochineniia,* book 8, p. 103.
15. Pavlenko, *Petr Velikii,* p. 239.
16. Ibid., p. 253.
17. *Istoriia Severnoi voiny,* p. 73.
18. Pavlenko, *Petr Velikii,* p. 261.
19. Solov'ev, *Sochineniia,* book 8, p. 211.
20. Anisimov, *Vremia petrovskikh reform,* p. 186.
21. Ibid., p. 187.
22. N.M. Kostomarov, *Mazepa,* reprint edition (Moscow, 1992), p. 176.
23. N.P. Eroshkin, *Istoriia gosudarstvennykh uchrezhdenii dorevoliutsionnoi Rossii,* third edition (Moscow, 1983), p. 88.
24. Pavlenko, *Petr Velikii,* p. 297.
25. Anisimov, *Vremia petrovskikh reform,* pp. 146–49.
26. *Istoriia Severnoi voiny,* p. 85.
27. Anisimov, *Vremia petrovskikh reform,* pp. 204 and 213.
28. M.S. Anderson, "Poltava and Europe," in J. Cracraft, ed., *Peter the Great Transforms Russia,* pp. 38 and 39.
29. S.F. Platonov, *Lektsii po russkoi istorii,* reprint edition (Moscow, 1993), p. 503.
30. M.S. Meier, *Osmanskaia imperiia v XVIII veke: Cherti strukturnogo krizisa* (Moscow, 1991), pp. 187–88.
31. Eroshkin, *Istoriia gosudarstvennykh uchrezhdenii,* p. 75.
32. Pavlenko, *Petr Velikii,* p. 333.
33. Anisimov, *Vremia petrovskikh reform,* p. 152.
34. Kliuchevskii, *Kurs russkoi istorii,* vol. 4, p. 150; V.Ia. Ulanov, "Preobrazovaniia upravleniia pri Petre Velikom," in *Tri veka: Rossiia ot Smuty do nashego vremeni.* Istoricheskii sbornik pod red. V. V. Kallasha, vol. 3 (Moscow, 1912), p. 254.
35. Pavlenko, *Petr Velikii,* p. 334.
36. Solov'ev, *Sochineniia,* book 8, p. 427.
37. Pavlenko, *Petr Velikii,* p. 371.
38. Solov'ev, *Sochineniia,* book 8, p. 464.
39. Ibid., p. 506.
40. Ibid., pp. 480–81.
41. See Bagger, *Reformy Petra Velikogo,* pp. 101–02.
42. L.V. Cherepnin, *Russkaia paleografiia* (Moscow, 1956), p. 477.
43. Anisimov, *Vremia petrovskikh reform,* pp. 278–79.
44. Ibid., p. 278.
45. Ibid., pp. 298–99.
46. Pavlenko, *Petr Velikii,* p. 379.
47. Anisimov, *Vremia petrovskikh reform,* p. 457.
48. Pavlenko, *Petr Velikii,* pp. 409–10.
49. E.V. Anisimov, *Podatnaia reforma Petra I* (Leningrad, 1982), p. 230.
50. Cited in Pavlenko, *Petr Velikii,* p. 424.
51. Anisimov, *Vremia petrovskikh reform,* p. 394.

52. *Polnoe sobranie zakonov Rossiiskoi imperii,* first series, vol. 6 (St. Petersburg, 1830), p. 317. For a convenient English translation of the regulation, see Alexander V. Muller (translator and editor), *The Spiritual Regulation of Peter the Great* (Seattle, 1972).

53. James Cracraft, "The Church Reforms of Peter the Great," in *Cracraft, Peter the Great Transforms Russia,* p. 168.

54. Anisimov, *Vremia petrovskikh reform,* p. 310.

55. See Pavlenko, *Petr Velikii,* p. 557, and Anisimov, *Vremia petrovskikh reform,* p. 435.

56. *Panegiricheskaia literatura petrovskogo vremeni* (Moscow, 1979), pp. 279–81.

57. MacKenzie and Curran, *A History of Russia,* p. 238.

58. Cited in Anisimov, *Vremia petrovskikh reform,* p. 8.

59. Ibid.

60. C.E. Black, *The Dynamics of Modernization* (New York, 1966), p. 121.

61. Marc Raeff, "Suggestions for Additional Reading," in his *Peter the Great Changes Russia,* p. 195.

62. Cynthia N. Whittaker, "The Reforming Tsar: The Redefinition of Autocratic Duty in Eighteenth-Century Russia," *Slavic Review,* vol. 51, no. 1 (Spring 1992), pp. 79 and 78, respectively.

Chapter 4

1. E.V. Anisimov, "Putniki, proshedshie ran'she nas," in the collection he edited entitled *Bezvremen'e i vremenshchiki: Vospominaniia ob 'epokhe dvortsovykh perevorotov' (1720–e—1760–e gody)* (Leningrad, 1991), p. 4.

2. Kliuchevskii, *Kurs russkoi istorii,* vol. 4, p. 238.

3. V.Ia. Ulanov, "Epokha dvortsovykh perevorotov (1725–1762)," in *Tri veka,* vol. 4 (Moscow, 1912), p. 331.

4. M.A. Boitsov, ". . . Klii strashnyi glas," in *So shpagoi i fakelom: Dvortsovye perevoroty v Rossii, 1725–1825* (Moscow, 1991), p. 9.

5. Kliuchevskii, *Kurs russkoi istorii,* vol. 4, p. 238.

6. E.V. Anisimov, "Smert' v kontorke," *Rodina,* 1993, no. 1, pp. 139–40.

7. See V.O. Kliuchevskii, "Byt i nravy russkogo svetskogo obshchestva okolo poloviny XVIII veka," in his *Neopublikovannye proizvedeniia* (Moscow, 1983), p. 98.

8. Ulanov, "Epokha dvortsovykh perevorotov," in *Tri veka,* vol. 4, p. 330.

9. V.S. Beliavskii, "Zolushka na trone Rossii," in *Na Rossiiskom prestole, 1725–1796: Monarkhi Rossiiskie posle Petra Velikogo* (Moscow, 1993), p. 7.

10. Anisimov, *Vremia petrovskikh reform,* p. 484.

11. Anisimov, *Podatnaia reforma,* pp. 283 and 265.

12. I.V. Kurukin, "Ten' Petra Velikogo," in *Na Rossiiskom prestole,* p. 71.

13. Ibid., p. 106.

14. Ibid., p. 79.

15. Ibid.

16. *Sbornik istoricheskikh materialov i dokumentov, otnosiashchikhsia k novoi russkoi istorii XVIII i XIX veka* (St. Petersburg, 1873), pp. 11–16.

17. See A.B. Kamenskii, "Rossiiskoe dvorianstvo v 1767 g. (K probleme konsolidatsii)," *Istoriia SSSR,* 1990, no. 1, pp. 58–77.

18. Cited in Solov'ev, *Sochineniia,* book 10, p. 204.
19. See A.G. Tartakovskii, *Russkaia memuaristika XVIII–pervoi poloviny XIX v.* (Moscow, 1991).
20. I.A. Kurliandskii, "Na ladoni sud'by," in *Na rossiiskom prestole,* p. 142.
21. Rossiiskii Gosudarstvennyi Arkhiv Drevnikh Aktov (RGADA), Moscow, fond 180, opis' 1, delo 16, list 1.
22. Cited in Kurliandskii, "Na ladoni sud'by," in *Na rossiiskom prestole,* p. 139.
23. Cited by E.V. Anisimov in his "Anna Ivanovna," *Voprosy istorii,* 1993, no. 4, p. 23 (English translations in *Russian Studies in History,* vol. 32, no. 4 [spring 1994], pp. 8–36 and in *The Emperors and Empresses of Russia: Rediscovering the Romanovs,* Donald J. Raleigh, ed. and A.A. Iskenderov, comp. [Armonk, N.Y., 1996], pp. 37–65).
24. See T.V. Chernikova, "Gosudarevo slovo i delo vo vremena Anny Ioannovny," *Istoriia SSSR,* 1989, no. 5, pp. 155–63.
25. See V. Stroev, *Bironovshchina i Kabinet ministrov* (Moscow, 1909); Alexander Lipski, "The 'Dark Era' of Anna Ivanovna," *American Slavic and East European Review,* vol. 15 (1956), pp. 477–88; Chernikova, "Gosudarevo slovo i delo vo vremena Anny Ioannovny," *Istoriia SSSR,* 1989, no. 5, pp. 155–63; and Anisimov, "Anna Ivanovna," *Voprosy istorii,* 1993, no. 4, pp. 25–31.
26. Evgenii Anisimov, for example, citing N.N. Repin: ibid., p. 28.
27. A.I. Iukht, "Finansy," in *Ocherki russkoi kul'tury XVIII v.* (Moscow, 1987), pt. 2, p. 118.
28. Kurliandskii, "Na ladoni sud'by," in *Na rossiiskom prestole,* p. 145.
29. Anisimov, "Putniki, proshedshie ran'she nas," in *Bezvremen'e i vremenshchiki,* p. 16.
30. L.G. Beskrovnyi, *Ocherki po istochnikovedeniiu voennoi istorii Rossii* (Moscow, 1957), p. 127.
31. P.P. Epifanov, "Voennoe delo," in *Ocherki russkoi kul'tury XVIII veka,* pt. 2, pp. 212 and 208, respectively.
32. Beskrovnyi, *Ocherki po istochnikovedeniiu voennoi istorii Rossii,* p. 127.
33. Anisimov, "Anna Ivanovna," *Voprosy istorii,* 1993, no. 4, p. 33.
34. RGADA, f. 6, d. 283, l. 7.
35. Ibid., f. 7, d. 745, l. 4.
36. Cited in S.F. Librovich, *Imperator pod zapretom* (St. Petersburg, 1912), p. 50.
37. Ibid., pp. 59–60.
38. Decree of 12 November 1740, in *Polnoe sobranie zakonov Rossiiskoi imperii,* first series, vol. 11, no. 8.289, pp. 303–04.
39. I. Shishkin, *Sobytiia v Peterburge v 1740 i 1741 gody* (St. Petersburg, 1858), p. 282.
40. *Vnutrennii byt Russkogo gosudarstva s 17 Oktiabria 1740 goda po 25 Noiabria 1741 goda po dokumentam, khraniashchimsia v Moskovskom arkhive Ministerstva iustitsii,* book I (Moscow, 1880), p. 339.
41. See Anisimov, *Rossiia v seredine XVIII veka: Bor'ba za nasledie Petra* (Moscow, 1986), pp. 6–42 (available in English translation as Evgeny V. Anisimov, *Empress Elizabeth: Her Reign and her Russia, 1741–1761,* edited, translated, and with a preface by John T. Alexander [Gulf Breeze, Fla., 1995]).

42. Ibid., p. 40.
43. Librovich, *Imperator pod zapretom,* p. 113.

Chapter 5

1. Anisimov, *Rossiia v seredine XVIII veka,* p. 28.
2. V.A. Bil'basov, *Istoriia Ekateriny Vtoroi,* vol. 2 (St. Petersburg, 1891), p. 437.
3. Anisimov, *Rossiia v seredine XVIII veka,* p. 42.
4. Translated from the original French into Russian as Konstantin Valishevskii [Waliszewski], *Doch' Petra Velikogo* (Moscow, 1911), p. 134.
5. Anisimov, *Rossiia v seredine XVIII veka,* p. 45.
6. V.P. Naumov, "Elizaveta Petrovna," *Voprosy istorii,* 1993, no. 5, p. 58 (English translations in *Russian Studies in History,* vol. 32, no. 4 [spring 1994], pp. 37–72 and in Raleigh, *The Emperors and Empresses of Russia,* pp. 67–100).
7. Solov'ev, *Sochineniia,* book 12, p. 33.
8. See S.O. Shmidt, "Vnutrenniaia politika Rossii serediny XVIII v.," *Voprosy istorii,* 1987, no. 3, pp. 42–58.
9. J.F. Brennan, *Enlightened Despotism in Russia: The Reign of Elizabeth, 1741–1762* (New York, 1987), p. 127.
10. Anisimov, *Rossiia v seredine XVIII veka,* p. 167.
11. On the "protective" stance of Lomonosov, see A.B. Kamenskii, "Lomonosov i Miller: dva vzgliada na istoriiu," in *Lomonosov: Sbornik statei i materialov,* vol. 9 (St. Petersburg, 1991), pp. 39–48.
12. Anisimov, *Rossiia v seredine XVIII veka,* p. 184.
13. Ibid., p. 201.
14. Ibid., p. 188.
15. Cited in ibid., p. 49.
16. Iu.V. Got'e, *Istoriia oblastnogo upravleniia v Rossii ot Petra I do Ekateriny II,* vol. 2 (Moscow, 1941), p. 135.
17. Platonov, *Lektsii po russkoi istorii,* p. 590.
18. Anisimov, *Rossiia v seredine XVIII veka,* p. 55.
19. A.I. Iukht, *Russkie den'gi ot Petra Velikogo do Aleksandra I* (Moscow, 1994), pp. 143 and 180.
20. Anisimov, *Rossiia v seredine XVIII veka,* p. 57.
21. S.M. Troitskii, *Russkii absoliutizm i dvorianstvo v XVIII v.* (Moscow, 1974), p. 162.
22. Anisimov, *Rossiia v seredine XVIII veka,* pp. 69–71.

Chapter 6

1. V.P. Naumov, "Udivitel'nyi samoderzhets: zagadki ego zhizni i tsarstvovaniia," in *Na Rossiiskom prestole* (Moscow, 1993), p. 284.
2. For a delightful survey of the architecture of the Russian manor house and the lifestyle inside, see Priscilla Roosevelt, *Life on the Russian Country Estate: A Social and Cultural History* (New Haven, 1995).
3. Isabel de Madariaga, *Russia in the Age of Catherine the Great* (New Haven, 1981), p. 89.

4. S.M. Troitskii, *Russkii absoliutizm i dvorianstvo v XVIII v.* (Moscow, 1974), p. 140.

5. I.V. Faizova, *Materialy Gerol'dmeisterskoi kontory kak istochnik po istorii Rossiiskogo dvorianstva XVIII stoletiia* (Saratov, 1990), pp. 42–57.

6. See "Mnenie byvshego imperatora Petra III," in *Russkii arkhiv,* 1871, p. 2055.

7. See: John T. Alexander, *Catherine the Great: Life and Legend* (New York, 1989), p. 15; A.B. Kamenskii, "Pod seniiu Ekateriny," *Vtoraia polovina XVIII veka* (St. Petersburg, 1992), pp. 133–37; and V.P. Naumov, "Udivitel'nyi samoderzhets," in *Na Rossiiskom prestole,* p. 324.

8. A.S. Myl'nikov, *Iskushenie chudom: "Russkii prints," ego prototipy i dvoiniki-samozvantsy* (Leningrad, 1991); by the same author, "Petr III," *Voprosy istorii,* 1991, nos. 4–5, pp. 43–58 (English translations in *Russian Studies in History,* vol. 32, no. 3 [winter 1993–94], pp. 30–56, and Raleigh, *The Emperors and Empresses of Russia,* pp. 101–33); Carol S. Leonard, "The Reputation of Peter III," *Russian Review,* vol. 47, no. 3 (July 1988), pp. 263–92; by the same author, *Reform and Regicide: The Reign of Peter III of Russia* (Bloomington, Ind., 1993).

9. P.Ia. Chaadaev, *Stat'i i pis'ma* (Moscow, 1987), p. 279.

10. *Russkie memuary: 1800–1825* (Moscow, 1989), p. 526.

11. See Alexander's *Catherine the Great,* especially the epilogue, pp. 329–41.

12. *Russkii arkhiv,* 1907, no. 9, p. 7.

13. MacKenzie and Curran, *A History of Russia, the Soviet Union, and Beyond,* p. 289.

14. O.A. Omel'chenko, *"Zakonnaia monarkhiia" Ekateriny II: Prosveshchennyi absoliutizm v Rossii* (Moscow, 1993), pp. 378–79.

15. Nicholas V. Riasanovsky, *The Image of Peter the Great in Russian History and Thought* (New York, 1985), p. 36.

16. *Zapiski imperatritsy Ekateriny Vtoroi* (St. Petersburg, 1907), p. 647.

17. Instructions published in *Sbornik Imperatorskogo russkogo istoricheskogo obshchestva,* vol. 7 (St. Petersburg, 1871), p. 348.

18. R.P. Bartlett, *Human Capital: The Settlement of Foreigners in Russia, 1762–1804* (Cambridge, Eng., 1979), p. 31.

19. RGADA, f. 10 (Kabinet Ekateriny II), op. 1, d. 12, l. 106.

20. *Zapiski imperatritsy Ekateriny Vtoroi,* pp. 174–75.

21. Ibid., p. 646.

22. D.M. Griffiths, "Of Estates, Charters and Constitutions," in David Griffiths and George E. Munro, trans. and eds., *Catherine II's Charters of 1785 to the Nobility and the Towns* (Bakersfield, Cal., 1991), pp. lii-liii and xxv, respectively.

23. *Zapiski imperatritsy Ekateriny Vtoroi,* pp. 626–27.

24. For an English translation of the *Duties of Man and Citizen,* see J.L. Black, *Citizens for the Fatherland: Education, Educators, and Pedagogical Ideals in Eighteenth Century Russia* (New York, 1979), pp. 209–66.

25. RGADA, f. 5, op. 1, d. 120, ff. 157–157 reverse.

26. A.S. Pushkin, *Polnoe sobranie sochinenii v desiati tomakh,* vol. 7 (Leningrad, 1978), pp. 242 and 245–46.

27. V.O. Kliuchevskii, *Istoricheskie portrety* (Moscow, 1991), p. 349.

28. N.K. Shil'der, *Imperator Aleksandr Pervyi,* vol. 1 (St. Petersburg, 1904), pp. 279–80.

Chapter 7

1. *Zapiski imperatritsy Ekateriny Vtoroi,* pp. 376–77.
2. Note for N.P. Rumiantsev, in f. 1, op. 1, d. 46, l. 1696, in RGADA.
3. Cited in V.A. Bil´basov, *Istoriia Ekateriny Vtoroi* (Berlin, n.d.), vol. 2, p. 270.
4. Cited in Solov´ev, *Sochineniia,* book 14, p. 280.
5. See Isabel de Madariaga, *Britain, Russia, and the Armed Neutrality of 1780: Sir James Harris's Mission to St. Petersburg during the American Revolution* (London, 1962).
6. Book translated from the German original as A.G. Brikner, *Istoriia Ekateriny Vtoroi,* part 3 (St. Petersburg, 1885), p. 418.
7. Cited in L.F. Segur, "Zapiski o prebyvanii v Rossii v tsarstvovanie Ekateriny II," in *Rossiia XVIII v. glazami inostrantsev* (Leningrad, 1989), p. 454.
8. Kliuchevskii, *Kurs russkoi istorii,* vol. 5, p. 56.
9. Draft in f. 10, op. 1, d. 17, l. 296, in RGADA. The document was published first in English by Marc Raeff in his "The Empress and the Vinerian Professor," in *Oxford Slavonic Papers, New Series,* vol. 7 (1974), p. 38, and then in Russian by Oleg Omel´chenko in his *"Zakonnaia monarkhiia" Ekateriny II,* p. 361.

Chapter 8

1. N.K. Shil´der, *Imperator Pavel Pervyi* (St. Petersburg, 1901), p. 248.
2. Roderick McGrew, *Paul I of Russia* (Oxford, 1992), p. 206.
3. N.Ia. Eidel´man, *Gran´ vekov* (Moscow, 1986), p. 71.
4. G.R. Derzhavin, *Sochineniia* (Moscow, 1985), p. 446.
5. *Tsareubiistvo 11 Marta 1801 goda* (St. Petersburg, 1908), p. 27.
6. Kliuchevskii, *Kurs russkoi istorii,* vol. 5, p. 175.
7. Cited in S.B. Okun´, *Istoriia SSSR. (Lektsii)* (Leningrad, 1974), pt. 1, p. 65.
8. Worthy of notice is the opinion of John P. LeDonne, who thinks this reform had an "anti-bureaucratic direction": see his *Ruling Russia* (Princeton, 1984), p. 61.
9. V.I. Semevskii, *Krest´ianskii vopros v Rossii v XVIII i pervoi polovine XIX veka* (St. Petersburg, 1888), vol. 1, p. 233.
10. V. Lapin, *Semenovskaia istoriia* (Leningrad, 1991), p. 57.
11. N.M. Karamzin, *Zapiska o drevnei i novoi Rossii* (Moscow, 1991), pp. 44–45 (available in English translation as Karamzin's *Memoir on Ancient and Modern Russia,* translated and edited by Richard Pipes [New York, 1966]).
12. McGrew, *Paul I of Russia,* pp. 355–56.
13. See Iu.A. Sorokin, "Rossiiskii imperator Pavel I," a candidate's dissertation completed at Tomsk University in 1989; and see also his "Pavel I," *Voprosy istorii,* 1989, no. 11, pp. 46–69, also in *Dinastiia Romanovykh* (Moscow, 1994) (translations in *Soviet Studies in History,* vol. 30, no. 3 [winter 1991], pp. 3–48 and in Raleigh, *The Emperors and Empresses of Russia,* pp. 178–215).

Conclusion

1. Jacques Le Goff, *Pour un autre Moyen Age: Temps, travail, et culture en Occident médiéval* (Paris, 1977).

Index

Aachen, 191
Åbo, 96, 190
Academy of Fine Arts, 234
Adrian, Patriarch, 74
Afanasiev, Iurii, 6
Akhmat, Khan of the Golden Horde, 19
Aland Islands, 110
Aleksei Mikhailovich (Peter I's father) 33, 36, 124, 147
Aleksei Petrovich (Peter I's son): 64, 122, 128, 132; marriage of, 96; confrontation with father, 104–107
Alexander I, 164, 169, 243, 263, 266, 276, 279, 280, 281
Alexander the Great, 75, 84
Allodial landholding, 15, 23
Amiens, 104
Amsterdam, 55, 69, 225
Anderson, M.S., 36
Anisimov, Evgenii: 1, 46, 58, 62, 68, 82, 87, 89, 102, 111, 114, 118, fn. 132, 157, 163, 176, 179, 181, 188; comparison of Peter's reign with that of Ivan IV, 50; court life under Elizabeth 174; effects of taxation on the peasantry in the post-Petrine period, 130; on the founding of the Senate by Peter I, 93; Industrialization process in Russia, 103; on Peter I's feelings toward his son, 106; on Peter I's tax reform, 109; on Peter I's testament, 124; on the significance of the Battle of Poltava, 91; views on the coup of 1741, 165, 168, 169; views on Ivan Mazepa, 86; views on Ivan Shuvalov, 177

Anna, Duchess of Holstein (daughter of Peter I), 94, 124, 126, 132, 139
Anna Ioannovna (Ivanovna), Duchess of Courland: ch. 4 passim, 139, 140, 141, 143, 145, 148, 149, 151, 152, 153, 155, 157, 158, 163, 170, 176, 208, 244, 278; character of, 145–147; commerce during reign of, 152; foreign policy under (ch.IV) 153–55; restriction of mandatory service requirement, 151; significance of her reign, 145. *See also* Succession Crisis of 1730
Anna Leopoldovna (Niece of Anna Ioannovna), 157, 159, 160, 161, 162, 163, 164, 170
Anti-Semitism, 173
Anti-Swedish Coalition, 68, 92
Anti-Turkish Alliance, 51, 59, 254
Anton-Ullrich, Prince of Brunswick-Lüneburg, 157, 159, 160, 161, 163, 164
Antropov, A., 236
Apraksin, Stepan Feodorovich, Field Marshal, 192
Archangel, 48, 51, 60, 76, 78, 79, 103, 137, 152
Argunov, I., 236
Armenia, 255
Aristocracy in Russia, 14, 140, 142
Assembly of the Land: 28, 29, 32, 33, 40; explanation of, 27–28; role in Russian history, 28
Astrakhan, 20, 60, 83
Ataman, 86

Augustus, Stanislaw. *See* Stanislaw Poniatowski
Augustus II, King of Poland (The Strong) 56, 59, 75, 80, 83, 84, 91, 104, 153
Augustus III, King of Poland, 154, 247
Austria, 59, 72, 128, 153, 154, 155, 189, 190, 191, 193, 247, 248, 250, 252, 254, 255, 258, 259, 260, 261
Austro-Russian Alliance, 92
Azov, 51, 52, 58, 67, 96, 249; sea of, 51, 95, 154; siege of, 51–52
Azov Fleet, 53, 80

Baku, 115
Baltic Region, 76, 83, 92, 95, 167, 191, 270, 285
Baltic Sea, 58, 59, 60, 68, 79, fn. 189
Bartlett, Roger P., historian, 211
Batu, Tatar khan, 10
Baturin, 88
Bavaria, 252
Bazhenov, V., 236, 238
Beauvais, 104
Beccaria, Cesare, 213
Bekleshov, A. A., Procurator General, 269
Belgrade, 259
Belorussia, 85, fn. 189, 250, 260
Berezina River, 85
Berezovo, 135, 148
Berlin, 193
Beskrovnyi, L.G., historian, 154, 155
Bestuzhev-Riumin, Aleksei Petrovich, 190, 191, 192
Betskoi, I.I.: 204, 234; plan to reform Russian education, 234–35
Bezborodko, Aleksandr Andreevich, 204, 239, 261, 281
Bilbasov, Vasilii, 168
Biron, Ernst-Johann (Bühren), 148–153, 156–159, 161, 168, 171, 247
"Bironovshchina," 149–151
Black, Cyril, 117, 119
Black Sea: 58, 72, 249, 251; fleet, 257
Blizhniaia kantseliariia. *See* Privy Chancellery
Bolshevik (October) Revolution of 1917, 4, 8, 179, 236, 281, 284
Boitsov, M.A., historian: on succession after Peter the Great, 123–24
Book of Household Management, 31
Bondsman (*kholop*) 51, 75
Borovikovskii, V., 236

Bortnianskii, D., 236
Bourgeoisie, 240
Boyar Council, 20, 21, fn. 22, 33, 51, 52, 53, 67, 81, 94; decline of, 41
Boyar Duma. *See* Boyar Council
Boyars, 15, 20, 23, 25, 29, 42, 63, fn. 142
Brailia, 95
Brandenburg, 192
Bratislava, 50
Brennan, James, historian, 173
Bruckner, Alexander, 253
Bucharest, 249, 259
Burnet, Gilbert, Archbishop of Salisbury, 56
Buturlin, Ivan Ivanovich, 132
Byzantium: 72, 244, 245, 257; Moscow as successor to Byzantium, 18

Cabinet of Her Imperial Majesty, 151
Cabinet of Ministers, 158, 160, 161, 172, 180
Cadet Corps, 234
Calais, 104
Cameralism, 107
Capitalism, 103
Carlowitz, Georg Carl von, 56
Carlsbad, 96
Caspian Sea, 115
Catherine I: 2, 94, 96, 105, 123, 124, 125, 126, 128, 129, 131, 133, 153; death of, 131, 132, 169; testament of, 133, 139
Catherine II, fn. 26, 28, fn. 43, 169, 184, 193 passim ch. VI, passim ch. VII, 266, 267, 268, 269, 271, 274, 275, 276, 277, 279, 284, 285; adherence to Enlightenment ideas, 204; administrative reform under, 209–10; attempts at education reform, 234–36; attempts to reform serfdom, 226–29; character of, 201–205; Charter to the Nobility, 230–31; Charter to State Peasants (Unpromulgated), 232; Charter to the Towns, 230, 231–32; death of, 262–63, 265, 268; "enlightened absolutism," under, 204, 205, 206, 246; foreign policy under, ch. 7 passim; foreign trade under, 224–25; "Fundamental Law" on provincial reform 1775, 222–24; Grand Instructions, 212–14, 260; "Greek project," 253–254; her part in the coup against Peter III, 199–200;

INDEX

Catherine II *(continued)*
  Legislative Commission, 211–16, 222, 237; nationality policy, 210–11; opinion of Radishchev, 240; polemic with Novikov, 237; reaction to the French Revolution, 260; secularization of church estates, 208–09; summation of Catherine's reign, 241–243; trip down the Volga River, 228
Catholicism: influence on Russia, 4, 74
Caucasus region, 115, 211, 250, 251, 255, 258, 259, 285
Central Asia, 60, 115, 250
Chaadaev, Peter: views on Catherine II, 201
Chancellery, 25, 33, 94
Chancellery secretary, 25
Charles II, of Spain, 59
Charles VI, Hapsburg Emperor, fn. 154
Charles XII, of Sweden, 70, 71, 75, 76, 83, 84, 85, 90, 92, 95, 110, 136
Charlotte Christine Sophie, of Brunswick-Wolfenbüttel, 96, 105, 126
Charter, received from Golden Horde, 14
Charter to the Nobility, 270
Charter to the State Peasants. *See* Catherine II
Charter to the Towns. *See* Catherine II
Cheliabinsk, 220
Cherepnin, L.V.: views on the Assemblies of the Land, 28, 29
Chernyshev, Ivan, Count, 182
Chétardie, Marquis de la, 147, 159, 165, 175, 190
Chief Procurator, 113
China, 31, 94, 99
Christianity. *See* Eastern Orthodoxy
Clergy: 74, 209; taxation on, 109
Code of Laws, 186
Colbert, Jean Baptiste, 182
Collegia: 107, 118, 268; Admiralty, 107, 131, 228, 269; Central Accounting Collegium, 107; Collegium of Economy, 209; Collegium of Foreign Affairs 101, 107, 131, 177, 261, 269; Collegium of Justice, 107; Collegium of State Expenditures,107; Collegium of State Revenues, 107, 131; Commerce Collegium, 107; creation of, 112–113; Ecclesiastical Collegium, 112; Holy Synod, 113, 118, 134, 141; Mining and Manufacturing Collegium, 107, 180; War Collegium, 100, 107, 131, 154, 269

Colton, Timothy, political scientist: views on reform, 37
Commanders: 138; under Ivan IV, 24, 65
Commission on Commerce, 137
Commission on Monetary Matters, 152
Commission on Taxation, 131
Companies, state mandated, 53
Complete Collection of Laws of the Russian Empire, 160
"Conditions" on Anna Ivanovna. *See* Succession Crisis of 1730
Conference at the Imperial Court, 172, 176, 177, 192, 208
Constantinople, 12, 18, 67, 92, 253, 257
Constituent Assembly, 143
Copper Bank, 184, 224
Cossacks: 32, fn. 32, 33, 35, 83, 86, 87, 88, 90, 118, 176, 210, 215, 220; revolt in Astrakhan, 83; influence on the Pugachev Uprising, 218
Council of Ministers, 81, 94
Council Secretary, 25
Courland. *See* Latvia
Cracraft, James, historian: views on the establishment of the Chief Procurator, 113
Crimea, 38, 44, 87, 154, 155, 211, 250, 251, 252, 254, 257, 258, 259
Crimean Khan, 44, 85
Crimean Khanate, 34, 44, 51, 251
Crimean Tatars, 249
Crimean War, 281, 284
Crisis of Traditionalism, 35–38, 83, 116, 281; in Russian culture, 36;
Crummey, Robert, historian 67
Czartoryski, Adam, 248

Dagestan, 115
Danilova, L.V., historian: fn. 13, fn. 30; views on Russian aristocracy, fn. 14; on allodial landholding, 15
Danzig, 104, 156, 260
Decembrist Uprising, 281
Declaration of Armed Neutrality, 253
"Decree on Single Inheritance," 99–100
Denmark, 59, 68, 70, 104, 128, 153, 164, 199, 245, 253
Derbent, 115
Derzhavin, G., 236, 238, 268
Deti boiarskie. *See* Middle Service People
Devier, Anton Manuilovich, General, 132
Diak. *See* Chancellery Secretary
Dnieper River, 87, 90, 258

Dniester River, 96, 259
Dolgorukaia, Ekaterina, 139, 142
Dolgorukii, Alexei Grigorievich, 137, 139, 140
Dolgorukii, Iurii, founder of Moscow, 9
Dolgorukii, Ivan Dmitrievich, 132, 136, 137, 139
Dolgorukii, Vasilii Lukich, 140, 250
Dolgorukii, Vasilii Vladimirovich, 140
Domostroi. See Book of Household Management
Don Cossacks, 83, 218, 220, 221, 258, 270, 272
Don River, 51, 52
Donskoi, Dmitrii: defeat of the Tatars at Kulikovo Field, 19
Dorpat. *See* Tartu
Dresden, 56
Duke of Courland, 55, 59, 126, 159
Duke of Holstein. *See* also Karl Friedrich
Duke of Marlborough, 84
Duke of Mecklenberg. *See* Leopold
Dumnyi Diak. See Council Secretary
Dunkirk, 104
Dvorianstvo. See Nobility

East India Company, 55
Eastern Orthodoxy, 3, 7, fn. 11, 17, 18, 30, 35, 73, 255, 285. *See also* Russian Orthodoxy
Education: during Muscovite period, 31; in early 18th century, 126. *See also* Catherine II
Eidelman, Natan, historian, 268, 276
Ekaterina Alekseevna. *See* Catherine II
Ekaterina Ioannovna, niece of Peter I, 104
Ekaterinburg, 220
Elagin, I. P., 238
Elector of Brandenburg. *See* Frederick II
Elizaveta Petrovna. *See* Elizabeth I
Elizabeth I (Daughter of Peter I): 94, 132, 139, 159, 162, 163, 164, ch. 5 passim, 195, 198, 211, fn. 213, 246, 253, 265; character of, 169–171; coup of 1741, 165–169, 170, 175, 176, 179; death of, 193, 194; foreign policy during the reign of, 188–193; her rise to the throne, 158, 163–64; industrial boom under, 182–83; legal reform under, 185–188; religiousness of, 173
England, 56, 59, 61, 67, 69, 72, 128, 168, 251, 252, 255, 257. *See also* Great Britain

Epifanov, P.P., historian, 154
Eropkin, Peter, 217
Estonia, 70, 76, 80, 91, 92, 111, 161
Eugene, Charles, Duke de Croy, 71
Europe: 4, 6, 7, 12, 28, 31, 36, 57, 58, 59, 65, 68, 72, 80, 90, 91, 103, 118, 119, 126, 132, 139, 149, 155, 173, 175, 181, 185, 189, 191, 192, 204, 206, 212, 225, 232, 240, 244, 252, 261, 267, 268, 274, 281
Europeanization of Russia, fn. 37, 67, 117, 128, 198, 206, 241
Evrosinia Fedorovna (mistress of Alexei Petrovich) 105

False Dmitrii, 200
Faisova, I. V., historian, 197
Farquharson, Andrew, 56
"Feeding." *See* Maintenance
Fedor Alekseevich, 37, 39, 41, 42, 124
Fedor Ivanovich (Ivan IV's son), 29
Felton, I., 236
Fermor, Villim Villimovich, General, 192
Feudalism in Russia, fn. 13
Finland, 96, 155, 190, 210
Fomin, I., 236
Fonvizin, D., 236
Foreign Policy. *See* various rulers
France: 46, 59, 104, 155, 170, 177, 182, 189, 190, 214, 245, 247, 248, 252, 253, 255, 257, 260, 267; cultural influence on Russia, 169; French styles at Elizabeth's court, 174
Frederick II, 54, 55, 59, 190, 191, 192, 247
Free Economic Society, 226
Freemasonry, 238, 239
French Revolution, 267, fn. 282
Froianov, I. Ia.: feudal relations in Kievan Rus, 13
Fur Tax, 110

Gadebusch, Battle of, 96
Gagarin, Matvei Petrovich: hanging of, 99
Galicia, 250
Galperin, G., historian: views on the Boyar Duma, 20
Gatchina, 267, 273
General Regulation. *See* Peter the Great
Genoa, 225
Georgia, 255
Germany, 159, 168
Gdansk. *See* Danzig
Giray, Devlet, 252

INDEX 301

Giray, Shahin, 252, 254
Godunov, Boris (1598–1605),29, 33
Golden Horde: 10, 14, 18, 19, 21; as model for Muscovite political and social development, 17
Golitsyn, Dmitrii Mikhailovich, Prince (ch.IV) 131, 139, 140, 142, 148, 248
Golitsyn, Mikhail Mikhailovich, 140, 147
Golitsyn, Vasilii Vasilievich, Prince, 37, 43
Golovkin, Gavrila Ivanovich, 91
Golovkin, Mikhail, 160
Golovin, Fedor Alekseevich, 53, 71.
Gordon, Patrick, 49
Gosti. *See* Leading Merchants
Gosudarev dvor. *See* Sovereign's Court
Gosudarev rodoslovets, 23
Gosudarev razriad, 23
Gote, Iurii, historian, 180
"Grand Embassy." *See* Peter the Great
Grand Princes, 19
Gränhamn Island, 111
Great Britain: 110, 153, 189, 190, 191, 245, 253, 258. *See also* England
Great Servitors. *See* Boyars
Greenwich Observatory, 56
Gregorian Calendar, 68
Greig, Samuel, Admiral, 258
Griaznov, Ivan, 220
Griffiths, David, historian, 232
Grodno, 83, 84
Grossjägersdorf, 192
Gubernii. *See* Provinces
Guilds: 224, 231, 232; definition of the first and second guilds, 112
Gumilev, Lev, historian, 11; affects of Mongol domination, 4; impact of the fall of Constantinople on Rus, 18; impact of the Golden Horde on development of Muscovite Rus, 10

Hangö, 97
Hanover, 91
Hapsburg Empire, 235
Helsingfors. *See* Helsinki
Helsinki, 96
Hetman. *See* Ukraine
Holland, 55, 56, 59, 104
Holy Roman Emperor, 71, 72
Holy Roman Empire, 56
Holy Synod. *See* Collegia
Holy Trinity Monastery, 47, 48
Horn, Henning Rudolf von, 81
Huizinga, Johan, 57

Iarlyk. *See* Charter
Iaroslavl, 19
Iasak. *See* Fur Tax
Iagushinskii, Pavel Ivanovich, Procurator-General of the Senate, 129
Iauza River, 48
Ilia Feodorovich, Son of Fedor Ivanovich, 42
India, 115
Intelligentsia: 283; Peter the Great's influence on, 120, 174
Iran, 255
Iulaev, Salavat, 220
Ivan Alekseevich (half brother of Peter), 42, 43, 45, 47, 126
Ivan III (1462–1505), 15, 19, 20, 26, fn. 43; his break with the Golden Horde,18
Ivan IV, The Terrible: fn. 22, 25, 27, 28, 35, 43, 50, 275; Boyar rule during Ivan's childhood, 23; conquest of Kazan, Astrakhan and Siberia,20; foreign policy under, 34; local government reform, 24
Ivan VI, 157, 158, 160, 161, 163, 164, 175, fn. 213
Izmailovo, 48

Janissaries, 95
Janković, Theodor, 235
Jelgava, 54, 55, 81, 140, 141, 148
Jews in Russia: 80, 211; Jewish Question, 262
Joint Stock Companies, 101
Joseph II, Austrian Emperor, 252, 254, 257, 259
Judaism, 148
Julian Calendar, 68
Julius Caesar, 75

Kaliningrad, 54, 55, 192
Kamennyi Zaton, 95
Kampfer, Engelbert, historian: views on Peter I's childhood, 45
Karakorum, Mongol capital, 12
Karl Friedrich, Duke of Holstein, 126, 132, 139, 153
Karl Peter Ulrich, 138, 139
Karamzin, N. M., historian, 275, 277
Kazan, 19, 20, 143, 220
Kerch, 67, 254
Kheraskov, M., 236, 238
Khmelnytsky, Bohdan, 87
Kholmogory, 164

Kholopy. See Bondsmen
Khotin, 249
Khvost, A.P., 15
Kiev, 9, 83, 84, 176
Kiev Academy, 36, 91
Kievan Rus: 9, 12, 13, 24; differences with Muscovite Rus, 11
Kinsky, Stephan Wilhelm von, 56
Kliuchevskii, Vasilii, historian: 43, 93, 124, 150, 243, 268; on the Era of Palace Revolutions, 122; views on Poland, 262; views on the Grand Embassy of Peter the Great, 61;
Kniazhnin, I., 236
Kobrin, V.B., 14
Kollmann, Nancy Shields, historian, 1, fn. 31–32, 37
Kolomenskoe, 44
Königsberg. *See* Kaliningrad
Konstantin Pavlovich, Son of Paul I, 253
Kosciuszko, Tadeusz, 260, 269
Kostomarov, Nikolai, 87
Kremlin, 42, 45, 46, 52, 217
Kumpanstva. *See* Companies
Kuchuk-Kainardji, Treaty of, 251
Kurakin, Boris: 138; views on reign of Sophia, 44
Kurbatov, Alexei, 68, fn. 82, 98
Kurliandskii, I.A., 146
Kurukin, I.V., 131, 138

Lake Ladoga, 76
Lake Pereiaslavl, 48, 49. *See* also Russian Navy
Latvia, 54, 81, 140, 153, 247, 250, 260
Law Code of 1649, 16, 30, 33, 206, 272
Leading Merchants, 27, 66
Lefort, Franz, 49, 53, 63
Lefortovo Palace, 66
Leibnitz, Gottfried Wilhelm, 61
Leonard, Carol, historian, 200
Leontiev, Konstantin, 23
Leopold, Duke of Mecklenburg, 104, 126, 157
Leopold II, Austrian Emperor, 259
Lesnaia, Battle of, 85
Lestocq, Armand, 162, 175
Leszczynski, Stanislaw, 83, 91, 154
Levitskii, D., 236
Librovich, S.F., historian, 160
Lithuanaia: 21, 84, 250, 260; war with Moscow, 20
Livonia, 76, 84, 92, 111, 150, 161, 210, 250
Lomonosov, Mikhail, 156, 174, 178
London, 56, 91, 191

Lopukhina, Evdokia (Peter's 1st wife) 49, 64, 128, 139
Lopukhina, Natalia Fedorovna, "Lopukhina Affair," 175, 190
Losenko, A., 236
Lotman, Iurii, historian, 79
Louis XIV, of France, 117
Louis XV, of France, 214
Louvre, 104
Löwenhaupt, Adam, Swedish General, 85
Löwenwolde, Karl von, 150, 160
Lublin, 260
Lvov, 251

MacKenzie, David, historian, 117
Magdeburg Law, 35
Maintenance, form of tax collection, 24, 98
Mamai, Khan of the Golden Horde, 19
Madariaga, Isabel de, historian: fn. 254; views on the freedom of the nobility, 197
Marfa Alekseevna, Tsarevna, 64
Maria Theresa, Empress of Austria, fn. 154, 173, 190
Mariia Fedorovna, 266, 267
Mattias, Erik, 165
Matveev, Andrei Artamonovich, 91, 98
Matveev, Artamon, 41, 42
Maurice of Saxony, 153
Mazepa, Ivan: 87, fn. 88, 88, 90; defection to the Swedes, 85–86
McGrew, Roderick, historian, 268, 276, 278
Mengden, Julie, 161
Menshikov, Alexander: 49, fn. 83, 88, fn. 88, 90, 91, 96, 125, 131, 132, 133, 134, 135, 136, 137, 148, 153; exile to Siberia, 135; Governor of St. Petersburg, 78
Meshchane. See Urban Inhabitants
Mestnichestvo: explanation of system, 22–23, 25, 37, 100
Merchantry, 103, 110, 112, 137, 232, 272
Middle Service People, 22
Mikhail Fedorovich, Tsar of Russia, 32, 33, 37, fn. 43, 124, 161
Mikhailov, Peter. *See* Peter the Great
Mikhelson, Ivan, Colonel, 220, 221
Miliukov, Pavel, historian, 61
Miloslavskii, Fedor Alekseevich (Peter the Great's half brother), 39, 41, 42
Miloslavskii, Ivan, 54

INDEX 303

Miloslavskiis, 41, 42, 43
Minsk, 250
Ministry of Commerce. *See* Paul I.
Ministry of State Domains.
    See Paul I.
Mirovich, Vasilii, 164, fn. 213
Mitau. *See* Jelgava
Modernization of Russia, 4, 117, 118, 119,
    128, 141, 143, 184, 214, 241, 281,
    283, 284, 286
Mogilev, 85
Moldavia: 94, 154, 249, 250, 251, 258;
    Moldavian steppe, 95
Molière, French playwright, 75, 205
Monastery Chancellery, 74
Mongol Conquest, consequences of, 10–12,
    14
Mongolia, 12
Monas, Sidney, historian, 4
Mons, Anna, 46, 49, 63, 125, 175
Mons, Villem, 125, 175
Montesquieu, 188, 206, 212
Moscow: 9, 10, 15, 18, 20, 22, 24, 25, 33
    (ch. II) 43, 47, 48, 51, 52, 53, 54, 56,
    57, 58, 59, 62, 63, 67, 75, 80, 81, 85,
    86, 91, 111, 136, 137, 139, 141, 142,
    143, 146, 148, 214, 220, 228, 234;
    Belyi Gorod section of, 64; German
    Quarter in, 46; "Hall of Comedy" in,
    75; Kitaigorod section of, fn. 217;
    Moscow Woolen Complex, 102;
    Plague Riot in, 217–218; Red Square
    in, 54; rivalry with Tver, 19; as Third
    Rome, 18; Zemlianoi Gorod section
    of, 64
Moscow Imperial University, 179, 239
Münnich, Burchard Christoph von, 150,
    154, 155, 157–160, 162, 168, 171, 175
Muscovite Rus: 9, 10, 13, 14, 17, 18, 19,
    20, 23, 238; differences with Kievan
    Rus: 11; Tatar administrative
    influence on, 10
Musketeers: 42, 56, 57, 63, 65, 72, 83, 99,
    118; conspiracy against Peter, 54, 62;
    uprising against Peter's ascension to
    the throne, 42–43, 47–48
Mylnikov, A. S., historian, 200

Naples, 105
Napoleon, 281
Nartov, Andrei, 42
Narva, 70, 71, 73, 75, 76, 80, 90. *See also*
    Northern War

Naryshkin, Kirill, 39
Naryshkin, L. K., 51
Naryshkin "Party," 41, 42
Naryshkina, Natalia Kirillovna, 39, 44, 47,
    49, 51
Naryshkina, Natalia (Sister of Peter I), 64
Natalia Alekseevna, 266
Nationalism, 244
Naumov, V.P., historian, 171, fn. 189, 194
Naval Academy, 101
Netherlands, 190, 245, 253
Neva River, 76, 77
Nevskii, Aleksander, 12, 19
News, first Russian newspaper, 75
Newton, Isaac, 56
Nicholas I, 201
Nikitin, R. 236
Nikon, Patriarch, 36
Nikonian Church, 45
Nobility: 32, 100, 108, 109, 114, 115, 118,
    119, 129, 140, 142, 143, 151, fn. 153,
    174, 180, 182, 183, 184, 185, 187,
    205, 213, 214, 218, 221, 223, 227,
    233, 237, 268, 270, 271, 273, 277;
    freedom from service and its
    consequences, 195–97, 198
Nolcken, Baron von, 167
Northern War: 71, 79, 111, 129, 155; Battle
    of Narva, 69–71; end of, 111; Treaty
    of Nystadt, 111
Norway, 110
Nöteborg, Swedish fortress, 76
Novikov, Nikolai Ivanovich, 237, 239, 240,
    269
Novgorod, 19, 70, 73, 76
Novodevichii Convent, 48, 64
Nystadt, 111, 155, 258. *See also* Northern
    War

Ochakov, 154, 157, 258
Office of Foreign Affairs, 75
Okolnichii, 20, 22
Okrugi. *See* Special Administrative Districts
Old Believers: 36, 42, 159, 173, 211;
    influence on Pugachev Uprising,
    218–219; participation in musketeer
    uprising against Peter, 42
Oldenburg, 150
Omel'chenko, Oleg, historian: views on
    Catherine as an enlightened
    absolutism, 205–206; view on Peter
    I's reform program, fn. 83, fn. 216,
    fn. 270

Oprichnina, 23
Order of Saint Andrew the Apostle, 72–73
Orenburg, 220
Orlov, A. G., 203, 249
Orthodoxy, 173, 188, 198, 201, 211, 229, 239, 266, 286
Osborne, Peregrine, Marquis of Carmarthen, 56
Ostermann, Heinrich Johann Friedrich (Andrei Ivanovich): 134, 136, 137, 150, 151, 162, 168, 175; rivalry with Menshikov, 134–36
Ottoman Empire, 34, 35, 51, 58, 59, 70, 87, 90, 92, 94, 95, 96, 115, 153, 154, 155, 189, 190, 191, 248, 249, 250, 251, 252, 254, 255, 257, 259
Oxford University, 56

Pale of Settlement, 211
Panchenko, A., historian: Russia in relation to Europe, 38
Panin, N. I., 204, 208, 248, 265
Panin, Peter, 250
Paris, 104, 177, 282
Parnu, 70
Pasha, Mustapha, 258
Pashkevich, V., 236
Paul I: 136, 169, 263, 265, passim VII; attempts to reform serfdom, 272–73; character of, 266; coup against Paul, 278, 281; domestic policy under, 269; establishment of Ministries, 269, 274; judicial reform, 270; military reforms, 273; revoking of Provincial reform, 269–70. *See also* Pavel Petrovich
Pavel Petrovich, Grand Duke, 239
Pavlenko, Nikolai, historian: 47, 58, fn.64, 71, fn. 83, 86, fn. 88, 89, 104, 106; the Finnish campaign of Peter I, 96; views on founding of the Senate by Peter I, 93
Peace of Belgrade, 154
Peasant Commune, 26, 81–82
Peasantry: 16, 26, 66, 100, 102, 110, 118, 129, 130, 148, 153, 168, 218, 232, 271; ascribed peasants, 102; court, 26; monastery 26, 208; peasant flight in the post-Petrine period, 130–131; seigniorial 26, 180;
Pernau. *See* Parnu
Persia, 94,
Peter I, the Great: 3, 4, 8, 38, ch. 2 passim, ch. 3 passim, ch. 4 passim, 165, 167,

Peter I, the Great *(continued)*
168, 169, 170, 175, 179, 180, 183, 184, 185, 200, 206, 208, 219, 228, 244, 261, 267, 283, 284; administrative reforms, 69, 89; building of Russian Navy 48–49; character of, 45–46; childhood, 39–46; commerce under, 103; death of, 115–116, 124, 129; death of Peter's mother, 51; foreign policy, 51–52, 57–61; General Regulation (bureaucratic reform) 107, 111, 114; "Grand Embassy," 53–58, 59, 60, 61, 84; industrialization under, 101–103; intellectual climate under, 61–62; life during Sophia's regency, 44–45; "Manifesto on the Invitation of Foreigners to Russia," 79; Military reforms, 69, 73; "Military Regulations," 101; Peter's attitude on service, 50; "Peter Mikhailov," 54; Petrine reforms, 82–83, 97–101, 116–121, 128–129; provincial reform under, 88–90; recruitment into the army under, 81–82, 118; reform of the calender, 68; Russian diplomacy under, 84; tax reform, 107–110; testament of Peter the Great (ch.IV) 124–125;
Peter II. *See* Petr Alekseevich
Peter III: 136, 169, 192, 193, 208, fn. 215, 218, 238, 246, 247, 267; character of, 194–95; coup against, 199–200
Peter and Paul Fortress, St. Petersburg, 79, 116, 175
Peterhof, St. Petersburg, 146
Petersburg Academy of Sciences, 132
Petr Alekseevich, Peter II: 123, 132, 134, 135, 136, 137, 138, 139, 142, 153, 170; death of, 136; reform of local government under, 138; testament of, 139
Petr Petrovich, 123
Pipes, Richard, historian: idea of society in 16th-century Russia, 28; on the Boyar Duma, 20; views on *votchina*, fn. 15
Platonov, S.F., historian, 92
Pogodin, M.P., historian, 117
Poland, 29, 33, 34, 44, 54, 59, 76, 80, 84, 87, 91, 94, 95, 96, 153, 154, 155, 189, 190, 211, 246, 247, 249, 250, 259, 262; partitions of, 250–51, 259–60; Polish Diet, 259–60; Polish Question, 247–48, 259–60; Russian war with, 42

Polish Commonwealth. *See*
    Polish-Lithuanian Commonwealth
Polish-Lithuanian Commonwealth, 84, 92,
    251, 260, 262
Poltava, Battle of, 90, 91, 97, 106
Pomerania, 96
Poniatowski, Stanislaw, 247, 251, 259
Popov, V. S., 243
Posad, 27
Potemkin, G. A., 204, 254, 257
Preobrazhenskii regiment, 91; disbandment
    of, 199
Preobrazhenskoe, 44, 46, 48, 52, 54, 63,
    111, 266; Peter's mock army at, 47
Presniakov, A. E., historian, 180
Pressburg, 50
Prikazy. See Chancelleries
"Prince-Caesar." *See* Fedor Romodanovskii
Privy Chancellery, 74
Prokopovich, Feofan, 91, 115
Prussia: 91, 154, 189, 190, 191, 192, 193,
    199, 239, 246, 247, 250, 251, 252,
    255, 258, 259, 260, 261, 273
Pruth River, 95, 96, 249
Pskov, 19, 73, 76, 95
Pufendorf, Samuel von, 62
Pugachev, Emelian: 217, 240, 266; uprising
    led by, 218–221
Pushkin, Alexander: 49, 79, 205, 281;
    views on Radishchev, 240
Pyrmont, 104

Queen Anne, of England, 91
Quitrents, 102

Radishchev, Alexander, 238, 239, 240,
    269; A Journey from Petersburg to
    Moscow, 240
Radoszkowicze, 85
Raeff, Marc, historian: historiography of
    Peter the Great, 120; intellectual
    climate during Peter I's reign, 61
Raneburg, 164
Razumovskii, Aleksei, 176, 177
Razumovskii, Kirill, 176, 177, 210
Regulation for the Main Magistracy, 112
Renaissance, the, 120
Repnin, N. V., 252
Revel. *See* Tallinn
Rhine River, 191
Riasanovsky, Nicholas, historian; on
    Catherine's attitude toward Peter I,
    206–207

Riazan, 20
Riga, 54, 55, 59, 70, 92, 104, 164, 192
Rokotov, F., painter, 236
Romanov Dynasty, 29, 124
Romanov, Filaret, patriarch of Moscow,
    33, fn. 43
Rome, 11, 72, 79
Romodanovskii, Fedor, 50, 57, 90, 97, 100
Ronne, Karl Edward von, General, 95
Rostov (the Great) 9, 19
Rumiantsev, P. A., 204, 210, 248, 249, 258
Rurikid Dynasty, 32
Rus, 9, 11, 12, 13, 14, 20. *See* Kievan Rus
Russian Law Code (Russkaia Pravda), 13
Russian Navy: building of, 48. *See* Peter
    the Great
Russian Orthodox Church, 18, 33, 74, 88,
    173, 178, 198, 209
Russian Women: position of in Russian
    society, 125–28;
Russo-Turkish War, 216, 225, 257, 258,
    259

Saardam Shipyards, 55. *See also* Peter the
    Great, "Grand Embassy"
Safonov, M., historian, 276
Saint Andrew, 72–73, 77, 176
Saint Peter's Basilica, 79
Saint Petersburg: 77, 81, 84, 91, 92, 95, 96,
    97, 103, 111, 139, 140, 157, 161, 162,
    164, 170, 177, 190, 191, 194, 198,
    234, 235, 246, 250, 257, 259, 260,
    267, 268, 275, 282; construction of,
    82; founding of, 77–80; coronation of
    Peter I as emperor, 111; Hermitage
    Museum in, 236
Saltykov, Peter, 193, 249
Saltykova, Daria, 228
Sanin, G.A., 59
Sarai, capital of the Golden Horde, 19
Saratov, 221
Saxony, 68, 83, 84, 190, 191
Schemberg, A.K., 151
Schismatics. *See* Old Believers
Schleswig, Duchy of, 59, 153, 199
School for Mathematics and Navigation,
    fn. 67, 69
Scotland, 72
Scythians, 72
Secret Chancellery: 105, 278; elimination
    of, 195; reestablishment of, 147, 148,
    151, 158
Semevskii, V. I., historian, 272

Senate: 113, 118, 130, 131, 136, 141, 151, 161, 162, 172, 176, 180, 185, 186, 212, 228, 233, 269, 271; founding of, 93–94; reform of 1763, 207–208
Serfdom: in Russia, 16, 33, 35, 103, 104, 108, 110, 118, 119, 185, 205, 209, 212, 214, 215, 217, 226, 227, 233, 240, 241, 272, 280, 283; in Ukraine, 35
Serfs, 25, 78, 180, 183, 184, 185, 187, 211, 220
Service princes, 20, 21
Seven Year's War, 188, 191, 199, 246
Shafirov, Peter, fn. 83, 92
Shaklovityi, Fedor, 48
Sharymov, A., 77
Shchapov, A.P., 42
Shcherbatov, M.M., Prince, 123, 237–38
Shepelev, Dmitrii Andreevich, 160
Shepeleva, Mavra Egorovna, 179
Sheremetev, Boris Petrovich, 49, 68, 76, 91, 100
Shilder, N.K., historian, 267
Shliakhetstvo. *See* Nobility
Shlisselburg Fortress, 76, 164, fn. 213, 239
Shubin, Alexei, sculptor, 171, 176
Shuvalov, Alexander, 179
Shuvalov, Ivan Ivanovich, 177, 178, 179, 187
Shuvalov, Peter, 179, 181, 182, 183, 184, 185, 186
Siberia, 20, fn. 26, 35, 38, 84, 99, 110, 135, 148, 159, 171, 175, 185, 215
Silesia, 191
Skavronskaia, Marta. *See* Catherine I
Slavophiles, 27, 238
Smolensk, 33, 39, 85, 210, 274
Smolensk War, 34
Smolnyi Institute, 235
Soloviev, Sergei, historian, 63, fn.64, fn. 82, 82, 98, 150; affect of Miloslavskii-Naryshkin rivalry on Peter: 41; views on Elizaveta Petrovna's character, 171; views on Ivan Mazepa, 86; views on Peter's punishment of the musketeer uprising, 57; views on Peter's striving toward the West, 54
Solzhenitsyn, Alexander, 6
Sophia, Tsarevna: 37, 43, 44, 63, 64, 133; as regent for Ivan and Peter I, 43–45
Sophie Auguste Friederike, Princess of Anhalt-Zerbst. *See* Catherine II

Sophie Dorothea, Princess of Wurtemberg, 266
Sorokin, Iurii Alekseevich, historian, 276, 278
Soul Tax, 108, 109, 112, 129, 131, 138, 152, 181, 231, 272
Sovereign's Court, 24
Soviet Union, 4, 6, 7
Spain, 19, 59, 245
Spiridov, G. A., Admiral, 204
Starov, I., 236
State Loan Bank, 183, 225
State Peasants: 27, 102, 109, 208, 233, 272; classification of, fn. 26
Stepennaia kniga, 25
Stettin, 96, 201
Stolnik, 22
Streltsy. See Musketeers
Sublime Porte, 80, 84, 92, 155
Succession Crisis of 1730: 138–144; attempt by nobles to enter political process, 142–43; "Conditions" on Anna Ivanovna, 140–142, 148, 208
Sudebnik of 1550, 23
Sumarokov, A., writer and poet, 236, 238
Supreme Privy Council: 133, 134, 136, 137, 138, 139, 140, 141, 142, 143, 151, 172, 208; creation of, 131, 140, 141
Susanin, Ivan, 161
Suvorov, A. V., 204, 248, 255, 258, 259, 260
Sweden: 29, 33, 54, 55, 58, 59, 67, 68, 70, 75, 83, 84, 104, 155, 167, 188, 190, 253, 258, 259; in the Great Northern War, 75–77, 90–91; Sweden as political model for Russia, 140
Swordbearers of the Teutonic Order, 12
Szczecin. *See* Stettin

Table of Ranks: 111, 114, 117, 131, 186, 187; introduction of, 114
Taganrog, 95, 249
Tallinn, 70, 92
Tamerlane, 19, 75
Tartu, 76, 80
Tatar khans, 10
Tatars: 5, 253; Nogay Tatars, 255
Tatar-Mongol Yoke, 9, 10, 12, 17
Tatishchev, Vasilii Nikitich, 98
Tbilisi, 255
Tiaglo, 27
Tiflis. *See* Tbilisi

INDEX

Time of Troubles, 29, 32, 34
Tokhtamysh, Khan of the Golden Horde, 19
Tolstoy, Petr Andreevich, 80, fn. 83, 105, 132
Torgau, 96
Torke, Hans-Joachim, 28
Torun, 91
Town Chamber, 65, 66
Townspeople, 27; classification of, 26
Trade Corporations, 112
Trediakovskii, Vasilii: his "Ode on the Victory over the Turks and Tatars and on the Capture of Khotin," 156
Troitskii, S. M., 186, 197
Trotti, Joachim Jacques, 167
Tsekha. See Trade Corporations
Tübingen, 177
Tver, 15; rivalry with Moscow, 19
Turks, 34, 52, 55, 58, 59, 67, 68, 72, 85, 92, 95, 96, 153, 157, 189

Ufa, 220
Ukraine: 35, 38, 85, 86, 87, 174, 176, 177, fn. 189, 210, 244, 250, 270, 273; changes during the reign of Peter I, 85–88; Hetman, 35, 85, 86–87, 92, 176, 177, 210
Ukrainian Orthodox Church, 36
Ukraintsev, Emelian, 67
Ulanov, V. Ia., historian, 93, 122
Ulozhenie. *See* Law Code
Unigeniture, Law of, 99
University of Jena, 134
Ural Metallurgical Industries, 224
Ural Mountains, 73, 211, 218, 220, 224
Urban Commune, 81
Urban Inhabitants, 231, 233
Ushakov, Andrei Ivanovich, 132, 147, 158
Ushakov, F. A., 204, 259
Uspenskii, B.A., historian, 79

Vallin-de la Mothe, J., 236
Vasilii III, 15, 20, 26
Vasnetsov, V. M., 5
Vedomosti. See News
Veliaminov, Ivan, 15
Venice, 56
Vernadsky, George, historian: view on Muscovite Rus and the Golden Horde, 10

Versailles, 159, 174
Viazemskii, A. A., Procurator General, 204, 210
Viazemskii, P. A., writer, 201
Vienna, 56, 59, 105, 257
Vladimir, town of, 84
Voevody. See Commanders
Volga region, 35, 38, 109, 215, 218
Volga River, 52, 211, 220, 228
Voltaire, 173, 177, 203
Volynskii, Artemii Petrovich, 143, 148, 156, 157
Vorobievo, 44
Voronezh, 52, 53, 65, 66, 67, 81
Vorontsev, Mikhail, 182, 192
Vorontsov, A. R., 204
Vorontsov, Roman, 238
Vorontsova, Elizaveta Romanovna, 195
Votchina. See Allodial Landholding
Vozgrin, V.E., 58
Voznitsyn, Petr, 53
Vyborg, 92, 111

Waliszewski, Konstantin, 168
Wallachia, 94, 251
War of Austrian Sucession. *See* Seven Year's War
War of Spanish Succession, 59
Warsaw, 96, 251, 260
Weber, Max, 32
Westphalia, 134
White Sea, 76
Whittaker, Cynthia, historian, 121
Whitworth, Charles, 91
Wilhelmine, Princess of Hesse-Darstadt. *See* Natalia Alekseeevna
William of Orange, 55, 56
Winter Palace, 167
Wittram, Reinhard, 100

Yanov, Alexander, historian, fn., 15

Zaporozhian Sich, 87
Zarubin-Chika, Ivan, 220
Zemskii Sobor. *See* Assembly of the Land
Zimin, A., historian: views on the Boyar Duma, 21
Zotov, Nikita, Peter's Tutor, 41

Aleksandr Borisovich Kamenskii was born in 1954 and educated in Moscow. He is currently at the Russian State Humanities University, where he is chair of the department of pre-1917 Russian history. In 1993, Professor Kamenskii was a Fulbright professor at the Department of History, Stanford University. He is the author of about seventy publications on eighteenth-century Russia. His book *Under Catherine's Shadow: The Second Half of the Eighteenth Century,* published in 1992, was the first biography of Catherine the Great to appear in Russia since tsarist times. His most recent publication is *The Life and Fate of Catherine the Great* (1997).

David Griffiths received his education at Swarthmore College, Columbia University, and Cornell University. He is professor of Russian history at the University of North Carolina at Chapel Hill, where he chairs the Curriculum in International Studies. He has published extensively on such themes as Catherine II, the Russian Enlightenment, Soviet historiography, and early Russian–American relations.